THE EVERYTHING

CHOCOLATE COOKBOOK

A chocolate-lover's dream collection of cookies,
cakes, brownies, candies, and confections

Laura Tyler Samuels

Adams Media Corporation
Holbrook, Massachusetts

An Everything® Series Book.
Everything® is a registered trademark of Adams Media Corporation.

Published by Adams Media Corporation
260 Center Street, Holbrook, MA 02343
www.adamsmedia.com

ISBN: 1-58062-405-7

Printed in the United States of America.

J I H G F E D C B

Library of Congress Cataloging-in-Publication data
available upon request from the publisher.

This publication is designed to provide accurate and authoritative information with regard to the subject matter covered. It is sold with the understanding that the publisher is not engaged in rendering legal, accounting, or other professional advice. If legal advice or other expert assistance is required, the services of a competent professional person should be sought.
— From a *Declaration of Principles* jointly adopted by a Committee of the American Bar Association and a Committee of Publishers and Associations

Many of the designations used by manufacturers and sellers to distinguish their products are claimed as trademarks. Where those designations appear in this book and Adams Media was aware of a trademark claim, the designations have been printed in initial capital letters.

Color insert photos by Foodpix®
Illustrations by Barry Littmann

This book is available at quantity discounts for bulk purchases.
For information, call 1-800-872-5627.

See the entire Everything® series at everything.com.

Contents

chapter one

Varieties and Ingredients

The difference between a good dessert and an unforgettable chocolate creation is the quality of ingredients you use. Start with the very best chocolate and partner it with the freshest, most natural ingredients. Also, make sure that no other flavor ever upstages or overwhelms the star of the show—chocolate.

Chocolate Varieties

Fortunately, chocolate is now available in a myriad of high caliber domestic and imported choices. Within "dark," "milk," and "white," chocolateries (chocolate manufacturers) offer a fascinating array of chocolate varieties. For example, one may offer a full-bodied taste against a backdrop of exotic spices. Another may boast a smooth, sophisticated flavor, embracing the essence of flowers or berries. And yet another may challenge your taste buds to detect a hint of sweet almonds.

Similar to creating a fine wine, chocolateries achieve different tastes and textures through painstakingly intricate designs of bean selection, roasting, blending, grinding, and conching, as well as select ratios of chocolate solids (known as chocolate liquor) and cocoa butter.

I highly recommend that you hold chocolate tastings on a regular basis, to get to know the subtle nuances of each. I also recommend that you start keeping track of which chocolate you would match with which recipe. For example, for an exquisite bittersweet mousse you may prefer the delicate tones of a Lindt Excellence couverture, whereas for a mocha torte you may prefer the smoldering richness of a Valrhona Pur Caraibe. As your expertise grows, you may even choose to blend varieties for special recipes.

Basic Chocolate Offerings

As I mentioned, these varieties fall within basic "dark," "milk," and "white" chocolate groupings. It's important to get acquainted with the characteristics of each of these offerings, so that you can customize recipes or design your own desserts and specialties with a minimum of trial and error.

Unsweetened Chocolate

Also known as "baker's chocolate," this is a solid form of chocolate, containing only chocolate liquor (chocolate solids), cocoa butter, an emulsifier (to help stabilize the cocoa butter), and sometimes a dash of vanilla or vanillin. Along with cocoa powder, this was the form of chocolate most often used by homemakers for baking and candy making until only 15 or 20 years ago. Today, the popularity of unsweetened chocolate has been replaced by the many varieties of bittersweet, semisweet, milk, and white chocolate.

If you decide to substitute unsweetened chocolate for bittersweet or semisweet chocolate in a recipe, be sure to compensate for the difference in sugar. And if you want to substitute unsweetened chocolate for

cocoa powder, remember to adjust the amount of butter or vegetable shortening; each ounce of unsweetened chocolate brings with it a tablespoon of cocoa butter. (There's no need to change sugar specifications—neither cocoa powder nor unsweetened chocolate contains any.) It's a bit more complicated to replace milk or white chocolate with unsweetened chocolate; you must calculate both sugar and dairy components.

Bittersweet Chocolate

A small amount of sugar is added to unsweetened chocolate to create this most sophisticated form of chocolate. Much like espresso or brut champagne, bittersweet chocolate is an acquired taste; one that should be carefully cultivated. If you are creating a dessert for true connoisseurs, a variety of bittersweet chocolate, as your primary ingredient, should be your first choice.

When substituting bittersweet for unsweetened chocolate, you'll want to adjust the sugar requirements. However, if you're using a bittersweet chocolate in place of a semisweet, you may *not* want to add more sugar; most bittersweet lovers prefer the natural reduction of sweetness. Also, you'll find with your tastings that chocolateries have very different opinions regarding what degree of sweetness defines "bittersweet." That's why it's important for you to conduct a taste test of each variety before using it. (Be sure to include Valrhona bittersweet varieties in your chocolate tastings. I find them to be among the most intriguing.)

The Legend of Quetzalcoatl

Quetzalcoatl, the man-god leader of the Toltec nation, was led into paradise by the sun god, and was given cocoa beans as a treasure to bring back to mankind. On his way home, evil sorcerers tricked Quetzalcoatl into drinking a potion that drove him insane and, taking his treasure, set him out to sea on a snake-covered raft.

Once at sea, Quetzalcoatl transformed into a mighty serpent god and returned to destroy the evil sorcerers, scattering the cocoa beans in the process. As he headed back out to sea, Quetzalcoatl empowered the cocoa beans to give birth to trees laden with their fruit, and vowed to return again with more gifts from the gods.

A Chocolatier's Pantry

If you're just getting started, these are the basics you'll want to start collecting:

- ❏ Nonalkalized cocoa powder
- ❏ Alkalized ("Dutch-processed") cocoa powder
- ❏ Sweetened ground chocolate
- ❏ Bittersweet, semisweet, milk, and white couvertures
- ❏ Dark, milk, and white coating compounds
- ❏ Chocolate chips
- ❏ Pure vanilla extract
- ❏ Pure almond extract
- ❏ Flavoring liqueurs, waters, and oils
- ❏ Instant espresso powder
- ❏ Fresh ground cinnamon, allspice, nutmeg, cloves, and ginger
- ❏ Powdered and superfine sugar
- ❏ Fresh almonds, walnuts, pecans, cashews, and hazelnuts
- ❏ Fresh and dried fruit
- ❏ Fruit preserves
- ❏ Peanut butter
- ❏ Mocha beans
- ❏ Sweetened coconut
- ❏ Heavy cream
- ❏ Sweet (unsalted) butter

Semisweet Chocolate

This European favorite contains slightly more sugar than a bittersweet variety. It is also the preference of most pastry chefs and chocolatiers worldwide, because of its smooth flavor and reliable consistency. If you're just getting started, you'll find semisweet chocolate (particularly an imported Callebaut couverture) to be the easiest to work with.

If you use semisweet chocolate in place of unsweetened or bittersweet, be sure to reduce the amount of sugar called for. If you're replacing milk or white chocolate, be sure to recalculate the sugar and dairy specs.

Sweet or German Chocolate

This is the sweetest form of dark chocolate. Don't overlook this choice when holding your chocolate tastings; you may find a new passion.

Milk Chocolate

Hands down, this is still America's first choice when it comes to nibbling chocolate. In addition to more sugar, powdered dairy products are added to create this sweet, gentle form of chocolate. These dairy additives also make milk chocolate more temperamental, more difficult to work with when melting and blending, and more susceptible to scorching when baking.

Other than using milk chocolate chips when a recipe calls for semisweet, it is not a good idea to substitute any form of milk chocolate when a recipe calls for dark. It is

Leading Chocolateries

Baker's Chocolate
800 Westchester Avenue
Rye Brook, NY 10573
(800) 431-1001

Barry Callebaut
1500 Suckle Highway
Pennsauken, NJ 08110
(800) 836-2626

Bloomer Chocolate
Bloomer Drive
East Greenville, PA 18041
(215) 679-4472

Guittard Chocolate
10 Guittard Road
Burlingame, CA 94010
(415) 697-4427

Hawaiian Vintage
   Chocolate
4614 Kilauea Avenue,
   Suite 435
Honolulu, HI 96816
(800) 429-6246

Hershey Foods
Post Office Box 810
Hershey, PA 17033
(717) 534-4200

Lindt and Sprungli
Stratham Industrial Park
1 Fine Chocolate Plaza
Stratham, NH 03885
(800) 338-0839

Merckens Chocolate
150 Oakland Street
Mansfield, MA 02048
(800) 637-2536

Nestle Foods
800 North Brand
Glendale, CA 91203
(818) 549-6000

Valrhona
1901 Avenue of the
   Stars, Suite 1800
Los Angeles, CA 90067
(310) 277-0401

also safest to limit the use of milk chocolate to recipes that do not require high baking temperatures; truffles, mousses, fillings, frostings, sauces, and beverages are safe choices. If you're just starting to work with milk chocolate, try the Guittard couvertures; they are among the richest and most consistent in flavor and behavior.

White Chocolate

Technically, there is no such thing as "white chocolate." Legally, a substance that does not contain chocolate solids cannot be called "chocolate." Since what we call white chocolate contains only the cocoa butter from the cocoa bean, it cannot be called

The Best White Chocolate is Ivory

White chocolate that contains cocoa butter, rather than vegetable fat substitutes, is actually ivory in color.

chocolate. However, in this book, for ease, I will refer to a formula of cocoa butter (or vegetable fats), sugar, dairy products, emulsifier, and vanilla or vanillin as white chocolate.

White chocolate is, by far, the sweetest variety of chocolate. As a dark chocolate snob, I never liked white chocolate for nibbling, and I was extremely reluctant to work with white chocolate as a professional—until I was asked to design a simple, petite white truffle using an ultra-rich imported variety. If your only acquaintance with white chocolate is molded Easter bunnies, you've probably only tasted an inexpensive blend containing cocoa butter substitutes. Have a white chocolate tasting using couvertures. You'll be surprised.

If you're new to working with chocolate, be warned that white chocolate is the most difficult form to work with. The two primary ingredients, cocoa butter and dairy products, are both highly temperamental. And, like milk chocolate, white chocolate is not a good substitute for dark, especially in recipes that require high baking temperatures.

Organic Chocolate

I embrace the ambition behind organic chocolate—to provide a chocolate grown free of pesticides and, in some cases, exploited laborers—I just haven't been able to find one that compares in flavor to traditionally grown varieties. But I haven't given up! I know one day soon there will be an organic chocolate that rivals the best in the world.

Sugar-Free Chocolate

For years, I found that sugar-free chocolate left a medicinal aftertaste similar to sugar-free sodas. However, there are now sugar-free chocolates that defy taste detection. Peter's Chocolate, a division of Nestle that specializes in professional-grade chocolate, makes an excellent sugar-free chocolate, rich in cocoa butter. To track down a retail source in your area, I would recommend visiting their Web site, which contains a list of distributors, then contacting a distributor in your area to see which retailers carry this product.

Forms of Chocolate

Chocolate is chocolate. Right? Wrong. Today, chocolate is available in many forms. And each form has specific strengths and challenges. The amount of chocolate liquor (or solids) will dictate how a chocolate behaves, as well as how a chocolate tastes. The percentage of cocoa butter (or what product is used in place of cocoa butter), will also help to determine flavor, texture, and performance. It's important for anyone who wants to work with chocolate to learn the characteristics of each form of chocolate and to understand how to use each to its best advantage.

Cocoa Powder

When most of the cocoa butter is removed from chocolate, this fine powder

Storage Times and Conditions

Moisture, heat, air, and light are chocolate's worst enemies. For all types and varieties, store chocolate in an airtight container in a dry, dark, cool place. I do not recommend the refrigerator or freezer because of the danger of moisture and condensation.

Dark Chocolate: All varieties of dark chocolate should stay at their most flavorful for a year.

Milk Chocolate: With dairy additives, for best results, milk chocolate should be used within six months.

White Chocolate: It's safest to use this fragile type of chocolate within three months.

"Pure, Unadulterated Extract"

That's how the first solid cocoa substance was marketed after a Dutch chemist, Coenraad Van Houten, invented a machine that would press most of the cocoa butter out of chocolate.

At the same time "dutching," a process that added potash to the cocoa to soften the flavor and help it dissolve in liquids more easily, was being developed. English manufacturers were skeptical, feeling cocoa butter was essential to the enjoyment of chocolate, but they were forced to invest in these presses to stay competitive with the Dutch.

Ironically, it was Englishman John Cadbury who, using the Dutch-designed equipment, refined the process, developing a way to make the pure cocoa powder we still use today.

remains. Since cocoa butter is filled with calories, cocoa powder is a good choice for reduced-fat recipes. However, the old saying, "The flavor's in the fat," holds very true for chocolate. When you remove the cocoa butter from the chocolate, you remove a great deal of the flavor. On the other hand, when you remove all or most of the temperamental cocoa butter, you have a form of chocolate that is much easier to work with.

There are two types of cocoa powder: (1) pure or natural cocoa powder, and (2) alkalized, or "Dutch-processed" cocoa powder. As a general rule, you may prefer to use natural cocoa powder when baking, as most recipes incorporate other forms of alkalization if necessary. When using cocoa powder to decorate a dessert, however, you may prefer the softer flavor of an alkalized version.

To convert a recipe from solid chocolate to cocoa powder, substitute 3 tablespoons of cocoa powder and 1 tablespoon of butter (or vegetable shortening) for each ounce of chocolate. And be careful not to confuse sweetened cocoa or hot chocolate mix for cocoa powder; your result will be too sweet.

Sweetened Ground Chocolate

For coating truffles, decorating desserts and drinks, and brewing hot chocolate, sweetened ground chocolate offers a mixture of chocolate, cocoa powder, sugar, and vanilla.

Couverture

At the other end of the spectrum is couverture. This form of chocolate has the

How to Get the Best Buys on Chocolate

The best way to buy chocolate is from a distributor. It's fresher and less expensive. Although most have minimum order requirements (usually $100–$150), not all require you to have a business or resale license. (In California, chocolate is a food product and is therefore not taxed. Call your local tax authority to see if chocolate is taxed where you live.) If you're a home chocolatier, you may want to form an informal chocolate co-op with friends or family.

Research the distributors in your area (you'll usually find them in the yellow pages under "Bakers' Supplies"). Find out what they carry (in what bulk quantities and pricing), what their minimum is, and how your co-op can buy from them. (You'll probably need to go to their facility to pick up your order, and they probably won't accept a personal check.) Also, find out what else they carry; you may be able to buy extracts, flavorings, dried fruit, pastry flour, or other items at a discount. Be organized and professional; most distributors don't have time to walk you through the features and benefits of each product they carry or to give you advice on which brand to buy.

The best way to learn more about the products they carry is to contact the manufacturers, or to network with pastry chefs, bakers, or chocolatiers.

Be wary of chocolate that's on sale. It's probably old.

Midges Are a Girl's Best Friend

Between the Tropic of Cancer and the Tropic of Capricorn, deep in the heart of the Theobroma cacao groves, midges are a welcome sight. It is these tiny insects that pollinate the flowers of chocolate trees, giving birth to bean-filled pods.

With the help of midges, fruit-bearing trees produce about 6,500 flowers per year, but only 1 to 2 percent of those flowers become pods. And although each pod contains an average of 30 seeds, after drying, the result is an annual yield of only one to two pounds of cocoa beans.

richest flavor and texture because it has the highest content of cocoa butter. Couverture is the most versatile form of chocolate; it can be used as an ingredient (cakes, cookies, candies, pastries, mousses, sauces, beverages), a ganache (truffle centers, cake toppings, glazes, fillings), a coating (when tempered), or—best of all—for nibbling. Most professional chocolatiers and pastry chefs prefer using couverture.

Some couverture is available in bits, rather than blocks. "Calets," "buttons," and "ribbons," are some of the names chocolateries use. Ask if this form is available through your specialty shop or distributor; it's much faster and easier to work with.

"Coating" or "Compound" Chocolate

Hot North American summers and sticky fingers triggered the invention of this form of chocolate. To successfully mass market the chocolate bar year-round, American manufacturers needed to find a way to raise the melting point of chocolate. They ultimately accomplished this by replacing all or most of the cocoa butter with vegetable fats.

As a bonus, with this substitution they found they no longer needed to temper the chocolate. ("Tempering" chocolate is a process used to bring the cocoa butter into balance so that the coating appears shiny and cloud/streak-free.) Compound chocolate is the most popular choice for mass-market candy and quick coating or molding jobs. Just keep in mind, like cocoa powder,

this form of chocolate will not provide the most vibrant flavor.

Chocolate Chips

Preformed chocolate chips are specially formulated to retain their shape even in high baking temperatures. As a result, they do *not* make a good choice when a recipe calls for chocolate; odds are they won't melt completely or blend thoroughly.

Milk and white chocolate chips are designed to resist scorching, so they can be safely substituted for dark chocolate chips in baking projects.

Ganache

This is not a form of chocolate you would buy, per se, but you will use ganache quite often in one form or another, and I find it's a term that confuses many who are just beginning to work with chocolate. Ganache is a blend of dark chocolate and cream. *Any* blend of dark chocolate and cream. The confusion comes in because, based on the ratio of chocolate to cream, ganache may take a fairly solid form, like a truffle; a creamy or whipped form, like a filling; or a fairly fluid form, like a glaze. Sometimes a flavoring is added. And sometimes butter is added, which, technically, makes it a ganache beurre.

Companion Ingredients

Over the years, you will blend dozens, maybe hundreds, of ingredients with

Imported Chocolates

Imported chocolates are as varied as the countries that produce them. Not only can you choose between creamy Swiss, spicy Brazilian, ultrarich French, and more, you can explore the flavor nuances between "cuvee" (chocolates made with an international blend of beans), "varietals" (chocolate using beans grown in one specific region), and "grand cru" (chocolates using one specific type of bean).

Keep in mind that, like wine, the country of origin doesn't guarantee quality. Most countries have a range of manufacturers, some offering fine chocolate, some offering an "affordable-quality" chocolate.

Pastry Chef's Pantry

If your focus will be on pastries, here's what you'll want in your pantry:

- ❏ Nonalkalized cocoa powder
- ❏ Alkalized ("Dutch-processed") cocoa powder
- ❏ Unsweetened chocolate
- ❏ Semisweet couverture
- ❏ All-purpose flour
- ❏ Cake flour
- ❏ Granulated and superfine sugar
- ❏ Dark and light brown sugar
- ❏ Powdered sugar
- ❏ Baking soda and baking powder
- ❏ Cream of tartar
- ❏ Cornstarch
- ❏ Ground cinnamon, allspice, nutmeg, cloves, and ginger
- ❏ Instant espresso powder
- ❏ Fresh almonds, walnuts, pecans, cashews, and hazelnuts
- ❏ Pure vanilla and pure almond extract
- ❏ Flavorings and liqueurs
- ❏ Honey
- ❏ Corn syrup
- ❏ Peanut butter
- ❏ Fresh fruit and preserves
- ❏ Sweetened coconut
- ❏ Extra-large eggs
- ❏ Sweet (unsalted) butter
- ❏ Heavy cream

chocolate. As a general rule, when selecting ingredients, choose fresh and natural, as opposed to artificial flavorings or substitutes. The price (and time) difference will be minimal in relation to the flavor rewards. (The exception to this rule would be fresh ingredients that have a high water content; in this case an extract would be a better choice.)

Here are a few specific exceptions to that rule, and a few tips to help you customize or design your own creations.

Baking Powder, Baking Soda, and Cream of Tartar

Baking powder contains baking soda, cream of tartar, and cornstarch, the combination of which causes batter to rise.

Baking soda is also used as a leavening agent, and in some cases, its alkaline base is used to balance other acidic ingredients.

Cream of tartar, an acid-based byproduct of the wine industry, helps to stabilize egg whites when making meringue. (An *unlined* copper bowl has the same effect, so if you use a copper bowl to beat egg whites, be sure to omit the cream of tartar.)

It is not a good idea to interchange any of these products, or to change the ratio of one or more in a recipe. And all three should be stored in separate airtight containers.

Butter

Sweet butter does not contain salt, has a lower water content, and usually has a

Sources for Chocolate and Other Ingredients

Albert Uster
9211 Gaither Road
Gaithersburg, MD 20877
(800) 231-8154

Assouline and Ting
314 Brown Street
Philadelphia, PA 19123
(800) 521-4491

Barry Callebaut
St. Albans Town Industrial
    Park
RD #2, Box 7
St. Albans, VT 05478
(802) 524-9711

Casa de Fruita
6680 Pacheco Pass Highway
Hollister, CA 95023
(800) 543-1702

Dairy Fresh Chocolate
57 Salem Street
Boston, MA 02113
(800) 336-5536

DeChoix Specialty Foods
58-25 52nd Avenue
Woodside, NY 11377
(800) 834-6881

Ferncliff House
Post Office Box 177
Tremont City, OH 45372
(937) 390-6420

Gourmail
126A Pleasant Valley, #401
Methuen, MA 01844
(800) 366-5900

Gourmand
2869 Towerview Road
Herndon, VA 22071
(800) 627-7272

Harry Wils and Co., Inc.
182 Duane Street
New York, NY 10013
(212) 431-9731

Istanbul Express
2434 Durant Avenue
Berkeley, CA 94704
(510) 848-3723

Kitchen Witch Gourmet Shop
127 N. El Camino Real,
    Suite D
Encinitas, CA 92024
(760) 942-3228

Paradigm
5775 SW Jean Road,
    Suite 106A
Lake Oswego, OR 97035
(800) 234-0250

Patisfrance
161 East Union Avenue
East Rutherford, NJ 07073
(800) PASTRY-1

Rafal Spice Company
2521 Russell
Detroit, MI 48207
(800) 228-4276

Sparrow
59 Waters Avenue
Everett, MA 02149
(800) 783-4116

The Sweet Shop
Post Office Box 573
Ft. Worth, TX 76101
(800) 222-2269

Swiss Connection
501 First Street
Orlando, FL 32824
(800) LE-SWISS

Tropical Nut and Fruit
1100 Continental Boulevard
Charlotte, NV 28273
(800) 438-4470

The Original Purveyors

The Olmec civilization, populating the lush jungles surrounding the Gulf of Mexico between 1400 and 400 B.C., is credited with discovering, and being the first to enjoy, the fruit of the Theobroma cacao.

However, the Mayans were the first to cultivate what they called "cacao" beans, establishing plantations around 300 A.D.

Next the Toltecs, inhabiting the lands abandoned by the Mayans, took pleasure in what they named "sun beans."

But it was the Aztecs, the civilization that flourished after the decline of the Toltecs, who would introduce xocolatl (a bitter drink made of cacao beans, chilies, vanilla, cinnamon, and water) to European explorers.

more pleasing flavor than regular butter. For best results, be sure to use very fresh butter in the consistency called for in the recipe. Butter takes on different characteristics at different temperatures, and those differences can have a dramatic effect on your end result.

If a recipe calls for butter to be at room temperature, leave the butter, covered, on your kitchen counter for an hour or two. If you're in a hurry, slicing the butter will speed the temperature adjustment. I do not recommend trying to bring butter to room temperature in the microwave; I find it changes the consistency.

If your grocery store offers more than one brand of butter, don't let price be the determining factor. Have a taste test. You'll be surprised at the range of flavors created among producers. And the most expensive brands don't always have the best flavor.

Champagne

Champagne is an exception to the "fresh and natural" rule. Having a very high water content, it's difficult to infuse a clear flavor note without adding too much moisture. Marc de Champagne (available at specialty shops), is among a select few flavorings that provide a true essence of this sparkling favorite.

Coffee

The combination of chocolate and coffee is more popular than ever for dessert creations. Another exception to the "fresh

and natural" rule, for the best results, use an instant espresso powder for coffee flavoring. (My favorite brand is Medaglia d'Oro, which is available in most grocery stores.) If you try to use a very strong cup of coffee, or even a brewed espresso, the intense flavor will be diluted by the water. If you try to use finely ground coffee or espresso beans, you will still detect a gritty quality in your finished product. Coffee liqueurs and quality coffee extracts are also better choices than the real thing.

Cream

When a recipe calls for cream, heavy cream, or whipping cream, look for "heavy cream." This usually indicates a cream with a high butterfat content (for the richest flavor) and one that is pasteurized, rather than ultra-pasteurized or sterilized. With the latter two processes, the cream is taken to higher temperatures to enable it to stay fresher longer. However, the higher temperatures rob the cream of flavor and texture.

If you have a choice of more than one brand of pasteurized cream with a high butterfat content, I would recommend you have a taste test. Also, be careful not to choose a cream with added flavorings.

Cream Cheese and Mascarpone Cream

The popularity of tiramisu introduced many of us to an elegant Italian cream cheese, called mascarpone. With a texture more similar to sour cream, mascarpone has a distinctly different flavor than our American version of cream cheese—a flavor well worth searching for. However, like everything else, different manufacturers provide different levels of quality, so sample as many as you can find.

When a recipe calls for cream cheese, you may want to consider substituting fresh mascarpone. If not, be sure to use a solid, rather than a whipped, version of cream cheese, unless otherwise specified.

20 Degrees of Chocolate

Theobroma cacao, the chocolate tree, is grown within 20 degrees of the equator, between the Tropic of Cancer and the Tropic of Capricorn, in Mexico, the Caribbean, Central and South America, Africa, and the South Pacific.

Edible Gold Leaf

For an elegant topping on enrobed truffles and confections, edible gold leaf is available in some specialty candy-making shops and art supply stores. Be sure it's tissue-thin, *edible* gold leaf (22 or 24 carat). The easiest way to apply this delicate topping is to use a sable brush.

Extracts, Flavorings, and Liqueurs

If you cannot find, or cannot use, a natural component for a flavoring, choose a pure extract or flavoring, rather than an artificial one. Your final result will be far better,

Edible Gold Leaf

A touch of gold leaf on top of any chocolate creation makes it even more elegant. Look for edible gold leaf in art supply stores or East Indian markets, or contact:

Easy Leaf Products
6001 Santa Monica Blvd.
Los Angeles, CA 90038
(800) 569-5323

and well worth the price and convenience difference.

Quality liqueurs are also a good source for flavorings. Choose liqueurs that you would be proud to serve as an aperitif, rather than a discount brand. And be careful not to confuse a fruit-flavored brandy with a fruit liqueur.

Flour

For most recipes, an all-purpose flour works very well. When a recipe calls for pastry flour or cake flour, it's designed for a lighter, softer flour. If you cannot find pastry or cake flour in your area, reduce each cup of all-purpose flour by 2 tablespoons. Pastry flour and cake flour can be interchanged with no measurement adjustment.

It is not a good idea to substitute whole-grain flour in pastry and dessert recipes; although arguably healthier, it's too dense.

Fruit

In most instances, the best choice for fruit flavoring is fresh fruit. However, with some recipes, or at certain times of the year, you may need to use an extract, preserve, or liqueur. I avoid canned and frozen fruits; the lackluster flavor just isn't worth the time and effort you have to put into handcrafted desserts and specialties. I would also recommend searching out specialty produce stores and stands. And consider organic fruit; many times the fruit looks and tastes better, in addition to being healthier and safer.

When customizing fruit desserts, try to substitute fruits with a similar texture and water content. And if there are nuts or spices in the recipe, you may also want to consider changing those to complement your new fruit selection.

Mocha Beans vs. Chocolate-Covered Coffee Beans

Mocha beans are bits of solid, coffee-flavored chocolate in the shape of coffee beans. They are absolutely delicious and work magic when used to decorate mocha creations. When your guests bite into them, they'll taste and feel only silken chocolate. Chocolate-covered coffee or espresso beans crunch when you bite into them, and tend to have a bitter, gritty characteristic. Some people love chocolate-covered beans, but not all, so it's much safer to use mocha beans when designing desserts for others.

Mocha beans can be expensive, so the best place to buy them is in bulk-candy stores where the store averages the cost of all the candy they stock, and charge a certain amount per pound, regardless of your selection. I also recommend American-made mocha beans over imported beans; they look and taste better.

Nuts

Nuts have always been a popular companion for chocolate. An easy, safe way to customize a recipe is by substituting one variety of nut for another. For most recipes, using toasted nuts will prove

And the Winner Is . . .

Can you match the country to how much chocolate is consumed, per person, per year?

1. Austria	A. 30 pounds
2. Belgium	B. 21 pounds
3. Denmark	C. 19 pounds
4. Finland	D. 18 pounds
5. France	E. 17 pounds
6. Ireland	F. 16 pounds
7. Italy	G. 15 pounds
8. Netherlands	H. 14 pounds
9. Spain	I. 12 pounds
10. Sweden	J. 11 pounds
11. Switzerland	K. 10 pounds
12. United Kingdom	L. 8 pounds
13. United States	M. 6 pounds
	N. 3 pounds

Answers: 1D, 2F, 3C, 4L, 5H, 6E, 7M, 8K, 9N, 10I, 11B, 12A, 13J

Chocolate in Bloom

"Bloom" is a term used to describe chocolate in which the cocoa butter has separated and risen to the top, creating gray streaks or a frosty appearance. This usually means the chocolate has experienced an unfriendly temperature change, or was not properly tempered to begin with. It can be tempered to bring the cocoa butter back into balance; however, if you buy chocolate and discover, upon unwrapping it, that it has bloomed, my advice is to take it back, especially if you're paying premium prices. It may be fine, but whatever caused it to bloom, may have also robbed the chocolate of flavor.

more flavorful than using raw nuts. This is easily accomplished by spreading shelled nutmeats on a cookie sheet and baking them for 10 to 20 minutes in a 325°F preheated oven. Be sure to check and turn the nuts every 5 minutes. (Almonds and hazelnuts tend to take a little longer than walnuts and pecans.) There's no need to grease the pan, as nuts contain a high percentage of natural oils. These oils also make nuts very susceptible to spoiling, so it's important to taste-test all nuts before using them (no matter how much you trust your supplier) and to store nuts in an airtight container in the freezer.

Spices

Spices are just coming into their own as companions to chocolate. The best spices are fragile and should be selected and stored with care. If possible, buy the spice in a whole or natural form, and grind, grate, or chop it just prior to use. I try to buy spices in small quantities, and when they lose their full flavor, I use them in simmering potpourris.

If you're designing or customizing a recipe, use just enough spice to intrigue your taste buds; the flavor of the spice should never overwhelm the flavor of the chocolate.

Sugar

Granulated sugar is the most widely used form of this ingredient. In most

recipes, if "sugar" is called for, this is the type to use.

For meringues and mousses, you'll find "superfine" sugar dissolves more easily, for a better result. (Look for it boxed, with brown and powdered sugar.) It can also be used as a substitute for granulated sugar.

Confectioners' or powdered sugar is granulated sugar that has been ground to a powder. (A small amount of cornstarch is added to prevent lumping.) Primarily used for confections, dusting, and decorating, confectioners' sugar can also work well in frostings, glazes, and sauces.

Brown sugar gets its flavor and color through the addition of molasses; the more molasses, the darker the sugar, and the more pronounced the caramel flavor. While in most cases light and dark brown sugars can be interchanged, it is not a good idea to substitute brown sugar for granulated sugar.

It is never a good idea to substitute sugar with artificial sweeteners. If you want or need to create sugar-free creations, there are cookbooks available that specialize in that area.

Vanilla versus Vanillin

As you're checking labels, be sure to notice if "vanilla" or "vanillin" is used as a flavoring. Vanilla is a natural flavoring extracted from vanilla beans. Vanillin is a synthetic flavoring designed to duplicate this flavor. Pure vanilla is always a better choice.

Calories Per Ounce

If you're counting calories, be sure to leave room for an ounce of chocolate!

Unsweetened =
about 135 calories

Bittersweet =
about 140 calories

Milk Chocolate =
about 145 calories

White Chocolate =
about 150 calories

Cocoa Powder =
about 80 calories

Chocolate-Tasting Gift Basket

You can design this basket with wrapped varieties, or create a blind tasting basket by providing varieties in plastic bags identified by a sticker with a symbol or tied with different colored ribbons that coordinate with a sealed description of the chocolate identities. Be sure to duplicate and include the tasting instructions and critique forms provided in "How to Host a Chocolate Tasting."

Chocolate tasting baskets also make festive or elegant centerpieces, and *very* popular door prizes and auction items!

As with all flavorings, different manufacturers offer different levels of quality. In addition, like varieties of chocolate, where and how the vanilla beans are grown and processed impacts the flavor. For example, Tahitian vanilla lays claim to a delicate floral tone, whereas vanilla from Madagascar boasts a spicy, robust flavor. Get to know different varieties, and match them to the character of your creations.

How to Host a Chocolate Tasting

Fun or fancy, chocolate-tasting parties are great for all ages and all interests. (They're also a great idea for fundraisers!)

Choose a Time When Your Guests Will Be at Their Best

You don't want your guests to be too sleepy, too hungry, or too full.

It's important that all their senses be alert and that they're relaxed. If you do serve a meal before the tasting, keep it light.

Choose a Peaceful Place

The fewer distractions, the more your guests can concentrate on nuances.

Unplug the phone, turn off noisy appliances, send the kids to the movies, give the dog a quiet bone, and ask the gardeners to take their blowers to the other side of town.

If you'd like music, choose something soft and relaxing.

Decide on One Type of Chocolate

It's best to focus on varieties of bittersweet chocolate only, semisweet chocolate only, milk chocolate only, or white chocolate only, and to have at least five different varieties to taste.

Create a Blind Taste Test

Place each variety on a separate plate, and identify it with a symbol or color, rather than a letter or number. Don't let your guests know the identity of the chocolaterie, or even if it is imported or domestic, before they've tasted and critiqued each selection.

Create a Beautiful Setting

Since you're treating your guests to the finest couvertures in the world, treat them to the good china, crystal, and linens.

Neutralize Fragrances

Remove potpourri, air fresheners, pets, fragrant flowers, and food aromas.

Ask your guests not to wear any perfume, aftershave, or scented lotions.

Dim the Lights

Nothing enhances chocolate like candlelight.

If you're tasting during the day, try to soften the sunlight.

Serve Fresh Spring Water

Champagne, Grand Marnier, coffee, and even milk are wonderful companions for chocolate, but when you're having a tasting, sipping plain room temperature water will help everyone's taste buds focus only on the chocolate.

Provide Your Guests with Instructions and Critique Forms

Chocolate Critique

1. To begin, select a sample and describe its aroma.
2. Place the same sample in your mouth and let it melt, without chewing. Describe your first flavor impression.
3. As it melts, describe its texture.
4. Now, has the flavor changed? Are new flavors appearing? Describe its "middle flavor."
5. Is the texture consistent, or is it changing as the chocolate melts?

Linger for a moment, then finally describe its "aftertaste."

Concentrate on Nuances

Encourage your guests to describe all of the aromas, flavors, and textures they're experiencing with each sample.

Do they detect: vanilla, berries, wine, coffee, tobacco, smoke, nuts, spices, caramel, flowers. . . ?

Is it: mild, harsh, mellow, acidic, sweet, bitter, balanced. . . ?

Does it feel: smooth, velvety, gritty, buttery, light, heavy, thick. . . ?

Reveal the Identities

You can wait until all your guests have completed their tastings and critiques to reveal each variety's identity, or you can hand out printed descriptions, as each guest finishes. (If you choose the latter, rolling the descriptions into scrolls and tying them with ribbons is a nice touch.) In either case, it's nice to include more than the name of the chocolate. For example, if you're having a tasting for semisweet chocolate, your descriptions may sound or look something like this:

(symbol/color)
Callebaut "811"

A Belgian chocolate, preferred by most chocolatiers and pastry chefs. Callebaut's exquisite worldwide bean selection and meticulous processing methods ensure a luxurious chocolate with a sophisticated, balanced flavor.

(symbol/color)
Lindt "Surfin"

A Swiss chocolate, using a blend of South American Criollo beans (a rare, delicate cocoa bean that makes up less than 10 percent of the world's harvest).

(symbol/color)
Cacao Barry "Favorite"

A French chocolate, using a blend of cocoa beans from throughout the world that are rich and consistent with traditional flavor identities.

(symbol/color)
Valrhona "Equatorial"

A French chocolate, revered for its aroma, body, and elegance; blended by an exclusive boutique, using cocoa beans from around the world.

(symbol/color)
El Rey "Bucare"

A Venezuelan "varietal" chocolate using a blend of aromatic cocoa beans grown exclusively in Venezuela.

Please note: I try to avoid including specific flavors (flowers, spices, etc.) in my descriptions. Taste, like art, is in the eye (or taste buds) of the beholder.

Symbol	Aroma	1st Flavor	Texture	Middle Flavor	Aftertaste

chapter two

Tools, Tips, and Techniques

Would you like to make a world-class truffle? How about an elegant torte? Or a show-stopping bombe? Each specialty requires specific tools and techniques. And with the right equipment and a few tips, you'll be on your way to building an exquisite chocolate repertoire.

I've organized the following tools between those you would need as a chocolatier, and those you would need as a pastry chef.

Tools for Chocolatiers

Dipping strawberries, coating truffles, crafting confections, molding specialties—if your primary interest is in being a chocolatier, there are a few special tools and some basic equipment that will make working with chocolate easier and more fun.

Airtight Containers

Chopping chocolate is messy. If you buy chocolate in bulk blocks, I would recommend that you chop it into small pieces and store it in an airtight container; it's much easier than trying to chop the exact amount you need each time you want to make something.

When making truffles, I find the easiest container for cooling, storing, and scooping the ganache is a shallow rectangular style with an airtight lid.

Airtight containers also keep your finished chocolate specialties fresher longer and protect them from absorbing unwanted flavors and aromas.

Aluminum Baking Sheets

Aluminum conducts heat or cold most efficiently. The ability to cool coated confections or molded chocolate quickly is one of the keys to a perfect end product. However, it is wise to cover the aluminum sheets with waxed paper or parchment paper before placing chocolate on them.

Brushes

For detailing molded chocolate specialties with contrasting colors and applying delicate toppings (like edible gold leaf), a set of high-quality sable brushes will turn your creations into pieces of art.

Candy Cups

Similar to cupcake or muffin cups, only smaller, candy cups are available in foil, paper, and glassine. Foil cups look elegant and can help form a decorative shape on the outside of some confections. Paper cups are the least expensive and are available in a variety of colors and festive patterns. Glassine cups are a bit sturdier and do not absorb oils from confections. You'll find the best selection at candy-making specialty shops.

Candy Thermometer

A candy thermometer has a range of 100 to 400°F. When creating chocolate confections, you may want to incorporate candy components. Like all thermometers, candy thermometers are fragile, and need to be handled and stored with care.

Chocolate Thermometer

A chocolate thermometer is not the same as a candy thermometer. A chocolate thermometer has a range of 40 to 130°F. When tempering chocolate and working with chocolate, it is critical to know and to control the *precise* temperature. Chocolate thermometers are fragile, and need to be handled and stored with care.

Chopping Blocks and Bowls

I prefer to chop chocolate on a wooden chopping block. Given that wood can retain other flavors and aromas, I keep one exclusively for chocolate.

I also keep a chopping bowl for chocolate, and another for chopping other ingredients and toppings.

Dipping Forks

Dipping forks come in a variety of shapes, including forks, ovals, rounds, and spirals. Similar in size and design to a dinner fork, these tools are available in wire with wood handles or in plastic. As their name implies, they are used for dipping truffles, fruit, nuts, and confections. I highly

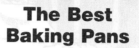

The Best Baking Pans

For most projects, high-quality, heavy aluminum or tin-plate steel pans will give you the best results; they conduct heat more quickly and evenly, and some are designed to insulate cakes and cookies from burning.

If you prefer dark, anodized aluminum or dark steel, both of which conduct heat more quickly, you'll want to reduce your baking temperature by 25°F. You may also need to reduce baking times, depending on the recipe and your oven.

In some instances (for example, soufflés) ceramic or glass is preferable to metal. Invest in high-quality pieces that are designed for your specialty.

Chocolate Gifts for Gardeners

Scented Geraniums

Chocolate trees need intense equatorial heat and humidity to thrive, but scented geraniums, which acclimate more easily to most parts of North America, are available in chocolate and chocolate mint. Look for scented geraniums near the herb section of your favorite nursery.

Cocoa Bean Mulch

To fill your entire garden with the aroma of chocolate, look for cocoa bean mulch, made from the discarded husks. In addition to mulching your flower beds, if you add a little to your garden paths, each time you step you'll release more of the rich, intoxicating chocolate fragrance.

recommend the wooden-handled wire variety. Although more difficult to find, they are much easier to use and more reliable.

Double Boilers

Many chocolatiers prefer using a double boiler to melt chocolate. I highly recommend a glass double boiler. It's important that you melt chocolate over hot—not boiling—water, so a glass version makes it much easier to keep an eye on the water.

You may also want to consider making your own double boiler by placing a stainless steel bowl over a glass pot. This saves you from the time, mess, and trouble of pouring the melted chocolate from the top of the double boiler into a mixing bowl. It also allows you to melt several different varieties (in different bowls) more quickly and easily.

If you do use this method, just make sure that the bowl fits securely within the pot, without the bottom of the bowl touching the water. It's important that the fit prevents any steam from escaping the pot, With steam, there's a danger of moisture getting into the chocolate, which will cause your chocolate to seize.

Glass Measuring Cups

Glass measuring cups are needed for measuring liquid ingredients. But the large 4-cup size also makes a great mixing bowl for some chocolate projects. And all sizes make great microwave-safe, easier-to-keep-an-eye-on-the-chocolate melting containers.

Sources for Equipment and Tools

A Cook's Wares
211 37th Street
Beaver Falls, PA 15010
(412) 846-9490

Beryl's Cake Decorating
   Equipment
Post Office Box 1584
North Springfield, VA 22151
(800) 488-2749

Bridge Kitchenware
   Corporation
214 E. 52nd Street
New York, NY 10022
(800) 274-3435

Candy Factory
12530 Riverside Drive
North Hollywood, CA 91607
(818) 766-8220

Chef's Catalog
3215 Commercial Avenue
Northbrook, IL 60062
(800) 338-3232

Chef's Collection
10631 Southwest 146th
   Place
Miami, FL 33186
(800) 590-CHEF

Crate & Barrel
Post Office Box 3210
Naperville, IL 60566
(800) 996-9960

J. B. Prince Company
36 E. 31st Street, 11th Floor
New York, NY 10016
(212) 683-3553

Kerekes
7107 13th Avenue
Brooklyn, NY 11228
(800) 525-5556

King Arthur Flour Baker's
   Catalog
Post Office Box 876
Norwich, VT 05055
(800) 777-4434

Kitchen Glamour
39049 Webb Court
Westland, MI 48185
(800) 641-1252

La Cuisine
323 Cameron Street
Alexandria, VA 22314
(800) 521-1176

Lamalle Kitchenware
36 West 25th Street
New York, NY 10010
(800) 660-0750

Matfer Kitchen and Bakery
   Supplies
16249 Stagg Street
Van Nuys, CA 91406
(800) 766-0799

Parrish's Cake Decorating
   Supplies, Inc.
225 West 146th Street
Gardena, CA 90248
(800) 736-8443

Previn
2044 Rittenhouse Square
Philadelphia, PA 19103
(215) 985-1996

Sur La Table
1765 Sixth Avenue
South, Seattle, WA 93134
(800) 243-0852

Sweet Celebrations
7009 Washington Avenue,
   South
Edina, MN 55439
(800) 328-6722

Today's Chef
413 Broadway
Bayonne, NJ 07002
(800) 989-1984

Williams Sonoma
Post Office Box 7456
San Francisco, CA 94120
(800) 541-2233

Wilton Enterprises, Inc.
2240 West 75th Street
Woodridge, IL 60517
(630) 963-7100

Zabar's
2245 Broadway
New York, NY 10024
(212) 496-1234

Grater

A stainless steel grater works very well for creating a variety of smaller chocolate shavings for decorating coated truffles and other confections.

Knives

It is extremely helpful to have a large, high-quality, heavy, sharp chef's knife to use when chopping bulk chocolate. It is also helpful to have several small, sharp paring knives for preparing various ingredients and toppings, and, of course, a convenient-to-use knife sharpener.

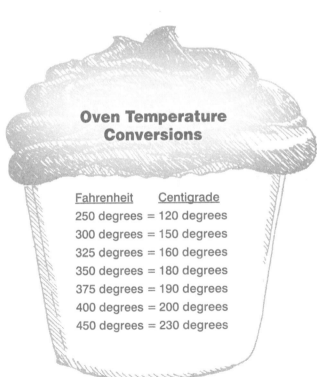

Oven Temperature Conversions

Fahrenheit	Centigrade
250 degrees	= 120 degrees
300 degrees	= 150 degrees
325 degrees	= 160 degrees
350 degrees	= 180 degrees
375 degrees	= 190 degrees
400 degrees	= 200 degrees
450 degrees	= 230 degrees

Marble Slab

If you'll be tempering chocolate, using the traditional method, you'll want to have a marble slab. Marble dissipates heat quickly; in fact it maintains a cooler temperature than most countertops and synthetic or wooden cutting boards.

Measuring Cups and Spoons

I prefer stainless steel and glass over plastic. I also recommend you keep more than one set of each on hand. Sometimes, when working with chocolate, you won't have time to stop and wash measuring devices before needing them again.

Microwave Oven

Microwave ovens can be used to melt chocolate. By using a microwave rather than a double boiler, you eliminate the danger of steam introducing unwanted moisture into the chocolate. However, you increase the danger of the chocolate overheating.

If you decide to use your microwave to melt chocolate, chop the chocolate into small pieces, place it in a microwave-safe bowl, and use no higher than a 50 percent power setting for no longer than one minute at a time. Be sure to stir the chocolate between exposures to disperse the heat, allowing the chocolate to melt more evenly. Stop microwaving the chocolate before it's completely melted to avoid overheating the chocolate. Stir it to melt and blend the last bits.

Mini-Muffin Pans

Aluminum mini-muffin pans are helpful when making confections that set in a candy cup (chocolate confections that are spooned or poured into candy cups while still warm and malleable). The mini-muffin pans add side support to fragile paper candy cups, and facilitate faster overall cooling.

Mixing Bowls

Some chocolatiers prefer using stainless steel mixing bowls, while others prefer clear glass. Choose a set of mixing bowls that are easy for you to use. If you're going to be melting chocolate in a makeshift double boiler, a stainless steel bowl is easiest to handle. However, if you plan to use the microwave, you're better off with a set of clear, ovenproof glass bowls. I use both, depending on the size and circumstance. I also prefer bowls with a pouring spout when working with chocolate in a liquid form.

The only bowls I would *not* recommend you use when working with chocolate are plastic bowls. Plastic can retain flavors and odors from your savory creations.

Molds

Chocolate molds are available in every size and shape, and for just about every theme you can think of, including sports, music, holidays, hobbies, professions, fraternal organizations, special interests, and

Equivalents for Liquid Ingredients		
1 (fluid) ounce	2 tablespoons	1/8 cup
2 ounces	4 tablespoons	1/4 cup
3 ounces	5 tablespoons	1/3 cup
4 ounces	8 tablespoons	1/2 cup
5 ounces	10 tablespoons	2/3 cup
6 ounces	12 tablespoons	3/4 cup
8 ounces	16 tablespoons	1 cup

even some popular cartoon characters. Similar in concept to ice cube trays, the best selections are available in shops that specialize in candy-making supplies. Some shops may even be able to special order molds that they don't normally carry in stock. If you do need to special order a mold, give your source plenty of lead time. There are minimum order requirements, so your molds will most likely be included in their next scheduled order.

Molding chocolate can be a nerve-wrenching art when you're working with couverture. However, it can also be just plain fun and easy if you work with coating chocolate. In fact, it's a great activity for kids! Basically, you simply melt the chocolate, pour it into a plastic dispenser, have the kids squirt it into plastic molds, tap the molds to release air bubbles, and refrigerate. And coating "chocolate" is now available in colors and flavors, which makes it even more fun for kids. In Chapter 11, "Decorations and Specialties," I'll go into more detail about using chocolate molds. There are also lots of classes available

through community education programs and candy-making shops.

Packaging

Candy-making specialty shops will have the best selection of packaging specifically designed for confections.

Boxes are more than square these days; tiny cardboard tuxedos, bowed treasure chests, and peekaboo hexagons are just the beginning. Available as small as a petite truffle, they also come in a variety of colors and patterns, including holographic.

Gift tins are an even better choice, as most keep confections airtight. Just keep in mind that tin also conducts and reflects hot and cold temperatures more dramatically than cardboard, so keep confection-filled tins in a cool place.

Since clear cellophane bags are a form of paper, they are preferable to using plastic bags for chocolate creations. With plastic, there's a danger of condensation, which can dull the chocolate. "Cello" bags are available in a variety of shapes and sizes, including ones large enough to package gift baskets.

And speaking of gift baskets, if you'll be putting unwrapped chocolate into a gift basket, be sure to use shred (or grass) that is designed for confections. With nonconfectionery shred, there's a danger of the color coming off onto the chocolate.

Confectionery foil, available in precut squares in a multitude of intense and pastel colors, is much thinner than other forms of foil. It is extremely easy to use, showcases the molded shape of your chocolates very nicely, and keeps chocolate creations more sanitary at parties. In fact, in some cases, it "creates" the piece. For example, chocolate fruit appears more realistic when covered by a foil in the color of its natural inspiration.

Parchment Paper

Parchment paper can be used to line cooling sheets; however, waxed paper works equally well, is easier to find, and is less expensive. When baking chocolate creations, I prefer to use parchment paper.

Pastry Bags

Pastry bags are helpful when decorating chocolate creations, when filling preformed truffle shells, or when "piping" ganache confections. A variety of tips are available to

International Conversions for Liquids		
AMERICAN	**METRIC**	**IMPERIAL**
1/4 teaspoon	1 ml	
1/2 teaspoon	2 ml	
1 teaspoon	5 ml	
1 tablespoon	15 ml	
2 tablespoons	30 ml	1 fluid ounce
1/4 cup	60 ml	2 ounces
1/3 cup	80 ml	3 ounces
1/2 cup	125 ml	4 ounces
2/3 cup	165 ml	5 ounces
3/4 cup	185 ml	6 ounces
1 cup	250 ml	8 ounces

help you create different designs. The most helpful tips for working with chocolate are star tips and writing tips. Pastry bags are available in several sizes. I keep a variety on hand. It's easiest, when selecting a size to use, to calculate filling the bag only half full. I find it's helpful to place the bag in a similarly sized cylindrical glass and fold back the top (as you would a collar) while filling, to help prevent a mess. Then I use a twist-tie to seal the bag just above the chocolate, to prevent the chocolate from oozing out the wrong end. I prefer synthetic pastry bags over traditional cloth, I find them easier to fill and use (they're more pliable), as well as being faster and easier to clean and dry.

Peelers

Stainless steel potato peelers are excellent tools for creating larger chocolate shavings for decorating.

Plastic Dispensers

Easier and less messy than pastry bags, plastic dispensers are now available with similar decorating tips (in some sizes). Again, I keep a variety of sizes on hand, and use them exclusively for chocolate to prevent the plastic from absorbing any conflicting flavors or aromas. A helpful cleaning tip is to squeeze as much of the remaining chocolate out as you can, then place the dispenser in the refrigerator. When the chocolate is solid, roll the dispenser to crack the chocolate, and then

Equivalents for Dry Ingredients	
3 teaspoons	1 tablespoon
2 tablespoons	1/8 cup
4 tablespoons	1/4 cup
5 tablespoons	1/3 cup
8 tablespoons	1/2 cup
16 tablespoons	1 cup

tap it out. With this method, valuable chocolate doesn't get washed down the drain, and cleanup is much easier.

Saucepans

You'll need saucepans to heat cream and other ingredients. Choose small, heavy-bottomed styles with pouring spouts.

Scale

A kitchen scale is invaluable when working with chocolate. The smartest way to buy chocolate is in bulk, so you'll need to be able to weigh it accurately. I recommend you invest in a small electronic scale; they're so much easier to use.

Scoops

Scoops enable you to measure and form truffles more easily than teaspoons. Invest in at least one high-quality, stainless steel scoop with a spring-loaded handle. The bowl should be 1 inch in diameter.

Sifter-Shaker

This is one of my favorite tools. It's a small container (1/2 cup to 1 cup) with a

screened top, in which I can put cocoa powder or powdered sugar, or any other topping that needs to be sifted while applying. Some varieties also come with an airtight lid that fits over, or replaces, the screened top.

Spatulas

I prefer using high-quality rubber spatulas for stirring chocolate, especially when melting chocolate. Unlike wooden spoons, they won't absorb other flavors and transfer them into the chocolate, and unlike stainless steel, it won't conduct the heat to your fingers. Rubber spatulas also make it easier to scrape pots and bowls clean. Be careful not to leave the rubber spatula in the chocolate while melting; use it to stir, and then remove it.

Wooden-handled stainless steel spatulas are helpful when spreading chocolate during traditional tempering. They also enable you to transfer confections from cooling sheets to serving dishes or candy cups without leaving fingerprints.

Synthetic Gloves

One of the questions I hear the most is, "Why does chocolate dry out my hands so much?" You would think with all that cocoa butter, chocolate would leave your hands soft and supple; unfortunately the opposite is true. By using second-skin synthetic gloves (like surgical gloves), your skin is protected. Also, if you're hand-rolling truffles or hand-working any number of other

International Weights	
US/UK	**METRIC**
1 ounce	30 grams
2 ounces	60 grams
4 ounces (¼ pound)	125 grams
5 ounces (⅓ pound)	155 grams
6 ounces	185 grams
7 ounces	220 grams
8 ounces (½ pound)	250 grams
10 ounces	315 grams
12 ounces (¾ pound)	375 grams
14 ounces	440 grams
16 ounces (1 pound)	500 grams
32 ounces (2 pounds)	1 kilogram

chocolate specialties, synthetic gloves will help insulate your warm body temperature from the chocolate, preventing it from melting as quickly.

Tabletop Tempering Machines

If you'll be making lots of coated truffles, dipped fruit, molded specialties, or coated confections, you may want to invest in an electric tempering machine.

To temper chocolate using the traditional method, you must bring the chocolate to a specified temperature, drop it to another specified temperature, then bring it to yet a third temperature, and hold it there. You must also stir the chocolate constantly. A tempering machine does all that for you and makes the task far easier, less time consuming, and more precise.

Tabletop tempering machines are available in different size capacities, but you need to handle and store them with care. If the electronic temperature-sensing device is damaged, the tempering pot's most important purpose is defeated.

Waxed Paper

Waxed paper is your best friend when it comes to working with chocolate. It insulates chocolate from unwanted reactions to cooling surfaces and makes cleanup much faster and easier. Keep plenty on hand.

Tools for Pastry Chefs

One of the things I love about being a pastry chef is all the tools, specialty pans, and serving dishes. If you want to be truly inspired, plan a special shopping trip, either in person or by catalog, to a gourmet baking supply shop like Williams-Sonoma or Sur La Table. To help you get started, here are some of the tools and pans that you're likely to use the most.

Cake Pans

Cake pans come in a myriad of shapes and sizes. As your repertoire grows, so will your collection of specialty pans. When starting out, for most projects you'll need at least two 8- or 9-inch round pans, one or two 8- or 9-inch square pans, a 13- by 9- by 2-inch rectangular pan, and/or a $9^1/_4$- by $5^1/_4$- by $2^3/_4$-inch loaf pan.

Springform pans are cake pans that are designed for cheesecakes, tortes, and other delicate desserts. The bottom of the pan is removable, and there is a clip on the outside of the pan that, when released, loosens the sides of the pan, allowing you to lift the contents out more easily. Springform pans are available in a standard round cake pan style and in a tube pan style.

Bundt pans are usually heavy-gauge, tube-style cake pans with high sides and a decorative shape. The shape "molds" your nonlayered cake while baking. For toppings, most bundt cake recipes call for a dusting of powdered sugar or a thin glaze (as opposed to a thick frosting) to showcase this distinctive shape. Bundt pans are available in a variety of shapes, including individual-serving and cupcake sizes.

Equivalents for Butter				
¹/₂ ounce	1 tablespoon			
1 ounce	2 tablespoons			
2 ounces	4 tablespoons	¹/₄ cup	¹/₂ stick	
4 ounces	8 tablespoons	¹/₂ cup	1 stick	¹/₄ pound
8 ounces	16 tablespoons	1 cup	2 sticks	¹/₂ pound
16 ounces	32 tablespoons	2 cups	4 sticks	1 pound

Craving Chocolate

Do you crave chocolate during stressful times? Or when your heart needs a hug? You're not just indulging your sweet tooth. Research has proven that eating chocolate triggers the release of serotonin, a natural antidepressant chemical produced by your brain. So, what you're really craving is the mild natural euphoria serotonin creates.

The good news is, not only are you putting yourself in a better mood by eating chocolate, you're also helping your heart.

Angel cake pans are usually a lighter weight aluminum with high sides, either in a tube-pan shape (with a removable bottom), or a long loaf-pan shape. It's essential that no form of grease or nonstick coating be present when baking an angel cake, as the delicate batter needs to climb up the sides of the pan. The cake will release easily if you place a piece of parchment paper in the bottom of the pan before baking, and slide a thin stainless steel spatula around the sides after the cake has baked and cooled. Also, never tap an angel cake to remove air bubbles before baking. It's those air bubbles that lift this heavenly cake.

Chopping Blocks and Bowls

Traditional chopping blocks and bowls are an easy and efficient way to chop chocolate, nuts, and other ingredients. Given that wood can retain other flavors and aromas, I keep a set exclusively for chocolate, another for pastry ingredients, and another for savory ingredients.

Cookie Sheets and Jelly Roll Pans

Keep at least three high-quality cookie sheets on hand that you use exclusively for baking cookies and pastries. In addition to cookie and pastry batters, jellyroll pans are perfect for toasting nuts.

Cooling Racks

Wire cooling racks enable air to circulate under the hot pans you remove from the oven to facilitate faster, more even

cooling. I prefer stainless steel to aluminum, and keep different shapes and sizes to accommodate different pans. If you're just getting started, two rectangular cooling racks will serve most purposes.

Cupcake and Muffin Pans

Cupcake and muffin pans now come in several sizes, from mini to monster, including a pan that bakes a batch of muffin tops!

Custard Cups and Soufflé Dishes

If creating custards, crème brûlées, or soufflés is your passion, invest in high-quality baking dishes that are specially designed for these desserts. A variety of sizes, colors, and decorative patterns allow you to bake and serve these elegant desserts in style.

Decorating Pedestal

Similar in design to a lazy Susan, decorating pedestals make topping and decorating far easier.

Double Boiler

A double boiler is a set of two pots; the top pot of which is cradled within the bottom pot, with enough space for hot water. As a pastry chef, you will be melting chocolate quite often (although probably rarely tempering it). Chocolate and other fragile ingredients are less likely to burn if melted over hot water rather than on the direct heat of a burner.

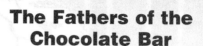

The Fathers of the Chocolate Bar

After studying the art of chocolate at the Caffarel factory in Turin, Italy, during the late 1700s, François-Louis Cailler moved to Switzerland and opened a chocolate factory. At that time chocolate was available only in dry or liquid form, but by 1819 Cailler had invented a series of machines that enabled him to produce the first solid chocolate that could be held and eaten as candy.

In the early 1900s, a caramel maker named Milton Hershey turned his considerable confectionery and promotional talents to chocolate and popularized the milk chocolate candy bar here in the United States.

Egg Separator

Infinitely easier than juggling the yolk between two broken eggshells, egg separators come in a variety of styles, from comical ceramic characters to stainless steel nests.

Electric Mixer

A high-quality electric mixer will save you time and energy and is essential for some dessert recipes. Most come with both a whisk and a paddle blade. You may also want to get an extra stainless steel mixing bowl, for convenience.

Antique Molds

Antique chocolate molds make wonderful decorative gifts for chocolatiers and chocolate lovers. Watch for them in antique stores and at flea markets, or contact:

Holcraft Collection
Post Office Box 792
211 El Cajon Avenue
Davis, CA 95616
(916) 756-3023

Measuring Cups and Spoons

The key to the art of baking is being very precise in timing, in temperatures, in ingredients, and, most importantly, in measurements. Invest in high-quality measuring cups, stainless steel for dry ingredients, and clear, ovenproof glass (with handles and pour spouts) for liquid ingredients. I also recommend that you invest in high-quality stainless steel measuring spoons for precision and durability.

Mixing Bowls

Some pastry chefs prefer using stainless steel mixing bowls, others prefer clear glass bowls, while others swear by heavy ceramic varieties. Choose a set of mixing bowls that are easy for you to use. And include at least one mixing bowl with a pouring spout.

The only bowls I would *not* recommend you use when making cakes and pastries, are plastic bowls. Plastic can retain flavors and odors from your savory creations.

Oven Thermometer

Baking is a very precise art, and many ovens fall out of calibration, so it's helpful to have an oven thermometer to help you keep an eye on your individual oven's exact temperatures.

Parchment Paper

I prefer parchment paper to waxed paper when baking. The nonstick surface makes

pan preparation and cleanup much faster and easier. More importantly, your results will be better and more consistent with parchment paper than with butter or shortening and flour, or spray-on nonstick coatings. Parchment paper comes in boxes similar to waxed paper, and is available in most grocery stores, as well as baking and candy-making specialty shops. If you're out of parchment paper, or can't find it, waxed paper can, in most instances, be substituted.

I usually precut several pieces in the sizes I use most often by placing several lengths on a cutting board, placing the cake pan or cookie sheet on top, and tracing the outside of the pan with a very sharp X-acto-style knife. If you prefer tracing the shape of the pan with a pencil and then cutting, be sure to cut just inside the marking, or to place the parchment with the traced side down, so your batter doesn't come in contact with the pencil marks.

Parfait Glasses

Clear parfait glasses are designed to showcase rich puddings, delicate mousses, fanciful fruits and sorbets, and even dessert beverages. Available in a variety of shapes and sizes, parfait glasses make even plain ice cream seem more festive.

Pastry Bags and Tips

Even as a home pastry chef, you'll be using pastry bags quite often for decorating, as well as for piping pastry doughs, cookies,

meringues, mousses, and ganaches. Pastry bags are available in several sizes. I keep a variety on hand. It's easiest, when selecting a size to use, to calculate filling the bag only half full. I find it's helpful to place the bag in a similarly sized cylindrical glass and fold back the top (as you would a collar) while filling, to help prevent a mess. Then I use a twist-tie to seal the bag just above the contents, to help prevent those contents from oozing out the wrong end. I prefer synthetic pastry bags over traditional cloth; I find them easier to fill and use (they're more pliable), as well as being faster and easier to clean and dry.

First Impressions

The packaging or serving dish you choose (or design) will create the first impression of your gift or dessert. Since you put so much time, effort, and expense into handmade chocolate specialties, showcase your pieces in packaging or on serving pieces that reflect their character and importance.

Sources for Tempering Pots

Even if you make chocolate confections only once a year, a tabletop tempering pot may be worth the investment. They save much time and frustration.

If you're part of a co-op or are starting a chocolate business, some distributors offer a promotional package that includes the tempering pot and bulk chocolate.

If not, investigate some of these sources:

Chandre Corporation offers the smallest tabletop electronic pots.

14 Catharine Street
Poughkeepsie, NY 12601
(800) 324-6252 or *www.chandre.com*

ACMC offers a larger capacity, lightweight electronic pot.

3194 Lawson Boulevard
Oceanside, NY 11572
(516) 766-1414

Hilliard's Chocolate System offers a large, sturdy, stainless steel unit.

275 East Center Street
West Bridgewater, MA 02379
(508) 587-3666

Tips for pastry bags are available in a wide range of designs. To begin, it's most helpful to have a star tip and a plain round tip. As you become more adept at decorating, you'll want to expand your tip selection.

When I was just getting started, I must confess, I was intimidated by these little bags. The pastry chefs I'd watched could go so fast and, with hardly a flick of their wrists, create pure visual magic. When I tried to duplicate what I'd seen, I ended up with a mess of squiggles, swirls, and stars that were uneven in volume and dimension. However, I soon discovered that the more you use a pastry bag, the more comfortable you become. And the more comfortable you become, the more skilled you become. And the more skilled you become, the more fun you have and the more creative you feel. So don't be shy. Practice on fun projects that don't have to be perfect, so when it's time to create a masterpiece, you'll be ready.

Pastry Blender

This tool with a series of thin, stainless steel blades formed in a broad "U" shape, and linked with a handle, offers an easy way to blend pastry ingredients.

Pastry Brushes

Most pastry chefs prefer high-quality pastry brushes that are similar in design to a small, wooden-handled paintbrush. A 1-inch wide bristle is fairly versatile, but keep at

least one brush exclusively for cakes and pastries; the ghosts of garlic or barbecue sauces don't mingle well with delicate dessert flavors.

Pie Pans

You have two choices in pie pans: aluminum, which conducts heat (and cold) more quickly; and ovenproof glass, which can double as a decorative serving dish. The standard size is a 9-inch round.

Plastic Dispensers

Plastic dispensers provide an easy, efficient way to decorate plates with special sauces, before placing the main chocolate dessert on them. Some styles also come with decorating tips, as a substitute for traditional pastry bags.

Rolling Pin

For most recipes, a 12-inch hardwood rolling pin, with a ball-bearing handle, will work best; some pastries require a slightly larger size. I also recommend that you dry wipe, rather than wash, your rolling pin clean, to prevent warping.

Saucepans

High-quality, heavy-bottomed saucepans will enable you to heat cream, sauces, and liquid ingredients more efficiently. I prefer saucepans with a pouring spout for additional ease.

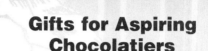

Gifts for Aspiring Chocolatiers

Here are some of my favorite items to give to aspiring chocolatiers. I try to give hard-to-find specialties or things they probably don't already have.

- Subscription to *Chocolatier* magazine
- Classes specific to working with chocolate
- Chocolate thermometer
- Wooden-handled wire dipping forks
- Sable paintbrushes
- High-quality spatulas
- Chocolate molds
- Chef's jacket
- Electronic scale
- Clear glass double boiler
- Marble slab
- Tabletop tempering pot
- Imported couvertures
- High-quality molding chocolates
- Chocolate truffle shells
- Petite chocolate cups
- Gourmet cocoa powders
- Marc de Champagne
- Flavoring liqueurs
- High-quality flavoring extracts

A World-Class Chocolate Vacation

The next time you plan a tour of Northern Europe, be sure to include these stops. You'll want to write or call ahead for reservations and current information on tours and exhibits, hours of operation, and admission prices.

Cadbury World
Linden Road
Bournville, England
Phone: (011 44 121) 451-4159

Chocolaterie S.A. Jacques N.V.
Industriestrasse 16
B-4700 Eupen, Belgium
Phone: (011 32 0) 87.59.29.11
Fax: (011 32 0) 87.59.29.29

SchokoLand Alprose
Chocolat Alprose S.A.
Via Rompada, P.O. Box 147
CH-6987, Caslano-Lugano, Switzerland
Phone: (011 41 91) 71.66.66
Fax: (011 41 91) 71.51.85

The Imhoff-Stollwerck Museum
Rheinauhafen, 50678
Cologne, Germany
Phone: (011 49 221) 931888-0
Fax: (011 49 221) 931888-14

Scale

For pastry chefs, a kitchen scale is invaluable when working with chocolate. The smartest way to buy chocolate is in bulk, so you'll need to be able to weigh it accurately. I recommend you invest in a small electronic scale—they're so much easier to use.

Scoops

I prefer scoops to teaspoons for measuring and shaping many cookie doughs. High-quality, stainless steel scoops with spring-loaded handles, are the easiest to use. The two most helpful bowl sizes are 1-inch in diameter, for bite-size cookies, and $1^{1}/_{2}$-inches in diameter.

Sifter

Many of our first attempts at baking result in a cake far heavier or more dense than we desire. One reason for this is that many new pastry chefs do not sift flour *before* measuring it. Since most flour compacts during storage, measuring it directly from the storage container will actually add more than what is intended by the recipe designer.

After measuring, sifters allow you to blend dry ingredients (like flour and baking soda or cocoa powder) more evenly before adding them to a batter. And finally, sifters make it easier for you to decorate desserts with spices, cocoa powder, and confectioners' sugar.

Some pastry chefs use wire strainers as sifters. I prefer a lightweight, handled, 4-cup traditional sifter for aerating flour and sifting ingredients. I use a "sifter-shaker," an 8-ounce container fitted with a wire lid, for decorating.

Spatulas

I prefer using high-quality, rubber spatulas for most stirring, scraping, folding, and quick batter spreading. Rubber is less likely than wood to retain other flavors and aromas. Rubber is also far more efficient than stainless steel when transferring batter from one container to another.

You'll also want a selection of wooden-handled stainless steel spatulas for decorating and to assist you with removing cakes and cookies from pans.

Trifle Dishes

A trifle dish is usually an elegantly simple clear bowl with a flat bottom and straight, high sides. I prefer trifle dishes with a pedestal to showcase these beautifully layered desserts.

Whisks

Wire whisks are essential tools for pastry chefs. Invest in high-quality stainless steel for beating, blending, and whipping eggs, sauces, and liquid ingredients. I also advise that you keep at least two sizes on hand for ease and efficiency.

Auctions

Quite often a bakery or restaurant will go out of business and will hire (or the court will hire) a professional auction company to liquidate their equipment. This is a great way for you to find professional-quality tools and equipment at a discounted price.

Watch your local paper for notices, or check the yellow pages of your phone book. Some auction houses specialize in food establishments, while others handle all types of businesses. Ask to be put on their mailing list and you'll receive regular notices by postcard.

Like flea markets, sometimes you'll find treasures and sometimes you'll find trash, so be persistent and patient.

Starting Your Own Chocolate Business

There are many kinds of chocolate businesses, from retail shops to specialty catering and mail order. However, I can tell you from personal experience, any business that focuses on chocolate is difficult. Chocolate is fragile and temperamental. It is affected by buying seasons, Mother Nature, narrow margins, and very stiff competition.

The smartest way to start your own chocolate business is to go to work for a similar business. Learn the techniques and see the ups and downs (and required hours). Talk to as many chocolate-business owners as you can. Ask them what they would do differently if they were to begin again. Then, get a lot of sleep—you'll need it!

Zester

A zester is a specialized peeler, primarily for the flavorful, aromatic, brightly-colored top layer of citrus fruit skins. Its blade is a series of tiny circles. Choose a high-quality, stainless steel design, with a sturdy handle for ease and efficiency. When preparing zest, be sure to wash the citrus thoroughly to remove residual pesticides, and to *not* scrape any of the bitter white pith that lies just beneath the top layer.

Techniques

Every time you try a new recipe, read a cookbook, or watch a cooking show, you will, most likely, learn a new technique. More importantly, every time you experiment, you will, most likely, develop a new technique of your very own. Old, traditional methods are being broken every day. New technology, scientific discoveries, time constraints, new tools, and even new chocolate varieties and ingredients give birth to new ways of doing things better, faster, or safer. I encourage you to experiment. Find out what works best for you.

In the meantime, here are a few basic techniques that are helpful to know for almost all chocolate projects. You'll find techniques specific to a specialty, with that specialty.

Chopping Chocolate

The best method for chopping chocolate is to prepare a clean, dry surface. I

prefer a wood cutting board or chopping block. A marble slab (recommended for tempering or cooling chocolate) may dull your knife, tile may hold unfriendly particles in its grout, and all other surfaces may be scratched in the process.

Break your slab or chunk of bulk chocolate into smaller pieces. Then, using a heavy 10-inch chef's knife, chop the chocolate into chocolate-chip-sized pieces that will melt quickly and easily.

You can also use a wooden chopping bowl; however, the weight of the knife makes using a cutting board easier. To use a chopping bowl, place small pieces of chocolate in the bowl and chop them into chip-sized pieces, using the stainless steel chopper that comes with the bowl.

I do not recommend using a food processor or other electric device to chop chocolate.

Melting Pure Chocolate

Chocolate burns easily. When melting chocolate that contains no other ingredients, keep in mind that you are not trying to cook the chocolate. In fact, the less heat, the better. And never try to melt chocolate over direct heat. There is an ongoing debate over the best method of melting chocolate. Here are four techniques. You decide what works best for you.

1. **Using a double boiler**: The wisdom behind the design of a double boiler (whether a set of two pots that fit together, or a bowl placed on top of a pot), is that the delicate chocolate, which is placed in the top pot or bowl, is insulated from the direct heat by a layer of water in the bottom pot, as well as a layer of air between the water and the top pot or bowl. The water should be hot, not boiling. The top pot or bowl should never be covered. And all precautions must be taken to prevent moisture (particularly steam) from contaminating the chocolate. If even a drop of moisture slips in, your chocolate will seize. It's also important that you gently stir the chocolate while melting. Do not whisk or beat the chocolate. You do not want to inject air into the chocolate. I also recommend that you remove the chocolate from the double boiler just before all the pieces melt completely. The residual heat should melt them during a final stir.

2. **Using a water bath**: This method is similar to that of a double boiler; however, this time, instead of suspending the bowl of chopped chocolate over the hot water, you place the bowl *in* the water. With this method, you must heat the water, and then turn off the source of the heat before placing the bowl of chopped chocolate in it. With this method, it is even more important to continuously stir the chocolate and to remove the bowl from the hot water before all the pieces are completely melted. You must also be even more careful to prevent moisture from damaging your chocolate.

3. **Using a microwave oven**: The upside to using a microwave is that the danger of moisture making its way into the chocolate is diminished. Also it's faster and

less messy. The downside is that chocolate burns more easily in a microwave. Never microwave chocolate on high. And never microwave chocolate for more than a minute without stirring. Be patient and be sure your microwave is clean and dry.

I recommend you use a medium power setting for dark chocolate, and a low power setting for milk and white chocolate. Again, I recommend you cease microwaving before all the pieces are completely melted, letting the heat of the mass complete the melting process. The amount of time needed will vary according to the amount of chocolate and your microwave oven. Set 1-minute

intervals initially, reducing the time as the chocolate begins to melt.

4. **Using an electric tempering machine**: Tempering machines are, by far, the safest method of melting pure chocolate. Specially designed to melt, as well as temper, chocolate, they also stir the chocolate continuously and hold it at the desired temperature.

Melting Chocolate with Other Liquid Ingredients

There are three methods for melting chocolate with other liquid ingredients:

1. **Melting the chocolate separately**: Melt the chocolate, using one of the techniques described above. Once melted, slowly stir in the liquid ingredient(s). Be sure that the chocolate and the liquid are approximately the same temperature. (Either cool the chocolate to room temperature or warm the liquid.) Never add cold liquid to warm chocolate; your chocolate will seize.

2. **Using the ingredient(s) to melt the chocolate**: Heat the cream, or other liquid ingredient in a heavy-bottomed saucepan. Just before the liquid begins to simmer, remove from the heat and pour over the finely chopped chocolate. Allow to sit, without stirring, for one minute. Stir gently to blend and to help the remaining bits of chocolate to finish melting.

3. **Melting the chocolate with the ingredient(s)**: Place the chopped chocolate and the liquid ingredient(s) together

A Cherished Stick

In the early days of chocolate, the chocolate drink was whipped with a stick called a "molinillo" to help blend the chocolate and create froth. When pots were designed to heat and serve chocolate, a hole was fashioned in the lid to hold this stick.

(be sure they are both at room temperature) and melt, using one of the techniques described in the last section. Be sure to stir continuously, and remove the mixture from the heat before all the chocolate pieces are completely melted. Then stir gently to help melt and blend the remaining bits.

Tempering Chocolate

Tempering couverture (cocoa butter-rich chocolate) is a method of bringing the cocoa butter into balance, so that the chocolate, when cooled, has a shiny appearance, a smooth texture, and a crisp snap. Chocolate that has fallen out of temper, due to an unfriendly change in temperature, will appear gray, frosty, or streaked, and is said to have "bloomed." In most instances, the bloomed chocolate can be melted down and brought back into temper; however, there is a chance that the temperature change also damaged the flavor.

Tempering chocolate is necessary when using couverture to dip fruit; to coat truffles or confections; to mold chocolate specialties; or to craft chocolate treats like rocky road, clusters, or bark. Tempering is *not* necessary when combining couverture with other liquid ingredients (which means most baking and pastry making), or when using a coating or compound chocolate from which the cocoa butter has been removed. There are three methods of tempering chocolate. Once again, you decide which one is best for you.

Why Chocolate "Seizes"

When chocolate transitions from a beautiful, shiny liquid form to a thick, dull mass, it's said to have "seized." There are three things that cause chocolate to seize.

1. **Moisture**: When just a few drops of moisture fall into pure chocolate, the chocolate will seize. However, when a larger amount of liquid is properly added to chocolate, it blends easily.
2. **Cold liquids**: Cold liquids, even in the proper ratios, will cause chocolate to seize. Be sure any liquids you add to chocolate are approximately the same temperature as the chocolate.
3. **Heat**: If the chocolate gets too hot it will seize. When melting chocolate, the temperature should never exceed 120°F for dark chocolate, 115°F for milk chocolate, and 110°F for white chocolate.

Once chocolate burns, there's no way to rescue it. However, some chocolate experts believe seized chocolate can be rescued by adding warm liquid to it or by adding a little butter to it.

Please note, these are general guidelines for temperatures. Each chocolaterie recommends specific temperatures for specific varieties, so consult the packaging, your specialty shop, your distributor, or even the chocolaterie for exact tempering settings.

1. **Traditional tempering**: Melt 1 pound of couverture, stirring continuously. Bring the temperature of the chocolate to *no higher than* 114°F for dark chocolate, 112°F for milk chocolate, and 110°F for white chocolate. (Be sure to remove the chocolate from the heat source just before reaching these temperatures, as the chocolate's temperature will continue to rise a bit.) Pour two thirds of the chocolate onto a clean, dry, cool slab of marble and, working gently, alternate spreading the chocolate and bringing the chocolate together until cooled to 80°F for dark chocolate, 78°F for milk chocolate, and 76°F for white chocolate. Finally, place the chocolate back in with the remaining melted chocolate, and stirring continuously, bring the temperature back up to 88°F for dark chocolate, 86°F for milk chocolate, and 84°F for white chocolate. Hold the chocolate at this temperature (over water of the same temperature) while dipping, coating, or pouring molds.

2. **Easy tempering**: Melt two thirds of a pound of couverture, stirring continuously. Bring the temperature of the chocolate to *no higher than* 114°F for dark chocolate, 112°F for milk chocolate, and 110°F for white chocolate. (Be sure to remove the chocolate from the heat source just before reaching these temperatures, as the chocolate's temperature will continue to rise a bit.) Gently stir in an additional one-third pound of chopped chocolate, a little at a time, until completely melted and blended. Your chocolate should be tempered.

3. **Electric tempering machines**: Place chopped chocolate in the tempering machine according to the capacity of the machine and your needs. Program the machine to melt dark chocolate to 114°F, milk chocolate to 112°F, and white chocolate to 110°F. When the specified temperature is reached, program the machine to drop the temperature to 80°F for dark chocolate, 78°F for milk chocolate, and 76°F for white chocolate. When these specified temperatures are reached, program the machine to elevate the temperature of the chocolate to 88°F for dark chocolate, 86°F for milk chocolate, and 84°F for white chocolate. When these temperatures are reached, your chocolate will be tempered, and your machine will hold the chocolate at the final temperature specified. The tempering machine will also stir your chocolate continuously throughout the tempering process, and while holding the chocolate in temper.

chapter three

Truffles and Confections

Handmade truffles and confections, using really good chocolate and fresh, whole ingredients, are far better than any you can buy through a retail shop or a catalog. Retailers must, by law, add preservatives. And most cannot use the highest quality ingredients; the end result would be far too expensive for most consumers.

Real chocolate truffles are surprisingly easy to make. So are many confections. And there's something very rewarding about giving friends and family a gift that you've taken the time to make especially for them.

Real Chocolate Truffles

Real chocolate truffles are bite-size bits of chocolate, cream, and a splash of flavoring (usually a cognac or liqueur), rolled in cocoa powder. Named after a gourmet mushroom (because of their similar size and shape), original truffles were not perfectly round. Today, some truffles in America have grown to the size of golf balls. Some are molded into domes or other shapes. And most are sealed in a hard shell of chocolate to extend their shelf life and to make shipping and handling easier.

If you've never tasted a *real* chocolate truffle, make one for yourself. Use your favorite nibbling chocolate, fresh cream, and your favorite liqueur or flavoring. I guarantee you'll fall in love.

Dark Chocolate Truffles

For each of the following recipes, choose your favorite variety of bittersweet or semisweet couverture. Before you begin, make sure all ingredients are at room temperature. If you coat, rather than enrobe, truffles, they must be stored in the refrigerator and will stay fresh for up to three weeks.

Amaretto Apricot Truffles

8 ounces dark chocolate, finely chopped
1/3 cup heavy cream
1 tablespoon almond liqueur
1 tablespoon apricot liqueur (or preserves)

Coating:
1/2 cup sliced almonds

1. Melt the chocolate and cream in the top of a double boiler over hot, not simmering, water. As the chocolate and cream melt together, stir gently with a rubber spatula without injecting any air into this mixture of ganache.

2. Remove the ganache from the top of the double boiler just before all the chocolate pieces are melted. Continue to stir the mixture. The residual heat will melt the remaining bits of chocolate. Set aside to cool to room temperature.

3.   When the ganache is cool but still in liquid form, stir in the almond and apricot liqueurs.

4.   Pour the ganache into an airtight container and refrigerate. (A shallow, wide container works best for cooling and scooping.)

5.   Toast and crumble the sliced almonds. Place in a small bowl, and set aside.

6.   When the ganache is firm enough to shape, scoop bite-size measures and form into irregular or round balls. Coat each truffle in almonds and place in a candy cup or on a serving dish.

Makes 20 bite-size truffles

Buttered Rum Truffles

8 ounces dark chocolate, finely chopped
1/4 cup heavy cream
3 tablespoons butter
1 tablespoon butterscotch liqueur
1 tablespoon dark rum

Coating:
1/2 cup superfine sugar
1/2 teaspoon nutmeg

1.   Melt the chocolate, cream, and butter in the top of a double boiler over hot, not simmering, water. As the chocolate, cream, and butter melt together, stir gently with a rubber spatula without injecting any air into this mixture of ganache.

2.   Remove the ganache from the top of the double boiler just before all the choco-

late pieces are melted. Continue to stir the mixture. The residual heat will melt the remaining bits of chocolate. Set aside to cool to room temperature.

3.   When the ganache is cool but still in liquid form, stir in the butterscotch liqueur and rum.

4.   Pour the ganache into an airtight container and refrigerate. (A shallow, wide container works best for cooling and scooping.)

5.   Sift together the sugar and nutmeg. Place in a small bowl and set aside.

6.   When the ganache is firm enough to shape, scoop bite-size measures and form into irregular or round balls. Coat each truffle in spiced sugar and place in a candy cup or on a serving dish.

Makes 20 bite-size truffles

Café Borja Truffles

8 ounces bittersweet chocolate, finely
*   chopped*
1/3 heavy cream
1 tablespoon orange liqueur
1 tablespoon instant espresso powder
1/2 teaspoon orange zest
1/8 teaspoon ground cinnamon

Coating:
3/4 cup candied orange peels, finely
*   chopped*

1.   Melt the chocolate and cream in the top of a double boiler over hot, not

(continued)

How to "Enrobe" Chocolate Truffles

Sealing a chocolate truffle in a hard shell of chocolate will prolong its shelf life, and make it easier to ship and handle. If you prefer to enrobe, rather than coat, truffles, you will need 12 to 16 ounces of tempered chocolate for each recipe in this book.

1.   Line two cookie sheets or jellyroll pans with waxed paper.

2.   Form the chilled ganache in round or irregular-shaped balls, place on lined cookie sheets, and warm to room temperature. If the ganache is too cold when you dip the truffles, the chocolate shells will crack as they cool.

3.   Gather and prepare whatever you plan to use for toppings. (If you plan to top your truffles with stripes or swirls of melted chocolate, you can delay this step.)

4.   If you plan to use couverture (which will give you a thinner coat and a richer flavor), temper the chocolate. If you plan to use compound chocolate (which is easier), bring it to the temperature recommended by the manufacturer.

5.   If you dip the truffles into the coating chocolate and set them on sheets to cool, the weight of the ganache will cause the coating chocolate under the truffle to disperse, and your truffle will not be sealed. If your truffle is not sealed, it must be refrigerated. There are two ways to prevent this: Either dip the truffles twice, or place the dipped truffles on chocolate disks, similar in size to the bottom of the truffles. To make the disks, simply pour a small circle of the coating chocolate onto the lined cookie sheet and allow it to harden.

6.   Working quickly, dip each truffle in the coating chocolate, tap gently to remove excess coating, place on a disk, and add the topping while the chocolate is still warm and receptive.

7.   Cool (refrigerate) as soon as possible, for 10 minutes. Cooling soon after dipping, in a cooling cabinet or refrigerator, creates a shiny coating. Do not put your trays in the freezer unless the coating chocolate has been specially formulated to freeze. And do not leave the truffles in the refrigerator for more than 10 minutes; you may lose the temper or attract condensation, which will create a "sugar bloom."

8.   If you're decorating the truffles by "lacing" them (drawing chocolate stripes, crisscrosses, or swirls), remove the truffles from the refrigerator, and place the trays in a cool area until you've finished dipping the entire batch. Decorate, and place them back in the refrigerator for a few more minutes.

9.   Place the truffles in candy cups, on serving dishes, or in airtight containers. (If completely sealed in a hard shell of chocolate, it's best if are not refrigerated.) Enrobed truffles can be stored for up to six weeks.

simmering, water. As the chocolate and cream melt together, stir gently with a rubber spatula without injecting any air into this mixture of ganache.

2.   Remove the ganache from the top of the double boiler just before all the chocolate pieces are melted. Continue to stir the mixture. The residual heat will melt the remaining bits of chocolate. Set aside to cool to room temperature.

3.   When the ganache is cool but still in liquid form, stir in the liqueur, espresso powder, orange zest, and cinnamon.

4.   Pour the ganache into an airtight container and refrigerate. (A shallow, wide container works best for cooling and scooping.)

5.   Place the chopped candied orange peel in a small bowl. Set aside.

6.   When the ganache is firm enough to shape, scoop bite-size measures and form into irregular or round balls. Coat each truffle in candied orange peel and place in a candy cup or on a serving dish.

Makes 20 bite-size truffles

Champagne Truffles

8 ounces dark chocolate, finely chopped
$1/3$ cup heavy cream
2 tablespoons Marc de Champagne*

Coating:
$1/2$ cup clear sugar crystals

(*continued*)

Truffle Shells

The easiest way to mold truffles, if you're planning to enrobe them, is to use specially designed, round, hollow chocolate shells, into which you pipe the ganache. These shells are available in a petite size (approximately 1-inch), and in a large size (approximately $1^{1}/_{2}$-inch). They are also available in dark, milk, or white chocolate. Truffle shells are difficult to find. You may have to special order them through a candy-making shop, or form a co-op and purchase cases of them through a distributor.

1. Melt the chocolate and cream in the top of a double boiler over hot, not simmering, water. As the chocolate and cream melt together, stir gently with a rubber spatula without injecting any air into this mixture of ganache.

2. Remove the ganache from the top of the double boiler just before all the chocolate pieces are melted. Continue to stir the mixture. The residual heat will melt the remaining bits of chocolate. Set aside to cool to room temperature.

3. When the ganache is cool but still in liquid form, stir in the Marc de Champagne.

4. Pour the ganache into an airtight container and refrigerate. (A shallow, wide container works best for cooling and scooping.)

5. Place the sugar crystals in a small bowl. Set aside.

6. When the ganache is firm enough to shape, scoop bite-size measures and form into irregular or round balls. Coat each truffle in sugar crystals and place in a candy cup or on a serving dish.

*Marc de Champagne is a concentrated flavoring. Natural champagne, in the required ratios, will not give you enough flavor.

Makes 20 bite-size truffles

Cherries Jubilee Truffles

8 ounces dark chocolate, finely chopped
1/3 cup heavy cream
1 tablespoon kirsch
1 tablespoon brandy

Coating:
1/2 cup glazed cherries

1. Melt the chocolate and cream in the top of a double boiler over hot, not simmering, water. As the chocolate and cream melt together, stir gently with a rubber spatula without injecting any air into this mixture of ganache.

2. Remove the ganache from the top of the double boiler just before all the chocolate pieces are melted. Continue to stir the mixture. The residual heat will melt the remaining bits of chocolate. Set aside to cool to room temperature.

3. When the ganache is cool but still in liquid form, stir in the kirsch and brandy.

4. Pour the ganache into an airtight container and refrigerate. (A shallow, wide container works best for cooling and scooping.)

5. Chop the glazed cherries. Place in a small bowl and set aside.

6. When the ganache is firm enough to shape, scoop bite-size measures and form into irregular or round balls. Coat each truffle in cherries and place in a candy cup or on a serving dish.

Makes 20 bite-size truffles

Espresso Truffles

8 ounces bittersweet chocolate, finely chopped
1/3 cup heavy cream

1 tablespoon coffee liqueur
1 tablespoon instant espresso powder

Coating:

4 ounces bittersweet chocolate, chilled

1. Melt the chocolate and cream in the top of a double boiler over hot, not simmering, water. As the chocolate and cream melt together, stir gently with a rubber spatula without injecting any air into this mixture of ganache.

2. Remove the ganache from the top of the double boiler just before all the chocolate pieces are melted. Continue to stir the mixture. The residual heat will melt the remaining bits of chocolate. Set aside to cool to room temperature.

3. When the ganache is cool but still in liquid form, stir in the coffee liqueur and espresso powder.

4. Pour the ganache into an airtight container and refrigerate. (A shallow, wide container works best for cooling and scooping.)

5. Using a stainless steel grater, shave the bittersweet chocolate into small bits. Place in a small bowl, cover, and refrigerate.

6. When the ganache is firm enough to shape, scoop bite-size measures and form into irregular or round balls. Coat each truffle in shaved chocolate and place in a candy cup or on a serving dish.

Makes 20 bite-size truffles

Fire and Ice Truffles

8 ounces dark chocolate, finely chopped
$1/3$ cup heavy cream
1 tablespoon cinnamon liqueur
1 tablespoon peppermint schnapps

Coating:

$1/2$ cup powdered sugar
$1/2$ teaspoon ground cinnamon

1. Melt the chocolate and cream in the top of a double boiler over hot, not simmering, water. As the chocolate and cream melt together, stir gently with a

(continued)

Chocolate Truffle-Making Gift Basket

I include chocolate couverture for the ganache, the recipient's favorite flavorings or liqueur, enrobing chocolate, special toppings or coatings, a dipping fork, a chocolate thermometer, fancy candy cups, and, of course, my favorite truffle-making cookbook!

rubber spatula without injecting any air into this mixture of ganache.

2.   Remove the ganache from the top of the double boiler just before all the chocolate pieces are melted. Continue to stir the mixture. The residual heat will melt the remaining bits of chocolate. Set aside to cool to room temperature.

3.   When the ganache is cool but still in liquid form, stir in the cinnamon liqueur and peppermint schnapps.

4.   Pour the ganache into an airtight container and refrigerate. (A shallow, wide container works best for cooling and scooping.)

5.   Sift together the powdered sugar and cinnamon. Place in a small bowl and set aside.

6.   When the ganache is firm enough to shape, scoop bite-size measures and form into irregular or round balls. Coat each truffle in the sugar and cinnamon mix, and place in a candy cup or on a serving dish.

Makes 20 bite-size truffles

French Truffles

8 ounces dark chocolate, finely chopped
1/3 cup heavy cream
2 tablespoons French cognac*

Coating:
1/2 cup alkalized cocoa powder

1.   Melt the chocolate and cream in the top of a double boiler over hot, not simmering, water. As the chocolate and cream melt together, stir gently with a rubber spatula without injecting any air into this mixture of ganache.

2.   Remove the ganache from the top of the double boiler just before all the chocolate pieces are melted. Continue to stir the mixture. The residual heat will melt the remaining bits of chocolate. Set aside to cool to room temperature.

3.   When the ganache is cool but still in liquid form, stir in the cognac.

4.   Pour the ganache into an airtight container and refrigerate. (A shallow, wide container works best for cooling and scooping.)

5.   Place the cocoa powder in a small bowl. Set aside.

6.   When the ganache is firm enough to shape, scoop bite-size measures and form into irregular or round balls. Coat each truffle in cocoa powder and place in a candy cup or on a serving dish.

*Grand Marnier, or any quality liqueur, can be substituted.

Makes 20 bite-size truffles

Honey Bear Truffles

8 ounces dark chocolate, finely chopped
1/4 cup heavy cream
3 tablespoons mascarpone cheese (or cream cheese)
2 tablespoons honey

Coating:
1/2 cup graham cracker crumbs

1. Melt the chocolate, cream, and mascarpone cheese in the top of a double boiler over hot, not simmering, water. As the chocolate, cream, and cheese melt together, stir gently with a rubber spatula without injecting any air into this mixture of ganache.

2. Remove the ganache from the top of the double boiler just before all the chocolate pieces are melted. Continue to stir the mixture. The residual heat will melt the remaining bits of chocolate.

3. Stir in the honey and set aside to cool to room temperature.

4. Pour the ganache into an airtight container and refrigerate. (A shallow, wide container works best for cooling and scooping.)

5. Place the graham cracker crumbs in a small bowl, and set aside.

6. When the ganache is firm enough to shape, scoop bite-size measures and form into irregular or round balls. Coat each truffle in graham cracker crumbs and place in a candy cup or on a serving dish.

Makes 20 bite-size truffles

Mandarin Spice Truffles

8 ounces dark chocolate, finely chopped
$^1/_3$ cup heavy cream
2 tablespoons orange liqueur
$^1/_2$ teaspoon ground ginger

Coating:
2 ounces dark chocolate, chilled
2 ounces milk chocolate, chilled

Tips for Using Truffle Shells

Truffle shells are fairly easy to use, especially if you keep these tips in mind:

1. Truffle shells are fragile; store them in a cool, dry place.
2. It's essential that the ganache is cool but still fluid when filling the shells. If the ganache is too warm, the thin shell will melt and lose its shape. If the ganache is not still fluid, air pockets may form.
3. Fill each shell to the top, leaving room to add a cap of enrobing chocolate (to seal the shell before dipping it).
4. The filled shells should be cool, but not cold, when dipping. If the shells are too cold, they may crack.

(continued)

1.   Melt the chocolate and cream in the top of a double boiler over hot, not simmering, water. As the chocolate and cream melt together, stir gently with a rubber spatula without injecting any air into this mixture of ganache.

2.   Remove the ganache from the top of the double boiler just before all the chocolate pieces are melted. Continue to stir the mixture. The residual heat will melt the remaining bits of chocolate. Set aside to cool to room temperature.

3.   When the ganache is cool but still in liquid form, stir in the orange liqueur and ginger.

4.   Pour the ganache into an airtight container and refrigerate. (A shallow, wide container works best for cooling and scooping.)

5.   Using a potato peeler, shave the dark and milk chocolate into small curls. Mix together, place in a small bowl, and set aside.

6.   When the ganache is firm enough to shape, scoop bite-size measures and form into irregular or round balls. Coat each truffle in chocolate curls and place in a candy cup or on a serving dish.

Makes 20 bite-size truffles

Mint Julep Truffles

8 ounces dark chocolate, finely chopped
$^1/_3$ cup heavy cream
1 tablespoon Kentucky bourbon
1 tablespoon peppermint schnapps

Coating:
$^1/_2$ cup chocolate-mint cookie crumbs

1.   Melt the chocolate and cream in the top of a double boiler over hot, not simmering, water. As the chocolate and cream melt together, stir gently with a rubber spatula without injecting any air into this mixture of ganache.

2.   Remove the ganache from the top of the double boiler just before all the chocolate pieces are melted. Continue to stir the mixture. The residual heat will melt the remaining bits of chocolate. Set aside to cool to room temperature.

3.   When the ganache is cool but still in liquid form, stir in the bourbon and peppermint schnapps.

4.   Pour the ganache into an airtight container and refrigerate. (A shallow, wide container works best for cooling and scooping.)

5.   Place the cookie crumbs in a small bowl. Set aside.

6.   When the ganache is firm enough to shape, scoop bite-size measures and form into irregular or round balls. Coat each truffle in crumbs and place in a candy cup or on a serving dish.

Makes 20 bite-size truffles

Monkey Junkie Truffles

8 ounces dark chocolate, finely chopped
$^1/_4$ cup heavy cream

3 tablespoons butter
2 tablespoons mashed bananas

Coating:
¹/₂ cup walnuts

1.   Melt the chocolate, cream, and butter, in the top of a double boiler over hot, not simmering, water. As the chocolate, cream, and butter melt together, stir gently with a rubber spatula without injecting any air into this mixture of ganache.

2.   Remove the ganache from the top of the double boiler just before all the chocolate pieces are melted. Continue to stir the mixture. The residual heat will melt the remaining bits of chocolate. Set aside to cool to room temperature.

3.   When the ganache is cool but still in liquid form, stir in the mashed bananas.

4.   Pour the ganache into an airtight container and refrigerate. (A shallow, wide container works best for cooling and scooping.)

5.   Toast and chop the walnuts. Place in a small bowl, and set aside.

6.   When the ganache is firm enough to shape, scoop bite-size measures and form into irregular or round balls. Coat each truffle in walnuts and place in a candy cup or on a serving dish.

Makes 20 bite-size truffles

A Truffle Cone

Truffles, spiraling to the sky, make an elegant centerpiece. You'll need:
   1 floral cone (approximately 10 inches high, with a 6-inch base)
   confectionery foil
   72-80 toothpicks
   36-40 petite white chocolate truffles (enrobed)
   36-40 petite dark or milk chocolate truffles (enrobed)
   18-24 petite fresh or silk rosebuds
   18-24 petite edible or chocolate leaves

1.   Begin with a Styrofoam floral cone.
2.   Cover the cone with confectionery foil.
3.   Starting at the base, attach a ring of truffles (alternating the flavor) by inserting a toothpick in the cone and skewering a truffle.
4.   Continue, alternating the truffle flavors, side-by-side and row-by-row.
5.   Add the rosebuds and leaves, and place on an elegant dish.

Rainforest Truffles

8 ounces dark chocolate, finely chopped
1/3 cup heavy cream
1 tablespoon rum
2 teaspoons banana liqueur
2 teaspoons coconut cream

Coating:
1/2 cup cashews

1.   Melt the chocolate and cream in the top of a double boiler over hot, not simmering, water. As the chocolate and cream melt together, stir gently with a

Chocolate Truffles and Liqueurs

Liqueurs (actually any form of alcohol) act as a natural preservative for chocolate truffles. The liqueurs used in recipes in this book are designed to enhance, rather than upstage, the flavor of the chocolate.

rubber spatula without injecting any air into this mixture of ganache.

2.   Remove the ganache from the top of the double boiler just before all the chocolate pieces are melted. Continue to stir the mixture. The residual heat will melt the remaining bits of chocolate. Set aside to cool to room temperature.

3.   When the ganache is cool but still in liquid form, stir in the rum, banana liqueur, and coconut cream.

4.   Pour the ganache into an airtight container and refrigerate. (A shallow, wide container works best for cooling and scooping.)

5.   Toast and chop the cashews. Place in a small bowl, and set aside.

6.   When the ganache is firm enough to shape, scoop bite-size measures and form into irregular or round balls. Coat each truffle in cashews and place in a candy cup or on a serving dish.

Makes 20 bite-size truffles

Raspberry Truffles

8 ounces dark chocolate, finely chopped
1/3 cup heavy cream
1 tablespoon raspberry liqueur
1 tablespoon seedless raspberry preserves

Coating:
1/2 cup chocolate sprinkles

1.   Melt the chocolate and cream in the top of a double boiler over hot, not

simmering, water. As the chocolate and cream melt together, stir gently with a rubber spatula without injecting any air into this mixture of ganache.

2. Remove the ganache from the top of the double boiler just before all the chocolate pieces are melted. Continue to stir the mixture. The residual heat will melt the remaining bits of chocolate. Set aside to cool to room temperature.

3. When the ganache is cool but still in liquid form, stir in the raspberry liqueur and preserves.

4. Pour the ganache into an airtight container and refrigerate. (A shallow, wide container works best for cooling and scooping.)

5. Place the chocolate sprinkles in a small bowl. Set aside.

6. When the ganache is firm enough to shape, scoop bite-size measures and form into irregular or round balls. Coat each truffle in sprinkles and place in a candy cup or on a serving dish.

Makes 20 bite-size truffles

Spiced Cider Truffles

8 ounces dark chocolate, finely chopped
$1/3$ cup heavy cream
2 tablespoons apple liqueur
1 teaspoon ground allspice

Coating:
$1/2$ cup cinnamon hard candy

1. Melt the chocolate and cream in the top of a double boiler over hot, not simmering, water. As the chocolate and cream melt together, stir gently with a rubber spatula without injecting any air into this mixture of ganache.

2. Remove the ganache from the top of the double boiler just before all the chocolate pieces are melted. Continue to stir the mixture. The residual heat will melt the remaining bits of chocolate. Set aside to cool to room temperature.

(continued)

A Chocolate Factory for Kids

"Sweet Surprises Candy Making Machine," by Express Ways (available at Toys Я Us), comes with everything kids need to make hollow chocolate-flavored confections with a secret message inside. Fortunately, adult supervision is required, so you get to join in the fun!

A Bittersweet Legend

Long ago and far away lived a beautiful princess, with exotic ebony eyes, dark silken skin, and a luxuriously full body. The gods had blessed her land with much treasure, and her people lived in euphoric harmony.

One day, word came that fierce plunderers were drawing near, so the king sent his only daughter deep into the rain forest to protect her. When days passed with no word, the princess ventured back to the palace. Her heart was torn to pieces when she found that all had been lost, including her beloved people.

She wandered aimlessly back into the rain forest, and to this very day, wherever her teardrops fall, a bittersweet treasure is born—a cocoa tree.

3.   When the ganache is cool but still in liquid form, stir in the apple liqueur and allspice.

4.   Pour the ganache into an airtight container and refrigerate. (A shallow, wide container works best for cooling and scooping.)

5.   Crumble the cinnamon candy. Place in a small bowl, and set aside.

6.   When the ganache is firm enough to shape, scoop bite-size measures and form into irregular or round balls. Coat each truffle in crumbled cinnamon candy and place in a candy cup or on a serving dish.

Makes 20 bite-size truffles

Milk Chocolate Truffles

For each of the following recipes, choose your favorite variety of milk chocolate couverture. Before you begin, make sure all ingredients are at room temperature. If you coat, rather than enrobe, truffles, they must be stored in the refrigerator and will stay fresh for up to three weeks.

Bavarian Truffles

8 ounces milk chocolate, finely chopped
$^1/_4$ cup heavy cream
1 tablespoon hazelnut liqueur
1 tablespoon orange liqueur

Coating:
$^1/_2$ cup hazelnuts

1. Melt the chocolate and cream in the top of a double boiler over hot, not simmering, water. As the chocolate and cream melt together, stir gently with a rubber spatula without injecting any air into this mixture of ganache.

2. Remove the ganache from the top of the double boiler just before all the chocolate pieces are melted. Continue to stir the mixture. The residual heat will melt the remaining bits of chocolate. Set aside to cool to room temperature.

3. When the ganache is cool but still in liquid form, stir in the hazelnut and orange liqueurs.

4. Pour the ganache into an airtight container and refrigerate. (A shallow, wide container works best for cooling and scooping.)

5. Toast, skin, and chop the hazelnuts. Place in a small bowl and set aside.

6. When the ganache is firm enough to shape, scoop bite-size measures and form into irregular or round balls. Coat each truffle in hazelnuts and place in a candy cup or on a serving dish.

Makes 20 bite-size truffles

Black Forest Truffles

8 ounces milk chocolate, finely chopped
3 tablespoons heavy cream
1 1/2 tablespoons kirsch
2 teaspoons almond liqueur

Coating:
1/2 cup powdered sugar, sifted

1. Melt the chocolate and cream in the top of a double boiler over hot, not simmering, water. As the chocolate and cream melt together, stir gently with a rubber spatula without injecting any air into this mixture of ganache.

2. Remove the ganache from the top of the double boiler just before all the chocolate pieces are melted. Continue to stir the mixture. The residual heat will melt the remaining bits of chocolate. Set aside to cool to room temperature.

3. When the ganache is cool but still in liquid form, stir in the kirsch and almond liqueur.

4. Pour the ganache into an airtight container and refrigerate. (A shallow, wide container works best for cooling and scooping.)

5. Place the powdered sugar in a small bowl. Set aside.

6. When the ganache is firm enough to shape, scoop bite-size measures and form into irregular or round balls. Coat each truffle in powdered sugar and place in a candy cup or on a serving dish.

Makes 20 bite-size truffles

Cappuccino Truffles

8 ounces milk chocolate
1/4 cup heavy cream
1 tablespoon coffee liqueur
1 tablespoon instant espresso powder
1/2 teaspoon ground cinnamon

(continued)

Coating:

¹/₂ cup sweet, ground chocolate
¹/₂ teaspoon cinnamon

1. Melt the chocolate and cream in the top of a double boiler over hot, not simmering, water. As the chocolate and cream melt together, stir gently with a rubber spatula without injecting any air into this mixture of ganache.

2. Remove the ganache from the top of the double boiler just before all the chocolate pieces are melted. Continue to stir the mixture. The residual heat will melt the

remaining bits of chocolate. Set aside to cool to room temperature.

3. When the ganache is cool but still in liquid form, stir in the coffee liqueur, espresso powder, and cinnamon.

4. Pour the ganache into an airtight container and refrigerate. (A shallow, wide container works best for cooling and scooping.)

5. Sift together the ground chocolate and cinnamon. Place in a small bowl and set aside.

6. When the ganache is firm enough to shape, scoop bite-size measures and form into irregular or round balls. Coat each truffle in chocolate mixture and place in a candy cup or on a serving dish.

Makes 20 bite-size truffles

Caramel Apple Truffles

8 ounces milk chocolate, finely chopped
2 tablespoons heavy cream
3 tablespoons butter
2 tablespoons apple liqueur
2 tablespoons dark brown sugar

Coating:

¹/₂ cup dry roasted peanuts

1. Melt the chocolate, cream, and butter in the top of a double boiler over hot, not simmering, water. As the chocolate, cream, and butter melt together, stir gently with a rubber spatula without injecting any air into this mixture of ganache.

The Slip of a Vowel

Cocoa beans are, technically, cacao beans, and were called the same until a commoner working in a London trading house inadvertently changed the spelling while processing paperwork.

2.   Remove the ganache from the top of the double boiler just before all the chocolate pieces are melted. Continue to stir the mixture. The residual heat will melt the remaining bits of chocolate. Set aside to cool to room temperature.

3.   When the ganache is cool but still in liquid form, stir in the apple liqueur and brown sugar.

4.   Pour the ganache into an airtight container and refrigerate. (A shallow, wide container works best for cooling and scooping.)

5.   Chop the peanuts. Place in a small bowl and set aside.

6.   When the ganache is firm enough to shape, scoop bite-size measures and form into irregular or round balls. Coat each truffle in peanuts and place in a candy cup or on a serving dish.

Makes 20 bite-size truffles

Cherry Cheesecake Truffles

8 ounces milk chocolate, finely chopped
2 tablespoons heavy cream
3 tablespoons cream cheese
2 tablespoons finely chopped maraschino
    cherries

Coating:
1 cup graham cracker crumbs

(continued)

How to Host a Chocolate Truffle-Making Party

It's far easier and more fun to make chocolate truffles with friends. Have each guest bring their favorite flavor of ganache, coating, and/or enrobing chocolate and toppings. (Also ask each guest to bring lined cookie sheets, scoops, etc.) Then, at the end of the party, like a cookie-swapping party, each guest can take home a selection of flavors!

1. Melt the chocolate, cream, and cream cheese in the top of a double boiler over hot, not simmering, water. As the chocolate, cream, and cream cheese melt together, stir gently with a rubber spatula without injecting any air into this mixture of ganache.

2. Remove the ganache from the top of the double boiler just before all the chocolate pieces are melted. Continue to stir the mixture. The residual heat will melt the remaining bits of chocolate. Set aside to cool to room temperature.

3. When the ganache is cool but still in liquid form, stir in the cherries.

4. Pour the ganache into an airtight container and refrigerate. (A shallow, wide container works best for cooling and scooping.)

5. Place the graham cracker crumbs in a small bowl. Set aside.

6. When the ganache is firm enough to shape, scoop bite-size measures and form into irregular or round balls. Coat each truffle in graham cracker crumbs and place in a candy cup or on a serving dish.

Makes 20 bite-size truffles

Chocolate Mint Truffles

8 ounces milk chocolate, finely chopped
$1/4$ cup heavy cream
2 tablespoons peppermint schnapps

Coating:
$3/4$ cup chocolate-coated mint candy

1. Melt the chocolate and cream in the top of a double boiler over hot, not simmering, water. As the chocolate and cream melt together, stir gently with a rubber spatula without injecting any air into this mixture of ganache.

2. Remove the ganache from the top of the double boiler just before all the chocolate pieces are melted. Continue to stir the mixture. The residual heat will melt the remaining bits of chocolate. Set aside to cool to room temperature.

3. When the ganache is cool but still in liquid form, stir in the peppermint schnapps.

4. Pour the ganache into an airtight container and refrigerate. (A shallow, wide container works best for cooling and scooping.)

5. Crumble the chocolate-coated mint candy. Place in a small bowl and set aside.

6. When the ganache is firm enough to shape, scoop bite-size measures and form into irregular or round balls. Coat each truffle in the crumbled candy and place in a candy cup or on a serving dish.

Makes 20 bite-size truffles

Honey Walnut Truffles

8 ounces milk chocolate, finely chopped
$1/4$ cup heavy cream
1 tablespoon honey
1 tablespoon whiskey

Coating:
$1/2$ cup walnuts

1.   Melt the chocolate and cream in the top of a double boiler over hot, not simmering, water. As the chocolate and cream melt together, stir gently with a rubber spatula without injecting any air into this mixture of ganache.

2.   Remove the ganache from the top of the double boiler just before all the chocolate pieces are melted. Continue to stir the mixture. The residual heat will melt the remaining bits of chocolate. When the chocolate is completely melted, stir in the honey. Set aside to cool to room temperature.

3.   When the ganache is cool but still in liquid form, stir in the whiskey.

Pour the ganache into an airtight container and refrigerate. (A shallow, wide container works best for cooling and scooping.)

4.   Toast and chop the walnuts. Place in a small bowl and set aside.

5.   When the ganache is firm enough to shape, scoop bite-size measures and form into irregular or round balls. Coat each truffle in walnuts and place in a candy cup or on a serving dish.

Makes 20 bite-size truffles

Irish Coffee Truffles

8 ounces milk chocolate, finely chopped
$^1/_4$ cup heavy cream
1 tablespoon brandy
1 tablespoon coffee liqueur
2 teaspoons instant espresso powder

Coating:
$^1/_2$ cup vanilla powder

1.   Melt the chocolate and cream in the top of a double boiler over hot, not simmering, water. As the chocolate and cream melt together, stir gently with a rubber spatula without injecting any air into this mixture of ganache.

2.   Remove the ganache from the top of the double boiler just before all the chocolate pieces are melted. Continue to stir the mixture. The residual heat will melt the remaining bits of chocolate. Set aside to cool to room temperature.

3.   When the ganache is cool but still in liquid form, stir in the brandy, coffee liqueur, and espresso powder.

4.   Pour the ganache into an airtight container and refrigerate. (A shallow, wide container works best for cooling and scooping.)

5.   Place the vanilla powder in a small bowl. Set aside.

6.   When the ganache is firm enough to shape, scoop bite-size measures and form into irregular or round balls. Coat each truffle in vanilla powder and place in a candy cup or on a serving dish.

Makes 20 bite-size truffles

Macadamia Macaroon Truffles

8 ounces milk chocolate, finely chopped
¹/₄ cup heavy cream
2 tablespoons coconut cream

Coating:
¹/₂ cup macadamia nuts, toasted and finely chopped

1. Melt the chocolate and cream in the top of a double boiler over hot, not simmering, water. As the chocolate and cream melt together, stir gently with a rubber spatula without injecting any air into this mixture of ganache.

2. Remove the ganache from the top of the double boiler just before all the chocolate pieces are melted. Continue to stir the mixture. The residual heat will melt the remaining bits of chocolate. Set aside to cool to room temperature.

3. When the ganache is cool but still in liquid form, stir in the coconut cream.

4. Pour the ganache into an airtight container and refrigerate. (A shallow, wide container works best for cooling and scooping.)

5. Toast and chop the macadamia nuts. Place in a small bowl and set aside.

6. When the ganache is firm enough to shape, scoop bite-size measures and form into irregular or round balls. Coat each truffle in macadamia nuts and place in a candy cup or on a serving dish.

Makes 20 bite-size truffles

Mudslide Truffles

8 ounces milk chocolate, finely chopped
¹/₄ cup heavy cream
1 tablespoon vodka
1 tablespoon Irish Cream liqueur
2 teaspoons instant espresso powder

Coating:
1 ounce dark chocolate, chilled
2 ounces milk chocolate, chilled
1 ounce white chocolate, chilled

1. Melt the chocolate and cream in the top of a double boiler over hot, not simmering, water. As the chocolate and cream melt together, stir gently with a rubber spatula without injecting any air into this mixture of ganache.

2. Remove the ganache from the top of the double boiler just before all the chocolate pieces are melted. Continue to stir the mixture. The residual heat will melt the remaining bits of chocolate. Set aside to cool to room temperature.

3. When the ganache is cool but still in liquid form, stir in the vodka, Irish Cream liqueur, and espresso powder.

4. Pour the ganache into an airtight container and refrigerate. (A shallow, wide container works best for cooling and scooping.)

5. Using a stainless steel grater, shave the dark, milk, and white chocolates into small bits. Mix together, place in a small bowl, and set aside.

6. When the ganache is firm enough to shape, scoop bite-size measures and form

into irregular or round balls. Coat each truffle in shaved chocolate and place in a candy cup or on a serving dish.

Makes 20 bite-size truffles

Peanut Butter Porcupines

8 ounces milk chocolate, finely chopped
¹/₄ cup heavy cream
2 tablespoons peanut butter

Coating:

1 cup mini chocolate chips

1.   Melt the chocolate and cream in the top of a double boiler over hot, not simmering, water. As the chocolate and cream melt together, stir gently with a rubber spatula without injecting any air into this mixture of ganache.

2.   Remove the ganache from the top of the double boiler just before all the chocolate pieces are melted. Continue to stir the mixture. The residual heat will melt the remaining bits of chocolate. When the chocolate is completely melted, stir in the peanut butter. Set aside to cool to room temperature.

3.   Pour the ganache into an airtight container and refrigerate. (A shallow, wide container works best for cooling and scooping.)

4.   Place the chocolate chips in a small bowl and set aside.

5.   When the ganache is firm enough to shape, scoop bite-size measures and form

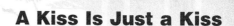

A Kiss Is Just a Kiss

Or is it? Hershey introduced a bite-size teardrop of solid milk chocolate in the early 1900s, which they called a "Kiss." Wrapped in foil, Hershey's Kisses continue to be one of their most popular offerings.

At about the same time, Perugina, a chocolate company in Italy, designed a bite-size dome of dark chocolate and hazelnuts. They called their treat a "Baci," which means "kiss" in Italian.

But Bacis come with a bonus! The creator, so the story goes, sent the first Baci to his lady, with a loving note hidden in the wrapping. So, to this day, each Baci carries with it a secret message.

(continued)

into irregular or round balls. Coat each truffle in chocolate chips and place in a candy cup or on a serving dish.

Makes 20 bite-size truffles

Pumpkin Pecan Truffles

8 ounces milk chocolate, finely chopped
3 tablespoons heavy cream
2 tablespoons solid pack pumpkin
1 tablespoon dark brown sugar
1 tablespoon pecan liqueur
$1/2$ teaspoon pumpkin pie spice

Coating:
$1/2$ cup pecans

1. Melt the chocolate and cream in the top of a double boiler over hot, not simmering, water. As the chocolate and cream melt together, stir gently with a rubber spatula without injecting any air into this mixture of ganache.

2. Remove the ganache from the top of the double boiler just before all the chocolate pieces are melted. Continue to stir the mixture. The residual heat will melt the remaining bits of chocolate. When the chocolate is completely melted, stir in the pumpkin and brown sugar. Set aside to cool to room temperature.

3. When the ganache is cool but still in liquid form, stir in the pecan liqueur and pumpkin pie spice.

4. Pour the ganache into an airtight container and refrigerate. (A shallow, wide container works best for cooling and scooping.)

5. Toast and chop the pecans. Place in a small bowl and set aside.

6. When the ganache is firm enough to shape, scoop bite-size measures and form into irregular or round balls. Coat each truffle in pecans and place in a candy cup or on a serving dish.

Makes 20 bite-size truffles

Strawberries and Cream Truffles

8 ounces milk chocolate, finely chopped
$1/4$ cup heavy cream
1 tablespoon Irish Cream liqueur
1 tablespoon seedless strawberry preserves

Coating:
$1/2$ cup vanilla cookie crumbs

1. Melt the chocolate and cream in the top of a double boiler over hot, not simmering, water. As the chocolate and cream melt together, stir gently with a rubber spatula without injecting any air into this mixture of ganache.

2. Remove the ganache from the top of the double boiler just before all the chocolate pieces are melted. Continue to stir the mixture. The residual heat will melt the remaining bits of chocolate. Set aside to cool to room temperature.

3. When the ganache is cool but still in liquid form, stir in the Irish Cream liqueur and strawberry preserves.

4.   Pour the ganache into an airtight container and refrigerate. (A shallow, wide container works best for cooling and scooping.)

5.   Place the cookie crumbs in a small bowl. Set aside.

6.   When the ganache is firm enough to shape, scoop bite-size measures and form into irregular or round balls. Coat each truffle in cookie crumbs and place in a candy cup or on a serving dish.

Makes 20 bite-size truffles

Tiramisu Truffles

8 ounces milk chocolate, finely chopped
2 tablespoons heavy cream
3 tablespoons mascarpone cheese
1 tablespoon rum
1 tablespoon coffee liqueur

Coating:
1/2 cup milk chocolate, chilled

1.   Melt the chocolate, cream, and mascarpone cheese in the top of a double boiler over hot, not simmering, water. As the chocolate, cream, and cheese melt together, stir gently with a rubber spatula without injecting any air into this mixture of ganache.

2.   Remove the ganache from the top of the double boiler just before all the chocolate pieces are melted. Continue to stir the mixture. The residual heat will melt the remaining bits of chocolate. Set aside to cool to room temperature.

3.   When the ganache is cool but still in liquid form, stir in the rum, and coffee liqueur.

4.   Pour the ganache into an airtight container and refrigerate. (A shallow, wide container works best for cooling and scooping.)

5.   Using a potato peeler, shave the chilled milk chocolate into small curls. Place in a small bowl and refrigerate.

6.   When the ganache is firm enough to shape, scoop bite-size measures and form into irregular or round balls. Coat each truffle in chocolate curls and place in a candy cup or on a serving dish.

Makes 20 bite-size truffles

Velvet Truffles

8 ounces milk chocolate, finely chopped
1/4 cup heavy cream
2 tablespoons chocolate liqueur*

Coating:
1/2 cup alkalized cocoa powder

1.   Melt the chocolate and cream in the top of a double boiler over hot, not simmering, water. As the chocolate and cream melt together, stir gently with a rubber spatula without injecting any air into this mixture of ganache.

2.   Remove the ganache from the top of the double boiler just before all the chocolate pieces are melted. Continue to stir the mixture. The residual heat will melt the

(continued)

remaining bits of chocolate. Set aside to cool to room temperature.

3.   When the ganache is cool but still in liquid form, stir in the chocolate liqueur.

4.   Pour the ganache into an airtight container and refrigerate. (A shallow, wide container works best for cooling and scooping.)

5.   Place the cocoa powder in a small bowl. Set aside.

6.   When the ganache is firm enough to shape, scoop bite-size measures and form into irregular or round balls. Coat each truffle in cocoa powder and place in a candy cup or on a serving dish.

*Any quality liqueur can be substituted.

Makes 20 bite-size truffles

White Chocolate Truffles

For each of the following recipes, choose your favorite variety of white chocolate couverture. Before you begin, make sure all ingredients are at room temperature. If you coat, rather than enrobe, truffles, they must be stored in the refrigerator and will stay fresh for up to three weeks.

Angel Truffles

8 ounces white chocolate, finely chopped
3 tablespoons heavy cream
2 tablespoons Irish Cream liqueur*

Coating:
1/2 cup vanilla powder

1.   Melt the chocolate and cream in the top of a double boiler over hot, not simmering, water. As the chocolate and cream melt together, stir gently with a rubber spatula without injecting any air into this mixture of ganache.

2.   Remove the ganache from the top of the double boiler just before all the chocolate pieces are melted. Continue to stir the mixture. The residual heat will melt the remaining bits of chocolate. Set aside to cool to room temperature.

3.   When the ganache is cool but still in liquid form, stir in the Irish Cream liqueur.

4.   Pour the ganache into an airtight container and refrigerate. (A shallow, wide container works best for cooling and scooping.)

5.   Place the vanilla powder in a small bowl. Set aside.

6.   When the ganache is firm enough to shape, scoop bite-size measures and form into irregular or round balls. Coat each truffle in vanilla powder and place in a candy cup or on a serving dish.

*Any quality liqueur can be substituted.

Makes 20 bite-size truffles

Butter Cream Dream Truffles

8 ounces white chocolate, finely chopped
2 tablespoons heavy cream
2 tablespoons butter
2 tablespoons butterscotch liqueur

Coating:

¹/₂ cup powdered sugar, sifted

1. Melt the chocolate, cream, and butter in the top of a double boiler over hot, not simmering, water. As the chocolate, cream, and butter melt together, stir gently with a rubber spatula without injecting any air into this mixture of ganache.

2. Remove the ganache from the top of the double boiler just before all the chocolate pieces are melted. Continue to stir the mixture. The residual heat will melt the remaining bits of chocolate. Set aside to cool to room temperature.

3. When the ganache is cool but still in liquid form, stir in the butterscotch liqueur.

4. Pour the ganache into an airtight container and refrigerate. (A shallow, wide container works best for cooling and scooping.)

5. Place the powdered sugar in a small bowl. Set aside.

6. When the ganache is firm enough to shape, scoop bite-size measures and form into irregular or round balls. Coat each truffle in powdered sugar and place in a candy cup or on a serving dish.

Makes 20 bite-size truffles

Chocolate Truffle Toppings

If you decide to enrobe your truffles (seal them in a hard shell of chocolate), toppings can add fun, elegance, or an additional flavor.

- Butterscotch Chips
- Candied Fruit Bits
- Candy Confetti
- Chocolate Chips
- Chocolate Shavings
- Chocolate Sprinkles
- Cinnamon Hearts
- Cocoa Powder
- Colored Candy Sprinkles
- Colored Sugar Crystals
- Dried Fruit Bits
- Edible Gold Leaf
- Mocha Beans
- Peanut Butter Chips
- Spices
- Sweetened Coconut
- Toasted Nuts
- Toffee Bits/Crumbled Pralines

Café Vienna Truffles

8 ounces white chocolate, finely chopped
3 tablespoons heavy cream
1 tablespoon coffee liqueur
1 tablespoon instant espresso powder
1 teaspoon ground cinnamon

Coating:
$1/2$ cup alkalized cocoa powder
$1/4$ teaspoon cinnamon

1. Melt the chocolate and cream in the top of a double boiler over hot, not simmering, water. As the chocolate and cream melt together, stir gently with a rubber spatula without injecting any air into this mixture of ganache.

2. Remove the ganache from the top of the double boiler just before all the chocolate pieces are melted. Continue to stir the mixture. The residual heat will melt the remaining bits of chocolate. Set aside to cool to room temperature.

3. When the ganache is cool but still in liquid form, stir in the coffee liqueur, espresso powder, and cinnamon.

4. Pour the ganache into an airtight container and refrigerate. (A shallow, wide container works best for cooling and scooping.)

5. Sift together the cocoa powder and cinnamon. Place in a small bowl and set aside.

6. When the ganache is firm enough to shape, scoop bite-size measures and form into irregular or round balls. Coat each truffle in the cocoa powder mixture and place in a candy cup or on a serving dish.

Makes 20 bite-size truffles

Cookies and Cream Truffles

8 ounces white chocolate, finely chopped
5 tablespoons heavy cream
2 tablespoons dark chocolate cookie crumbs

Coating:
$1/2$ cup dark chocolate cookie crumbs

1. Melt the chocolate and cream in the top of a double boiler over hot, not simmering, water. As the chocolate and cream melt together, stir gently with a rubber spatula without injecting any air into this mixture of ganache.

2. Remove the ganache from the top of the double boiler just before all the chocolate pieces are melted. Continue to stir the mixture. The residual heat will melt the remaining bits of chocolate. Set aside to cool to room temperature.

3. When the ganache is cool but still in liquid form, stir in 2 tablespoons of cookie crumbs.

4. Pour the ganache into an airtight container and refrigerate. (A shallow, wide container works best for cooling and scooping.)

5. Place the remaining cookie crumbs in a small bowl. Set aside.

6. When the ganache is firm enough to shape, scoop bite-size measures and form into irregular or round balls. Coat each truffle in cookie crumbs and place in a candy cup or on a serving dish.

Makes 20 bite-size truffles

Eggnog Truffles

8 ounces white chocolate, finely chopped
3 tablespoons heavy cream
1 tablespoon brandy
1 tablespoon orange liqueur
1 teaspoon nutmeg

Coating:
½ cup sweetened, ground chocolate

1. Melt the chocolate and cream in the top of a double boiler over hot, not simmering, water. As the chocolate and cream melt together, stir gently with a rubber spatula without injecting any air into this mixture of ganache.

2. Remove the ganache from the top of the double boiler just before all the chocolate pieces are melted. Continue to stir the mixture. The residual heat will melt the remaining bits of chocolate. Set aside to cool to room temperature.

3. When the ganache is cool but still in liquid form, stir in the brandy, orange liqueur, and nutmeg.

4. Pour the ganache into an airtight container and refrigerate. (A shallow, wide container works best for cooling and scooping.)

5. Place the sweetened, ground chocolate in a small bowl. Set aside.

6. When the ganache is firm enough to shape, scoop bite-size measures and form into irregular or round balls. Coat each truffle in chocolate and place in a candy cup or on a serving dish.

Makes 20 bite-size truffles

Latte Truffles

8 ounces white chocolate, finely chopped
3 tablespoons heavy cream
1 tablespoon coffee liqueur
1 tablespoon instant espresso powder

Coating:
½ cup vanilla powder
1 teaspoon instant espresso powder

1. Melt the chocolate and cream in the top of a double boiler over hot, not simmering, water. As the chocolate and cream melt together, stir gently with a rubber spatula without injecting any air into this mixture of ganache.

2. Remove the ganache from the top of the double boiler just before all the chocolate pieces are melted. Continue to stir the mixture. The residual heat will melt the remaining bits of chocolate. Set aside to cool to room temperature.

3. When the ganache is cool but still in liquid form, stir in the coffee liqueur and espresso powder.

4. Pour the ganache into an airtight container and refrigerate. (A shallow, wide

(continued)

container works best for cooling and scooping.)

5. Sift together the vanilla powder and espresso powder. Place in a small bowl and set aside.

6. When the ganache is firm enough to shape, scoop bite-size measures and form into irregular or round balls. Coat each truffle in the vanilla powder mixture and place in a candy cup or on a serving dish.

Makes 20 bite-size truffles

Margarita Gold Truffles

8 ounces white chocolate, finely chopped
3 tablespoons heavy cream
1 tablespoon tequila
1 tablespoon Grand Marnier
1 teaspoon lime zest

Coating:
¹/₂ cup yellow sugar crystals

1. Melt the chocolate and cream in the top of a double boiler over hot, not simmering, water. As the chocolate and cream melt together, stir gently with a rubber spatula without injecting any air into this mixture of ganache.

2. Remove the ganache from the top of the double boiler just before all the chocolate pieces are melted. Continue to stir the mixture. The residual heat will melt the remaining bits of chocolate. Set aside to cool to room temperature.

3. When the ganache is cool but still in liquid form, stir in the tequila, Grand Marnier, and lime zest.

4. Pour the ganache into an airtight container and refrigerate. (A shallow, wide container works best for cooling and scooping.)

5. Place the yellow sugar crystals in a small bowl. Set aside.

6. When the ganache is firm enough to shape, scoop bite-size measures and form into irregular or round balls. Coat each truffle in sugar crystals and place in a candy cup or on a serving dish.

Makes 20 bite-size truffles

Peaches and Cream Truffles

8 ounces white chocolate, finely chopped
3 tablespoons heavy cream
1 tablespoon peach liqueur
1 tablespoon Irish Cream liqueur

Coating:
4 ounces white chocolate, chilled

1. Melt the chocolate and cream in the top of a double boiler over hot, not simmering, water. As the chocolate and cream melt together, stir gently with a rubber spatula without injecting any air into this mixture of ganache.

2. Remove the ganache from the top of the double boiler just before all the chocolate pieces are melted. Continue to stir the

mixture. The residual heat will melt the remaining bits of chocolate. Set aside to cool to room temperature.

3.   When the ganache is cool but still in liquid form, stir in the peach and Irish Cream liqueurs.

4.   Pour the ganache into an airtight container and refrigerate. (A shallow, wide container works best for cooling and scooping.)

5.   Using a potato peeler, shave the white chocolate into small curls. Place in a small bowl and refrigerate.

6.   When the ganache is firm enough to shape, scoop bite-size measures and form into irregular or round balls. Coat each truffle in white chocolate curls and place in a candy cup or on a serving dish.

Makes 20 bite-size truffles

Praline Truffles

8 ounces white chocolate, finely chopped
3 tablespoons heavy cream
2 tablespoons pecan liqueur

Coating:
¹/₂ cup toffee bits or crumbled pecan
*   pralines*

1.   Melt the chocolate and cream in the top of a double boiler over hot, not simmering, water. As the chocolate and cream melt together, stir gently with a rubber spatula without injecting any air into this mixture of ganache.

2.   Remove the ganache from the top of the double boiler just before all the chocolate pieces are melted. Continue to stir the mixture. The residual heat will melt the remaining bits of chocolate. Set aside to cool to room temperature.

3.   When the ganache is cool but still in liquid form, stir in the pecan liqueur.

4.   Pour the ganache into an airtight container and refrigerate. (A shallow, wide container works best for cooling and scooping.)

5.   Place the toffee bits or crumbled pralines in a small bowl. Set aside.

6.   When the ganache is firm enough to shape, scoop bite-size measures and form into irregular or round balls. Coat each truffle in the toffee or pralines and place in a candy cup or on a serving dish.

Makes 20 bite-size truffles

Rainbow Truffles

8 ounces white chocolate, finely chopped
3 tablespoons heavy cream
1 tablespoon seedless strawberry preserves
1 tablespoon orange juice concentrate
¹/₂ teaspoon lemon zest
¹/₂ teaspoon lime zest

Coating:
¹/₂ cup candy confetti

1.   Melt the chocolate and cream in the top of a double boiler over hot, not simmering, water. As the chocolate and

(continued)

cream melt together, stir gently with a rubber spatula without injecting any air into this mixture of ganache.

2.　Remove the ganache from the top of the double boiler just before all the chocolate pieces are melted. Continue to stir the mixture. The residual heat will melt the remaining bits of chocolate. Set aside to cool to room temperature.

3.　When the ganache is cool but still in liquid form, stir in the strawberry preserves, orange juice concentrate, lemon zest, and lime zest.

4.　Pour the ganache into an airtight container and refrigerate. (A shallow, wide container works best for cooling and scooping.)

5.　Place the candy confetti in a small bowl. Set aside.

6.　When the ganache is firm enough to shape, scoop bite-size measures and form into irregular or round balls. Coat each truffle in confetti and place in a candy cup or on a serving dish.

Makes 20 bite-size truffles

Raspberry Sparkle Truffles

8 ounces white chocolate, finely chopped
3 tablespoons heavy cream
1 tablespoon Marc de Champagne*
1 tablespoon raspberry liqueur

Coating:
¹/₂ cup clear sugar crystals

1.　Melt the chocolate and cream in the top of a double boiler over hot, not simmering, water. As the chocolate and cream melt together, stir gently with a rubber spatula without injecting any air into this mixture of ganache.

2.　Remove the ganache from the top of the double boiler just before all the chocolate pieces are melted. Continue to stir the mixture. The residual heat will melt the remaining bits of chocolate. Set aside to cool to room temperature.

3.　When the ganache is cool but still in liquid form, stir in the Marc de Champagne and raspberry liqueur.

4.　Pour the ganache into an airtight container and refrigerate. (A shallow, wide container works best for cooling and scooping.)

5.　Place the sugar crystals in a small bowl. Set aside.

6.　When the ganache is firm enough to shape, scoop bite-size measures and form into irregular or round balls. Coat each truffle in the sugar crystals and place in a candy cup or on a serving dish.

*Marc de Champagne is a concentrated flavoring. Natural champagne, in the required ratios, will not give you enough flavor.

Makes 20 bite-size truffles

Spiced Pear Truffles

8 ounces white chocolate, finely chopped
3 tablespoons heavy cream
2 tablespoons pear liqueur
¹/₄ teaspoon ground cloves

Coating:
¹/₂ cup macaroon crumbs

1. Melt the chocolate and cream in the top of a double boiler over hot, not simmering, water. As the chocolate and cream melt together, stir gently with a rubber spatula without injecting any air into this mixture of ganache.

2. Remove the ganache from the top of the double boiler just before all the chocolate pieces are melted. Continue to stir the mixture. The residual heat will melt the remaining bits of chocolate. Set aside to cool to room temperature.

3. When the ganache is cool but still in liquid form, stir in the pear liqueur and ground cloves.

4. Pour the ganache into an airtight container and refrigerate. (A shallow, wide container works best for cooling and scooping.)

5. Place the macaroon crumbs in a small bowl. Set aside.

6. When the ganache is firm enough to shape, scoop bite-size measures and form into irregular or round balls. Coat each truffle in macaroon crumbs and place in a candy cup or on a serving dish.

Makes 20 bite-size truffles

Sunrise in Paradise Truffles

8 ounces white chocolate, finely chopped
3 tablespoons heavy cream
1 tablespoon rum
2 teaspoons Key Largo liqueur
1 teaspoon orange liqueur
1 teaspoon grenadine

Coating:
¹/₂ cup pink, yellow, and orange sugar crystals

1. Melt the chocolate and cream in the top of a double boiler over hot, not simmering, water. As the chocolate and cream melt together, stir gently with a rubber spatula without injecting any air into this mixture of ganache.

2. Remove the ganache from the top of the double boiler just before all the chocolate pieces are melted. Continue to stir the mixture. The residual heat will melt the remaining bits of chocolate. Set aside to cool to room temperature.

3. When the ganache is cool but still in liquid form, stir in the rum, Key Largo liqueur, orange liqueur, and grenadine.

4. Pour the ganache into an airtight container and refrigerate. (A shallow, wide container works best for cooling and scooping.)

5. Mix the sugar crystals together. Place in a small bowl and set aside.

6. When the ganache is firm enough to shape, scoop bite-size measures and form into irregular or round balls. Coat each

(continued)

truffle in sugar crystals and place in a candy cup or on a serving dish.

Makes 20 bite-size truffles

Valentine Truffles

8 ounces white chocolate, finely chopped
3 tablespoons heavy cream
2 tablespoons cinnamon liqueur

Coating:
1/2 cup red sugar crystals

1. Melt the chocolate and cream in the top of a double boiler over hot, not simmering, water. As the chocolate and cream melt together, stir gently with a rubber spatula without injecting any air into this mixture of ganache.

2. Remove the ganache from the top of the double boiler just before all the chocolate pieces are melted. Continue to stir the mixture. The residual heat will melt the remaining bits of chocolate. Set aside to cool to room temperature.

3. When the ganache is cool but still in liquid form, stir in the cinnamon liqueur.

4. Pour the ganache into an airtight container and refrigerate. (A shallow, wide container works best for cooling and scooping.)

5. Place the red sugar crystals in a small bowl. Set aside.

6. When the ganache is firm enough to shape, scoop bite-size measures and form into irregular or round balls. Coat

---

Chocolate Truffle Coatings

If you're serving a variety of truffles and you want to coat (rather than enrobe) them, you may want to use different coatings to identify the flavors. Here are some ideas:

- Chocolate Sprinkles
- Cocoa Powder
- Colored Sugar Crystals
- Cookie/Graham Cracker Crumbs
- Finely Chopped, Toasted Nuts
- Grated Chocolate
- Mini Chocolate Chips
- Powdered Sugar
- Sugar and Spice
- Superfine Sugar
- Sweetened Coconut
- Vanilla Powder

each truffle in the red sugar crystals and place in a candy cup or on a serving dish.

Makes 20 bite-size truffles

Zabaglione Truffles

8 ounces white chocolate, finely chopped
3 tablespoons heavy cream
2 tablespoons Marsala or sweet sherry
$^1/_2$ teaspoon lemon zest

Coating:
$^1/_2$ cup alkalized cocoa powder

1.   Melt the chocolate and cream in the top of a double boiler over hot, not simmering, water. As the chocolate and cream melt together, stir gently with a rubber spatula without injecting any air into this mixture of ganache.

2.   Remove the ganache from the top of the double boiler just before all the chocolate pieces are melted. Continue to stir the mixture. The residual heat will melt the remaining bits of chocolate. Set aside to cool to room temperature.

3.   When the ganache is cool but still in liquid form, stir in the Marsala or sweet sherry and lemon zest.

4.   Pour the ganache into an airtight container and refrigerate. (A shallow, wide container works best for cooling and scooping.)

5.   Place the cocoa powder in a small bowl. Set aside.

6.   When the ganache is firm enough to shape, scoop bite-size measures and form into irregular or round balls. Coat each truffle in cocoa powder and place in a candy cup or on a serving dish.

Makes 20 bite-size truffles

Truffle Kisses

An alternative to scooping and rolling truffles is to "pipe" the ganache into chocolate kiss shapes: When the ganache is cool enough to hold its shape, place it in a pastry bag fitted with a $^1/_2$-inch round or star tip. Pipe bite-size cones or swirls onto a cookie sheet lined with wax paper. Refrigerate until set. Coat with cocoa powder, serve.

Chocolate Grapes

We first created this centerpiece for one of our winery clients. Chocolate truffles, coated with cocoa powder or grated chocolate, are piled into the shape of a cluster of grapes, and decorated with chocolate grape leaves and chocolate "tendrils." (See Chapter 11 to make the chocolate leaves and chocolate dough.) Here's a scaled down version:

>*24 petite chocolate truffles (coated)*
>*2 chocolate grape leaves*
>*2 chocolate tendrils (molded out of chocolate dough)*

1. Place approximately half of the truffles in a loose triangular shape, on an elegant dish.

2. Use the remaining truffles to create two more loose layers on top, the way grape clusters form naturally.

3. Add the chocolate grape leaves and tendrils!

Chocolate Fudge

Sweeter than a truffle, chocolate fudge is a thick, rich, moist, silken bite of chocolate. There are many recipes for chocolate fudge. Some require complex timing and techniques; however, I've found these evaporated milk-based fudge recipes to be just as delicious and far less frustrating.

Bittersweet Espresso Fudge

>$1^1/_2$ cups superfine sugar
>2 tablespoons butter
>$^1/_2$ cup (4 ounces) evaporated milk
>$^1/_3$ cup marshmallow cream
>12 ounces bittersweet chocolate, finely chopped
>2 teaspoons pure vanilla extract
>2 tablespoons instant espresso powder
>1 cup almonds, toasted and roughly chopped

1. Line the bottom of an 8-inch square baking pan with waxed or parchment paper. Lightly butter the sides of the pan.

2. In a heavy-bottomed saucepan, combine the sugar, butter, and evaporated milk, stirring constantly, over medium heat. When the mixture comes to a boil, reduce the heat to low, and continue stirring for 5 minutes.

3. Remove the pan from the heat, and fold in the marshmallow cream.

4. Fold in the finely chopped chocolate. Stir until the chocolate is completely melted and the mixture is smooth.

5. Gently fold in the vanilla extract, espresso powder, and almonds, blending until smooth.

6. Pour the fudge into the prepared pan, cover with plastic wrap, and refrigerate. Chill for at least 2 hours.

7. When firm, run a warm stainless steel spatula around the sides of the pan to free the fudge. Remove the parchment

paper bottom. Cut into bite-size squares, and place in candy cups, on a serving dish, or in an airtight container. Fudge can be stored at room temperature for up to a week.

Makes 36 bite-size squares

Butter Crunch Fudge

1 cup superfine sugar
1 cup dark brown sugar, firmly packed
2 tablespoons butter
$^1/_2$ cup (4 ounces) evaporated milk
$^1/_2$ cup marshmallow cream
8 ounces milk chocolate, finely chopped
2 teaspoons butterscotch liqueur
$^1/_2$ cup butterscotch chips
$^1/_2$ cup peanut brittle, roughly chopped

1. Line the bottom of an 8-inch square baking pan with waxed or parchment paper. Lightly butter the sides of the pan.

2. In a heavy-bottomed saucepan, combine the sugars, butter, and evaporated milk, stirring constantly, over medium heat. When the mixture comes to a boil, reduce the heat to low, and continue stirring for 5 minutes.

3. Remove the pan from the heat, and fold in the marshmallow cream.

4. Fold in the finely chopped chocolate. Stir until the chocolate is completely melted and the mixture is smooth.

5. Gently fold in the liqueur, butterscotch chips, and peanut brittle, blending until smooth.

6. Pour the fudge into the prepared pan, cover with plastic wrap, and refrigerate. Chill for at least 2 hours.

7. When firm, run a warm stainless steel spatula around the sides of the pan to free the fudge. Remove the parchment paper bottom. Cut into bite-size squares, and place in candy cups, on a serving dish, or in an airtight container. Fudge can be stored at room temperature for up to a week.

Makes 36 bite-size squares

Cinnamon Spice Fudge

1 cup superfine sugar
2 tablespoons butter
$^1/_3$ cup evaporated milk
$^1/_2$ cup marshmallow cream
8 ounces white chocolate, finely chopped
2 teaspoons cinnamon liqueur
$^1/_4$ cup tiny candy cinnamon hearts
1 teaspoon ground allspice

1. Line the bottom of an 8-inch square baking pan with waxed or parchment paper. Lightly butter the sides of the pan.

2. In a heavy-bottomed saucepan, combine the sugar, butter, and evaporated milk, stirring constantly, over medium heat. When the mixture comes to a boil, reduce the heat to low, and continue stirring for 5 minutes.

3. Remove the pan from the heat, and fold in the marshmallow cream.

(continued)

4.   Fold in the finely chopped chocolate. Stir until the chocolate is completely melted and the mixture is smooth.

5.   Gently fold in the liqueur, hearts, and spice, blending until smooth.

6.   Pour the fudge into the prepared pan, cover with plastic wrap, and refrigerate. Chill for at least 2 hours.

7.   When firm, run a warm stainless steel spatula around the sides of the pan to free the fudge. Remove the parchment paper bottom. Cut into bite-size squares, and place in candy cups, on a serving dish, or in an airtight container. Fudge can be stored at room temperature for up to a week.

Makes 36 bite-size squares

Classic Fudge

2 cups superfine sugar
2 tablespoons butter
$^1/_2$ cup (4 ounces) evaporated milk
$^1/_2$ cup marshmallow cream
8 ounces semisweet chocolate, finely
    chopped
2 teaspoons pure vanilla extract
1 cup walnuts, toasted and roughly
    chopped

1.   Line the bottom of an 8-inch square baking pan with waxed or parchment paper. Lightly butter the sides of the pan.

2.   In a heavy-bottomed saucepan, combine the sugar, butter, and evaporated milk, stirring constantly, over medium heat.

When the mixture comes to a boil, reduce the heat to low, and continue stirring for 5 minutes.

3.   Remove the pan from the heat, and fold in the marshmallow cream.

4.   Fold in the finely chopped chocolate. Stir until the chocolate is completely melted and the mixture is smooth.

5.   Gently fold in the vanilla extract and walnuts, blending until smooth.

6.   Pour the fudge into the prepared pan, cover with plastic wrap, and refrigerate. Chill for at least 2 hours.

7.   When firm, run a warm stainless steel spatula around the sides of the pan to free the fudge. Remove the parchment paper bottom. Cut into bite-size squares, and place in candy cups, on a serving dish, or in an airtight container. Fudge can be stored at room temperature for up to a week.

Makes 36 bite-size squares

Congo Fudge

$^1/_2$ cup superfine sugar
1 cup light brown sugar, firmly packed
2 tablespoons butter
$^1/_2$ cup (4 ounces) evaporated milk
$^1/_2$ cup marshmallow cream
4 ounces semisweet chocolate, finely
    chopped
4 ounces milk chocolate, finely chopped
2 teaspoons pure vanilla extract
$^1/_2$ cup (4 ounces) glazed fruit bits
$^1/_2$ cup Brazil nuts, toasted and roughly
    chopped

1. Line the bottom of an 8-inch square baking pan with waxed or parchment paper. Lightly butter the sides of the pan.

2. In a heavy-bottomed saucepan, combine the sugars, butter, and evaporated milk, stirring constantly, over medium heat. When the mixture comes to a boil, reduce the heat to low, and continue stirring for 5 minutes.

3. Remove the pan from the heat, and fold in the marshmallow cream.

4. Fold in the finely chopped chocolate. Stir until the chocolate is completely melted and the mixture is smooth.

5. Gently fold in the vanilla extract, fruit bits, and Brazil nuts, blending until smooth.

6. Pour the fudge into the prepared pan, cover with plastic wrap, and refrigerate. Chill for at least 2 hours.

7. When firm, run a warm stainless steel spatula around the sides of the pan to free the fudge. Remove the parchment paper bottom. Cut into bite-size squares, and place in candy cups, on a serving dish, or in an airtight container. Fudge can be stored at room temperature for up to a week.

Makes 36 bite-size squares

White Chocolate Fudge

1 cup superfine sugar
2 tablespoons butter
¹/₃ cup evaporated milk
¹/₂ cup marshmallow cream
8 ounces white chocolate, finely chopped

2 teaspoons pure vanilla extract
1 cup cashews, toasted and roughly chopped

1. Line the bottom of an 8-inch square baking pan with waxed or parchment paper. Lightly butter the sides of the pan.

2. In a heavy-bottomed saucepan, combine the sugar, butter, and evaporated milk, stirring constantly, over medium heat. When the mixture comes to a boil, reduce the heat to low, and continue stirring for 5 minutes.

3. Remove the pan from the heat, and fold in the marshmallow cream.

4. Fold in the finely chopped chocolate. Stir until the chocolate is completely melted and the mixture is smooth.

5. Gently fold in the vanilla extract and cashews, blending until smooth.

6. Pour the fudge into the prepared pan, cover with plastic wrap, and refrigerate. Chill for at least 2 hours.

7. When firm, run a warm stainless steel spatula around the sides of the pan to free the fudge. Remove the parchment paper bottom. Cut into bite-size squares, and place in candy cups, on a serving dish, or in an airtight container. Fudge can be stored at room temperature for up to a week.

Makes 36 bite-size squares

Rocky Road

Not being able to find rocky road made with *dark* chocolate (my father's favorite) started me on the path to becoming a chocolatier. One day I boldly decided to make some. How hard could it be? Chocolate, marshmallows, and nuts. Simple. Several attempts later (which my father loved, no matter how imperfect), I learned that the chocolate needed to be tempered, that I needed to taste all the ingredients before using (our grocery store had allowed packaged walnuts to go rancid), and that large marshmallows worked better than small. I also learned which ratios produced the best balance.

ET's Favorite Rocky Road

12 ounces milk chocolate
$10^1/_2$ ounces large marshmallows
$^1/_3$ cup Reese's Pieces
$^2/_3$ cup dry roasted peanuts

1. Line the bottom of an 8-inch square baking pan with waxed or parchment paper.
2. Temper the chocolate (see Chapter 2 for tempering directions). Cool to room temperature.
3. Working quickly, gently fold the marshmallows, Reese's Pieces, and peanuts into the chocolate.
4. Pour into the prepared pan and refrigerate for 10 to 20 minutes.
5. When set, run a warm stainless steel spatula around the sides of the pan to free the rocky road. Remove the parchment paper bottom. Cut into chunks and place on a serving dish or in an airtight container. Rocky road is best if served and stored (or hidden!) at room temperature and will stay fresh for up to 3 weeks.

Makes 36 bite-size squares

Ray's Favorite Rocky Road

12 ounces semisweet chocolate
$10^1/_2$ ounces large marshmallows
1 cup walnuts, toasted and roughly chopped

1. Line the bottom of an 8-inch square baking pan with waxed or parchment paper.
2. Temper the chocolate (see Chapter 2 for tempering directions). Cool to room temperature.
3. Working quickly, gently fold the marshmallows and walnuts into the chocolate.
4. Pour into the prepared pan and refrigerate for 10 to 20 minutes.
5. When set, run a warm stainless steel spatula around the sides of the pan to free the rocky road. Remove the parchment paper bottom. Cut into chunks and place on a serving dish or in an airtight container. Rocky road is best if served and stored (or hidden!) at room temperature and will stay fresh for up to 3 weeks.

Makes 36 bite-size squares

Rudolph's Favorite Rocky Road

12 ounces white chocolate
10¹/₂ ounces large marshmallows
³/₄ cup glazed red cherries, halved
¹/₄ cup crumbled candy canes

1. Line the bottom of an 8-inch square baking pan with waxed or parchment paper.
2. Temper the chocolate (see Chapter 2 for tempering directions). Cool to room temperature.
3. Working quickly, gently fold the marshmallows, cherries, and crumbled candy canes into the chocolate.
4. Pour into the prepared pan and refrigerate for 10 to 20 minutes.
5. When set, run a warm stainless steel spatula around the sides of the pan to free the rocky road. Remove the parchment paper bottom. Cut into chunks and place on a serving dish or in an airtight container. Rocky road is best if served and stored (or hidden!) at room temperature and will stay fresh for up to 3 weeks.

Makes 36 bite-size squares

Chocolate Clusters

For a museum opening, I was asked to design an array of bite-size white chocolate treats—on the morning of the event! Limited time gave birth to a collection of these new sensations, which quickly became almost as popular as our chocolate truffles.

Aloha Clusters

8 ounces white chocolate
¹/₄ cup glazed pineapple bits
¹/₄ cup sweetened coconut flakes
¹/₂ cup macadamia nuts, toasted and
*   roughly chopped*

1. Place 24 foil or paper candy cups in mini-muffin tins.
2. Temper the chocolate (see Chapter 2 for tempering directions). Cool to room temperature.
3. Working quickly, gently fold the pineapple bits, coconut, and macadamia nuts into the chocolate. When all ingredients are completely coated, place a teaspoonful in each candy cup.
4. Chill for 10 minutes.
5. When set, place on a serving dish or in an airtight container. Clusters are best if served and stored at room temperature and will stay fresh for up to 6 weeks.

Makes 24 clusters

Banana Nut Clusters

8 ounces semisweet chocolate
¹/₂ cup dried bananas, roughly chopped
¹/₂ cup almonds, toasted and roughly
*   chopped*

1. Place 24 foil or paper candy cups in mini-muffin tins.
2. Temper the chocolate (see Chapter 2 for tempering directions). Cool to room temperature.

(continued)

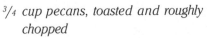

3.   Working quickly, gently fold the bananas and almonds into the chocolate. When all ingredients are completely coated, place a teaspoonful in each candy cup.

4.   Chill for 10 minutes.

5.   When set, place on a serving dish or in an airtight container. Clusters are best if served and stored at room temperature and will stay fresh for up to 6 weeks.

Makes 24 clusters

Bing Cherry Clusters

8 ounces semisweet chocolate
1 cup dried Bing cherries

1.   Place 24 foil or paper candy cups in mini-muffin tins.

2.   Temper the chocolate (see Chapter 2 for tempering directions). Cool to room temperature.

3.   Working quickly, gently fold the cherries into the chocolate. When the cherries are completely coated, place a teaspoonful in each candy cup.

4.   Chill for 10 minutes.

5.   When set, place on a serving dish or in an airtight container. Clusters are best if served and stored at room temperature and will stay fresh for up to 6 weeks.

Makes 24 clusters

Bittersweet Praline Clusters

8 ounces bittersweet chocolate

³/₄ cup pecans, toasted and roughly
*   chopped*
¹/₄ cup toffee bits or crumbled pralines

1.   Place 24 foil or paper candy cups in mini-muffin tins.

2.   Temper the chocolate (see Chapter 2 for tempering directions). Cool to room temperature.

3.   Working quickly, gently fold the pecans and toffee or pralines into the chocolate. When all ingredients are completely coated, place a teaspoonful in each candy cup.

4.   Chill for 10 minutes.

5.   When set, place on a serving dish or in an airtight container. Clusters are best if served and stored at room temperature and will stay fresh for up to 6 weeks.

Makes 24 clusters

Black and White Clusters

8 ounces white chocolate
1 cup semisweet chocolate chips

1.   Place 24 foil or paper candy cups in mini-muffin tins.

2.   Temper the chocolate (see Chapter 2 for tempering directions). Cool to room temperature. Be sure the tempered chocolate is cool enough, so the chips don't melt.

3.   Working quickly, gently fold the chocolate chips into the white chocolate. When the chips are completely coated, place a teaspoonful in each candy cup.

4. Chill for 10 minutes.

5. When set, place on a serving dish or in an airtight container. Clusters are best if served and stored at room temperature and will stay fresh for up to 6 weeks.

Makes 24 clusters

Blueberry Clusters

8 ounces milk chocolate
1 cup dried blueberries

1. Place 24 foil or paper candy cups in mini-muffin tins.

2. Temper the chocolate (see Chapter 2 for tempering directions). Cool to room temperature.

3. Working quickly, gently fold the blueberries into the chocolate. When the blueberries are completely coated, place a teaspoonful in each candy cup.

4. Chill for 10 minutes.

5. When set, place on a serving dish or in an airtight container. Clusters are best if served and stored at room temperature and will stay fresh for up to 6 weeks.

Makes 24 clusters

Chocolate Mint Clusters

8 ounces semisweet chocolate
1 cup chocolate-mint chips

1. Place 24 foil or paper candy cups in mini-muffin tins.

2. Temper the chocolate (see Chapter 2 for tempering directions). Cool to room temperature. Be sure the tempered chocolate is cool enough, so the chips don't melt.

3. Working quickly, gently fold the mint chips into the chocolate. When the chips are completely coated, place a teaspoonful in each candy cup.

4. Chill for 10 minutes.

5. When set, place on a serving dish or in an airtight container. Clusters are best if served and stored at room temperature and will stay fresh for up to 6 weeks.

Makes 24 clusters

A Heart Like No Other

It was romantic Richard Cadbury, son of chocolate pioneer John Cadbury, who in 1861 was the first to fill a heart-shaped box with chocolate confections. This delicious way of saying "I love you" remains a favorite way to celebrate Valentine's Day all over the world.

Cranberry Clusters

8 ounces white chocolate
1 cup dried cranberries

1. Place 24 foil or paper candy cups in mini-muffin tins.
2. Temper the chocolate (see Chapter 2 for tempering directions). Cool to room temperature.
3. Working quickly, gently fold the cranberries into the chocolate. When the cranberries are completely coated, place a teaspoonful in each candy cup.
4. Chill for 10 minutes.
5. When set, place on a serving dish or in an airtight container. Clusters are best if served and stored at room temperature and will stay fresh for up to 6 weeks.

Makes 24 clusters

Mocha Bean Clusters

8 ounces milk chocolate
¹/₂ cup mocha beans*
¹/₂ cup hazelnuts, toasted and roughly chopped

1. Place 24 foil or paper candy cups in mini-muffin tins.
2. Temper the chocolate (see Chapter 2 for tempering directions). Cool to room temperature.
3. Working quickly, gently fold the mocha beans and hazelnuts into the chocolate. When all ingredients are completely coated, place a teaspoonful in each candy cup.
4. Chill for 10 minutes.
5. When set, place on a serving dish or in an airtight container. Clusters are best if served and stored at room temperature and will stay fresh for up to 6 weeks.

   *Mocha beans are pieces of solid, coffee-flavored chocolate, shaped like coffee beans.

Makes 24 clusters

Peanut Butter Clusters

8 ounces milk chocolate
1 cup peanut butter chips

1. Place 24 foil or paper candy cups in mini-muffin tins.
2. Temper the chocolate (see Chapter 2 for tempering directions). Cool to room temperature. Be sure the tempered chocolate is cool enough, so the chips don't melt.
3. Working quickly, gently fold the peanut butter chips into the chocolate. When the chips are completely coated, place a teaspoonful in each candy cup.
4. Chill for 10 minutes.
5. When set, place on a serving dish or in an airtight container. Clusters are best if served and stored at room temperature and will stay fresh for up to 6 weeks.

Makes 24 clusters

Sweet Harvest Clusters

8 ounces milk chocolate
1/2 cup mixed dried fruit bits
1/2 cup dry roasted mixed nuts, roughly
chopped

1. Place 24 foil or paper candy cups in mini-muffin tins.

2. Temper the chocolate (see Chapter 2 for tempering directions). Cool to room temperature.

3. Working quickly, gently fold the fruit bits and mixed nuts into the chocolate. When all ingredients are completely coated, place a teaspoonful in each candy cup.

4. Chill for 10 minutes.

5. When set, place on a serving dish or in an airtight container. Clusters are best if served and stored at room temperature and will stay fresh for up to 6 weeks.

Makes 24 clusters

Walnut Spice Clusters

8 ounces white chocolate
1/2 cup candied ginger, roughly chopped
1/2 cup walnuts, toasted and roughly
chopped

1. Place 24 foil or paper candy cups in mini-muffin tins.

2. Temper the chocolate (see Chapter 2 for tempering directions). Cool to room temperature.

3. Working quickly, gently fold the ginger and walnuts into the chocolate.

(continued)

How to Host a Chocolate Cluster-Making Party

The potential ingredient combinations for chocolate clusters are endless. Ask each guest to bring chocolate and their favorite dry ingredient(s). Or give each guest a list of ingredients to bring to ensure a wide selection. Place each ingredient in the center of the table or along a buffet table and let your guests' imaginations take over.

Another idea is to give your guests a theme, and ask them to bring coordinating ingredients. For example, Hawaiian, Mardi Gras, Kid Stuff, etc.

As with a cookie-swapping party, at the end, your guests can take home a selection of flavors.

When all ingredients are completely coated, place a teaspoonful in each candy cup.

4. Chill for 10 minutes.

5. When set, place on a serving dish or in an airtight container. Clusters are best if served and stored at room temperature and will stay fresh for up to 6 weeks.

Makes 24 clusters

Chocolate Turtles

Originally, a puddle of caramel and chocolate formed a "shell" over buttery pecan "legs" for these charming treats. But I can never resist creating variations.

Cold Hands, Warm Hearts

For years, confectioneries preferred hiring women partly because their body temperatures were slightly lower than men's; therefore, the chocolate didn't melt on their fingertips as quickly.

Classic Pecan Turtles

6 ounces semisweet chocolate
100 pecan halves (about 1 cup), toasted
8 ounces vanilla caramels
1 tablespoon water
1 teaspoon pecan liqueur

1. Line cookie sheets with waxed or parchment paper.

2. Temper the chocolate (see Chapter 2 for tempering directions). Cool to room temperature.

3. Place four pecan halves together, forming a "+" sign, to create the legs of your turtles.

4. Melt the caramels, water, and liqueur in the top of a double boiler over simmering water. Cool slightly.

5. Place a dollop of caramel over the pecan legs, covering half of each pecan, to create the bodies of your turtles. Set aside to cool for 10 minutes.

6. Place a dollop of chocolate over the caramel.

7. Place in the refrigerator for 10 minutes.

8. When set, place on a serving dish or in an airtight container. Turtles are best if served and stored at room temperature and will stay fresh for up to 6 weeks.

Makes 25 turtles

Caramel Apple Turtles

6 ounces milk chocolate
100 walnut halves (about 1 cup), toasted
8 ounces chocolate caramels
1 tablespoon water
1 teaspoon apple liqueur
1/4 cup dried apple bits

1. Line cookie sheets with waxed or parchment paper.
2. Temper the chocolate (see Chapter 2 for tempering directions). Cool to room temperature.
3. Place four walnut halves together, forming a "+" sign, to create the legs of your turtles.
4. Melt the caramels, water, and liqueur in the top of a double boiler over simmering water. Cool slightly.
5. Place a dollop of caramel over the walnut legs, covering half of each walnut, to create the bodies of your turtles. Set aside to cool for 10 minutes.
6. Place a dollop of chocolate over the caramel.
7. Sprinkle apple bits on top of your turtle's chocolate shell. Place in the refrigerator for 10 minutes.
8. When set, place on a serving dish or in an airtight container. Turtles are best if served and stored at room temperature and will stay fresh for up to 6 weeks.

Makes 25 turtles

Sweet and Tart Turtles

6 ounces white chocolate
100 almonds (about 1 cup), skinned and toasted
8 ounces vanilla caramels
1 tablespoon water
1 teaspoon almond liqueur
1/4 cup dried apricot bits

1. Line cookie sheets with waxed or parchment paper.
2. Temper the chocolate (see Chapter 2 for tempering directions). Cool to room temperature.
3. Place four almonds together, forming a "+" sign, to create the legs of your turtles.
4. Melt the caramels, water, and liqueur in the top of a double boiler over simmering water. Cool slightly.
5. Place a dollop of caramel over the almond legs, covering half of each almond, to create the bodies of your turtles. Cool for 10 minutes.
6. Place a dollop of chocolate over the caramel.
7. Sprinkle apricot bits on top of your turtle's chocolate shell. Place in the refrigerator for 10 minutes.
8. When set, place on a serving dish or in an airtight container. Turtles are best if served and stored at room temperature and will stay fresh for up to 6 weeks.

Makes 25 turtles

Pralines

Although not chocolate, these sweet crunchy delights make wonderful ingredients and toppings for chocolate truffles, confections, and desserts.

$^1/_4$ cup superfine sugar
$^1/_4$ cup light brown sugar, firmly packed
$^1/_8$ teaspoon cream of tartar
1 teaspoon pure vanilla extract
2 tablespoons water
$^1/_2$ cup pecans,* toasted and chopped

1.   Line a cookie sheet with waxed or parchment paper.

2.   Using a wooden spoon, combine the sugars, cream of tartar, vanilla, and water in a heavy-bottomed saucepan or skillet. Place over medium heat, stirring continuously for approximately 4 to 6 minutes.

3.   When the mixture turns a dark honey color, remove from heat and add the nuts. Working quickly, blend thoroughly.

4.   Pour the mixture onto the parchment paper and spread into a thin layer.

5.   When *completely* cool, crumble and store in an airtight container. Pralines are best if used and stored at room temperature and should stay fresh for up to 6 weeks.

*Traditional pralines are made with pecans; however, other nuts may be substituted.

Here are a few easy recipes for desperately delicious chocolate confections.

Buried Treasures

A delicious surprise is buried in these mocha-flavored treasures.

$^3/_4$ cup powdered sugar
$^1/_4$ cup alkalized cocoa powder
1 tablespoon instant espresso powder
$1^1/_4$ cups crumbled vanilla cookies
$^1/_2$ cup almonds, toasted and finely chopped
2 tablespoons coffee liqueur
$1^1/_2$ tablespoons light corn syrup
36 mocha beans*

1.   Sift together $^1/_2$ cup of the powdered sugar, 2 tablespoons of the cocoa powder, and the espresso powder. Mix in the cookie crumbs and chopped nuts.

2.   Fold in the liqueur and corn syrup.

3.   Cover and chill for at least an hour.

4.   Sift together the remaining sugar and cocoa powder to create a coating mixture. Form a 1-inch ball with the chilled mixture around each mocha bean. Roll each ball in the coating mixture.

5.   Place in candy cups, on a serving dish, or in an airtight container. Buried Treasures are best if served at room temperature, but should be stored in the refrigerator. They should stay fresh for up to 3 weeks.

*Mocha beans are pieces of solid, coffee-flavored chocolate, shaped like coffee beans.

Makes 36 Buried Treasures

Raspberry Rochers

These chocolate-coated treats are a sweeter, crunchier version of a nut cluster.

2 cups almonds, blanched and slivered
³/₄ cup powdered sugar
2 tablespoons raspberry liqueur
8 ounces semisweet chocolate

1. Preheat the oven to 325°F.
2. In a small bowl, mix the almonds, sugar, and liqueur until thoroughly blended and slightly moist.
3. Spread the mixture on a cookie sheet and bake for 30 minutes, *mixing every 3 to 4 minutes* to ensure even toasting and to prevent burning. (After about 20 minutes the sugar should begin to crystallize around the almonds.) Remove the mixture and continue mixing while cooling.
4. Temper the chocolate (see Chapter 2 for tempering directions). Cool to room temperature.
5. Line a cookie sheet with waxed paper.
6. When the almond mixture is room temperature, break into bite-size pieces and gently fold into the chocolate.
7. Once coated, place the Raspberry Rochers on the lined cookie sheet and refrigerate for 10 minutes.
8. Place in candy cups, on a serving dish, or in an airtight container. Rochers are best if served and stored at room temperature and should stay fresh for up to 6 weeks.

Makes 48 Raspberry Rochers

Veroniques

An exotic heart of gold lies hidden under an armor of buttery pecans and irresistible chocolate.

¹/₄ cup butter
1 cup powdered sugar
¹/₄ cup Grand Marnier
1 teaspoon orange zest
2 tablespoons crumbled pralines or toffee bits
200 pecan halves (about 2 cups), toasted
4 ounces semisweet chocolate

1. Line cookie sheets with waxed or parchment paper.
2. Cream the butter, using an electric mixer on medium-high speed. Add the sugar. Reduce the mixer speed to medium and add the Grand Marnier, orange zest, and crumbled pralines or toffee bits, one at a time, stopping to scrape the sides of the bowl with a rubber spatula before each addition.
3. Place a dollop (about ¹/₂ teaspoon) of the mixture between two pecan halves.
4. Cover and chill for at least an hour.
5. Temper the chocolate (see Chapter 2 for tempering directions). Cool to room temperature.
6. Dip each Veronique in tempered chocolate, then chill for 5 minutes.
7. When set, place in candy cups, on a serving dish, or in an airtight container. Veroniques are best if served and stored at room temperature and will stay fresh for up to 6 weeks.

Makes 100 Veroniques

Are You a Candy Connoisseur?

Can you match these famous chocolate snacks with their design?

1. Baby Ruth

2. Boeri

3. Clark Bar

4. Dove Bar

5. Fiat Cremino

6. Gianduiotti

7. Goo Goo Cluster

8. Kit Kat Bar

9. Milky Way

10. Toblerone

A. Dark chocolate mixed with almonds, layered with milk chocolate mixed with hazelnuts

B. Vanilla nougat and caramel covered in milk chocolate

C. Brandied cherries in a dark chocolate log

D. Italian nougat in dark, milk, or white chocolate

E. Crumbly peanut butter covered in milk chocolate

F. A high-quality solid dark or milk chocolate bar

G. Crisp wafers covered in milk chocolate

H. A triangle of chocolate and hazelnut paste

I. Nougat, roasted peanuts, and caramel, covered with milk chocolate

J. Milk chocolate, caramel, marshmallow, and peanuts

Answers: 1I, 2C, 3E, 4F, 5A, 6H, 7J, 8G, 9B, 10D

chapter four

Cookies, Brownies, and Bars

The most wonderful thing about cookies, brownies, and bars is that they can take on so many different personalities. Fun, elegant, healthy, naughty—these bite-size treats have it all.

Like truffles and confections, start with your favorite nibbling chocolate, add high-quality ingredients, and don't be afraid to experiment with your favorite nut, fruit, or flavoring substitutions.

Cookies

Nestlé® Toll House® Cookies

One legend claims these cookies came to be when their creator, lacking the time to melt the chocolate for fudge cookies, left the chocolate in chunks. Whatever their origin, these simple little cookies are still America's favorite.

> 2 cups flour
> 1 teaspoon baking soda
> ¹/₂ teaspoon salt
> 1 cup sweet butter, softened
> ³/₄ cup sugar
> ³/₄ cup dark brown sugar, firmly packed
> 1 teaspoon pure vanilla extract
> 2 large eggs, warmed to room
>   temperature
> 2 cups semisweet chocolate chips
> 1 cup walnuts, toasted and chopped

1. Preheat the oven to 375°F. Line cookie sheets with parchment paper or lightly coat with butter and flour.

2. Sift together the flour, baking soda, and salt. Set aside.

3. Cream the butter using an electric mixer on a medium-high speed. Add the sugars and vanilla, one at a time, scraping the sides of the bowl before each addition. Adjust your mixer to a medium speed. Add the eggs, one at a time, beating until thoroughly blended.

4. Adjust your mixer to a low speed. Slowly add the flour mixture until lightly blended. Fold in the chocolate chips and nuts, a third at a time.

5. For bite-size cookies, use a scoop with a 1-inch diameter or a teaspoon. Place mounds of batter on the prepared cookie sheets. Bake for approximately 10 to 12 minutes. Cool on the pans for 5 minutes, then remove and place on cooling racks.

Makes about 120 bite-size cookies

Mocha Chip Cookies

A close cousin to the Toll House cookie, this variety adds cocoa and coffee flavorings, and replaces walnuts with hazelnuts.

> 1¹/₂ cups flour
> ¹/₄ cup nonalkalized cocoa powder
> ¹/₄ cup instant espresso powder
> 1 teaspoon baking soda

¹/₂ teaspoon salt
1 cup butter, softened
³/₄ cup sugar
³/₄ cup dark brown sugar, firmly packed
1 teaspoon coffee liqueur (optional)
1 teaspoon chocolate liqueur (optional)
2 eggs, warmed to room temperature
2 cups semisweet chocolate chips
1 cup hazelnuts, toasted, skinned, and chopped

1.   Preheat the oven to 375°F. Line cookie sheets with parchment paper or lightly coat with butter and flour.

2.   Sift together the flour, cocoa powder, espresso powder, baking soda, and salt. Set aside.

3.   Cream the butter using an electric mixer on a medium-high speed. Add the sugars and liqueurs, one at a time, scraping the sides of the bowl before each addition. Adjust your mixer to a medium speed. Add the eggs, one at a time, beating until thoroughly blended.

4.   Adjust your mixer to a low speed. Slowly add the flour mixture until lightly blended. Fold in the chocolate chips and nuts.

5.   For bite-size cookies, use a scoop with a 1-inch diameter or a teaspoon. Place mounds of batter on the prepared cookie sheets. Bake for approximately 10 to 12 minutes. Cool on the pans for 5 minutes, then remove and place on cooling racks.

Makes about 120 bite-size cookies

Easy as 1-2-3

Here are three tips to make your baking easier and more fun.

1.   Before you begin, read through the entire recipe and make sure you have all the ingredients and equipment on hand.

2.   Prepare the pans or cookie sheets you'll be using (line with parchment paper, lightly coat with butter and flour, etc.), and prepare and premeasure the ingredients (chop the chocolate, toast the nuts, sift the flour, etc.).

3.   Relax and have fun. Slip into something comfortable . . . put on your favorite music or video . . . light a few candles . . . whatever puts you in a creative mood.

Angel Chip Cookies

On the other side of the Toll House family are these heavenly little bites, featuring white chocolate chips and macadamia nuts.

2 cups flour
1 teaspoon baking soda
¹/₂ teaspoon salt
1 cup butter, softened
³/₄ cup sugar
³/₄ cup light brown sugar, firmly packed
1 teaspoon pure vanilla extract
2 eggs, warmed to room temperature
2 cups white chocolate chips
1 cup macadamia nuts, toasted and
    chopped

Flavorings

Artificial flavorings are easier to find and less expensive, but "pure" or "natural" extracts are well worth the additional cost and even the extra time it may take to find them. Since you'll be using the best chocolate, partner it with the best flavorings.

1.   Preheat the oven to 375°F. Line cookie sheets with parchment paper or lightly coat with butter and flour.

2.   Sift together the flour, baking soda, and salt. Set aside.

3.   Cream the butter using an electric mixer on a medium-high speed. Add the sugars and vanilla, one at a time, scraping the sides of the bowl before each addition. Adjust your mixer to a medium speed. Add the eggs, one at a time, beating until thoroughly blended.

4.   Adjust your mixer to a low speed. Slowly add the flour mixture until lightly blended. Fold in the white chocolate chips and nuts.

5.   For bite-size cookies, use a scoop with a 1-inch diameter or a teaspoon. Place mounds of batter on the prepared cookie sheets. Bake for approximately 10 to 12 minutes. Cool on the pans for 5 minutes, then remove and place on cooling racks.

Makes about 120 bite-size cookies

Almond Crunch Cookies

Almonds, toffee, and coconut turn these Toll House cookies into a crunchy delight.

2 cups flour
1 teaspoon baking soda
¹/₂ teaspoon salt
1 cup butter, softened
³/₄ cup sugar
³/₄ cup dark brown sugar, firmly packed
1 teaspoon pure almond extract

2 eggs, warmed to room temperature
$^1/_2$ cup toffee bits
$^1/_2$ cup sweetened, flaked coconut
$^1/_2$ cup mini semisweet chocolate chips
$^1/_2$ cup almonds, toasted and chopped

1. Preheat the oven to 375°F. Line cookie sheets with parchment paper or lightly coat with butter and flour.

2. Sift together the flour, baking soda, and salt. Set aside.

3. Cream the butter using an electric mixer on a medium-high speed. Add the sugars and almond extract, one at a time, scraping the sides of the bowl before each addition. Adjust your mixer to a medium speed. Add the eggs, one at a time, beating until thoroughly blended.

4. Adjust your mixer to a low speed. Slowly add the flour mixture until lightly blended. Fold in the toffee bits, coconut, chocolate chips, and nuts.

5. For bite-size cookies, use a scoop with a 1-inch diameter or a teaspoon. Place mounds of batter on the prepared cookie sheets. Bake for approximately 10 to 12 minutes. Cool on the pans for 5 minutes, then remove and place on cooling racks.

Makes about 120 bite-size cookies

Peanut Butter Pleasers

These creamy, peanut butter-chocolate chip cookies are guaranteed to melt in your mouth.

2 cups flour
1 teaspoon baking soda
$^1/_2$ teaspoon salt
1 cup butter, softened
$^1/_2$ cup creamy peanut butter
$^3/_4$ cup sugar
$^3/_4$ cup dark brown sugar, firmly packed
1 teaspoon pure vanilla extract
1 egg, warmed to room temperature
2 cups milk chocolate chips

1. Preheat the oven to 375°F. Line cookie sheets with parchment paper or lightly coat with butter and flour.

2. Sift together the flour, baking soda, and salt. Set aside.

3. Cream the butter using an electric mixer on a medium-high speed. Add the peanut butter, sugars, and vanilla, one at a time, scraping the sides of the bowl before each addition. Adjust your mixer to a medium speed. Add the egg, beating until thoroughly blended.

4. Adjust your mixer to a low speed. Slowly add the flour mixture until lightly blended. Fold in the chocolate chips.

5. For bite-size cookies, use a scoop with a 1-inch diameter or a teaspoon. Place mounds of batter on the prepared cookie sheets. Bake for approximately 10 to 12 minutes. Cool on the pans for 5 minutes, then remove and place on cooling racks.

Makes about 120 bite-size cookies

Oatmeal Chocolate Chip

Another American favorite, this recipe turns Toll House cookies into a healthier treat.

> 1 cup flour
> 1 teaspoon baking soda
> ¹/₂ teaspoon salt
> 1 cup butter, softened
> ¹/₂ cup sugar
> 1 cup dark brown sugar, firmly packed
> 1 teaspoon pure vanilla extract
> 2 eggs, warmed to room temperature
> 3 cups rolled oats
> 2 cups semisweet chocolate chips

1. Preheat the oven to 375°F. Line cookie sheets with parchment paper or lightly coat with butter and flour.
2. Sift together the flour, baking soda, and salt. Set aside.
3. Cream the butter using an electric mixer on a medium-high speed. Add the sugars and vanilla, one at a time, scraping the sides of the bowl before each addition. Adjust your mixer to a medium speed. Add the eggs, one at a time, beating until thoroughly blended.
4. Adjust your mixer to a low speed. Slowly add the flour mixture until lightly blended. Fold in the oats and chocolate chips.
5. For bite-size cookies, use a scoop with a 1-inch diameter or a teaspoon. Place mounds of batter on the prepared cookie sheets. Bake for approximately 10 to 12 minutes. Cool on the pans for

5 minutes, then remove and place on cooling racks.

Makes about 150 bite-size cookies

Sam's Olympic Treats

Here's a world-class treat, starring bananas, coconut, cashews, and chocolate kisses. You'll need a helper for these cookies—someone to unwrap the kisses, and to press them into the cookies as they come out of the oven.

> 1¹/₂ cups flour
> 1 teaspoon baking soda
> 1 teaspoon salt
> 1 cup butter, softened
> ³/₄ cup sugar
> ³/₄ cup dark brown sugar, firmly packed
> 1 teaspoon pure vanilla extract
> ¹/₄ cup mashed bananas
> 2 eggs, warmed to room temperature
> 3 cups rolled oats
> 1 cup sweetened, flaked coconut
> 1 cup cashews, toasted and chopped
> 40 chocolate kisses, unwrapped

1. Preheat the oven to 375°F. Line cookie sheets with parchment paper or lightly coat with butter and flour.
2. Sift together the flour, baking soda, and salt. Set aside.
3. Cream the butter using an electric mixer on a medium-high speed. Add the sugars, vanilla, and mashed bananas, one at a time, scraping the sides of the bowl

before each addition. Adjust your mixer to a medium speed. Add the eggs, one at a time, beating until thoroughly blended.

4. Adjust your mixer to a low speed. Slowly add the flour mixture until lightly blended. Fold in the oats, coconut, and nuts.

5. For Olympic-size cookies, use a scoop with a 1^1/$_2$-inch diameter or a tablespoon. Place mounds of batter on the prepared cookie sheets. Bake for approximately 12 to 14 minutes. As soon as the cookies come out of the oven, press a kiss into each. Cool on the pans for 5 minutes, then remove and place on cooling racks.

Makes about 60 Olympic-size cookies

Confetti Fudge Cookies

Dark, chewy chocolate, studded with colorful M&M's, these cookies make every day a celebration.

> 6 ounces semisweet chocolate, finely
>   chopped
> 2 cups flour
> ^{1}/$_2$ cup nonalkalized cocoa powder
> 1 teaspoon baking soda
> ^{1}/$_2$ teaspoon salt
> ^{3}/$_4$ cup butter, warmed to room temperature
> ^{3}/$_4$ cup sugar
> ^{3}/$_4$ cup dark brown sugar, firmly packed
> 1 tablespoon unsulphured molasses
> 2 teaspoons pure vanilla extract
> 2 eggs, warmed to room temperature
> 2 cups M&M's
> ^{1}/$_4$ cup powdered sugar, sifted

(continued)

Flour Power

The way you measure and incorporate flour can make or break your cookies. Flour may compact during storage. Sifting prior to measuring ensures better accuracy. Sifting again to blend similar powdered ingredients allows for more even blending. And, most importantly, when incorporating flour into your batter, sprinkle the flour mixture in a little at a time, just until it's evenly blended. Avoid overmixing.

(Sifting is also essential when measuring powdered sugar.)

1. Preheat the oven to 350°F. Line cookie sheets with parchment paper or lightly coat with butter and flour.

2. Melt the chocolate in the top of a double boiler over hot (not simmering) water, stirring continuously. Remove from heat and set aside to cool to room temperature.

3. Sift together the flour, cocoa powder, baking soda, and salt. Set aside.

4. Cream the butter using an electric mixer on a medium-high speed. Add the sugars, molasses, and vanilla, one at a time, scraping the sides of the bowl before each addition. Adjust your mixer to a medium speed. Add the eggs, one at a time, beating until thoroughly blended.

5. Adjust your mixer to a low speed. Slowly add the melted chocolate and flour mixture, one at a time, until lightly blended. Fold in the M&M's.

6. For bite-size cookies, use a scoop with a 1-inch diameter or a teaspoon. Place mounds of batter on the prepared cookie sheets. Bake for approximately 10 to 12 minutes. Cool on the pans for 5 minutes, then remove and place on cooling racks.

7. When cool, dust with powdered sugar.

Makes about 120 bite-size cookies

Zach's Monster Bites

Rumor has it these super chocolaty, chocolate and butterscotch chip cookies are served in the Star Wars Café. Each bite has so much chocolate, it tastes like two!

8 ounces semisweet chocolate, finely
   chopped
$^1/_4$ cup butter, warmed to room temperature
$^1/_4$ cup flour
$^1/_2$ teaspoon baking powder
$^1/_4$ teaspoon salt
2 eggs, warmed to room temperature
$1^1/_2$ teaspoons pure vanilla extract
$^3/_4$ cup dark brown sugar, firmly packed
$^1/_2$ cup semisweet chocolate chips
$^1/_2$ cup butterscotch chips
$^1/_2$ cup walnuts, toasted and chopped

1. Preheat the oven to 325°F. Line cookie sheets with parchment paper or lightly coat with butter and flour.

2. Melt the chocolate and butter in the top of a double boiler over hot (not simmering) water, stirring continuously. Remove from heat and set aside to cool to room temperature.

3. Sift together the flour, baking powder, and salt. Set aside.

4. Beat together the eggs and vanilla, using an electric mixer on a medium speed, until frothy. Add the sugar and beat until thick. Using a rubber spatula, scrape the sides of the bowl.

5. Adjust your mixer to a low speed. Slowly add the chocolate mixture and flour mixture, one at a time, until lightly blended. Fold in the chips and nuts.

6. For monster-size cookies, use a scoop with a $1^1/_2$-inch diameter or a tablespoon. Place mounds of batter on the

prepared cookie sheets. Bake for approximately 12 to 14 minutes. Cool on the pans for 5 minutes, then remove and place on cooling racks.

Makes about 30 monster cookies

Mocha Eclipse

These ultrarich bites of bittersweet chocolate, chocolate chips, and mocha beans are the ultimate cookie for chocolate connoisseurs.

> 8 ounces bittersweet chocolate, finely
>   chopped
> $1/4$ cup butter, warmed to room tempera-
>   ture
> 3 tablespoons flour
> 1 tablespoon nonalkalized cocoa powder
> $1/2$ teaspoon baking powder
> $1/4$ teaspoon salt
> 2 eggs, warmed to room temperature
> 1 tablespoon coffee liqueur
> $2/3$ cup sugar
> 2 tablespoons instant espresso powder
> 1 cup semisweet chocolate chips
> $1/2$ cup mocha beans*

1.   Preheat the oven to 325°F. Line cookie sheets with parchment paper or lightly coat with butter and flour.

2.   Melt the chocolate and butter in the top of a double boiler over hot (not simmering) water, stirring continuously. Remove from heat and set aside to cool to room temperature.

(continued)

Separating Eggs

Separating egg whites and yolks is simple, but needs to be done carefully.

1.   Gently tap a fresh egg on the rim of a bowl to crack it in half.
2.   Transfer the yolk between the two halves, encouraging the whites to fall into the bowl. (Be careful not to let the ragged edge of the shell pierce and break the yolk.)
3.   Or place a stainless steel egg separator over a bowl and pour the yolk into the center; the whites will fall into the bowl.
4.   Or crack an egg into a cute little pottery-face egg separator, and pour the whites out through the mouth. (Look for these separators at craft fairs.)

Gifts for Cookie Makers

All you need are cookie sheets and mixing bowls to make cookies, right? Well, right and wrong. There are lots of fun gifts for cookie makers.

- *Death by Chocolate Cookies* by Marcel Desaulniers
- Cookie press
- Cookie cutters
- Cookie decorating kit
- Insulated cookie sheets
- Wire cooling racks
- Character egg separators
- High-quality measuring spoons and cups
- High-quality spatulas and whisks
- A nest of clear glass mixing bowls
- Stand mixer
- Parchment paper
- Gift tins or boxes
- Domestic and imported couvertures
- Flavored chocolate chips
- Toffee bits
- Mocha beans
- Candied ginger
- High-quality extracts
- Instant espresso powder

3. Sift together the flour, cocoa powder, baking powder, and salt. Set aside.

4. Beat together the eggs and coffee liqueur using an electric mixer on a medium speed, until frothy. Add the sugar and espresso powder; beat until thick. Using a rubber spatula, scrape the sides of the bowl.

5. Adjust your mixer to a low speed. Slowly add the chocolate and flour mixture, one at a time, until lightly blended. Fold in the chocolate chips and mocha beans.

6. For bite-size cookies, use a scoop with a 1-inch diameter or a teaspoon. Place mounds of batter on the prepared cookie sheets. Bake for approximately 12 to 14 minutes. Cool on the pans for 5 minutes, then remove and place on cooling racks.

*Mocha beans are pieces of solid, coffee-flavored chocolate, shaped like coffee beans.

Makes about 60 bite-size cookies

Kelly's Kisses

My all-time favorites, I designed these peppermint meringue cookies years ago, but I never found the perfect name for them until someone very special came into our lives.

3 egg whites, warmed to room temperature
¹/₈ teaspoon cream of tartar
¹/₄ teaspoon pure peppermint extract
3 drops red food coloring
²/₃ cups superfine sugar
¹/₃ cup mini chocolate chips

1. Preheat the oven to 200°F. Line cookie sheets with parchment paper.

2. Beat the egg whites with the cream of tartar, peppermint extract, and food coloring until soft peaks form, using an electric mixer on a medium speed. Scrape the sides of your bowl.

3. Adjust the mixer to a high speed and gradually sprinkle in the sugar, whipping until stiff peaks form. Lightly fold in the mini chips.

4. For bite-size cookies, use a teaspoon. Place mounds of meringue on the prepared cookie sheets. Bake for 30 minutes. Turn off the oven, but leave the meringues in the oven for an additional 30 minutes. Remove and place the pans on cooling racks.

Makes about 36 bite-size cookies

Mocha Praline Kisses

These mocha-flavored meringue kisses have a sweet, nutty crunch.

> 3 egg whites, warmed to room temperature
> 1/8 teaspoon cream of tartar
> 1/3 cup superfine sugar
> 1/3 cup light brown sugar, firmly packed
> 2 tablespoons nonalkalized cocoa powder
> 1 tablespoon instant espresso powder
> 1/3 cup crumbled pecan pralines

1. Preheat the oven to 200°F. Line cookie sheets with parchment paper.

2. Beat the egg whites with the cream of tartar until soft peaks form, using an electric mixer on a medium speed. Scrape the sides of your bowl.

3. Adjust the mixer to a high speed and gradually sprinkle in the sugars, cocoa powder, and espresso powder, whipping until stiff peaks form. Lightly fold in the pralines.

4. For bite-size cookies, use a teaspoon. Place mounds of meringue on the prepared cookie sheets. Or place the meringue in a pastry bag fitted with a 1/2-inch round tip, and pipe in cone shapes on the prepared cookie sheets. Bake for 30 minutes. Turn off the oven, but leave the meringues in the oven for an additional 30 minutes. Remove and place the pans on cooling racks.

Makes about 36 bite-size cookies

Chocolate Cherry Swirls

Here's another technique for making chocolate meringue cookies.

> 3 ounces semisweet chocolate, finely chopped
> 3 egg whites, warmed to room temperature
> 1/8 teaspoon cream of tartar
> 2/3 cups superfine sugar
> 1/3 cup maraschino cherries, drained and chopped

1. Preheat the oven to 200°F. Line cookie sheets with parchment paper.

2. Melt the chocolate in the top of a double boiler over hot (not simmering)

(continued)

The Best Training Ground

Making cookies is a great way for young pastry chefs to get started. In addition to being a fun way to begin learning how to cook, making cookies helps teach planning skills, decision-making skills, shopping skills, measuring skills, reading and direction-following skills, and timing skills. It also helps build confidence, creativity, and self-esteem.

And cookies made by little hands make extra-special gifts for friends, family members, charities, and fundraisers.

water, stirring continuously. Remove from heat and set aside to cool to room temperature.

3. Beat the egg whites with the cream of tartar and sugar until combined, using an electric mixer on a medium speed. Heat in the top of a double boiler over simmering water, stirring continuously with a wire whisk, until the egg whites are hot and the sugar is dissolved. Remove from heat and, using an electric mixer on a medium-high speed, whip until the meringue is stiff and cooled, but not dry.

4. Lightly fold in the melted chocolate and cherry bits.

5. Place the meringue in a pastry bag fitted with a $1/2$-inch star tip. Pipe bite-size swirls onto cookie sheets lined with parchment paper, and bake for 30 minutes. Turn off the oven, but leave the meringues in the oven for an additional 30 minutes. Remove and place the pans on cooling racks.

Makes about 36 bite-size cookies

Pistachio Puffs

These delicate bites of rich pistachios, tangy tangerine peels, and sweet white chocolate chips are lighter than air.

$1/4$ *cup candied tangerine peels, chopped*
$3/4$ *cup pistachios, skinned and chopped*
1 cup white chocolate chips
1 cup powdered sugar, sifted
1 egg white, warmed to room temperature and slightly beaten

1.   Preheat the oven to 325°F. Line cookie sheets with parchment paper or lightly coat with butter and flour.

2.   Mix together the candied tangerine peels, pistachios, chips, and powdered sugar. Add the egg white and mix until thoroughly blended.

3.   Using a teaspoon, place mounds of the cookie batter on the prepared cookie sheets, at least 2 inches apart. Bake for 15 to 18 minutes, until edges are a light golden brown. Cool on the cookie sheets, placed on wire cooling racks.

Makes about 36 bite-size cookies

Hazelnut Crisps

Delicate and spicy, these crispy treats are a great accent for ice cream.

2 tablespoons ground hazelnuts
1 cup rolled oats
1 teaspoon ground allspice
$^{1}/_{2}$ cup butter
$^{3}/_{4}$ cup dark brown sugar, firmly packed
2 tablespoons brewed coffee
1 egg, warmed to room temperature
1 tablespoon hazelnut liqueur
$^{1}/_{4}$ cup mini semisweet chocolate chips

1.   Preheat the oven to 350°F. Line cookie sheets with parchment paper or lightly coat with butter and flour.

2.   Mix the ground hazelnuts, oats, and allspice. Set aside.

Taking the Fall

For years, chocolate was blamed for skin breakouts. Not true. Medical research has found no direct correlation between chocolate and blemishes. So how did this misconception get started?

Stress and depression *have* been proven to cause acne. These two factors can also cause you to crave chocolate, because chocolate triggers your brain to release serotonin, a natural antidepressant.

So, poor little chocolate, while being blamed for embarrassing blemishes, was actually working hard to eliminate the real culprit—stress.

(continued)

Every Step of the Way

Let your protégé help with every step in this cookie-making process.

1. Choose a recipe together.
2. Check your pantry to see what equipment and ingredients you already have. Then make a list of what you need.
3. Make a special trip to the grocery and/or kitchen store. Buy only cookie-making supplies. (Buying other groceries dilutes the magic.)
4. Prep the pans and preheat the oven.
5. Premeasure the ingredients.
6. Make the batter. Scoop, roll, and decorate the cookies.
7. Time the baking, checking periodically for doneness.
8. Cool and decorate the cookies.
9. Clean up.
10. Pour a big glass of milk and enjoy your masterpieces!

3. Heat the butter, brown sugar, and coffee in a heavy-bottomed saucepan over a low heat, stirring continuously. When the butter is melted, increase the heat to a medium setting and, stirring continuously, simmer for 1 minute. Remove the saucepan from the heat and place in a bowl of ice water. Whisk the mixture for 3 minutes.

4. Remove the pan from the ice water and whisk in the egg and hazelnut liqueur, then fold in the oat mixture and mini chocolate chips. Place the saucepan back in the ice water for 5 minutes.

5. Using a teaspoon, place mounds of the cookie batter on the prepared cookie sheets, at least 2 inches apart. Bake for 10 to 12 minutes. Cool on the cookie sheets, placed on wire cooling racks.

Makes about 24 bite-size cookies

Florentines

A thin layer of chewy honey-coated almonds sits atop a swirl of rich, dark chocolate.

2 tablespoons butter
$^1/_3$ cup heavy cream
2 tablespoons honey
$^1/_4$ cup light brown sugar, firmly packed
1 cup almonds, sliced and lightly toasted
1 teaspoon orange zest
1 tablespoon Grand Marnier
$^1/_4$ cup flour
$^1/_8$ teaspoon salt

Bottom Coating:

8 ounces dark chocolate, tempered

1. Preheat the oven to 350°F. Line cookie sheets with parchment paper or lightly coat with butter and flour.
2. Combine the butter, cream, honey, and sugar in a heavy-bottomed saucepan. Slowly bring to a boil over a low heat, stirring continuously.
3. Remove from heat and fold in the almonds, orange zest, and Grand Marnier. Fold in the flour and salt.
4. Using a scoop with a 1-inch diameter or a teaspoon, place round mounds of batter on the prepared cookie sheets at least 3 inches apart. Bake for 10 minutes. Cool on the pans for 5 minutes, then remove and place on cooling racks.
5. When the cookies are completely cool, coat the bottoms of the cookies with swirls of chocolate. Refrigerate, chocolate side up, for 5 minutes.

Makes about 24–30 cookies

Heartbreak Shortbread Cookies

These are hearts you'll love to break. Brown sugar shortbread cookies are shaped into hearts and dipped into dark and white chocolates.

1 cup butter, softened
1/2 cup light brown sugar, firmly packed
2 1/2 cups flour

(continued)

Candied Fruit Peels

Candied fruit peels can be substituted for nuts, chocolate chips, and other toppings.

I'll use an orange as an example, but you can use this same technique for any citrus fruit. You'll need 2 medium oranges, 1 cup sugar, and 1 cup water:

1. Wash and dry the oranges. Using the palm and heel of your hand, gently roll the oranges on a solid work surface to loosen the peels. Slice the oranges in quarters. Using your fingers, separate the peel from the fruit and as much of the bitter white pith as possible. Slice the peels into 1/4-inch strips.
2. In a heavy-bottomed saucepan, combine the sugar and water; stirring continuously over a medium heat, bring to a simmer, creating a hot syrup.
3. Reduce the heat to low and add the orange peels. Simmer on a low heat for 1 hour, turning the peels often to soak evenly. Remove from heat and continue soaking at room temperature for 24 hours.
4. Drain the peels and dry them on a wire rack for 3 hours. Store in an airtight container.

Toasting Nuts

For most recipes, using toasted nuts will prove more flavorful than using raw nuts.

To toast nuts: Spread shelled nutmeats on a cookie sheet and bake them in a preheated 325°F oven for 10 to 20 minutes. Be sure to check and turn the nuts every 5 minutes. (Almonds and hazelnuts tend to take a little longer than walnuts and pecans.) There's no need to grease the pan—nuts contain a high percentage of natural oils. These oils also make nuts very susceptible to spoiling, so it's important to taste-test all nuts before using them and to store nuts in an airtight container in the freezer.

To skin hazelnuts: After toasting, while still warm, place the hazelnuts in a towel and rub them together. The force of the nuts rubbing against each other will remove most of the skins.

To skin or blanch almonds: Prior to toasting, drop the almonds into boiling water. After 1 minute, remove the nuts to a bowl of cold water. The skins should slip off easily. If not, repeat the process.

Coating:
4 ounces white chocolate
4 ounces bittersweet chocolate

1.   Cream the butter using an electric mixer on a medium-high speed. Add the brown sugar, beating until fluffy.

2.   Adjust the mixer to a low speed and slowly add the flour until thoroughly blended and smooth.

3.   Divide the dough into 2 parts, cover, and refrigerate for several hours.

4.   Preheat the oven to 300°F. Line cookie sheets with parchment paper or leave them uncoated.

5.   Lightly dust a flat surface with flour. Roll each mixture of dough to a $1/3$-inch thickness. Cut $1^1/2$-inch or 2-inch cookies using a heart-shaped cookie cutter. Place on cookie sheets and bake for 25 minutes. Remove from oven and place on wire racks to cool.

6.   Temper the chocolates. (See Chapter 2 for tempering directions). Cool to room temperature. Line cookie sheets with waxed paper. When the cooled cookies and tempered chocolate are approximately the same temperature, dip half of each cookie in the white chocolate. Place in the refrigerator for approximately 5 minutes, until set. Then dip the other half of each cookie in the dark chocolate. Place in the refrigerator for approximately 5 minutes, until set.

Makes about 60 cookies

Mocha Sugar Cookies

Here's a recipe for old-fashioned sugar cookies with a new mocha flavor.

> 2^1/$_4$ cups flour
> ^{1}/$_4$ cup nonalkalized cocoa powder
> ^{1}/$_4$ cup instant espresso powder
> 1 teaspoon baking soda
> 1 teaspoon cream of tartar
> 1 cup butter, softened
> 1^1/$_2$ cups superfine sugar
> 1 egg, warmed to room temperature
> 1 teaspoon pure vanilla extract

Coating:

> ^{1}/$_4$ cup sugar

1.   Sift together the flour, cocoa powder, espresso powder, baking soda, and cream of tartar. Set aside.

2.   Cream the butter using an electric mixer on a medium-high speed. Add the sugar, beating until fluffy. Adjust the mixer to a medium speed and add the egg and vanilla, beating until thoroughly blended.

3.   Adjust the mixer to a low speed and slowly add the flour mixture until lightly blended.

4.   Divide the dough into 2 parts; cover, and refrigerate for several hours.

5.   Preheat the oven to 375°F. Line cookie sheets with parchment paper or leave them uncoated.

6.   Lightly dust a flat surface with flour. Roll each mixture of dough to a ^{1}/$_4$-inch thickness. Cut out shapes with your favorite cookie cutters and sprinkle with sugar. Or

Young Designers

Designing cookie recipes is a wonderful way to build confidence, creativity, and self-esteem, especially for young ones.

1.   Begin with a basic Toll House or a chocolate cookie recipe.
2.   Substitute like for like. For example, replace vanilla extract with almond extract, walnuts with cashews, chocolate chips with toffee bits, etc.
3.   Keep it simple. Most new designers want to put everything they love into their first recipe. Make sure you maintain a balance between cookie dough and chips, nuts, or candy bits.
4.   Keep a special recipe journal, documenting your new designs.
5.   Choose a name for the new cookie.
6.   Plan a special party or presenta-tion to introduce the new cookie.

(continued)

roll into balls and flatten with the bottom of a glass that has been dipped in sugar. Place on cookie sheets and bake for 5 to 8 minutes. Remove from oven and place on wire racks to cool.

Makes 40–60 cookies

Chocolate Almond Butter Cookies

Snowmen with freckles? This recipe gives a whole new look, and flavor, to traditional cookie-press butter cookies.

> 1 cup grated semisweet chocolate
> 2^1/$_2$ cups flour
> ^{1}/$_2$ teaspoon baking powder
> ^{1}/$_4$ teaspoon salt
> 1 cup butter
> ^{3}/$_4$ cup sugar
> 1 egg, warmed to room temperature
> 2 teaspoons pure almond extract
> toppings (sprinkles, candied fruit,
>   nuts, etc.)

1. Preheat the oven to 375°F. Line cookie sheets with parchment paper or lightly coat with butter and flour.
2. Refrigerate the chocolate until cool. Grate the chocolate. Refrigerate the grated chocolate in an airtight container while preparing the cookie batter.
3. Sift together the flour, baking powder, and salt. Set aside.
4. Cream the butter using an electric mixer on a medium-high speed. Add the sugar. Adjust the mixer to a medium speed. Add the egg and almond extract, one at a time, scraping the sides of the bowl before each addition.
5. Adjust your mixer to a low speed, and slowly add the flour mixture until lightly blended. Slowly add the grated chocolate until evenly blended.
6. Refrigerate the dough for at least 1 hour.
7. Feed the dough through a cookie press, decorate, and bake for 8 to 10 minutes. Cool on the pans for 5 minutes, then remove and place on cooling racks.

Makes about 48 bite-size cookies

Cocoa Butter Cookies

These chocolate cookie-press cookies are rich and creamy.

> 2 cups flour
> ^{1}/$_2$ cup nonalkalized cocoa powder
> ^{1}/$_2$ teaspoon baking powder
> ^{1}/$_4$ teaspoon salt
> 1 cup butter, softened
> ^{1}/$_4$ cup mascarpone cheese
> 1 cup sugar
> 1 egg
> 1 teaspoon pure vanilla extract
> toppings (sprinkles, candied fruit, nuts, etc.)

1. Preheat the oven to 375°F. Line cookie sheets with parchment paper or lightly coat with butter and flour.

2.   Sift together the flour, cocoa powder, baking powder, and salt. Set aside.

3.   Cream together the butter and cheese, using an electric mixer on a medium-high speed. Add the sugar. Adjust the mixer to a medium speed. Add the egg and vanilla, one at a time, scraping the sides of the bowl before each addition.

4.   Adjust your mixer to a low speed, and slowly add the flour mixture until lightly blended.

5.   Refrigerate the dough for at least 1 hour.

6.   Feed the dough through a cookie press, decorate, and bake for 8 to 10 minutes. Cool on the pans for 5 minutes, then remove and place on cooling racks.

Makes about 48 bite-size cookies

Oatmeal Streusel Cookies

Apples, dates, walnuts, and chocolate snuggle between swirls of oats and honey in these refrigerator cookies.

Base Layer:
1 cup flour
¹/₂ teaspoon baking soda
¹/₄ teaspoon salt
¹/₂ cup butter, softened
¹/₄ cup sugar
³/₄ cup dark brown sugar, firmly packed
1 egg, warmed to room temperature
2 tablespoons honey
1¹/₂ cups rolled oats

Cookie-Making Parties for Kids

This is a great way to celebrate a birthday, graduation, or rainy day.

1.   Design sandwich-cookie invitations.
2.   Decorate your kitchen like a cookie factory.
3.   Make shopping for ingredients part of the party.
4.   Organize the guests into cookie-making teams.
5.   Provide imaginative aprons, smocks, or chef's hats.
6.   Take extra safety precautions around the oven and hot pans.
7.   Invite the guests' parents for a cookie tasting and awards presentation.
8.   Give each cookie-maker or team member an award—"Best Sifter," "Best Scooper," "Best Chocolate Chip Cookies." Decorated wooden spoons make great trophies!

(continued)

Streusel Layer:
¹/₄ cup chopped dried apples
¹/₄ cup chopped dates
¹/₄ cup sugar
1 teaspoon ground cinnamon
2 tablespoons lemon juice
¹/₃ cup water
¹/₄ cup chopped walnuts, toasted
4 ounces semisweet chocolate, finely chopped

1. Sift together the flour, baking soda, and salt. Set aside.
2. Cream the butter using an electric mixer on a medium-high speed. Add the sugars, beating until fluffy. Adjust the mixer to a medium speed and add the egg and honey, beating until thoroughly blended.
3. Adjust the mixer to a low speed and slowly add the flour mixture and oats until lightly blended.
4. Divide the dough into 2 parts, cover, and refrigerate for several hours.
5. In a heavy-bottomed saucepan, combine the apples, dates, sugar, cinnamon, lemon juice, and water. Cook over a medium heat, stirring continuously, until mixture thickens. Remove from heat and stir in walnuts. Set aside to cool.
6. When the dough is firm and the streusel filling is cool: Remove dough from refrigerator and flatten, between two pieces of waxed paper, into two 7-inch by 11-inch rectangles. Remove the waxed paper and spread half of the streusel filling and half of the chopped chocolate on each rectangle.

Roll each rectangle up into an 11-inch log; wrap tightly in waxed paper, then in plastic wrap. Refrigerate overnight or until firm.

7. When logs are firm: Preheat the oven to 375°F. Line cookie sheets with parchment paper or lightly coat with butter and flour. Slice logs into ¹/₄-inch cookies, place on cookie sheets, and bake for 8 to 10 minutes. Remove from oven and place on wire racks to cool.

Makes about 60 cookies

Lemon Pecan Butterballs

These delicate little cookies have just a hint of chocolate, and literally melt in your mouth.

³/₄ cup flour
¹/₄ cup nonalkalized cocoa powder
¹/₂ cup toasted pecans, finely chopped
¹/₂ cup butter
¹/₄ cup powdered sugar
1 tablespoon lemon juice
1 teaspoon lemon zest

Coating:
3 tablespoons powdered sugar
1 tablespoon alkalized cocoa powder
¹/₄ teaspoon ground nutmeg

1. Preheat the oven to 350°F. Line cookie sheets with parchment paper or lightly coat with butter and flour.
2. Sift together the flour and cocoa powder. Blend in the pecans. Set aside.
3. Cream the butter using an electric mixer on a medium-high speed. Add the

sugar, lemon juice, and lemon zest, one at a time, scraping the sides of the bowl before each addition.

4. Adjust your mixer to a low speed. Slowly add the flour mixture until lightly blended.

5. Sift together the remaining powdered sugar, cocoa powder, and nutmeg.

6. For bite-size cookies, use a scoop with a 1-inch diameter or a teaspoon. Roll scoops of the batter into balls, place on the prepared cookie sheets and bake for 12 to 14 minutes. Roll in coating mixture while still warm and place on wire racks to cool.

Makes about 60 bite-size cookies

Cocoa Nut Macaroons

Chocolate and cashew nuts are added to these chewy coconut favorites.

> 6 ounces semisweet chocolate, finely
>   chopped
> 2 egg whites, warmed to room temperature
> $^1/_2$ cup light brown sugar, firmly packed
> 2 tablespoons alkalized cocoa powder
> 1 teaspoon pure vanilla extract
> 2 cups sweetened flaked coconut
> 1 cup cashews, toasted and chopped

1. Preheat the oven to 375°F. Line cookie sheets with parchment paper or lightly coat with butter and flour.

2. Melt the chocolate in the top of a double boiler over hot (not simmering) water, stirring continuously. Remove from heat and set aside to cool to room temperature.

3. Beat the egg whites, using an electric mixer on a medium-high speed, until soft peaks form. Slowly add the sugar, beating until the mixture thickens. Add the cocoa powder and vanilla, beating until lightly blended.

4. Adjust your mixer to a low speed. Slowly add the melted chocolate until lightly blended. Fold in the coconut and cashews.

5. For bite-size cookies, use a scoop with a 1-inch diameter or a teaspoon. Place mounds of batter on the prepared cookie sheets. Bake for approximately 12 to 14 minutes. Cool on the pans for 5 minutes, then remove and place on cooling racks.

Makes about 24 bite-size cookies

Fudge Snaps

If you love gingersnaps, try this chocolate fudge variation.

> 6 ounces semisweet chocolate, finely
>   chopped
> 2 cups flour
> $^1/_2$ cup nonalkalized cocoa powder
> 1 teaspoon baking soda
> $^1/_2$ teaspoon salt
> 2 teaspoons ground cinnamon
> 1 tablespoon ground ginger
> $^3/_4$ cup butter, warmed to room temperature
> 1 cup dark brown sugar, firmly packed
> $^1/_4$ cup unsulphured molasses
> 1 egg, warmed to room temperature
> 1 tablespoon lemon zest

Coating:
$^1/_4$ cup sugar

(continued)

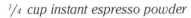
1. Preheat the oven to 350°F. Line cookie sheets with parchment paper or lightly coat with butter and flour.

2. Melt the chocolate in the top of a double boiler over hot (not simmering) water, stirring continuously. Remove from heat and set aside to cool to room temperature.

3. Sift together the flour, cocoa powder, baking soda, salt, cinnamon, and ginger. Set aside.

4. Cream the butter using an electric mixer on a medium-high speed. Add the sugar and molasses, one at a time, scraping the sides of the bowl before each addition. Adjust your mixer to a medium speed. Add the egg, beating until thoroughly blended.

5. Adjust your mixer to a low speed. Slowly add the melted chocolate and flour mixture, one at a time, until lightly blended.

6. For bite-size cookies, use a scoop with a 1-inch diameter or a teaspoon. Roll scoops of the batter into balls, then roll the balls in sugar. Place the balls on the prepared cookie sheets, press into disks, and bake for 10 to 12 minutes. Cool on the pans for 5 minutes, then remove and place on cooling racks.

Makes about 60 bite-size cookies

Bittersweet Almond Biscotti

These crunchy dippers are perfect for an afternoon energy boost.

1¹/₂ cups flour
²/₃ cup nonalkalized cocoa powder

¹/₄ cup instant espresso powder
2 teaspoons baking powder
¹/₄ teaspoon salt
1¹/₄ cups sugar
1¹/₂ cups almonds, toasted and chopped
1 cup bittersweet chocolate, chopped into chip-size pieces
4 eggs, warmed to room temperature
1 teaspoon pure almond extract

1. Preheat the oven to 325°F. Line cookie sheets with parchment paper.

2. Sift together the flour, cocoa powder, espresso powder, baking powder, and salt. Mix in the sugar, almonds, and chocolate pieces. Set aside.

3. Whisk together the eggs and almond extract. Fold in the flour mixture, forming a dough.

4. Divide the dough in half. Roll each half into a log approximately 2 inches wide by 12 inches long by 1 inch high. Flatten each log slightly and bake for 40 minutes. Remove from oven and place the cookie sheet on a wire rack to cool for 30 minutes.

5. Remove logs from cookie sheet and, using a knife with a serrated edge, cut into ¹/₂-inch slices. Place the slices on parchment-lined cookie sheets and bake for 20 minutes. Remove from oven and place pans on wire racks to cool completely.

Makes about 48 dippers

Brownies

Classic Brownies

Simple, light, and classic, this is how brownies began.

> 4 ounces unsweetened chocolate, finely
>   chopped
> $^3/_4$ cup butter, cut into $^1/_4$-inch cubes
> 1 cup flour
> 1 teaspoon baking powder
> $^1/_4$ teaspoon salt
> $1^1/_2$ cups sugar
> 1 teaspoon pure vanilla extract
> 3 large eggs, warmed to room temperature
> 1 cup walnuts, toasted and chopped

1.   Preheat the oven to 350°F. Lightly coat the sides of an 8-inch baking pan with butter and flour. Line the bottom of the pan with parchment paper.

2.   Melt the chocolate and butter in the top of a double boiler over hot (not simmering) water, stirring continuously. Remove from heat and set aside to cool for a few minutes.

3.   Sift together the flour, baking powder, and salt. Set aside.

4.   Blend the sugar into the chocolate mixture a little at a time. Add the vanilla.

5.   Stir the eggs into the mixture one at a time.

6.   Fold the flour mixture into the chocolate mixture just until lightly blended. Gently fold in the walnuts.

(continued)

Chocolate Pizza Parties for Teens

This can be a potluck party, where guests are invited to bring their favorite topping, or you can provide all the fixings.

1.   Use a Toll House cookie or basic brownie recipe for the pizza crust. (Leave out the chocolate chips and/or nuts, and bake the dough in pizza pans.)
2.   Provide a "sauce" to help hold the toppings. This can be whipped cream, mascarpone, custard, or ganache. Be careful not to use a "sauce" that will make the crust soggy.
3.   Provide a buffet of toppings so each guest can design an individual slice or work together to build a community pizza.

7. Spread the batter evenly into the prepared pan and bake for 25 to 30 minutes. Remove the brownies from the oven, and place them on a cooling rack for at least 1 hour before cutting.

Makes 9–16 brownies

Chewy Chunky Brownies

Chewier than a classic brownie, these treats have an additional chocolate chip surprise.

> 4 ounces semisweet chocolate, finely chopped
> 1/2 cup butter, cut into 1/4-inch cubes
> 2 large eggs, warmed to room temperature
> 1 cup dark brown sugar, firmly packed
> 1/4 teaspoon salt
> 1 teaspoon pure vanilla extract
> 1/2 cup flour, sifted
> 3/4 cup semisweet chocolate chips
> 3/4 cup walnuts, toasted and chopped

1. Preheat the oven to 350°F. Lightly coat the sides of an 8-inch baking pan with butter and flour. Line the bottom of the pan with parchment paper.

2. Melt the chocolate and butter in the top of a double boiler over hot (not simmering) water, stirring continuously. Remove from heat and set aside to cool for a few minutes.

3. Whisk the eggs together. Gradually whisk in the sugar, salt, and vanilla.

4. Fold the chocolate mixture into the egg mixture.

5. Fold in the flour, just until lightly blended. Gently fold in the chocolate chips and walnuts.

6. Spread the batter evenly into the prepared pan and bake for 25 to 30 minutes. Remove the brownies from the oven, and place them on a cooling rack for at least 1 hour before cutting.

Makes 9–16 brownies

Black Tie Brownies

More like a bite-size torte, in this elegant brownie the walnuts are ground and replace most of the flour. Italian cream cheese adds an extraordinary richness. And a swirl of whipped cream, topped with curls of bittersweet chocolate, gives a formal finishing touch.

> 8 ounces semisweet chocolate, finely chopped
> 1/2 cup butter, cut into 1/4-inch cubes
> 1/4 cup mascarpone cheese, warmed to room temperature
> 4 large eggs, separated
> 3/4 cup sugar, divided
> 2 tablespoons cognac
> 1 tablespoon instant espresso powder
> 3/4 cup walnuts, toasted and ground
> 1/4 cup flour, sifted
> 1/4 teaspoon cream of tartar

Topping:
> 1 cup heavy cream, chilled
> 1/4 cup superfine sugar
> 1/2 cup bittersweet chocolate curls

1. Preheat the oven to 350°F. Lightly coat the sides of an 8-inch baking pan with butter and flour. Line the bottom of the pan with parchment paper.

2. Melt the chocolate, butter, and mascarpone cheese in the top of a double boiler over hot (not simmering) water, stirring continuously. Remove from heat and set aside to cool for a few minutes.

3. Using an electric mixer set on a medium speed, beat the egg yolks and $1/2$ cup of the sugar together until thick.

4. Adjust your mixer to a low speed and gradually add the chocolate mixture, cognac, espresso powder, walnuts, and flour, one at a time. Set aside.

5. With a clean, dry mixer and bowl, beat the egg whites at a medium-high speed. Sprinkle in the cream of tartar and continue beating until soft peaks form. Adjust your mixer to a high speed and sprinkle in $1/4$ cup sugar. Beat until firm peaks form. (Be careful not to overmix.)

6. Lightly fold a third of the egg whites into the batter. Repeat until all the egg whites are incorporated.

7. Spread the batter evenly into the prepared pan and bake for 30 to 40 minutes. Remove the brownies from the oven, and place them on a cooling rack for at least 1 hour before cutting. If the brownies cool unevenly, with the edges higher than the center, gently press the edges down. Then cut and decorate these brownies with the bottom side up.

(continued)

Preparing Pans

Taking a minute to prep your pans (even nonstick pans) will make removing your brownies and other desserts much easier.

1. Place the pan on parchment or waxed paper and trace a line around the outside. Cut just inside the line for the best fit.
2. Rub a *light* coating of butter on the sides of the pan.
3. Sprinkle a small amount of flour in the pan and tip the pan, coating the sides.
4. Invert the pan over your sink and gently tap to remove any excess flour.
5. Place the parchment or waxed paper in the bottom, and your pan is ready.

8. Just before serving, whip the cream with the superfine sugar, using an electric mixer on a high speed until soft peaks form. Decorate each brownie individually with a dollop of whipped cream and bitter-sweet chocolate curls.

Makes 16 (2-inch-square) brownies

Peanut Butter Swirl Brownies

A layer of peanut butter sweetened with brown sugar swirls through the top layer of these brownies.

4 ounces unsweetened chocolate, finely
    chopped
$3/4$ cup butter, cut into $1/4$-inch cubes
1 cup flour
1 teaspoon baking powder
$1/4$ teaspoon salt
$1^1/2$ cups sugar
1 teaspoon pure vanilla extract
3 large eggs, warmed to room temperature
1 cup walnuts, toasted and chopped

Peanut Butter Swirl:
$1/2$ cup creamy peanut butter
$1/4$ cup mascarpone cheese
2 tablespoons flour
2 tablespoons light brown sugar, firmly
    packed
1 egg, warmed to room temperature

1. Preheat the oven to 325°F. Lightly coat the sides of an 8-inch baking pan with butter and flour. Line the bottom of the pan with parchment paper.

2. Melt the chocolate and butter in the top of a double boiler over hot (not boiling) water, stirring continuously. Remove from heat and set aside to cool for a few minutes.

3. Sift together the flour, baking powder, and salt. Set aside.

4. Blend the sugar into the chocolate mixture, a little at a time. Add the vanilla.

5. Stir the eggs into the mixture, one at a time.

6. Fold the flour mixture into the chocolate mixture just until lightly blended. Gently fold in the walnuts. Set aside.

It's All About Image

Some of the most elegant gift boxes in the chocolate industry are the gold boxes that hold Godiva Chocolates. Who owns Godiva?

A. Golden Grain Macaroni Company
B. Lindt & Sprungli
C. Campbell Soup Company
D. Nestle Food Company

Answer: C—Campbell Soup Company

7. In a separate bowl, cream together the peanut butter, mascarpone cheese, flour, and brown sugar. Beat the remaining egg into the mixture. Set aside.

8. Spread three-quarters of the batter into the prepared pan. Spoon the peanut butter mixture on top of the batter in nine equal parts evenly spaced. Spoon the remaining brownie batter in and around the peanut butter mounds. Using the tip of a knife, gently swirl the two top layers together. Bake for 45 minutes. Remove the brownies from the oven, and place them on a cooling rack for at least 1 hour before cutting.

Makes 9–16 brownies

Rocky Road Brownies

These brownies are topped with a "rocky" marshmallow frosting.

4 ounces semisweet chocolate, finely chopped
¹/₂ cup butter, cut into ¹/₄-inch cubes
2 large eggs, warmed to room temperature
¹/₂ cup sugar
¹/₂ cup light brown sugar, firmly packed
¹/₄ teaspoon salt
1 teaspoon pure vanilla extract
¹/₂ cup flour, sifted
1 cup milk chocolate chips

Topping:
3 egg whites, warmed to room temperature
¹/₂ cup powdered sugar
¹/₂ cup walnuts, toasted and chopped

1. Preheat the oven to 350°F. Lightly coat the sides of an 8-inch baking pan with butter and flour. Line the bottom of the pan with parchment paper.

2. Melt the chocolate and butter in the top of a double boiler over hot (not boiling) water, stirring continuously. Remove from heat and set aside to cool for a few minutes.

3. Whisk the eggs together. Gradually whisk in the sugars, salt, and vanilla.

4. Fold the chocolate mixture into the egg mixture.

5. Fold in the flour just until lightly blended. Gently fold in the chocolate chips.

6. Spread the batter evenly into the prepared pan and bake for 25 to 30 minutes. Remove the brownies from the oven, and place them on a cooling rack for 30 minutes, then in the refrigerator for an additional 30 minutes.

7. When the baked brownies are completely cool, prepare the frosting: Beat the egg whites with an electric mixer on a medium-high speed until frothy. Sprinkle in the powdered sugar and continue beating until the mixture becomes the consistency of marshmallow cream. Fold in the walnuts.

8. Remove the baked brownies from the refrigerator and spread the marshmallow frosting on top, leaving swirls and soft peaks. Bake for an additional 10 to 15 minutes, until the peaks turn golden. Remove the brownies from the oven and place them on a cooling rack for at least an hour. To cut these sticky treats, dip a sharp knife in hot water and wipe dry before each cut.

Makes 9–16 brownies

Triple Treat Brownies

Butterscotch chips and coconut join walnuts for these chewy treats.

> 4 ounces semisweet chocolate, finely chopped
> 1/2 cup butter, cut into 1/4-inch cubes
> 2 large eggs, warmed to room temperature
> 1 cup dark brown sugar, firmly packed
> 1/4 teaspoon salt
> 1 teaspoon pure vanilla extract
> 1/2 cup flour, sifted
> 1/2 cup butterscotch chips
> 1/2 cup sweetened coconut
> 1/2 cup walnuts, toasted and chopped

1. Preheat the oven to 350°F. Lightly coat the sides of an 8-inch baking pan with butter and flour. Line the bottom of the pan with parchment paper.

2. Melt the chocolate and butter in the top of a double boiler over hot (not boiling) water, stirring continuously. Remove from heat and set aside to cool for a few minutes.

3. Whisk the eggs together. Gradually whisk in the sugar, salt, and vanilla.

4. Fold the chocolate mixture into the egg mixture.

5. Fold in the flour, just until lightly blended. Gently fold in the butterscotch chips, coconut, and walnuts.

6. Spread the batter evenly into the prepared pan and bake for 25 to 30 minutes. Remove the brownies from the oven, and place them on a cooling rack for at least 1 hour before cutting.

Makes 9–16 brownies

White Chocolate Brownies

These are classic brownies, made with white chocolate.

> 4 ounces white chocolate, finely chopped
> 1/2 cup butter, cut into 1/4-inch cubes
> 1 cup flour
> 1 teaspoon baking powder
> 1/4 teaspoon salt
> 1 cup sugar
> 1 teaspoon pure vanilla extract
> 2 large eggs, warmed to room temperature
> 1 cup walnuts, toasted and chopped

1. Preheat the oven to 325°F. Lightly coat the sides of an 8-inch baking pan with butter and flour. Line the bottom of the pan with parchment paper.

2. Melt the chocolate and butter in the top of a double boiler over hot (not boiling) water, stirring continuously. Remove from heat and set aside to cool for a few minutes.

3. Sift together the flour, baking powder, and salt. Set aside.

4. Blend the sugar into the chocolate mixture, a little at a time. Add the vanilla.

5. Stir the eggs into the mixture, one at a time.

6.   Fold the flour mixture into the chocolate mixture just until lightly blended. Gently fold in the walnuts.

7.   Spread the batter evenly into the prepared pan and bake for 40 minutes. Remove the brownies from the oven, and place them on a cooling rack for at least 1 hour before cutting.

Makes 9–16 brownies

Royal Raspberry Brownies

These white chocolate brownies have a layer of flavored cream cheese, and are crowned with fresh raspberries and mint leaves.

4 ounces white chocolate, finely chopped
¹/₂ cup butter, cut into ¹/₄-inch cubes
1 cup flour, sifted
1 teaspoon baking powder
¹/₄ teaspoon salt
1 cup sugar
1 teaspoon pure vanilla extract
2 large eggs, warmed to room temperature
1 cup walnuts, toasted and chopped

Cream Cheese Filling:
8 ounces cream cheese, chilled
2 tablespoons flour
¹/₄ cup powdered sugar
3 tablespoons seedless raspberry preserves
1 large egg, warmed to room temperature

Topping:
1 cup heavy cream, chilled
¹/₄ cup superfine sugar
16 fresh raspberries
16 small fresh mint leaves (optional)

1.   Preheat the oven to 325°F. Lightly coat the sides of an 8-inch baking pan with butter and flour. Line the bottom of the pan with parchment paper.

2.   Melt the chocolate and butter in the top of a double boiler over hot (not boiling) water, stirring continuously. Remove from heat and set aside to cool for a few minutes.

3.   Sift together 1 cup flour, baking powder, and salt. Set aside.

4.   Blend the sugar into the chocolate mixture, a little at a time. Add the vanilla.

5.   Stir 2 eggs into the mixture, one at a time.

6.   Fold the flour mixture into the chocolate mixture just until lightly blended. Gently fold in the walnuts. Set aside.

7.   In a separate bowl, blend together the cream cheese, 2 tablespoons flour, powdered sugar, and raspberry preserves. Beat in the remaining egg. Set aside.

8.   Spread two-thirds of the brownie batter evenly into the prepared pan. Spread the cream cheese mixture over the top. Top with the remaining brownie batter. Using the tip of a knife, gently swirl the two top layers. Bake for 45 minutes. Remove the brownies from the oven, and place them on a cooling rack for at least 1 hour before cutting.

9.   Just before serving, whip the cream with the superfine sugar, using an electric mixer on a high speed. Place in a pastry bag fitted with a star tip, and pipe a star on top of each brownie. Place a fresh raspberry, upside down, in the center of each

(continued)

star. Tuck a fresh mint leaf next to each raspberry.

Makes 9–16 brownies

Crème Brûlée Brownies

If you love the flavor of crème brûlée, try these white chocolate brownies with orange candied walnuts.

Candied Walnuts:
1 cup walnuts, coarsely chopped
$1/3$ cup powdered sugar
1 tablespoon orange liqueur

Brownie Batter:
4 ounces white chocolate, finely chopped
$1/2$ cup butter, cut into $1/4$-inch cubes
2 large eggs, warmed to room temperature
1 cup sugar
$1/4$ teaspoon salt
1 teaspoon orange zest
$1/2$ cup flour, sifted

Topping:
$1/2$ cup light brown sugar, firmly packed
$1^1/2$ tablespoons boiling water

1.   Preheat the oven to 325°F. Lightly coat the sides of an 8-inch baking pan with butter and flour. Line the bottom of the pan with parchment paper. Set aside.

2.   In a small bowl, mix the walnuts, sugar, and liqueur until thoroughly blended and slightly moist.

3.   Spread the mixture on a cookie sheet and bake for 30 minutes, *mixing every 3 to 4 minutes* to ensure even toasting and to prevent burning. (After about 20 minutes the sugar should begin to crystallize around the walnuts.) Remove the mixture and continue mixing while cooling.

4.   Melt the chocolate and butter in the top of a double boiler over hot (not boiling) water, stirring continuously. Remove from heat and set aside to cool for a few minutes.

5.   Whisk the eggs together. Gradually whisk in the sugar, salt, and orange zest.

6.   Fold the chocolate mixture into the egg mixture.

7.   Fold in the flour just until lightly blended. Gently fold in the candied pecans.

8.   Spread the batter evenly into the prepared pan and bake for 25 to 30 minutes. Remove the brownies from the oven, and place them on a cooling rack for 30 minutes, then in the refrigerator for an additional 30 minutes.

9.   When the brownies are completely cool, move the oven's broiler rack to the highest position, and preheat the broiler. Mix the brown sugar and boiling water into a paste. Remove the brownies from the refrigerator, and spread a thin layer of the brown sugar paste over the top. Place the brownies under the broiler for a few minutes until the top turns brown and bubbly. Remove the brownies from the oven and chill before serving. To cut these special treats, dip a sharp knife in hot water and wipe dry before each cut.

Makes 9–16 brownies

Bars

Peanut Butter S'Mores

Here's a way to add a peanut butter surprise to everyone's favorite camping treat.

> 4 graham crackers
> 2 teaspoons creamy peanut butter
> 2 milk chocolate bars
> 8 large marshmallows, sliced in half

1.   Preheat the oven to 350°F. Cover a cookie sheet with foil.

2.   Snap a rectangular graham cracker in half, creating 2 squares. Spread a $1/4$-teaspoon circle of peanut butter in the center of each square.

3.   On one square, place a square of chocolate on top of the peanut butter.

4.   Place four marshmallow halves on top of the chocolate.

5.   Add another square of chocolate, and another graham cracker square, peanut butter side down. Repeat to make 3 more S'Mores.

6.   Place in the oven and bake for 5 to 7 minutes. Place on cooling racks for a few minutes before eating.

Makes 4 S'Mores

Crispy Fruit Bars

Imagine your favorite rice cereal cookie, seasoned with dried fruit bits and frosted with creamy milk chocolate.

Frosting:

> 8 ounces milk chocolate, finely chopped
> $1/2$ cup heavy cream, warmed to room
>   temperature
> 2 tablespoons butter, warmed to room
>   temperature
> 2 tablespoons alkalized cocoa powder
> 1 tablespoon dark brown sugar, firmly
>   packed

Crispy Base:

> 3 tablespoons butter
> 10 ounces marshmallows
> $1/2$ cup dried fruit bits
> $1/2$ teaspoon nutmeg
> 6 cups crispy rice cereal

1.   Lightly coat the sides of a 9-inch by 13-inch baking pan with butter and flour. Line the bottom of the pan with parchment paper. Set aside.

2.   Melt the chocolate, cream, butter, cocoa powder, and brown sugar in the top of a double boiler over hot (not simmering) water, stirring continuously. Remove from heat and set aside to cool for about 2 hours.

Makes 24–28 bars

Coconut Cashew Chocolate Bars

These chewy, chunky chocolate bars are quick and easy to make.

 2 cups chocolate cookie crumbs
 1 cup chocolate chips
 1 cup sweetened coconut
 1 cup cashews, toasted and chopped
 14 ounces sweetened condensed milk
 $^1/_4$ cup butter, melted

1.   Preheat the oven to 350°F. Lightly coat the sides of a 9-inch by 13-inch baking pan with butter and flour. Line the bottom of the pan with parchment paper.

2.   Mix together the cookie crumbs, chocolate chips, coconut, and cashews. Stir in the condensed milk and melted butter.

3.   Press the mixture evenly into the pan and bake for 15 to 20 minutes. Remove from the oven and place on a cooling rack.

Makes 24–28 bars

Toasted Almond Bars

A light layer of egg whites and toasted almonds covers a base of dark chocolate.

Base Layer:
 1 cup flour
 $^1/_4$ cup nonalkalized cocoa powder
 $^1/_2$ teaspoon baking soda
 $^1/_4$ teaspoon salt
 $^1/_2$ cup butter, softened
 $^1/_2$ cup sugar

 2 tablespoons rum
 1 cup chocolate chips

Top Layer:
 4 egg whites, warmed to room temperature
 $^1/_8$ teaspoon cream of tartar
 1 teaspoon pure almond extract
 1 cup superfine sugar
 $1^1/_2$ cups almonds, toasted and ground
 $^1/_2$ cup almonds, sliced

1.   Preheat the oven to 325°F. Lightly coat the sides of a 9-inch by 13-inch baking pan with butter and flour. Line the bottom of the pan with parchment paper.

2.   Sift together the flour, cocoa powder, baking soda, and salt. Set aside.

3.   Cream together the butter and sugar using an electric mixer on a medium-high speed. Add the rum. Adjust the mixer to a low speed and add the flour mixture and chocolate chips. The mixture should have a crumbly texture.

4.   Press the mixture into the prepared pan and bake for 15 to 20 minutes. Remove the base layer from the oven, and place it on a cooling rack for 30 minutes, then in the refrigerator for an additional 30 minutes.

5.   When the base layer is completely cool, prepare the top layer: Beat the egg whites, cream of tartar, almond extract, sugar, and ground almonds with an electric mixer on a medium-high speed until thoroughly blended and frothy.

6.   Gently pour the egg white mixture over the chocolate base. Sprinkle with

sliced almonds. Bake for an additional 20 to 25 minutes, until golden brown. Remove the bars from the oven and place them on a cooling rack for at least an hour.

Makes 24–28 bars

Bittersweet Ginger Mint Bars

A cloud of creamy mint, featuring bits of bittersweet chocolate and candied ginger, floats atop a rich chocolate base.

Base Layer:
4 ounces unsweetened chocolate, finely chopped
$1/2$ cup butter, cut into $1/4$-inch cubes
1 cup flour
$1/2$ teaspoon baking powder
2 tablespoons instant espresso powder
$1/8$ teaspoon salt
2 eggs, warmed to room temperature
1 cup sugar
1 teaspoon vanilla extract

Top Layer:
3 egg whites, warmed to room temperature
$1/4$ teaspoon pure mint extract
$1/2$ cup powdered sugar
3 drops green food coloring (optional)
2 ounces bittersweet chocolate, chopped into chip-size pieces
$1/4$ cup candied ginger, chopped into chip-size pieces

1. Preheat the oven to 350°F. Lightly coat the sides of a 9-inch by 13-inch baking pan with butter and flour. Line the bottom of the pan with parchment paper.

2. To make the base layer: Melt the chocolate and butter in the top of a double boiler over hot (not simmering) water, stirring continuously. Remove from heat and set aside to cool to room temperature.

3. Sift together the flour, baking powder, espresso powder, and salt. Set aside.

4. Beat together the eggs and sugar, using an electric mixer on a high speed,

(continued)

Chocolate Medals

If you're planning a backyard or company Olympics, molds are available for large and small medals that can be poured in dark, milk, or white chocolate. When set, wrap in gold, silver, or bronze confectionery foil and attach a ribbon!

until thick. Adjust the mixer to a low speed and add the chocolate mixture and vanilla. Fold in the flour mixture until lightly blended.

5.　Pour the batter into the prepared pan and bake for 15 to 20 minutes. Remove the base layer from the oven, and place it on a cooling rack for 30 minutes, then in the refrigerator for an additional 30 minutes.

6.　When the base layer is completely cool, prepare the top layer: Beat the egg whites and mint extract with an electric mixer on a medium-high speed until frothy. Sprinkle in the powdered sugar and continue beating until the mixture becomes the consistency of marshmallow cream. Add the food coloring, drop by drop, until the mixture reaches the color you desire. Fold in the bittersweet chocolate and candied ginger.

7.　Remove the base layer from the refrigerator and spread the mint cream on top, leaving swirls and soft peaks. Bake for an additional 10 to 15 minutes, until the peaks turn golden. Remove the bars from the oven and place them on a cooling rack for at least an hour. To cut these sticky treats, dip a sharp knife in hot water and wipe dry before each cut.

Makes 24–28 bars

Baklava Bars

Spiced walnuts, almonds, and honey, sprinkled with mini chocolate chips, crown a buttery base.

Base Layer:
1/2 cup butter, chilled and cut into 1/4-inch cubes
1/2 cup dark brown sugar, firmly packed
1 teaspoon vanilla
1 cup flour
1 egg white, slightly beaten

Top Layer:
2/3 cup butter, cut into 1/4-inch cubes
1/2 cup light brown sugar, firmly packed
1/2 cup honey
1/2 cup walnuts, toasted and chopped
1/2 cup almonds, toasted and chopped
1/4 cup mascarpone cheese
1/2 teaspoon ground cinnamon
1/8 teaspoon ground cloves
1 cup mini semisweet chocolate chips

1.　Preheat the oven to 350°F. Lightly coat the sides of an 8-inch baking pan with butter and flour. Line the bottom of the pan with parchment paper.

2.　Cream together the butter and brown sugar using an electric mixer on a high speed. Add the vanilla. Adjust your mixer to a medium speed and add the flour, a little at a time, until lightly blended.

3.　Press the dough evenly into the pan and, using a pastry brush, lightly paint the top with egg white. Bake for 25 minutes, until golden brown. Remove the base layer from the oven, and place it on a cooling rack for 30 minutes, then in the refrigerator for an additional 30 minutes.

4.　When the base layer is completely cool, prepare the top layer: Mix the butter,

brown sugar, and honey in a heavy-bottomed saucepan over a low heat. Simmer, without stirring, for 5 minutes. Remove from heat and set aside.

5. In a separate bowl, mix the walnuts, almonds, mascarpone cheese, cinnamon, and cloves. Gently fold the honey mixture into the walnut mixture.

6. Remove the base layer from the refrigerator. Pour the honey mixture over it, sprinkle with chocolate chips, and bake for 20 minutes. Remove the bars from the oven, and place them on a cooling rack for at least an hour. To cut these sticky treats, dip a sharp knife in hot water and wipe dry before each cut.

Makes 16–24 bars

White Chocolate Cranberry Bars

Tart dried cranberries float in a spiced white chocolate, cream cheese filling atop a crunchy base.

Base Layer:
1/2 cup flour
3/4 cup rolled oats
1/2 cup dark brown sugar, firmly packed
3/4 cup butter, chilled and cut into 1/4-inch cubes

Filling:
6 ounces white chocolate, finely chopped
1/4 cup heavy cream, warmed to room temperature

8 ounces cream cheese, warmed to room temperature
1/4 cup sugar
1 tablespoon pure almond extract
1/2 teaspoon allspice
2 egg yolks, warmed to room temperature
2 tablespoons almonds, toasted and ground
1 cup dried cranberries

Topping:
1 cup white chocolate curls

1. Preheat the oven to 325°F. Lightly coat the sides of an 8-inch baking pan with butter and flour. Line the bottom of the pan with parchment paper.

2. Mix together the flour, oats, and brown sugar. Cut the butter into the mixture with a pastry blender. When the mixture is crumbly, press it evenly into the pan and bake for 20 minutes. Remove this base layer from the oven, and place it on a cooling rack for 30 minutes, then in the refrigerator for an additional 30 minutes.

3. When the base layer is completely cool, prepare the top layer: Melt the chocolate and cream in the top of a double boiler over hot (not boiling) water, stirring continuously. Remove from heat and set aside to cool for a few minutes.

4. Combine the cream cheese with the sugar, almond extract, and allspice, using an electric mixer on a high setting. Beat until fluffy. Adjust your mixer to a medium speed, and add the egg yolks, one at a time.

(continued)

5.　Fold in the ground almonds, chocolate mixture, and cranberries, one at a time.

6.　Remove the base layer from the refrigerator. Spread the cream cheese mixture over the base layer, and bake for 60 minutes. Turn off the oven and leave the bars in for an additional hour. Remove the bars from the oven and place on a rack to cool completely.

7.　When completely cool, cut with a sharp knife dipped in hot water and dried, and top with white chocolate curls.

Makes 16–24 bars

Caramel Latte Bars

An espresso-flavored base holds toasted pecans, floating in white chocolate and caramel.

Base Layer:

2¹/₂ cups flour
¹/₄ cup instant espresso powder
1 cup butter, softened
¹/₂ cup sugar
1 egg, warmed to room temperature

Top Layer:

1 cup butter
²/₃ cup dark brown sugar, firmly packed
¹/₄ cup corn syrup
2¹/₂ cups pecans, toasted and chopped
1 cup white chocolate chips

1.　Preheat the oven to 375°F. Lightly coat the sides of a 9-inch by 13-inch baking pan with butter and flour. Line the bottom of the pan with parchment paper.

2.　Sift together the flour and espresso powder. Set aside.

3.　Cream the butter using an electric mixer on a medium-high speed. Add the sugar, beating until fluffy. Adjust your mixer to a medium speed. Add the egg, beating until thoroughly blended.

4.　Adjust your mixer to a low speed. Slowly add the flour mixture until lightly blended.

5.　Press the batter evenly into the pan and bake for 20 minutes. Remove this base layer from the oven, and place it on a cooling rack. Reduce the oven temperature to 325°F.

6.　Melt the remaining butter in a heavy-bottomed saucepan, over medium heat. Add the brown sugar and corn syrup, stirring continuously. When the mixture comes to a boil, stop stirring for 2 minutes. Stir in the pecans.

7.　Spread this pecan mixture over the base layer, and bake for 20 minutes. Remove the bars from the oven and quickly sprinkle the white chocolate chips on top. Gently press the chips into the hot caramel. Bake for 3 minutes. Place on a rack to cool completely.

Makes 24–28 bars

chapter five

Muffins and Morning Treats

When Europeans first started drinking chocolate, they preferred it in the morning, particularly if they had a hangover. Through the ages, hot chocolate remained a favorite morning drink. Today, with our love for chocolate expanding and new varieties of chocolate becoming available, chocolate is moving into the mainstream of muffins and other morning treats. Here are a few recipes to help get your day off to the right start.

Muffins

Midnight Muffins

Ultra-rich and elegant, these bittersweet chocolate muffins have a filling of cream cheese and chocolate chips, and are especially good in the wee hours of the morning.

Filling:
6 ounces cream cheese, softened
3 tablespoons sugar
1 egg, warmed to room temperature
1/4 cup miniature dark chocolate chips

Muffins:
4 ounces bittersweet chocolate, finely chopped
3 tablespoons butter, sliced into 1/4-inch cubes
3/4 cup flour
2 teaspoons instant espresso powder
1/2 teaspoon baking powder
1/8 teaspoon salt
1 egg, warmed to room temperature
1/4 cup sugar
1/4 cup milk
1 tablespoon raspberry liqueur

1. Preheat the oven to 350°F. Line 12 standard muffin-pan cups with cupcake papers.

2. To make the filling: Beat together the cream cheese, sugar, and egg, using an electric mixer on a medium speed, until smooth. Adjust the mixer to a low speed and blend in the chocolate chips. Set aside.

3. Melt the chocolate and butter in the top of a double boiler over hot (not simmering) water, stirring continuously. Remove from heat and set aside to cool to room temperature.

4. Sift together the flour, espresso powder, baking powder, and salt. Set aside.

5. Whisk together the egg, sugar, milk and liqueur. Whisk in the melted chocolate mixture. Fold in the flour mixture until lightly blended.

6. Fill the muffin cups 1/3 full with muffin batter. Place a tablespoon of cream cheese in the center of each, and top with remaining batter. Bake for 20 to 25 minutes, or until a cake tester inserted in center comes out clean. Serve hot out of the oven.

Makes 12 muffins

California Sunrise Muffins

Start your day with fresh orange juice, squeezed into these bittersweet chocolate muffins. (These treats taste even better with an ice cold glass of champagne!)

Streusel Filling:

$1/4$ cup superfine sugar
$1/4$ cup flour
2 tablespoons butter, chilled
$1/8$ teaspoon ground allspice
$1/4$ cup maraschino cherries, drained and
   chopped

Muffins:

2 cups flour
1 teaspoon baking powder
$1/2$ teaspoon baking soda
$1/4$ teaspoon salt
1 cup light brown sugar, firmly packed
2 tablespoons orange zest
$1/4$ cup fresh-squeezed orange juice
2 tablespoons grenadine
$1/4$ cup butter, melted
$1/4$ cup milk, warmed to room temperature
1 egg, warmed to room temperature and
   slightly beaten
4 ounces bittersweet chocolate, grated

1. Preheat the oven to 350°F. Line 12 standard muffin-pan cups with cupcake papers.

2. To make the streusel filling: Combine sugar, flour, butter, and allspice with a fork or pastry blender until crumbly. Mix in the cherries. Set aside.

3. Sift together the flour, baking powder, baking soda, and salt.

4. Stir in the brown sugar, orange zest, orange juice, grenadine, butter, milk, and egg, one ingredient at a time. Mix only until dry ingredients are moistened and combined. Fold in the bittersweet chocolate.

5. Fill the muffin cups $1/3$ full with muffin batter. Sprinkle the streusel filling over the muffins and top with remaining batter. Bake for 30 to 35 minutes, or until a cake tester inserted in center comes out clean. Serve hot out of the oven.

Makes 12 muffins

Center Story

Muffins, cakes, and pastries bake from the outside in. When you insert a toothpick or tester to see if your treat is done, it's important to place the tester in the center of the item.

Apple and Cinnamon Muffins

These brown sugar-topped apple muffins are even better when baked in a special muffin-top pan. Available at most better kitchen and specialty shops, the cavities in this pan are wider and shallower, so the muffins are mostly the most delicious part—the top!

Topping:

¹/₃ cup light brown sugar, firmly packed
¹/₃ cup flour
3 tablespoons butter, chilled
1 teaspoon ground cinnamon
¹/₄ cup pecans, toasted and chopped

Muffins:

1³/₄ cups flour
¹/₄ cup nonalkalized cocoa powder
1 teaspoon baking powder
¹/₂ teaspoon baking soda
¹/₄ teaspoon salt
¹/₂ cup butter, softened
1 cup light brown sugar, firmly packed
2 eggs, warmed to room temperature
1 cup chopped fresh, tart apples

1.   Preheat the oven to 350°F. Lightly coat the sides and bottoms of a muffin-top pan with butter and flour, or line 18 standard muffin-pan cups with cupcake papers.

2.   Combine topping ingredients with a fork or pastry blender until crumbly. Set aside.

3.   Sift together the flour, cocoa powder, baking powder, baking soda, and salt. Set aside.

4.   Cream the butter using an electric mixer on a medium-high speed. Add the brown sugar, beating until fluffy. Adjust your mixer to a medium speed and add the eggs, beating until thoroughly blended.

5.   Adjust your mixer to a low speed. Add the flour mixture until lightly blended. Fold in the apples.

6.   Fill the muffin cups ²/₃ full with muffin batter. Sprinkle topping over each muffin and bake for 40 to 45 minutes, or until a cake tester inserted in center comes out clean. Serve hot out of the oven.

Makes 18 muffins

Ginger Chip Bran Muffins

These healthy muffins have two surprises—chocolate chips and candied ginger.

1 cup flour
2 teaspoons baking powder
¹/₂ teaspoon baking soda
¹/₂ teaspoon salt
2 cups bran
1 cup rolled oats
¹/₂ cup milk chocolate chips
¹/₄ cup candied ginger, chopped
¹/₃ cup butter, softened
¹/₂ cup light brown sugar, firmly packed
1 egg
1 cup buttermilk

1.   Preheat the oven to 400°F. Line 12 standard muffin-pan cups with cupcake papers.

2. Sift together the flour, baking powder, baking soda, and salt. Add the bran, oats, chocolate chips, and ginger. Mix well and set aside.

3. Cream the butter using an electric mixer on a medium-high speed. Add the brown sugar, beating until fluffy. Adjust your mixer to a medium speed and add the egg, beating until thoroughly blended.

4. Using a fork, alternate adding small portions of the flour mixture and buttermilk until lightly blended. The batter should be lumpy.

5. Fill the muffin cups ²/₃ full and bake for 20 to 25 minutes, or until a cake tester inserted in center comes out clean. Serve hot out of the oven.

Makes 12 muffins

Peanut Butter Kiss Muffins

A giant milk chocolate kiss hides inside each of these peanut butter mini-muffins.

Topping:
1 cup dry roasted peanuts, chopped
2 tablespoons light brown sugar, firmly
  packed

Muffins:
1¹/₂ cups flour
1 teaspoon baking powder
¹/₂ teaspoon baking soda
¹/₄ teaspoon salt
¹/₂ cup butter, softened
¹/₂ cup creamy peanut butter
¹/₂ cup sugar
1 egg, warmed to room temperature
24 chocolate kisses, unwrapped

(continued)

Gifts for Morning Treat Makers

If you don't have a specialty kitchen shop in your area, you can find great gifts through mail-order catalogs and Web sites.

- Muffin-top pans
- Mini-muffin pans
- Muffin bundt pans
- Miniature loaf pans
- Crepe pans
- Serving baskets with warmers
- Pastry blenders
- Ceramic or pottery mixing bowls
- High-quality measuring spoons and cups
- High-quality spatulas and whisks
- Egg separators
- Unique muffin cups
- Parchment paper
- Stand mixer
- Domestic and imported couvertures
- Gourmet cocoa powders
- Cappuccino chips
- Dried cherries or blueberries
- High-quality extracts
- Chocolate-flavored coffee beans

1. Preheat the oven to 350°F. Lightly coat the sides and bottoms of a mini-muffin pan with butter and flour, or line 24 mini-muffin pan cups with cupcake papers.

2. Combine topping ingredients with a fork. Set aside.

3. Sift together the flour, baking powder, baking soda, and salt. Set aside.

4. Cream the butter using an electric mixer on a medium-high speed. Add the peanut butter and sugar, beating until fluffy. Adjust your mixer to a medium speed and add the egg, beating until thoroughly blended.

5. Adjust your mixer to a low speed. Add the flour mixture until lightly blended.

Chocolate Coffee Beans

On special mornings, brew coffee made with chocolate-flavored coffee beans. These are regular and decaffeinated beans infused with chocolate and other flavors. Look for them at your local coffee bean shop, or contact Gloria Jean's at (800) 946-8528 or *www.gloriajeans.com.*

6. Fill the muffin cups ¹/₃ full with muffin batter. Place a chocolate kiss in each and fill ²/₃ full with batter. Sprinkle topping over each muffin and bake for 25 to 30 minutes. Cool on wire racks.

Makes 24 mini-muffins

Eggnog Muffins

These simple little white chocolate muffins are wonderful on cold winter mornings.

> 4 ounces white chocolate, finely chopped
> ¹/₄ cup milk, warmed to room temperature
> 1¹/₂ cups flour
> 1 teaspoon baking soda
> ¹/₄ teaspoon salt
> ¹/₄ teaspoon nutmeg
> ¹/₄ cup butter, softened
> ¹/₂ cup sugar
> 1 egg, warmed to room temperature
> 1 tablespoon brandy
> 1 teaspoon orange liqueur
> 1 teaspoon orange zest
> ¹/₂ cup milk

1. Preheat the oven to 350°F. Line 12 standard muffin-pan cups with cupcake papers.

2. Melt the chocolate and ¹/₄ cup milk in the top of a double boiler over hot (not simmering) water, stirring continuously. Remove from heat and set aside to cool to room temperature.

3. Sift together the flour, baking soda, salt, and nutmeg. Set aside.

4. Cream the butter using an electric mixer on a medium-high speed. Add the sugar, beating until fluffy. Adjust your mixer to a medium speed and add the egg, brandy, liqueur, and orange zest, beating until thoroughly blended.

5. Adjust your mixer to a low speed and blend in the melted chocolate. Then, alternate adding small portions of the flour mixture and $^1/_2$ cup milk until lightly blended.

6. Fill the muffin cups $^2/_3$ full and bake for 20 to 25 minutes, or until a cake tester inserted in center comes out clean. Serve hot out of the oven.

Makes 12 muffins

Red, White, and Blueberry Muffins

Cranberries and white chocolate chips join blueberries in these patriotic muffins.

2 cups flour
1 teaspoon baking powder
$^1/_2$ teaspoon baking soda
$^1/_4$ teaspoon salt
$^1/_2$ cup butter
1 cup sugar
2 eggs, warmed to room temperature
1 teaspoon pure vanilla extract
$^1/_2$ cup milk
$^1/_2$ cup dried cranberries
$^1/_2$ cup dried blueberries
$^1/_2$ cup white chocolate chips

(continued)

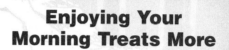

Enjoying Your Morning Treats More

Wouldn't you love to wake up to fresh baked (or made) morning treats? Here's a tip for the next best thing: Prepare as much as you can the night before.

1. Prep the pans and set up your cooling racks.
2. Prep the ingredients: Chop chocolate or nuts, separate eggs, sift flour, wash and slice fresh fruit, etc.
3. Premeasure the ingredients.
4. Sift together the dry ingredients.
5. Set up your mixer or any other equipment you'll need.
6. Set a special table or breakfast-in-bed tray.

1. Preheat the oven to 375°F. Line 18 standard muffin-pan cups with cupcake papers.

2. Sift together the flour, baking powder, baking soda, and salt. Set aside.

3. Cream the butter using an electric mixer on a medium-high speed. Add the sugar, beating until fluffy. Adjust your mixer to a medium speed and add the eggs and vanilla, beating until thoroughly blended.

4. Adjust your mixer to a low speed and alternate adding small portions of the flour mixture and milk until lightly blended. Fold in the cranberries, blueberries, and white chocolate chips.

6. Fill the muffin cups $2/3$ full and bake for 20 to 25 minutes, or until a cake tester inserted in center comes out clean. Serve hot out of the oven.

Makes 18 muffins

Tea Breads and Coffee Cakes

Holiday Crowns

These charming tea bread alternatives to fruitcake are jeweled with glazed fruit and, when baked in muffin-size bundt pans, magically transform into small crowns.

$1^1/2$ *cups flour*
$1/2$ *teaspoon allspice*
$1^1/2$ *cups almonds, toasted and ground*
7 eggs, warmed to room temperature and separated
1 cup superfine sugar, divided

6 tablespoons butter, melted
2 tablespoons cognac
6 ounces semisweet chocolate, grated
8 ounces glazed fruit bits

Topping:
powdered sugar, sifted

1. Preheat the oven to 375°F. Lightly coat each cavity of a muffin-size bundt pan with butter and flour.

2. Sift together the flour, allspice, and ground almonds. Set aside.

3. Beat the egg whites, using an electric mixer on a high speed, until soft peaks form. Sprinkle in $1/2$ cup sugar, beating until stiff peaks form. Set aside.

4. In a separate bowl, beat the egg yolks and remaining $1/2$ cup sugar using an electric mixer on a high speed until thick. Adjust your mixer to a medium speed. Add the melted butter and cognac, beating until thoroughly blended. Adjust your mixer to a low speed. Sprinkle in the flour mixture until lightly blended.

5. Fold a third of the egg whites into the batter. Fold in the remaining egg whites. Fold in the chocolate and fruit bits.

6. Pour the batter into the prepared pan, and bake for 30 minutes, or until a cake tester inserted in center comes out clean. Cool in the pan on a wire rack for 10 minutes, then remove from pan, and let cool completely on a wire rack. Dust with powdered sugar prior to serving.

Makes 12 crowns

Chocolate Nut Banana Bread

Chocolate-coated cashews make this banana bread extra special.

3 ounces milk chocolate
$^1/_2$ cup cashews, toasted and chopped into
    large pieces
2 cups flour
1 teaspoon baking powder
1 teaspoon baking soda
$^1/_4$ teaspoon salt
$^1/_2$ cup butter
1 cup sugar
2 eggs, warmed to room temperature
3 ripe bananas, mashed

1. Preheat the oven to 350°F. Line a cookie sheet with waxed paper. Lightly coat the sides of a 9-inch by 5-inch by 3-inch loaf pan with butter and flour. Line the bottom of the loaf pan with parchment paper.

2. Place the chocolate in a microwave-safe bowl. Heat for 1 minute on medium power. Remove and stir slowly and thoroughly. Continue heating for 30 seconds at a time, then stirring, until melted. Set aside to cool to room temperature.

3. When the chocolate is cool but still in a liquid form, fold the cashews into the chocolate, then spread the mixture in a thin layer on the cookie sheet. Refrigerate for 10 minutes. When set, break into small pieces.

4. Sift together the flour, baking powder, baking soda, and salt. Set aside.

5. Cream the butter using an electric mixer on a medium-high speed. Add the sugar, beating until fluffy. Adjust your mixer to a medium speed and add the eggs, one at a time, beating until thoroughly blended. Mix in the mashed bananas.

6. Adjust your mixer to a low speed and sprinkle in the flour mixture until lightly blended. Fold in the chocolate-coated cashews.

7. Pour into the loaf pan and bake for 40 to 45 minutes, or until a cake tester inserted in center comes out clean. Remove from oven and cool on wire rack. Slice and serve.

Makes 8 servings

Serving Baskets with Warmers

These are the greatest invention since muffin cups! A simple bread-basket is packaged with a small sealed cloth bag filled with warming crystals. You heat the bag in the microwave and place it back in the basket under a cloth napkin filled with bread or muffins.

Lemon Latte Tea Bread

White chocolate and candied lemon peels sweeten this coffee-flavored tea bread.

> 1¹/₄ cups flour
> ¹/₄ cup instant espresso powder
> ¹/₂ teaspoon baking powder
> ¹/₂ teaspoon baking soda
> ¹/₄ teaspoon salt
> ¹/₂ cup butter, softened
> 1 cup sugar
> 2 eggs, warmed to room temperature
> 2 tablespoons lemon juice
> ¹/₂ cup buttermilk
> ¹/₂ cup candied lemon peels, chopped
> ¹/₂ cup white chocolate, grated

Topping:
candied lemon peels

1. Preheat the oven to 350°F. Lightly coat the sides of a 9-inch by 5-inch by 3-inch loaf pan with butter and flour. Line the bottom of the loaf pan with parchment paper.

2. Sift together the flour, espresso powder, baking powder, baking soda, and salt. Set aside.

3. Cream the butter using an electric mixer on a medium-high speed. Add the sugar, beating until fluffy. Adjust your mixer to a medium speed and add the eggs, one at a time, beating until thoroughly blended. Mix in the lemon juice.

4. Adjust your mixer to a low speed and alternate adding the flour mixture and buttermilk, until lightly blended. Fold in the lemon peels and white chocolate.

5. Pour into the loaf pan and bake for 50 to 60 minutes, or until a cake tester inserted in center comes out clean. Remove from oven, top with candied lemon peels, and cool on wire rack. Slice and serve.

Makes 8 servings

Praline Streusel Coffeecake

White chocolate, crumbled pralines, and pecans hide within this coffeecake.

Streusel Filling and Topping:
¹/₂ cup light brown sugar, firmly packed
2 tablespoons butter, chilled
2 tablespoons flour
1 teaspoon cinnamon
¹/₄ cup crumbled pralines
¹/₂ cup pecans, toasted and chopped
³/₄ cup white chocolate curls

Cake Batter:
1¹/₂ cups flour
2 teaspoons baking powder
¹/₂ teaspoon baking soda
¹/₄ teaspoon salt
1 egg, warmed to room temperature
³/₄ cup sugar
¹/₃ cup butter, melted
¹/₂ cup milk
1 teaspoon pure vanilla extract

1. Preheat the oven to 350°F. Lightly coat the sides of an 8-inch square or round baking pan with butter and flour. Line the bottom of the pan with parchment paper.

2. Combine all the streusel ingredients except the white chocolate with a fork until crumbly. Set aside.

3. Sift together the flour, baking powder, baking soda, and salt. Set aside.

4. Beat the egg, using an electric mixer on a medium speed, until frothy. Add the sugar and melted butter, and beat until thoroughly blended. Beat in the milk and vanilla.

5. Adjust your mixer to a low speed and add the flour mixture until lightly blended.

6. Pour half of the batter into the prepared pan. Sprinkle half of the streusel mixture and $^1/_2$ cup of the white chocolate over the batter. Spoon the remaining batter evenly over the top, and sprinkle with the remaining streusel mixture. Bake for 30 to 40 minutes, or until a cake tester inserted in center comes out clean. Cool on a wire rack for 10 minutes, remove from pan, and top with the remaining white chocolate curls before serving.

Makes about 8 servings

Mocha Crumbcake

Sour cream and hazelnuts enhance this simple, delicious coffeecake.

> $1^1/_2$ *cups flour*
> $^1/_4$ *cup nonalkalized cocoa powder*
> $^1/_4$ *cup instant espresso powder*
> 1 *teaspoon baking powder*
> $^1/_2$ *teaspoon baking soda*

> $^1/_4$ *teaspoon salt*
> $^1/_2$ *cup hazelnuts, toasted, skinned, and ground*
> $^1/_2$ *cup butter*
> 1 *cup sugar*
> 3 *eggs, warmed to room temperature*
> 1 *teaspoon pure vanilla extract*
> $^3/_4$ *cup sour cream*

Topping:
> $^1/_2$ *cup sugar*
> $^1/_4$ *cup flour*
> 2 *tablespoons butter, chilled*
> 1 *teaspoon ground cinnamon*
> 2 *tablespoons powdered sugar, sifted*

(continued)

The Manner of Making Coffee, Tea, and Chocolate

Don't bother looking for this in your favorite bookstore. It was written in 1685 by Philippe Dufour, and is thought to be the first published cookbook containing recipes for chocolate.

1. Preheat the oven to 350°F. Lightly coat a 9-inch tube pan with butter and flour.

2. Sift together the flour, cocoa powder, espresso powder, baking powder, baking soda, and salt. Mix in the ground hazelnuts and set aside.

3. Cream the butter using an electric mixer on a medium-high speed. Add the sugar, beating until fluffy. Adjust your mixer to a medium speed and add the eggs and vanilla, beating until thoroughly blended.

4. Adjust your mixer to a low speed and alternate adding small portions of the flour mixture and sour cream until lightly blended.

5. Pour the batter into the prepared pan and bake for 50 to 60 minutes, or until a cake tester inserted in center comes out clean.

6. Combine topping ingredients, except the powdered sugar, with a fork until crumbly. Sprinkle topping over baked cake and return to oven for 10 minutes. Remove from oven and cool on a wire rack for 10 minutes. Remove from pan, sprinkle powdered sugar on top, and serve.

Makes about 10 servings

Morning Pastries

Chocolate Almond Croissants

If chocolate-filled croissants are a little too rich or messy for you, try these light, flaky alternatives.

4 tablespoons warm water, divided
$3^1/_2$ teaspoons sugar, divided
1 teaspoon active dry yeast
$1^1/_2$ cups flour
$^1/_2$ teaspoon salt
$^1/_2$ cup warm milk
2 teaspoons pure almond extract
$^1/_2$ cup butter, chilled
flour for dusting
8 teaspoons grated semisweet chocolate

Topping:
1 egg, warmed to room temperature
$^1/_2$ teaspoon pure almond extract
$^1/_2$ teaspoon water
$^1/_4$ cup almonds, sliced
1 teaspoon superfine sugar

1. Combine 2 tablespoons of warm water with $^1/_2$ teaspoon sugar in a small glass bowl. Sprinkle the yeast over the top. Set aside, without stirring, for 10 minutes. (If your yeast is active, this mixture should foam. If it does not, begin again with fresh, *active* yeast.)

2. Lightly coat the inside of a medium-size glass bowl with butter. Set aside.

3. Sift together the flour, 3 teaspoons of sugar, and salt. Set aside.

4. In a separate bowl, combine the yeast mixture, 2 tablespoons warm water, warm milk, and almond extract. Sprinkle in the flour mixture a little at a time, stirring and folding until the dough is smooth. Place the dough in the buttered bowl, cover with a light towel, and set aside for 1 hour in a warm, draft-free room to rise.

5. When the dough has risen, lightly dust the chilled butter with flour and, using a rolling pin, roll into a 3-inch square. Set aside.

6. Divide the dough in half and roll, on a flour-dusted surface, into two 3-inch squares. Place the butter between the two layers of dough, seal in plastic wrap, and refrigerate for 30 minutes.

7. Place the chilled dough on a flour-dusted surface, and lightly roll into a 12-inch square. Fold the dough in half twice, and roll into a 12-inch square again. Fold in half twice, again, seal in plastic wrap, and refrigerate for 30 minutes.

8. Repeat step 7 and refrigerate for 8 hours.

9. Lightly coat a baking sheet with butter. Set aside. Roll and fold the dough two more times, then roll into a 12-inch by 8-inch rectangle. Cut the rectangle into eight 4-inch by 3-inch strips. Sprinkle each strip with 1 teaspoon grated chocolate and, using your fingers, create the croissants by rolling the strips from corner to corner. Place on the prepared baking sheet, seam side down, curving slightly. Cover with a light towel and set aside for 1 hour to rise.

10. Preheat oven to 425°F. Whisk the egg with the almond extract and water. Using a pastry brush, paint the tops of the croissants. Sprinkle with almonds and sugar and bake for 15 to 20 minutes, or until golden brown. Cool on wire racks for a few minutes before serving.

Makes 8 croissants

Cherry Chip Scones

Tart, dried cherries and sweet chocolate chips make these scones a perfect way to start your day.

> *2 cups flour*
> *1 tablespoon baking powder*
> *$^1\!/_2$ teaspoon salt*
> *$^1\!/_4$ cup superfine sugar*
> *$^1\!/_3$ cup dried cherries*
> *$^1\!/_3$ cup semisweet chocolate chips*
> *1 cup heavy cream*
> *flour for dusting*
> *2 tablespoons butter, melted*

1. Preheat the oven to 425°F. Line a cookie sheet with parchment paper.

2. Sift together the flour, baking powder, salt, and sugar. Mix in the cherries and chocolate chips.

3. Using a fork, stir in the cream until the dough is thoroughly blended and sticky.

4. Dust a clean, dry working surface with flour. Place the dough on the surface and dust the top of the dough with flour. Knead the dough by pushing it away from you and then folding it back over itself. Do this about 10 to 12 times, turning it slightly each time, so that it comes full circle.

5. Divide the dough into 12 to 18 servings, and form into disks or triangles. Place on the lined or an uncoated cookie sheet, brush with melted butter, and bake for 15 to 20 minutes, until golden brown. Serve hot out of the oven.

Makes 12–18 scones

Chocolate Beignets

Mornings in the French Quarter of New Orleans always begin with hot puffs of delicate dough smothered in powdered sugar. Here's a chocolate version of this world-class treat.

> $1/2$ cup flour
> 2 tablespoons nonalkalized cocoa powder
> $1/2$ cup water
> 1 tablespoon sugar
> $1/4$ teaspoon salt
> 2 tablespoons butter, sliced into $1/4$-inch cubes
> 2 eggs, warmed to room temperature
> $1/2$ teaspoon pure vanilla extract
> $1/2$ cup vegetable shortening

Topping:
powdered sugar, sifted

1. Sift together the flour and cocoa powder. Set aside.

2. Combine the water, sugar, salt, and butter in a heavy-bottomed saucepan. Bring to a boil over a medium heat, melting the butter.

3. Remove from heat and add the flour mixture quickly with a wooden spoon until lightly blended. Return to heat and continue stirring briskly, until dough separates from the sides of the saucepan and forms a ball.

4. Remove from heat and add the eggs, one at a time; beat with an electric mixer on a medium speed until the dough is smooth and shiny, and holds its shape. Beat in the vanilla.

5. Place an ovenproof serving dish in the oven and turn the oven on low. Sift the powdered sugar into a wide, shallow bowl. Set aside. Preheat the vegetable shortening in a skillet or electric frying pan to 350°F. Divide the dough into 12 rounded mounds. Fry 6 at a time, continuously turning until golden brown. Remove, drain on paper towels, and place in the dish in the oven to keep warm.

6. When all the beignets are cooked, smother in powdered sugar, and serve hot.

Makes 12 beignets

Espresso Donut Pops

What could be better than donuts and coffee, all in one? These donut-hole-size treats are so easy to pop into your mouth, you can take them on the road.

> 4 ounces bittersweet chocolate, finely chopped
> $1^3/4$ cups cake flour
> 2 tablespoons nonalkalized cocoa powder
> 2 tablespoons instant espresso powder
> 1 teaspoon baking powder
> $1/2$ teaspoon salt
> $1/2$ cup superfine sugar
> $1/3$ cup milk, warmed to room temperature
> 1 egg, warmed to room temperature
> $1^1/2$ tablespoons butter, melted
> flour for dusting
> $1/2$ cup vegetable shortening

1. Melt the chocolate in the top of a double boiler over hot (not simmering) water,

stirring continuously. Remove from heat and set aside to cool to room temperature.

2. Sift together the cake flour, cocoa powder, espresso powder, baking powder, salt, and sugar. Set aside.

3. Whisk together the milk, egg, melted butter, and melted chocolate until thoroughly blended. Fold in the flour mixture, a little at a time, just until the dry ingredients are moistened.

4. Place the dough on a flour-dusted surface. Dust your hands with flour and knead the dough by pushing it away from you, folding it back over itself, and turning it a quarter turn. Repeat 4 to 6 times, or until the dough is smooth. Do not overknead.

5. Lightly coat a baking sheet with flour. Shape the dough into one large disk, 1/2-inch thick. Place the dough on the baking sheet, seal in plastic wrap, and freeze for 15 minutes or until firm.

6. Line a cookie sheet with waxed paper. Remove the dough from the freezer and cut out 1-inch rounds using a cookie cutter. Place the donut pops on the prepared cookie sheet. Knead the dough scraps into another 1/2-inch thick disk. Freeze for 15 minutes and cut more pops out of the remaining dough.

7. Preheat the vegetable shortening in a skillet or electric frying pan to 375°F. Drop the pops into the hot oil and turn continuously until golden brown. Remove, drain on paper towels, and place on wire racks to cool.

Makes about 2 1/2 dozen pops

Chocolate Fritters

Fried in butter, these old-fashioned apple fritters are even better with chocolate.

> 3 tart apples
> 3/4 cup flour
> 1/4 cup nonalkalized cocoa powder
> 1 teaspoon baking powder
> 1/2 teaspoon cinnamon
> 1/4 teaspoon salt
> 1/3 cup light brown sugar, firmly packed
> 3/4 cup milk, warmed to room temperature
> 2 eggs, warmed to room temperature
> 2 tablespoons butter, melted
> 3–4 tablespoons butter (for frying)

Topping:
powdered sugar, sifted

1. Peel, core, and chop the apples. Set aside.

2. Sift together the flour, cocoa powder, baking powder, cinnamon, salt, and brown sugar. Set aside.

3. Whisk together the milk, eggs, and melted butter. Fold in the flour mixture until lightly blended. Fold in the apples.

4. Melt 1 tablespoon of butter in a large skillet over medium-high heat. When hot, spoon 1/2 cup portions of the batter into the pan. Fry about 4 fritters at a time, each with a tablespoon of butter, until golden brown. Serve hot, sprinkled with powdered sugar.

Makes 12–16 fritters

Special Treats

Peaches and Cream Crunchy Oat Crisp

Here's a way to get your morning serving of oats that's far more fun than oatmeal. Fresh peaches and creamy white chocolate are topped with buttery, crunchy oats in this healthy crisp.

Peaches and Cream Layer:

1 tablespoon flour
1 tablespoon light brown sugar, firmly packed
$^1/_8$ teaspoon salt
$^1/_2$ teaspoon ground cinnamon
$^1/_4$ teaspoon ground nutmeg
1 tablespoon lemon juice
4 cups peeled and sliced fresh, ripe peaches
1 teaspoon vanilla
1 tablespoon Irish cream liqueur
$^1/_4$ cup white chocolate curls

Cobbler Layer:

$^1/_4$ cup rolled oats
$^1/_4$ cup flour
$^1/_4$ cup light brown sugar, firmly packed
$^1/_4$ cup butter, cut into $^1/_4$-inch cubes
$^1/_4$ cup pecans, toasted and chopped

1. Preheat the oven to 350°F. Lightly coat 4 single-serving baking dishes with butter.

2. To make the peach layer: Sift together the flour, brown sugar, salt, cinnamon, and nutmeg. Set aside.

3. Place the lemon juice in a mixing bowl large enough to hold the peaches. As you peel and slice the fresh peaches, coat them with lemon juice.

4. Sprinkle the vanilla extract and liqueur over the peaches and mix. Sprinkle the flour mixture over the peaches, and mix lightly. Place the peach mixture in the prepared baking dishes. Sprinkle with white chocolate curls. Set aside.

5. To make the crunchy oat cobbler: Combine the oats, flour, brown sugar, and butter using a fork or pastry blender until crumbly. Mix in the pecans.

6. Spoon small mounds of the oat mixture over the peaches. Bake for 40 to 45 minutes, or until the oat cobbler is golden brown and crunchy. Serve hot.

Makes 4 servings

Pears Zabaglione

In this alternative to oatmeal, you'll also get a serving of egg—the fun way. Fresh pears are topped with crumbled oatmeal chocolate chip cookies, baked in Marsala wine, and topped with traditional zabaglione.

Pears:

$^1/_2$ cup Marsala wine
$^1/_4$ cup water
$^1/_2$ teaspoon cinnamon

2 fresh ripe pears
1 tablespoon lemon juice
1 cup crumbled oatmeal chocolate chip
  cookies
1 tablespoon light brown sugar, firmly
  packed
1 tablespoon butter, melted
1 egg white, warmed to room temperature
  and slightly beaten

Zabaglione:

1 egg yolk, warmed to room temperature
1 tablespoon sugar
1 tablespoon Marsala wine

1. Preheat the oven to 375°F. Lightly coat a baking dish, large enough to accommodate 4 pear halves, with butter. Mix together the Marsala wine, water, and cinnamon. Pour into the baking dish.

2. Peel and core the pears. Scoop a small, round cavity out of the heart of each pear half. Coat the pears in lemon juice and place in the baking dish.

3. Mix together the crumbled oatmeal chocolate chip cookies, sugar, and butter. Mix in the egg white.

4. Spoon a generous serving of the mixture into the heart of each pear half and bake for 20 minutes. Remove from the oven and set aside.

5. To make the zabaglione: Remove the top pot from a small double boiler. In the bottom of the double boiler, heat water to a simmer.

6. While the water is heating, place the egg yolk and sugar into the top of the double boiler (away from the heat). Using an electric mixer set on a medium-high speed, beat until thickened.

7. Adjust your mixer to a medium-low speed and slowly add the Marsala wine. Place the mixture over the simmering water and continue beating until thickened. Spoon onto the baked pears and serve immediately.

Makes 4 servings

Some Customs Should Never Die

In the seventeenth century, queens and courtiers had the right idea. Mornings began with "levees," or breakfast in bed, which was a leisurely ritual featuring a bowl of hot liquid chocolate.

Chocolate Chip Bread Pudding

Bananas, raisins, honey wheat bread, and yogurt snuggle in with milk chocolate chips for this healthy morning treat.

$^1/_2$ cup golden raisins
$^1/_2$ cup apple juice
1 teaspoon ground cinnamon
$^1/_4$ teaspoon salt
1 teaspoon pure vanilla extract
2 ripe bananas, sliced
$^1/_2$ cup milk chocolate chips
1 cup lightly toasted honey wheat bread, cut into cubes
$^1/_2$ cup milk, warmed to room temperature
1 tablespoon honey
$^1/_4$ cup dark brown sugar, firmly packed

1. Preheat the oven to 400°F. Lightly coat 4 single-serving baking dishes with butter.

2. In a heavy-bottomed saucepan, bring the raisins, apple juice, cinnamon, salt, and vanilla to a simmer.

3. Remove from heat and stir in the bananas, chocolate chips, and bread. Mix the milk and honey together and add to the banana mixture. Spoon into the baking dishes, sprinkle with brown sugar, and bake for 25 to 30 minutes. Serve hot out of the oven.

Makes 4 servings

Susie Q's

This is a wonderful Mother's Day treat. Almond lace tuiles cradle strawberries and chocolate chips floating in a whipped lemon cream. For an elegant presentation, serve on chilled plates, lightly dusted with powdered sugar and decorated with a slice of lemon, a strawberry, and a sprig of fresh mint.

Almond Tuiles:
1 egg, warmed to room temperature and slightly beaten
$^1/_3$ cup almonds, toasted and ground
$^1/_4$ cup butter
$^1/_4$ cup light brown sugar, firmly packed
3 tablespoons flour
$^1/_8$ teaspoon salt
1 tablespoon heavy cream
1 teaspoon pure almond extract
2 ounces semisweet chocolate, finely chopped

Lemon Cream:
1 cup heavy cream, chilled
$^1/_4$ cup superfine sugar
2 tablespoons lemon curd
2 cups fresh strawberries, sliced
$^1/_2$ cup miniature chocolate chips

1. To prepare the almond tuiles: Preheat the oven to 375°F. Line cookie sheets with parchment paper or lightly coat with butter and flour.

2. In a heavy-bottomed saucepan, mix together the egg, almonds, butter, brown sugar, flour, salt, cream, and almond extract. Bring to a simmer over a medium heat, stirring constantly.

3. Pour 6 teaspoonfuls (evenly spaced) of the batter onto each cookie sheet. Bake for 6 to 8 minutes. Remove from oven and

carefully lift each tuile off the cookie sheet and drape over a wooden spoon handle suspended horizontally across two bowls. (This will form the tuiles into a taco shape.) Set aside to cool completely.

4.   When the tuiles are cool: Place the chopped semisweet chocolate in a microwave-safe bowl. Heat for 1 minute on medium power. Remove and stir slowly and thoroughly. Continue heating for 30 seconds at a time, then stirring, until melted. Cool for a few minutes, then dip the edge of each tuile in the chocolate. Set aside to cool.

5.   To make the lemon cream: Whip together the cream, sugar, and lemon curd, using an electric mixer on a high speed, until stiff peaks form. Fold in the strawberries and chocolate chips. Spoon into the almond tuiles and serve.

Makes about 12 Susie Q's

Main Courses

Chocolate Crepes

This elegant dessert turns into a glorious breakfast treat when filled with honey yogurt and topped with fresh fruit. It's easier (and more fun) to make these with a buddy; so one can cook the crepes, while the other fills and tops them.

Crepes:
$1/2$ cup flour
1 tablespoon nonalkalized cocoa powder
1 tablespoon superfine sugar

2 eggs, warmed to room temperature
$3/4$ cup milk, warmed to room temperature
1 teaspoon pure almond extract
2 tablespoons butter, melted

Filling:
3 cups wild berry yogurt, chilled
3 tablespoons honey

Topping:
2 cups fresh blackberries
$1/4$ cup crunchy granola
$1/4$ cup white chocolate curls

1.   Sift together the flour, cocoa powder, and sugar. Set aside.

2.   Whisk together the eggs, milk, and almond extract. Gradually sprinkle in the flour mixture, blending until smooth. Mix in the melted butter. Set aside for 1 hour.

3.   To make the filling: Mix together the yogurt and honey. Set aside.

4.   Coat a crepe pan (or a shallow 7-inch nonstick frying pan) with butter. Heat over a medium-low heat. Pour approximately $1/4$ cup of crepe batter into the pan and tip the pan, coating the entire bottom of the pan. Cook for 1 to 2 minutes, flip, and cook for another minute. Place on a warm serving plate.

5.   Spoon approximately $1/4$ cup yogurt onto the center of the crepe. Loosely roll the crepe up and top with fresh blackberries, granola, and white chocolate curls. Serve immediately.

Makes 8–12 crepes

Sammy Cakes with Chocolate Butter

These traditional buttermilk pancakes are filled with miniature chocolate chips. For special occasions, serve them with chocolate butter!

Chocolate Butter:
¹/₂ cup butter, slightly softened
2 tablespoons ground sweetened chocolate

Sammy Cakes:
1 cup flour
2 teaspoons baking powder
¹/₂ teaspoon salt
2 teaspoons sugar
3 eggs, warmed to room temperature
1 teaspoon brown sugar, firmly packed
¹/₂ cup buttermilk
2 tablespoons butter, melted
¹/₂ cup miniature chocolate chips

1. To prepare the chocolate butter: Cream the butter using an electric mixer on a medium-high speed. Add the ground chocolate and beat until fluffy. Refrigerate.

2. To make the Sammy Cakes: Sift together the flour, baking powder, sugar, and salt. Set aside.

3. Beat the eggs, using an electric mixer on a high speed, until light and fluffy. Adjust your mixer to a medium speed. Sprinkle in the flour mixture and brown sugar and beat until smooth.

4. Stir in the buttermilk, butter, and chocolate chips until lightly blended. Do not overmix.

5. Heat a griddle or heavy skillet. Pour spoonfuls of batter onto the hot surface, creating 1¹/₂-inch disks, and cook until bubbles form on the surface. Flip and cook until golden brown on both sides. Serve hot off the griddle.

Makes about 16 bite-size pancakes

Tiramisu Waffles

Here's a way for you to enjoy all the flavors of the popular Italian dessert, first thing in the morning!

Topping:
1 cup heavy cream, chilled
¹/₄ cup superfine sugar
1 teaspoon Kahlua
2 teaspoons rum
¹/₂ cup milk chocolate curls

Waffles:
1 cup flour
¹/₂ teaspoon baking powder
¹/₂ teaspoon baking soda
¹/₂ teaspoon salt
1 tablespoon instant espresso powder
2 eggs, warmed to room temperature
1 cup mascarpone cheese
¹/₂ cup butter, melted
2 tablespoons rum
2 ounces milk chocolate, grated

(continued)

Chocolate Morning Syrups

Here's a great way for you to start designing your own specialties. Chocolate syrups that can be used on morning treats are a wonderful addition to your pantry. They also make unique gifts, especially when given in enchanting bottles or elegant decanters.

Since a dark chocolate color is not always compatible with morning treats, I recommend using white (which is technically clear) crème de cacao or white chocolate liqueur, blended with a base of maple or fruit syrups, flavorings, and/or spices.

Here are some ideas for flavorings:

Vanilla extract	Almond extract
Mint extract	Liqueurs
Eaux de vie	Brandies
Fresh fruit/preserves	Dried fruit
Nuts	Cinnamon
Allspice	Ginger
Cloves	Nutmeg
Vanilla beans	Coconut Cream
Instant espresso	
Peanut Butter powder	

1. Place a base syrup in a heavy-bottomed saucepan over a very low heat. (Calculate the amount of base syrup you need by the size of your bottle or pitcher and the type of flavorings you're planning to use. For example, if you're adding only an extract and/or some ground spices, you can almost fill your bottle or pitcher with base syrup. If you're planning to add bulky ingredients, like fruit, leave additional room.)

2. Add the crème de cacao or chocolate liqueur to taste. Blend well.

3. Add other flavorings. Remember to start with a small amount, flavoring to taste. Blend well.

4. Pour into a bottle or pitcher and use or cool. If your syrup contains perishable ingredients, cover and refrigerate.

1. To make the topping: Whip together the cream, sugar, Kahlua, and rum, using an electric mixer on a high speed, until stiff peaks form. Refrigerate.

2. To make the waffles: Sift together the flour, baking powder, baking soda, salt, and espresso powder. Set aside.

3. Beat the eggs using an electric mixer on a high speed until light and fluffy.

4. Adjust your mixer to a low speed. Alternate adding the flour mixture and mascarpone cheese until lightly blended. Blend in the butter and rum. Fold in the grated chocolate.

5. Heat the waffle iron. Pour the batter onto the bottom half of the waffle iron until it spreads to about 1 inch from the edge. Close the waffle iron. Keep the iron closed until the batter stops steaming. Open and place the waffles on serving dishes. Decorate with the whipped cream topping and chocolate curls.

Makes 4 waffles

Ooh La La Toast

Chocolate swirls through this naughty French toast. And when topped with hot, spiced Grand Marnier syrup . . . ooh la la!

Chocolate Brioche:

2 tablespoons warm water
2¹/₂ tablespoons superfine sugar divided
1 tablespoon active dry yeast
1¹/₄ cups flour
¹/₄ cup cake flour

1 teaspoon ground cinnamon
1 teaspoon plus 1 pinch salt
5 eggs, warmed to room temperature
2 tablespoons milk, chilled
¹/₂ cup plus 1 tablespoon butter, cut into ¹/₄-inch cubes
2 ounces semisweet chocolate, finely chopped
¹/₄ cup heavy cream, warmed to room temperature
1 tablespoon cocoa powder
1 teaspoon orange zest

Spiced Grand Marnier Syrup:

1¹/₂ cups maple syrup
¹/₂ cup Grand Marnier
1 teaspoon orange zest
¹/₈ teaspoon cinnamon
¹/₈ teaspoon allspice
¹/₈ teaspoon ginger
¹/₈ teaspoon cloves

French Toast:

3 eggs, warmed to room temperature
¹/₄ cup cream
¹/₈ teaspoon pure vanilla extract
¹/₂ teaspoon sugar
4 slices Chocolate Brioche bread
1 tablespoon butter

1. To make the chocolate brioche: Combine the warm water and ¹/₂ tablespoon sugar in a small glass bowl. Sprinkle the yeast over the top. Set aside, without stirring, for 10 minutes. (If your yeast is active, this mixture should foam. If it does not, begin again with fresh, *active* yeast.)

2.   Lightly coat the inside of a medium-size glass bowl with butter. Set aside.

3.   Sift together the flours, cinnamon, $1^1/_2$ tablespoons sugar, and 1 teaspoon salt. Place in the bowl of an electric stand mixer fitted with a dough hook.

4.   On a low speed, add 2 eggs and the chilled milk to the flour mixture. Add the yeast mixture. Add 2 more eggs. Increase the speed slightly, and beat for 5 minutes or until the dough pulls away from the sides of the bowl. (If the mixture seems too dry, add a little more milk.)

5.   Adjust to a medium speed and add $^1/_2$ cup butter, a little at a time, beating until the butter is thoroughly absorbed.

6.   Place the dough in the buttered bowl, cover with a light towel, and set aside for 1 hour in a warm, draft-free room to rise.

7.   After an hour, deflate the dough, by punching it in the center. Cover with plastic wrap and refrigerate overnight.

8.   Melt the semisweet chocolate, cream, and 1 tablespoon butter in the top of a double boiler over hot, not simmering, water, stirring continuously. Set aside to cool to room temperature. Slightly beat the remaining egg, and divide in half. Cover and refrigerate half of the beaten egg. To the other half, add the remaining $^1/_2$ tablespoon sugar, cocoa powder, and orange zest, blend into the chocolate mixture. Cover and refrigerate.

9.   Lightly coat a 7-inch by 14-inch loaf pan with butter and flour. Lightly dust a flat, dry surface with flour. Place the dough on the surface. Lightly dust the top of the dough with flour. Using a rolling pin lightly dusted with flour, roll the dough into a 7-inch by 14-inch rectangle. Fold in quarters, turn, and roll again.

10.   Fold, turn, and roll the dough into a $6^1/_2$-inch by $13^1/_2$-inch rectangle. Spread the chocolate mixture over the dough. Using your fingers, roll (like a jellyroll) the wide side of the rectangle, creating a $13^1/_2$-inch log. Place the log of dough, seam side down, in the prepared pan. Place in a warm, draft-free room for 2 hours.

11.   Preheat the oven to 325°F. Add a pinch of salt to the remaining beaten egg. Brush the top of the dough with the egg glaze, and bake for 20 minutes. Turn the loaf, and bake for another 15 minutes, or until golden brown. Cool on a wire rack.

12.   To make the spiced Grand Marnier syrup: Combine all syrup ingredients in a heavy-bottomed saucepan, and warm over a low heat, stirring occasionally, while making the toast.

13.   To make the French toast: Beat together the eggs, cream, vanilla, and sugar in a wide, shallow dish. Place the bread in the egg batter, and soak for a minute. Turn the bread over and soak the other side.

14.   Heat the butter in a heavy-bottomed skillet over a medium heat. Sauté the toast in the hot butter until golden brown on both sides. Serve with hot spiced Grand Marnier syrup.

Makes 4 servings

Apple Lace Omelet

White chocolate curls melt into a beautiful lace pattern and sweeten apples, tucked in a light, fluffy omelet. Toasted almonds and sprinkles of chocolate sugar add a finishing touch.

Topping:

2 teaspoons superfine sugar
1 teaspoon sweetened ground chocolate
sliced almonds, toasted

Filling:

1 cup sliced, peeled, and cored apples
1 tablespoon lemon juice
2 tablespoons butter
1 tablespoon light brown sugar, firmly packed
¹/₄ cup white chocolate curls

Omelet:

4 eggs, warmed to room temperature and separated
1 tablespoon cream
1 tablespoon butter, melted
¹/₈ teaspoon pure almond extract
1 teaspoon sugar
¹/₂ teaspoon salt
2 tablespoons butter

1. To make the topping: Mix together the sugar and ground chocolate. Set aside.

2. To make the filling: Coat the apple slices with lemon juice as you slice them. Melt the butter in a heavy-bottomed skillet over medium heat. Mix in the brown sugar, and stir until completely dissolved. Add the apple slices, and cook, turning the slices constantly, for 10 minutes. Remove from heat, but keep the apples warm while you prepare the omelet.

3. To make the omelets: Whisk the egg yolks together with the cream, butter, almond extract, sugar, and salt until thickened.

4. In a separate bowl, beat the egg whites, using an electric mixer on a high speed, until stiff peaks form. Fold the egg whites into the egg yolks in 3 increments.

5. Melt 1 tablespoon of butter in a 9-inch omelet or frying pan over a low heat. Pour half of the egg batter into the pan. Cook, without stirring, until firm and light golden brown on the bottom. Flip and lightly brown the other side.

6. Place on a warm serving dish. Layer half of the omelet with ¹/₂ cup apples and 2 tablespoons white chocolate curls. Fold the omelet in half, sprinkle with toasted almonds and the sugar-chocolate mixture, and serve.

Makes 2 servings

chapter six

Pies, Tarts, and Pastries

Who doesn't covet the chocolate éclairs, chocolate fruit tarts, and chocolate cream pies displayed in the windows of bakeries and pastry shops. Most of us don't have time or think we couldn't master the techniques needed to create these sensations. Some of us even settle for whipping up a close-but-no-cigar instant substitute.

Today, classes and videos are available to demystify the art of pastry making. New tools, tips, and equipment save time and make the process more fun. And, for busy home chefs, premade crusts, shells, gourmet fillings, and glazes, can be combined with your favorite chocolate couverture for a custom creation.

Pies

Heaven-Sent Pie

Light enough to float over your table, this cloud of chocolate is topped with cherries in spiked chantilly cream.

Chocolate Base:
4 egg whites, warmed to room temperature
1/4 teaspoon cream of tartar
3/4 cup superfine sugar
2 tablespoons nonalkalized cocoa powder
1 teaspoon pure vanilla extract
1/4 cup grated semisweet chocolate

Topping:
1 cup heavy cream, chilled
1 tablespoon superfine sugar
1 tablespoon Grand Marnier
1 cup Bing cherries, pitted and sliced
2 tablespoons semisweet chocolate curls

1. Preheat the oven to 300°F. Lightly coat a 9-inch glass, pie-shaped baking dish with butter and flour.

2. Beat the egg whites, using an electric mixer on a high speed, until soft peaks form. Sprinkle in the cream of tartar and sugar, and beat until stiff peaks form. Adjust the mixer to a low speed. Lightly mix in the cocoa powder and vanilla. Gently fold in the grated chocolate without deflating the mixture.

3. Pour the batter into the prepared pan. Smooth and swirl the top and create a 6-inch round by 1/4-inch deep, indentation in the center. Bake for 1 hour. Remove from the oven and cool on a wire rack. (While cooling, the center should fall slightly.)

4. To make the topping: Whip the heavy cream until soft peaks form. Sprinkle in the sugar and Grand Marnier and beat until stiff peaks form. Fold in the cherries and refrigerate. When ready to serve, spoon the cherry mixture into the center of the cooled chocolate pie, and sprinkle with chocolate curls.

Makes 8–10 servings

How to Make Perfect Pie Crusts and Tart Shells

Using a Food Processor

The invention of the food processor was a miracle for the art of making pie crusts and tart shells. The investment is worth it for this task alone.

1. Make sure your food processor is clean and dry. Place the steel blade in the unit.
2. For best results, thoroughly chill all ingredients.
3. Place the flour, sugar, and salt in the food processor and briefly mix by turning it on and off.
4. Add the butter and process until the mixture becomes the texture of cornmeal.
5. In a mixing bowl, whisk together the egg yolk(s) and cream.
6. Add the egg mixture to the flour mixture, and process until a ball forms. (You can add a little more cream if the dough appears to be too dry.)
7. Remove the ball of dough from your food processor. On a lightly floured surface flatten the ball into a disk, seal in plastic wrap, and refrigerate overnight.

Using Your Fingers

There's something fun and very gratifying about making pie crusts and tart shells the way pastry chefs have been making them from the beginning of time—with your fingers.

1. Wash your hands.
2. Make sure your flat working surface is clean and dry. For best results, thoroughly chill all ingredients.
3. Sift the flour into a small pile on your working surface. Make a small well in the center of the flour. Place the sugar and salt in the well.
4. Slice the butter into $1/4$-inch cubes. Place the butter in the well and, using your fingers, mix together the butter, sugar, and salt.
5. Place the egg yolk(s) in the well and use your fingers to mix into the butter mixture. Mix in the cream.
6. Add the flour to the mixture a little at a time, mixing with your fingers until the mixture becomes the texture of coarse crumbs. Press the mixture into a ball.
7. Lightly flour a flat surface and knead the dough until it becomes smooth, and peels off the work surface in one piece.
8. Flatten the ball into a disk, seal in plastic wrap, and refrigerate overnight.

Bittersweet Chiffon Pie

The light texture of this pie belies its rich, bittersweet flavor.

Pie Crust:

1¼ cups chocolate cookie crumbs
1 tablespoon instant espresso powder
¼ cup sugar
⅓ cup butter, melted

Filling:

4 ounces bittersweet chocolate, finely chopped
1 tablespoon instant espresso powder
¼ cup cold water
2 teaspoons unflavored gelatin
4 eggs, separated and warmed to room temperature
½ cup superfine sugar, divided
½ cup heavy cream, chilled

Topping:

1 cup bittersweet chocolate curls

1. Preheat the oven to 350°F. To make the crust: Mix together the cookie crumbs, espresso powder, and sugar. Drizzle in the melted butter, and blend. Press into the bottom and sides of a lightly buttered 9-inch pie pan, and bake for 10 minutes. Cool on a wire rack. (Turn the oven off.)

2. Melt the chocolate in the top of a double boiler over hot (not simmering) water, stirring continuously. Remove from heat and set aside to cool to room temperature. Stir in the espresso powder.

3. Place the cold water in a small glass bowl. Sprinkle the gelatin over the water and set aside to soften.

4. Beat together the egg yolks and ¼ cup sugar, in the top of a double boiler, using a wooden spoon. Heat over hot, not simmering, water, stirring constantly, until the mixture thickens and coats the spoon. Add the gelatin mixture and stir until the gelatin is dissolved. Remove from heat and fold in the melted chocolate. Refrigerate for 1 hour, or until the mixture is cool and the consistency of unbeaten egg whites.

5. Whip the cream, using an electric mixer on a high speed, until soft peaks form. Sprinkle in 2 tablespoons of the remaining sugar and beat until stiff peaks form. Refrigerate.

6. When the chocolate mixture is cooled, gently fold a third of the whipped cream into the chocolate mixture. Repeat until all the whipped cream is incorporated. Refrigerate.

7. Whip the egg whites, using an electric mixer on a high speed, until soft peaks form. Sprinkle in the remaining sugar and beat until stiff peaks form. Gently fold a third of the egg whites into the chocolate mixture. Repeat until all egg whites are incorporated. Pour the mixture into the cooled pie crust, cover, and refrigerate for 6 to 8 hours. Top with chocolate curls and serve.

Makes 8–10 servings

Chocolate Cream Pie

This old-fashioned pie, crowned with golden meringue, is still simple, rich, and delicious.

Pie Crust:
1¹/₄ cups flour, sifted
1 tablespoon sugar
¹/₄ teaspoon salt
¹/₂ cup butter, chilled
1 egg yolk, chilled
1 tablespoon heavy cream, chilled

Filling:
6 ounces semisweet chocolate, finely chopped
1 cup milk, warmed to room temperature
1 cup heavy cream, warmed to room temperature
¹/₄ cup cornstarch
¹/₄ cup sugar
3 egg yolks, warmed to room temperature
1 teaspoon pure vanilla extract

Meringue Topping:
3 egg whites, warmed to room temperature
¹/₂ teaspoon pure vanilla extract
¹/₈ teaspoon cream of tartar
²/₃ cup superfine sugar

1.   Preheat the oven to 400°F. Prepare the pie crust according to directions on page 157. Press the dough into a lightly buttered 9-inch pie pan. Bake for 15 minutes, or until golden brown, and set aside to cool. (Turn off the oven.)

The Art of Rolling Dough

Rolling dough to an even thickness without it sticking to your working surface or rolling pin and, more importantly, without losing its future flakiness, is an art.

1. Cool your working surface by placing something from the freezer on it for a few minutes.
2. Dry the surface thoroughly, and lightly dust with flour. Place your dough on the surface. Lightly dust the dough and your rolling pin with flour.
3. Roll from the center out, in one direction then another. Turn the dough, and redust, as necessary. Try to use as little additional flour as possible.
4. Roll to a thickness of ¹/₄ inch to ¹/₈ inch, and trim to approximately 2 inches larger than your pan.

(continued)

2.   Place the chocolate in the top of a double boiler. Mix together the milk and cream. Sprinkle in the cornstarch and stir until smooth and thoroughly blended. Mix in the sugar. Pour over the chocolate and heat over simmering water, stirring, for 10 minutes or until the mixture thickens. Cover and continue cooking, stirring occasionally, for another 10 minutes.

3.   Beat the egg yolks, using a wooden spoon, until smooth. Stir a third of the hot, chocolate mixture into the egg yolks, mixing thoroughly. Stir the egg yolk mixture into the remaining hot chocolate mixture. Cook for another 5 minutes. Remove from heat, stir in the vanilla, and pour into the cooled crust. Cover and refrigerate for at least 4 hours.

4.   When the pie is cooled and set, preheat the oven to 400°F. Whisk together the egg whites, vanilla, cream of tartar, and sugar in a glass bowl that can be used as the top of a double boiler. Place over simmering water and continue whisking for 2 minutes, until the egg whites are hot and the sugar has dissolved.

5.   Remove from heat and beat, using an electric mixer on a medium speed, until soft peaks form. Spoon over the pie, sealing the chocolate with meringue. Using a metal spatula, create swirls and peaks in the meringue. Bake for 7 to 10 minutes, or until the meringue is golden. Cool on a wire rack.

Makes 8–10 servings

Hot Fudge Brownie Pie

A buttery crust, a rich chocolate-walnut filling, and a scoop of vanilla ice cream are all smothered in thick, sticky, hot fudge.

Pie Crust:
1¹/₄ cups flour, sifted
1 tablespoon sugar
¹/₄ teaspoon salt
¹/₂ cup butter, chilled
1 egg yolk, chilled
1 tablespoon heavy cream, chilled

Filling:
4 ounces semisweet chocolate, finely chopped
¹/₂ cup butter, cut into ¹/₄-inch cubes
3 eggs, warmed to room temperature
¹/₂ cup sugar
2 tablespoons alkalized cocoa powder
¹/₂ cup walnuts, toasted and chopped

Hot Fudge Topping:
4 ounces semisweet chocolate, finely chopped
¹/₂ cup alkalized cocoa powder
¹/₂ cup sugar
¹/₂ cup evaporated milk
¹/₂ cup light corn syrup
1 teaspoon pure vanilla extract
vanilla ice cream
walnuts, toasted and chopped

1.   Preheat the oven to 400°F. Prepare the pie crust, according to directions on page 157. Press the dough into a lightly buttered 9-inch pie pan. Bake for 15 minutes or until golden brown, and set aside to cool.

2.   Melt the chocolate and butter in the top of a double boiler over hot (not simmering) water, stirring continuously. Remove from heat and set aside to cool to room temperature.

3.   Beat together the eggs and sugar, using an electric mixer on a medium speed, until thick. Mix in the cocoa powder. Fold in the melted chocolate and walnuts.

4.   Cover the edge of the baked pie crust with aluminum foil to prevent it from burning. Pour the batter into the cooled crust. Bake for 40 to 45 minutes, uncovering the pie crust edge for the last 5 to 10 minutes. Cool on a wire rack.

5.   To prepare the hot fudge: Melt the chocolate in the top of a double boiler over hot (not simmering) water, stirring continuously. Remove from heat and set aside to cool to room temperature.

6.   Combine the cocoa powder and sugar in a heavy-bottomed saucepan. Stir in the evaporated milk, creating a thick, smooth paste. Add the corn syrup. Bring the mixture to a boil over a medium heat, stirring constantly. Remove from heat and fold in the melted chocolate and vanilla. Cool to room temperature, then refrigerate. Warm in the microwave on a medium setting before serving.

7.   To serve, place individual slices of pie on serving dishes. Place a scoop of vanilla ice cream on top of each slice, and top with fudge sauce and a light sprinkling of walnuts.

Makes 8–10 servings

Placing the Dough in the Pan

When rolled to a thickness of $1/4$ inch to $1/8$ inch, pie and tart pastry becomes fairly fragile. To safely place it in your baking pan:

1.   Loosely roll the circle of dough over your rolling pin.
2.   Center the dough over your baking pan and unroll, leaving the dough slack.
3.   Hold the top edge of the dough up off the rim of the pan while gently pressing it into the bottom and sides of the pan.
3.   When the dough is in place, carefully roll the rolling pin over the rim of the pan to cut off any excess dough.
4.   Cover and refrigerate for at least 1 hour before baking.

Chocolate Potpourri

Dried cocoa bean husks makes a wonderful base for chocolate potpourri that makes a wonderful gift for friends who love chocolate. Here are some ideas for companion ingredients:

Spicy Potpourri
Cinnamon sticks
Whole allspice
Whole cloves
Orange peels
Vanilla beans

Sweet Potpourri
Rose petals
Lavender
Wild berries
Orchid bark
Tahitian vanilla beans

Refreshing Potpourri
Eucalyptus leaves
Mint oil
Small pine cones
Redwood bark
Coco tops

Amaretto Ice Pie

Cool and rich, this frozen chocolate cream pie sits in a crunchy crust of almonds and chocolate cookie crumbs.

Pie Crust:
1 cup chocolate cookie crumbs
$1/4$ cup almonds, toasted and chopped
$1/4$ cup sugar
$1/3$ cup butter, melted

Filling:
8 ounces semisweet chocolate, finely chopped
$3/4$ cup mascarpone cheese, warmed to room temperature
$1/4$ cup milk, warmed to room temperature
$1/2$ cup sugar
2 tablespoons Amaretto liqueur
1 tablespoon dark rum
2 cups heavy cream, whipped

Topping:
$1/2$ cup almonds, sliced and toasted

1. Preheat the oven to 350°F. To make the crust: Mix together the cookie crumbs, almonds, and sugar. Drizzle in the melted butter and blend. Press into the bottom and sides of a lightly buttered 9-inch pie pan and bake for 10 minutes. Cool on a wire rack. (Turn the oven off.)

2. Melt the chocolate in the top of a double boiler over hot (not simmering) water, stirring continuously. Remove from heat and set aside to cool to room temperature.

3. Beat together the mascarpone cheese, milk, sugar, Amaretto, and rum, using an electric mixer on a medium speed, until thoroughly blended. Fold in the whipped cream and the cooled melted chocolate.

4. Pour into the cooled crust. Seal in an airtight container, and freeze overnight. Before serving, top with sliced almonds.

Makes 8–10 servings

Chocolate Mudslide Pie

Chocolate ice cream is laced with vodka, scooped into a Kahlua crust, and topped with whipped Irish Cream for this potent pie.

Pie Crust:
1¼ cups chocolate cookie crumbs
2 tablespoons instant espresso powder
¼ cup sugar
⅓ cup butter, melted
2 tablespoons Kahlua liqueur

Filling:
4 cups chocolate ice cream, softened
¼ cup vodka, chilled

Topping:
1 cup heavy cream, chilled
2 tablespoons superfine sugar
¼ cup Irish Cream liqueur
dark, milk, and white chocolate curls

1. Preheat the oven to 350°F. To make the crust: Mix together the cookie crumbs, espresso powder, and sugar. Drizzle in the melted butter, and blend. Press into the bottom and sides of a lightly buttered 9-inch pie pan, and bake for 10 minutes. Cool on a wire rack. (Turn the oven off.)

2. When the crust is cool, drizzle the Kahlua over the crust. Set aside.

3. Blend the chocolate ice cream and vodka using an electric mixer on a low speed. Spoon into the crust, smooth the top, seal in an airtight container, and freeze overnight.

4. When ready to serve, whip the cream, using an electric mixer on a high speed, until soft peaks form. Sprinkle in the sugar and Irish Cream liqueur, beating until stiff peaks form. Spread the whipped cream over the pie and top with chocolate curls.

Makes 8–10 servings

Turtle Truffle Pie

A layer of buttery pecans is covered with a layer of creamy caramel, which is covered with a layer of rich milk chocolate truffle filling, which is smothered with chocolate curls.

Pie Crust:
1¼ cups flour, sifted
1 tablespoon sugar
¼ teaspoon salt
½ cup butter, chilled
1 egg yolk, chilled
1 tablespoon heavy cream, chilled

(continued)

Caramel Layer:
1 cup pecans, toasted and chopped
³/₄ cup heavy cream, warmed to room temperature
1¹/₄ cups sugar
¹/₃ cup light corn syrup

Chocolate Truffle Layer:
8 ounces milk chocolate, finely chopped
¹/₄ cup heavy cream
2 tablespoons butter, cut into ¹/₄-inch cubes
1 tablespoon butterscotch liqueur
1 tablespoon pecan liqueur

Topping:
2 cups milk chocolate curls

1.   Preheat the oven to 400°F. Prepare the pie crust, according to directions on page 157. Press the dough into a lightly buttered 9-inch pie pan. Bake for 15 minutes or until golden brown, and set aside to cool.

2.   To make the caramel layer: Spread the pecans evenly in the bottom of the baked, cooled pie crust.

3.   Combine the cream, sugar, and corn syrup in a heavy-bottomed saucepan. Bring the mixture to a boil over a low heat, stirring with a wooden spoon only until the sugar dissolves. When the temperature reaches 244°F, pour the mixture into a stainless steel bowl or pot. Stir every few minutes while the mixture cools. When the caramel has cooled but is still in a liquid form, gently pour over the pecans. Set aside.

4.   To make the chocolate truffle layer: Melt the chocolate, cream, and butter in the top of a double boiler over hot (not simmering) water, stirring continuously. Remove from heat and set aside to cool to room temperature. Stir in the liqueurs. Gently pour over the caramel layer. Cover and refrigerate overnight. Top with chocolate curls and serve.

Makes 8–10 servings

Pumpkin Dream Pie

Chocolate, pumpkin, and cream cheese fill a graham cracker crust, and are topped with a spiced pecan whipped cream.

Pie Crust:
1¹/₄ cups graham cracker crumbs
¹/₄ cup light brown sugar, firmly packed
¹/₃ cup butter, melted

Filling:
4 ounces milk chocolate, finely chopped
1 pound cream cheese, softened
³/₄ cup sugar
¹/₄ cup solid pack pumpkin
1 teaspoon ground pumpkin pie spice
2 eggs, warmed to room temperature

Topping:
1 cup heavy cream, chilled
2 tablespoons superfine sugar
¹/₄ teaspoon nutmeg
¹/₄ cup pecans, toasted and chopped

1.   Preheat the oven to 325°F. To make the crust: Mix together the graham cracker crumbs and brown sugar. Drizzle in the melted butter and blend. Press into the bottom and sides of a lightly buttered 9-inch pie pan, and bake for 12 minutes. Cool on a wire rack.

2.   Melt the chocolate in the top of a double boiler over hot (not simmering) water, stirring continuously. Remove from heat and set aside to cool to room temperature.

3.   Cream the cream cheese, using an electric mixer on a medium-high speed, until fluffy. Sprinkle in the sugar, beating until thoroughly blended. Adjust your mixer to a medium speed and blend in the pumpkin, pumpkin pie spice, and eggs, one at a time. Fold in the cooled melted chocolate.

4.   Pour into the cooled crust and bake for 45 minutes or until firm. Remove from the oven and cool on a wire rack.

5.   To make the topping: Whip the cream, using an electric mixer on a high speed, until soft peaks form. Sprinkle in the sugar and nutmeg, beating until firm peaks form. Fold in the pecans, and refrigerate. Before serving, top the pie with the pecan cream.

Makes 8–10 servings

Gifts for Pie and Tart Makers

Kitchen and cake decorating shops are great sources for pie, tart, and pastry tools, equipment, and ingredients. Cake decorating shops often have premade fillings, or instant gourmet fillings, and they usually have a large selection of decorations. Here are some ideas for the pie or tart baker in your life.

- Pie pans
- Ceramic pie dishes
- Tart pans
- Pastry blender
- Marble rolling pin and slab
- Pastry bag and tip set
- High-quality measuring spoons and cups
- High-quality spatulas and whisks
- Egg separator
- Nest of clear glass mixing bowls
- Food processor
- Stand mixer
- Domestic and imported couvertures
- Gourmet cocoa powders
- High-quality extracts
- Flavoring liqueurs
- Gourmet fruit preserves
- Premade/instant gourmet fillings
- Premade glaze

Weight and Bake

If you want to prebake your pie or tart crust before adding the filling, you must weigh the bottom and sides of the crust down while baking.

1. Remove the dough-lined pan from the refrigerator.
2. Place parchment paper or foil in the pan, over the dough.
3. Fill the pan with pie weights or dry beans, and bake according to the time and temperature specified in the recipe.
4. Cool on a wire rack. When cool, remove the weights and paper or foil.

Sweet and Sour Apple Pie

Sweet white chocolate chips play hide-and-seek with tart dried cherries in this rich sour cream apple pie.

Pie Crust:
1¼ cups flour, sifted
1 tablespoon sugar
¼ teaspoon salt
½ cup butter, chilled
1 egg yolk, chilled
1 tablespoon heavy cream, chilled

Apple Layer:
4 tart apples
2 tablespoons lemon juice
¼ cup butter, melted
½ cup light brown sugar, firmly packed
1 tablespoon flour
¼ cup dried tart cherries
¼ cup white chocolate chips

Sour Cream Layer:
2 eggs, warmed to room temperature
½ cup sugar
1¼ cups sour cream, warmed to room temperature
1 teaspoon ground cinnamon
1 tablespoon apple liqueur
1 tablespoon cherry liqueur

Crumb Topping:
½ cup light brown sugar, firmly packed
¼ cup flour
2 tablespoons butter, chilled

1. Preheat the oven to 400°F. Prepare the pie crust, according to directions on page 157. Press the dough into a lightly buttered 9-inch pie pan and refrigerate.

2. To make the apple layer: Peel, core, and slice the apples. Coat with lemon juice. Sprinkle the apples with melted butter, brown sugar, and flour, one at a time, mixing to coat the apples. Add the cherries and chocolate chips, mixing thoroughly. Spoon into the prepared crust and bake for 30 minutes.

3. To make the sour cream layer: Whisk together the eggs and sugar. Whisk in the sour cream, cinnamon, and liqueurs. Set aside until the pie has baked for 30 minutes. Pour the sour cream mixture over the apple-cherry layer, and bake for an additional 30 minutes, or until the sour cream layer is firm. (If the edge of the pie crust starts getting too dark, cover with a strip of foil.)

4. To make the crumb topping: Combine topping ingredients with a fork or pastry blender until crumbly. Set aside until the pie has baked for the additional 30 minutes. Sprinkle topping over the sour cream layer and bake for 10 minutes. Remove from oven and cool on a wire rack.

Makes 8–10 servings

American Chocolate

There are two types of chocolate manufactured in the United States: those that are intended for mass merchandising in the form of candy or small baking bars; and those that are designed to be used by professional pastry chefs and chocolatiers.

Overall, mass-market chocolates are sweeter (to accommodate America's ultrasweet tooth), not quite as flavorful, and a bit less refined (to assure a lower price). Like coffee, the more flavorful the bean, the higher the cost, and the more elaborate the processing procedure, the more expensive.

Couvertures, the other type of chocolate made in America, contain the most flavorful beans and a high percentage of cocoa butter; they are processed much like their finest European competitors.

Coconut Cream Pie

The addition of white chocolate makes this traditional favorite even more delicious.

Pie Crust:

1 cup macaroon cookie crumbs
¹/₄ cup macadamia nuts, chopped
¹/₄ cup sugar
¹/₃ cup butter, melted

Filling:

4 ounces white chocolate, finely chopped
³/₄ cup milk, warmed to room temperature
³/₄ cup heavy cream, warmed to room
temperature
¹/₄ cup cornstarch
¹/₄ cup sugar
3 egg yolks, warmed to room temperature
1 teaspoon pure vanilla extract
2 cups sweetened, shredded coconut

Meringue Topping:

3 egg whites, warmed to room
temperature
¹/₂ teaspoon pure vanilla extract
¹/₈ teaspoon cream of tartar
²/₃ cup superfine sugar

1.   Preheat the oven to 350°F. To make the crust: Mix together the cookie crumbs, nuts, and sugar. Drizzle in the melted butter, and blend. Press into the bottom and sides of a lightly buttered 9-inch pie pan, and bake for 10 minutes. Cool on a wire rack. (Turn the oven off.)

2.   Place the chocolate in the top of a double boiler. Mix together the milk and cream. Sprinkle in the cornstarch, stirring until smooth and thoroughly blended. Mix in the sugar. Pour over chocolate and heat over simmering water, stirring, for 10 minutes, or until the mixture thickens. Cover and continue cooking, stirring occasionally, for another 10 minutes.

3.   Beat the egg yolks, using a wooden spoon, until smooth. Stir a third of the hot chocolate mixture into the egg yolks, mixing thoroughly. Stir the egg yolk mixture into the remaining hot chocolate mixture. Cook for another 5 minutes. Remove from heat. Cool for a few minutes. Stir in the vanilla, fold in all but 2 tablespoons of the coconut, and pour into the cooled crust. Cover and refrigerate for at least 4 hours.

4.   When the pie is cooled and set, preheat the oven to 350°F. Whisk together the egg whites, vanilla, cream of tartar, and sugar in a glass bowl that can be used as the top of a double boiler. Place over simmering water and continue whisking for 2 minutes, until the egg whites are hot and the sugar has dissolved.

5.   Remove from heat and beat, using an electric mixer on a medium speed, until soft peaks form. Spoon over the pie, sealing the chocolate with meringue. Using a metal spatula, create swirls and peaks in the meringue. Sprinkle on the reserved 2 tablespoons of coconut, and bake for 15 minutes, or until the meringue is golden. Cool on a wire rack.

Makes 8–10 servings

Summer Ice Pie

For white chocolate purists, this frozen pie is exquisite by itself, and even better when smothered with sliced strawberries, peaches, kiwis, or any summer fruit.

Pie Crust:
1¹/₄ cups vanilla cookie crumbs
¹/₄ cup sugar
¹/₃ cup butter, melted

Filling:
8 ounces white chocolate, finely chopped
3 cups heavy cream, chilled
1 teaspoon pure vanilla extract
¹/₃ cup sugar

Topping:
2 cups sliced fresh fruit OR
2 cups white chocolate curls

1. Preheat the oven to 350°F. To make the crust: Mix together the cookie crumbs, and sugar. Drizzle in the melted butter, and blend. Press into the bottom and sides of a lightly buttered 9-inch pie pan, and bake for 10 minutes. Cool on a wire rack. (Turn the oven off.)

2. Melt the chocolate in the top of a double boiler over hot (not simmering) water, stirring continuously. Remove from heat and set aside to cool to room temperature.

3. Whip the cream, using an electric mixer on a high speed, until soft peaks form. Sprinkle in the vanilla and sugar, beating until stiff peaks form. Gently fold in the cooled melted chocolate.

4. Pour the chocolate mixture into the cooled crust. Seal in an airtight container, and freeze overnight.

5. Before serving, top with fresh fruit or white chocolate curls.

Makes 8–10 servings

Flaky Secret

Investing in a marble slab and rolling pin will make rolling pie crusts and tart shells easier and more successful. The marble stays cold longer, and the pastry dough is less likely to stick, which means you won't need as much dusting flour, which means flakier crusts and shells!

Tarts

Heart-to-Heart Tart

This elegant tart is filled with rich truffle ganache, and topped with a black and white marbled glaze. Be sure to use your favorite nibbling chocolate.

Chocolate Tart Shell:
1 cup flour
$^1/_4$ cup nonalkalized cocoa powder
$^1/_2$ cup sugar
$^1/_2$ cup butter, chilled and cut into $^1/_4$-inch cubes
1 egg yolk, chilled
1 teaspoon heavy cream, chilled

Truffle Filling:
12 ounces dark chocolate, finely chopped
$^3/_4$ cup heavy cream, warmed to room temperature
3 tablespoons of your favorite liqueur

Black and White Glaze:
3 ounces dark chocolate, finely chopped
$^1/_4$ cup butter, cut into $^1/_4$-inch cubes
1 teaspoon light corn syrup
1 ounce white chocolate, finely chopped

1. Preheat the oven to 400°F. Prepare the tart shell according to directions on page 157. Press the dough into four lightly buttered 4-inch fluted tart pans with removable bottoms. Bake for 15 minutes, or until golden brown, and set aside to cool.

2. Melt the chocolate and cream in the top of a double boiler over hot (not simmering) water, stirring continuously. Remove from heat and set aside to cool to room temperature. Stir in the liqueur and fill each tart shell about $^3/_4$ full. Cover and refrigerate.

3. To make the glaze: Melt the dark chocolate, butter, and corn syrup in the top of a double boiler over hot (not simmering) water, stirring continuously. Remove from heat and set aside.

4. Melt the white chocolate in a small heatproof bowl in the microwave, on a low setting. Heat in 15-second increments, and stir between heatings, being careful not to overheat. Set aside.

5. Gently spread a thin layer of the dark chocolate glaze on top of each tart. Spoon three dollops of the melted white chocolate on top of the dark chocolate glaze. Using a small sable paintbrush, lightly swirl the two chocolates together, creating a marbled effect. Set aside to cool and set.

Makes 4 small tarts

The Queen of Tarts

Fresh raspberries, whipped cream, and sliced almonds crown a rich, dark chocolate tart.

Almond Tart Shell:
1 cup flour
$^1/_4$ cup almonds, toasted and ground
$^1/_4$ cup sugar
$^1/_2$ cup butter, chilled and cut into $^1/_4$-inch cubes
1 egg yolk, chilled
1 teaspoon heavy cream, chilled

Chocolate Filling:

8 ounces semisweet chocolate
1 cup milk, warmed to room temperature
2 tablespoons butter, cut into $^1/_4$-inch cubes
2 tablespoons raspberry liqueur
3 eggs, warmed to room temperature
2 egg yolks, warmed to room temperature
$^1/_4$ cup sugar

Topping:

$^1/_4$ cup heavy cream, warmed to room
temperature
$^1/_4$ cup mascarpone cheese, warmed to
room temperature
1 teaspoon dark rum
1 tablespoon powdered sugar, sifted
12 perfect, fresh raspberries
$^1/_2$ cup almonds, sliced and toasted

1.   Preheat the oven to 400°F. Prepare the tart shell according to directions on page 157. Press the dough into a lightly buttered 9$^1/_2$-inch fluted tart pan with a removable bottom. Bake for 15 minutes, or until golden brown, and set aside to cool.

2.   Melt the chocolate, milk, and butter in the top of a double boiler over hot (not simmering) water, stirring continuously. Remove from heat and set aside to cool to room temperature. Stir in the raspberry liqueur.

3.   When the tart shell and chocolate mixture have cooled: preheat the oven to 350°F. Whisk together the eggs, egg yolks, and sugar until thoroughly blended. Fold in the chocolate mixture. Pour into the tart shell and bake for 20 minutes, or until set. Remove from oven, cool on a wire rack, and refrigerate (covered) until ready to serve.

4.   When ready to serve: Whip the heavy cream, mascarpone cheese, and rum, using an electric mixer on a high speed, until soft peaks form. Sprinkle in the sugar, beating until stiff peaks form. Spoon into a pastry bag with a 1-inch star tip, and pipe 12 stars around the outside rim of the tart. Place a fresh raspberry, upside down, on top of each cream star. Sprinkle the almonds in the center of the raspberry crown, and serve.

Makes 8–12 servings

Copper Magic

When egg whites are whisked or beaten in a copper bowl, a chemical reaction stabilizes the whites and helps to increase their volume. If you use a copper bowl, omit any cream of tartar called for in the recipe.

Mocha Toffee Tart

Caramelized milk blends with chocolate and coffee to form a rich base for this tart, topped with crunchy toffee and pecans.

Mocha Tart Shell:

1 cup flour
¹/₂ cup sugar
2 tablespoons nonalkalized cocoa powder
2 tablespoons instant espresso powder
¹/₂ cup butter, chilled and cut into ¹/₄-inch cubes
1 egg yolk, chilled
1 teaspoon heavy cream, chilled

Mocha Filling:

4 ounces bittersweet chocolate, finely chopped
¹/₄ cup instant espresso powder
1 cup sweetened condensed milk
¹/₂ cup butter, cut into ¹/₄-inch cubes
²/₃ cup light brown sugar, firmly packed
2 tablespoons light corn syrup

Topping:

¹/₂ cup pecans, toasted and chopped
¹/₄ cup toffee bits

1. Preheat the oven to 400°F. Prepare the tart shell according to directions on page 157. Press the dough into a lightly buttered 9¹/₂-inch tart pan with a removable bottom. Bake for 15 minutes, or until golden brown, and set aside to cool.

2. Melt the chocolate in the top of a double boiler over hot (not simmering) water, stirring continuously. Remove from heat and set aside to cool to room temperature. Stir in the espresso powder.

3. Combine the condensed milk, butter, brown sugar, and corn syrup in a heavy-bottomed nonstick saucepan. Bring to a boil over a low heat, stirring constantly. Continue stirring and simmering for 5 to 10 minutes, until the mixture thickens and turns a pale caramel color. Remove from heat and cool to room temperature.

4. Fold the melted chocolate into the caramel mixture, and pour into the baked tart shell. Cover and refrigerate for several hours.

5. Sprinkle with pecans and toffee, and serve.

Makes 8–12 servings

Strawberry Tart

A chocolate surprise hides within this traditional pastry cream tart.

Butter Tart Shell:

1¹/₄ cups flour
¹/₄ cup sugar
¹/₂ cup butter, chilled and cut into ¹/₄-inch cubes
1 egg yolk, chilled
1 teaspoon heavy cream, chilled

Pastry Cream:

1 tablespoon sugar
2 teaspoons flour
¹/₂ tablespoon cornstarch
1 egg yolk, slightly beaten
¹/₂ cup milk, warmed to room temperature
¹/₄ teaspoon pure vanilla extract
¹/₈ teaspoon pure almond extract
¹/₂ cup grated semisweet chocolate

Strawberries and Glaze:

¹/₂ cup apricot preserves
2 tablespoons Grand Marnier
1 tablespoon superfine sugar
4 cups fresh strawberries, sliced

1.   Preheat the oven to 400°F. Prepare the tart shell according to directions on page 157. Press the dough into a lightly buttered 9¹/₂-inch fluted tart pan with a removable bottom. Bake for 15 minutes, or until golden brown, and set aside to cool.

2.   To make the pastry cream: Sift together the sugar, flour, and cornstarch. Whisk in the egg yolk, beating until smooth and light. Set aside.

3.   Bring the milk to a boil in a stainless steel saucepan. Slowly pour the hot milk into the egg yolk, whisking until all the milk is incorporated. Pour the mixture into the saucepan and, stirring continuously, bring to a simmer over medium heat. Continue stirring for 1 minute. Remove from heat and mix in the vanilla and almond extracts. Set aside to cool. Fold in the grated chocolate.

4.   To make the glaze: Combine the apricot preserves, Grand Marnier, and sugar in a heavy-bottomed saucepan. Bring to a simmer over a medium heat, stirring continuously. Remove from heat. Using a pastry brush, coat the inside of the tart shell with the preserves. Set aside.

5.   Spread the pastry cream in the tart shell. Arrange the sliced strawberries on the pastry cream. Brush the strawberries with the apricot glaze, and serve.

Makes 8–10 servings

Three Bean Chocolate

Cocoa beans naturally evolved in two basic varieties. The coveted criollo bean is produced by a rare fragile plant and offers a delicate, sophisticated flavor. Forastero beans, while not as flavorful as criollos, grow in far greater abundance.

In an attempt to produce a stronger criollo plant or a more flavorful forastero bean, planters developed a third type by crossbreeding the two natural varieties. The result was the trinitario.

Most chocolates today are a blend of two or all three of these beans, except Grand Cru chocolates, which uses one bean exclusively.

Callebaut

Most chocolatiers and pastry chefs (both professional and amateur) have a love for Callebaut. Their exquisite bean selection and meticulous processing methods ensure a luxurious couverture with a consistent taste and performance. And, as the largest chocolate factory in the world, the volume discounts Callebaut receives when buying beans enables them to offer you exceptional chocolates at comparatively low prices.

There is also a North American division of Callebaut that offers a transcontinental chocolate! The chocolate base, or liquor, is brought from Belgium and processed in Vermont using American sugar and dairy products. The prices reflect the savings in tariffs, and the taste mirrors that of its Belgian cousins.

Fall Harvest Tart

Spiced apples rest on a chocolate-pumpkin pastry cream that lies within a hazelnut tart shell. Chocolate leaves add a special topping.

Hazelnut Tart Shell:

1 cup flour
$1/4$ cup hazelnuts, toasted, skinned, and ground
$1/4$ cup sugar
$1/2$ cup butter, chilled and cut into $1/4$-inch cubes
1 egg yolk, chilled
1 teaspoon heavy cream, chilled

Chocolate-Pumpkin Pastry Cream:

2 ounces milk chocolate, finely chopped
1 tablespoon solid-pack pumpkin
$1/8$ teaspoon pumpkin pie spice
1 tablespoon sugar
2 teaspoons flour
$1/2$ tablespoon cornstarch
1 egg yolk, slightly beaten
$1/2$ cup milk, warmed to room temperature

Spiced Apples:

2 cups peeled, cored, and thinly sliced apples
2 tablespoons lemon juice
$1/4$ cup butter
2 tablespoons light brown sugar, firmly packed
$1/2$ teaspoon apple pie spice
$1/2$ teaspoon pure vanilla extract

Glaze:

¹/₂ cup apricot preserves
2 tablespoons apple liqueur
1 tablespoon superfine sugar
chocolate leaves (optional)

1.   Preheat the oven to 400°F. Prepare the tart shell according to directions on page 157. Press the dough into a lightly buttered 9¹/₂-inch tart pan with a removable bottom. Bake for 15 minutes, or until golden brown, and set aside to cool.

2.   To make the chocolate-pumpkin pastry cream: Melt the chocolate in the top of a double boiler over hot (not simmering) water, stirring continuously. Remove from heat and set aside to cool to room temperature. Stir in the pumpkin and spice.

3.   Sift together the sugar, flour, and cornstarch. Whisk in the egg yolk, beating until smooth and light. Set aside.

4.   Bring the milk to a boil in a stainless steel saucepan. Slowly pour the hot milk into the egg yolk, whisking until all the milk is incorporated. Pour the mixture into the saucepan and, stirring continuously, bring to a simmer over medium heat. Continue stirring for 1 minute. Remove from heat and set aside to cool. Fold in the chocolate-pumpkin mixture. Set aside.

5.   To make the spiced apples: Coat the apple slices with lemon juice as you slice them. Brown the butter in a heavy-bottomed skillet over medium heat. Mix in the brown sugar, and stir until completely dissolved. Blend in the spice and vanilla. Add the apple slices, and cook, turning the slices

constantly, for 5 to 7 minutes. Remove from heat and set aside to cool.

6.   To make the glaze: Combine the apricot preserves, apple liqueur, and sugar in a heavy-bottomed saucepan. Bring to a simmer over a medium heat, stirring continuously. Remove from heat. Using a pastry brush, coat the inside of the tart shell with the preserves. Spoon the pastry cream into the tart shell. Arrange the apple slices on top of the pastry cream. Paint the apples with glaze. Refrigerate.

7.   Before serving, randomly place chocolate leaves on top.

Makes 8–10 servings

Tuscan Tart

A classic Italian chocolate cheese tart, flavored with Amaretto, is covered with fresh, spiced pears.

Butter Tart Shell:

1¹/₄ cups flour
¹/₄ cup sugar
¹/₂ cup butter, chilled and cut into ¹/₄-inch cubes
1 egg yolk, chilled
1 teaspoon heavy cream, chilled

Filling:

3 cups ricotta cheese, warmed to room temperature
¹/₂ cup sugar
¹/₄ cup nonalkalized cocoa powder
4 eggs, warmed to room temperature
2 tablespoons Amaretto liqueur

(continued)

Spiced Pears:

2 cups water
¹/₂ cup sugar
¹/₄ teaspoon whole cloves
2 ripe pears

Glaze:

¹/₂ cup apricot preserves
2 tablespoons Amaretto liqueur
1 tablespoon superfine sugar
¹/₈ teaspoon allspice

1. Preheat the oven to 350°F. Prepare the tart shell according to directions on page 157. Press the dough into a lightly buttered 9¹/₂-inch fluted tart pan with a removable bottom, and refrigerate.

2. Cream the ricotta, using an electric mixer on a medium speed, until smooth. Blend in the sugar and cocoa powder. Add the eggs, one at a time, beating until thoroughly mixed. Add the Amaretto liqueur. Pour into the tart shell and bake for 45 minutes or until firm in the center. Cool on a wire rack.

3. To make the spiced pears: Bring the water, sugar, and cloves to a boil in a heavy-bottomed saucepan over a medium heat. Peel the pears, slice them in half, and remove the core. Place the pear halves in the hot syrup, cover, and simmer on a low heat for 10 to 12 minutes or until tender. Remove from heat and set aside to cool in the syrup.

4. When the tart and the pears are cool, drain the pears on a paper towel, slice, and arrange on top of the tart. Set aside.

5. To make the glaze: Combine the apricot preserves, Amaretto, and sugar in a heavy-bottomed saucepan. Bring to a simmer over a medium heat, stirring continuously. Remove from heat. Using a pastry brush, paint the pears with glaze and serve.

Makes 8–10 servings

Rocky Road Supreme Tart

Here's a fun tart for family celebrations. A milk chocolate truffle base supports walnuts, marshmallows, cherries, and chocolate chips in sweetened whipped mascarpone cheese.

Shortbread Tart Shell:

1¹/₄ cups flour
¹/₄ cup light brown sugar, firmly packed
¹/₂ cup butter, chilled and cut into ¹/₄-inch cubes
1 teaspoon heavy cream, chilled

Chocolate Truffle Layer:

8 ounces milk chocolate, finely chopped
¹/₃ cup heavy cream, warmed to room temperature
2 tablespoons butter, cut into ¹/₄-inch cubes

Rocky Road Layer:

1 cup heavy cream, chilled
1 cup mascarpone cheese, chilled
¹/₄ cup sugar, divided
2 tablespoons alkalized cocoa powder
1 cup walnuts, toasted and chopped

1 cup miniature marshmallows
*1 cup maraschino cherries, drained and
   halved*
¹/₂ cup milk chocolate chips

1. Preheat the oven to 400°F. Prepare the tart shell according to directions on page 157. Press the dough into a lightly buttered 9¹/₂-inch fluted tart pan with a removable bottom. Bake for 15 minutes, or until golden brown, and set aside to cool.

2. To make the chocolate truffle layer: Melt the chocolate, cream, and butter in the top of a double boiler over hot (not simmering) water, stirring continuously. Remove from heat and set aside to cool to room temperature. Pour into the cooled tart shell.

3. To make the rocky road layer: Whip the cream, using an electric mixer on a high speed, until soft peaks form. Sprinkle in half of the sugar, and beat just until combined. Cover and refrigerate.

4. Cream the mascarpone cheese, using an electric mixer on a medium speed, until soft. Blend in the remaining 2 tablespoons of sugar and cocoa powder. Gently fold in the whipped cream, walnuts, marshmallows, cherries, and chocolate chips, one ingredient at a time. Spoon onto the tart and serve.

Makes 8–10 servings

Chocolate Books for Kids

These delightful books for young readers have chocolate story lines!

Ages 4–8:
The Last Chocolate Cookie by Jamie Rix
Chocolate Island by Karen Dolby
Cocoa Ice by Diana Appelbaum
Chocolatina by Erik Kraft
The Ghost Who Ate Chocolate by Susan Saunders
Hot Fudge by James Howe

Ages 9–12:
Charlie and the Chocolate Factory by Roald Dahl
Cam Jansen and the Chocolate Fudge Mystery by David A. Adler
The Case of the Chocolate Fingerprints by Parker C. Hinter
The Chocolate Touch by Patrick Skene Catling
The Chocolate Sundae Mystery by Gertrude Chandler Warner
The Chocolate-Covered Contest by Carolyn M. Keene
The Cocoa Commotion by Melissa Peterson
Mary Marony and the Chocolate Surprise by Suzy Kline

Key Largo Tart

Papaya, mango, pineapple, banana, kiwi, star fruit, passion fruit . . . use one or more of your favorite tropical fruits to top this sweet, white chocolate tart.

Cashew Tart Shell:
1 cups flour
¹/₄ cup cashews
¹/₄ cup sugar
¹/₂ cup butter, chilled and cut into ¹/₄-inch cubes
1 egg yolk, chilled
1 teaspoon heavy cream, chilled

White Chocolate Filling:
8 ounces white chocolate, finely chopped
³/₄ cup milk, warmed to room temperature
2 tablespoons butter, cut into ¹/₄-inch cubes
3 tablespoons Key Largo liqueur
3 eggs, warmed to room temperature
2 egg yolks, warmed to room temperature
¹/₄ cup sugar

Tropical Fruit and Glaze:
4 cups sliced or cubed fresh tropical fruit
2 tablespoons lemon juice
¹/₂ cup apricot preserves
2 tablespoons Key Largo liqueur
1 tablespoon superfine sugar
¹/₄ cup sweetened shredded coconut, toasted

1.   Preheat the oven to 400°F. Prepare the tart shell according to directions on page 157. Press the dough into a lightly buttered 9¹/₂-inch fluted tart pan with a removable bottom. Bake for 15 minutes, or until golden brown, and set aside to cool.

2.   Melt the chocolate, milk, and butter in the top of a double boiler over hot (not simmering) water, stirring continuously. Remove from heat and set aside to cool to room temperature. Stir in the liqueur.

3.   To make the white chocolate filling: Preheat the oven to 350°F. Whisk together the eggs, egg yolks, and sugar until thoroughly blended. Fold in the chocolate mixture. Pour into the tart shell and bake for 20 minutes, or until set. Remove from the oven, and cool on a wire rack.

4.   To make the tropical fruit and glaze: Peel and slice or cube the tropical fruit, coating the fruit with lemon juice as you work. Place the fruit on the white chocolate filling.

5.   Combine the apricot preserves, liqueur, and sugar in a heavy-bottomed saucepan. Bring to a simmer over a medium heat, stirring continuously. Remove from heat. Using a pastry brush, paint the tropical fruit with the preserves.

6.   To toast the coconut: Preheat the oven to 350°F. Spread the coconut on a nonstick cookie sheet. Toast for 3 to 7 minutes, or until golden brown, tossing every few minutes to toast evenly. Sprinkle on top of the glazed fruit and serve.

Makes 8–10 servings

Lemon Tarts

A tart lemon glaze crowns sweet white chocolate and is decorated with swirls of white chocolate hearts. For a special topping, add sugared violets and fresh mint.

Pecan Tart Shell:
1 cup flour
$^1/_4$ cup pecans, toasted and ground
$^1/_4$ cup sugar
$^1/_2$ cup butter, chilled and cut into $^1/_4$-inch cubes
1 egg yolk, chilled
1 teaspoon heavy cream, chilled

White Chocolate Layer:
8 ounces white chocolate, finely chopped
$^1/_3$ cup heavy cream
2 tablespoons butterscotch liqueur

Lemon Layer:
2 eggs, warmed to room temperature
2 egg yolks, warmed to room temperature
2 tablespoons sugar
$^1/_2$ cup lemon juice
$^1/_3$ cup butter, warmed to room temperature

Topping:
2 ounces white chocolate, finely chopped
12 sugared violets (optional)
4–8 small, fresh mint leaves (optional)

1.   Preheat the oven to 400°F. Prepare the tart shell according to directions on page 157. Press the dough into four lightly buttered 4-inch tart pans with removable bottoms. Bake for 15 minutes, or until golden brown, and set aside to cool.

2.   To make the white chocolate layer: Melt the chocolate and cream in the top of a double boiler over hot (not simmering) water, stirring continuously. Remove from heat and set aside to cool to room temperature. Stir in the liqueur, and fill each tart shell about half full. Set aside.

3.   To make the lemon layer: In a glass bowl that can be used as the top of a double boiler, whisk together the eggs, egg yolks, sugar, and lemon juice. Place over simmering water and continue to whisk for 10 minutes or until mixture thickens.

4.   Remove from heat, add butter, and whisk until smooth. Cool for a few minutes. Spoon over the white chocolate filling in each tart. Set aside.

5.   To make the topping: Melt the white chocolate in a small heatproof bowl in the microwave, on a low setting. Heat in 15-second increments and stir between heatings, being careful not to overheat. Place small dots of white chocolate, approximately 1 inch apart, in a circle approximately 1 inch from the outside of the tart shell. Create a smaller circle within the first. Using a toothpick, draw a line through the center of each dot in the outer circle, connecting each to the next. A ring of small hearts will form. Repeat, connecting the dots in the inner circle.

6.   Refrigerate to set. Place 3 sugared violets and 1 or 2 mint leaves (or a fresh edible flower) in the center of each tart before serving.

Makes 4 tarts

Irish Crème Brûlée Tart

White chocolate sweetens, and Irish Cream liqueur flavors classic crème brûlée, which rests in a spiced tart shell.

Spiced Tart Shell:

1¹/₄ cups flour
¹/₄ cup sugar
¹/₂ teaspoon ground cinnamon
¹/₂ teaspoon ground nutmeg
¹/₄ teaspoon ground ginger
¹/₄ teaspoon ground cloves
¹/₂ cup butter, chilled and cut into ¹/₄-inch cubes
1 egg yolk, chilled
1 teaspoon heavy cream, chilled

Holiday Prep Party

There are really fun molds available for every holiday. Invite friends of all ages over to mold, assemble, decorate, and package chocolate specialties. Your results can be used for gifts, package toppers, or fundraisers.

Crème Brulee:

4 ounces white chocolate, finely chopped
2 tablespoons Irish Cream liqueur
1 cup heavy cream
1 teaspoon pure vanilla extract
6 egg yolks, warmed to room temperature
3 tablespoons sugar

Topping:

²/₃ cup light brown sugar, firmly packed
2 tablespoons powdered sugar

Preheat the oven to 400°F. Prepare the tart shell according to directions on page 157. Press the dough into a lightly buttered 9¹/₂-inch fluted tart pan with a removable bottom. Bake for 15 minutes or until golden brown and set aside to cool.

2. Melt the chocolate in the top of a double boiler over hot (not simmering) water, stirring continuously. Remove from heat and set aside to cool to room temperature. Stir in the Irish Cream liqueur. Set aside.

3. Combine the cream and vanilla in a heavy-bottomed saucepan, and bring to a boil over a low heat.

4. In a glass bowl that can be used as the top of a double boiler, whisk together the egg yolks and sugar. Place the bowl over simmering water and continue to whisk until the egg yolks heat and lighten in color. Turn off the stove, and remove the bowl from the double boiler. Slowly pour the boiling cream into the egg yolks, and whisk continuously. Put the bowl back over the hot water for 7 to 10 minutes, whisking occasionally, until the mixture thickens.

5.   Remove the bowl from the double boiler and place in a larger bowl containing ice water. Fold in the melted chocolate. Leave in the ice water bath, stirring occasionally, until cool. Pour into the tart shell, cover, and refrigerate.

6.   When set, preheat your broiler. Sift the brown sugar evenly over the tart. Cover the baked edge of the tart shell with foil, and place the tart under the broiler until the sugar is melted and golden. Set aside to cool.

7.   Just before serving, place a paper doily over the tart, and sift a light dusting of powdered sugar over the doily. Carefully remove the doily. For an extra special touch, place white chocolate roses in the center.

Makes 8–10 servings

Pastries

Chocolate Rosettes

Lighter than air, these easy, delicate chocolate pastries melt in your mouth. You'll need a rosette iron, which can be found in most kitchen and specialty shops.

> 3 cups flour
> ¹/₄ cup nonalkalized cocoa powder
> ¹/₂ teaspoon salt
> 4 eggs, warmed to room temperature
> ¹/₄ cup superfine sugar
> 2 cups milk, warmed to room temperature
> vegetable oil
> powdered sugar

1.   Sift together the flour, cocoa powder, and salt. Set aside.

2.   Beat together the eggs, sugar, and milk. Sprinkle in the flour mixture, beating until smooth. Set aside.

3.   Preheat 2 inches of vegetable oil to 350°F in a skillet or electric frying pan. Heat the rosette iron in the oil. Blot the excess oil on a paper towel. Dip the bottom of the rosette iron in the batter, being careful not to cover the iron in batter. Place the iron in the hot oil. Using a fork, gently ease the batter off the iron. Turn the rosettes in the hot oil for a few minutes, cooking evenly. Remove from oil, drain on paper towels, dust with powdered sugar, and serve.

Makes 6–8 servings

Petits Choux Kisses

A trio of bite-size chocolate cream puffs, stuffed with scoops of ice cream and dusted with powdered sugar, makes a light, delicious dessert after a rich meal.

Chocolate Kisses:
> ¹/₂ cup flour, sifted
> 1 tablespoon nonalkalized cocoa powder
> 2 eggs, warmed to room temperature
> ¹/₂ cup water
> ¹/₄ teaspoon salt
> ¹/₄ cup butter, cut into ¹/₄-inch cubes
> ¹/₂ tablespoon superfine sugar

Glaze:
> 1 egg, beaten
> ¹/₈ teaspoon salt

(continued)

Filling and Topping:

ice cream
powdered sugar

1. Preheat the oven to 425°F. Line baking sheets with parchment paper. Sift together the flour and cocoa powder. Set aside. Crack each egg into an individual bowl and set aside.

2. Combine the water, salt, butter, and sugar in a heavy-bottomed saucepan, and bring to a boil. Remove from heat, add the flour mixture, and beat quickly with a wooden spoon for 1 minute or until smooth. The mixture should pull away from the sides of the pan and form a ball.

3. Beat in the eggs, one at a time. The mixture should be shiny and slide off the spoon. Place the dough in a pastry bag fitted with a 1/4-inch plain tip, and pipe 1-inch mounds onto the prepared pans.

4. Mix together the egg and salt. Using a pastry brush, paint the top of each cream puff with this egg glaze, gently smoothing down the peak. Bake for 20 to 25 minutes. Place on wire racks to cool.

5. To serve, slice the cream puffs, place a small scoop of ice cream inside, and dust with powdered sugar.

Makes about 2 dozen bite-size puffs

Scare Wees

These little chocolate monsters will scare rainy-day blues away. Chocolate choux puffs are stuffed with chocolate pudding and decorated with cute monster faces.

1 recipe Petits Choux Kisses (page 181)
1 recipe Chocolate Pudding (page 249)
12 ounces white chocolate, finely chopped
powdered coloring for chocolate
24 candy-coated chocolates (like M&M's)
1/2 cup tiny candy beads
24 blanched, slivered almond pieces

1. Preheat the oven to 425°F. Prepare the chocolate choux batter. Pipe into 2-inch mounds and bake for 30 to 40 minutes. Cool on wire racks. Slice in half horizontally.

2. Prepare the chocolate pudding as directed, and chill.

3. Spoon chilled chocolate pudding onto the bottom halves of the choux puffs, and place the tops over the pudding.

4. Melt the white chocolate in the top of a double boiler over hot (not simmering) water, stirring until smooth. If you want to make more than one color of chocolate, separate the chocolate into different bowls. Blend in the powdered coloring. Powdered coloring is very concentrated, so sprinkle in just a little bit at a time, until the color you desire is achieved. Do not use liquid food coloring; your chocolate will seize. Set the colored chocolate aside to cool.

5. Using a toothpick, dab a tiny amount of chocolate onto the center of one of the flat sides of each of the candy-coated chocolate pieces. Place a tiny candy bead on top of the chocolate to create the eyes.

6. Spoon warm colored chocolate on top of each choux puff, encouraging the chocolate to drip down into a nose shape.

7. Place two eyes in the colored chocolate, and sprinkle with additional candy beads.

8. Place two almond slivers in the chocolate pudding to create fangs, and serve!

Makes 12 monsters

Sweet Williams

Slices of fresh strawberries are coated in semisweet chocolate and tucked inside these petite cream puffs, which are topped with a dollop of rich dark chocolate.

Cream Puffs:
1 cup flour, sifted
4 eggs, warmed to room temperature
1 cup water
¹/₂ teaspoon salt
¹/₂ cup butter, cut into ¹/₄-inch cubes
¹/₂ teaspoon pure vanilla extract

Glaze:
1 egg, beaten
¹/₈ teaspoon salt

Filling:
8 ounces semisweet chocolate, finely chopped
2 cups fresh strawberries, sliced
2 cups heavy cream, chilled
¹/₄ cup superfine sugar

(*continued*)

The Chemistry of Chocolate

New research is finding small amounts of inherent chemicals in chocolate that may provide holistic benefits:

• Caffeine—Although, not always considered a benefit, caffeine in chocolate acts as a natural stimulant.

• Cannabinoids—These chemicals may encourage your brain's production of natural painkilling elements.

• Phenylethylamine—Falling in love, as well as chocolate, produces this stimulating substance in your brain.

• Polyphenois—These antioxidants help prevent cholesterol from forming in your arteries.

• Serotonin—An antidepressant naturally produced in your brain, small amounts of serotonin are also found in chocolate.

• Theobromine—Similar to caffeine, this natural chemical is a form of amphetamine.

Frosting:

4 ounces semisweet chocolate, finely chopped
1 cup heavy cream, warmed to room temperature
1/4 cup butter, cut into 1/4-inch cubes
1 tablespoon light corn syrup

1. Preheat the oven to 425°F. Line baking sheets with parchment paper. Sift the flour and set aside. Crack each egg into an individual bowl and set aside.

2. Combine the water, salt, butter, and vanilla in a heavy-bottomed saucepan, and bring to a boil. As soon as the butter is completely melted, remove from heat, add the flour, and beat quickly with a wooden spoon for 1 minute or until smooth. The mixture should pull away from the sides of the pan and form a ball.

3. Beat in the eggs, one at a time. The mixture should be shiny, and slide off the spoon. Drop by tablespoonfuls onto the prepared pans.

4. Mix together the egg and salt. Using a pastry brush, paint the top of each cream puff with this egg glaze, and bake for 25 to 35 minutes, or until golden brown. Place on wire racks to cool.

5. To make the filling: Melt the chocolate in the top of a double boiler over hot (not simmering) water, stirring continuously. Remove from heat and set aside to cool to room temperature. Line cookie sheets with waxed paper.

6. Wash and slice strawberries. Blot each slice dry between paper towels. Dip each slice in melted chocolate and place on the waxed paper. Refrigerate for 10 minutes to set the chocolate.

7. Whip the cream, using an electric mixer on a high speed, until soft peaks form. Sprinkle in the sugar, and beat until stiff peaks form. Cover and refrigerate.

8. To make the frosting: Melt the chocolate, cream, butter, and syrup in the top of a double boiler over hot (not simmering) water, stirring continuously. Remove from heat and set aside to cool for about 30 minutes.

9. Slice each cream puff. Place a dollop of whipped cream on the bottom of each. Place chocolate-coated strawberry slices on top of the whipped cream. Place another dollop of whipped cream on top of the strawberries. Cover with the cream puff top, and spoon frosting on top.

Makes about 2 dozen cream puffs

Chantilly Choux Heart

Perfect anytime you want to say, "I love you." Choux pastry is piped into a heart shape and filled with a special raspberry chantilly cream. A dark chocolate glaze, white chocolate curls, and fresh raspberries add a romantic topping.

Choux Heart:

1 cup flour, sifted
4 eggs, warmed to room temperature
1 cup water
1/2 teaspoon salt
1/2 cup butter, cut into 1/4-inch cubes
1 teaspoon pure almond extract

Egg Glaze:

1 egg, beaten
¹/₈ teaspoon salt

Chantilly Filling:

2 cups heavy cream, chilled
¹/₄ cup superfine sugar
¹/₂ cup grated semisweet chocolate
¹/₄ cup fresh raspberries

Glaze and Toppings:

4 ounces semisweet chocolate, finely
*   chopped*
¹/₃ cup butter, cut into ¹/₄-inch cubes
2 teaspoons light corn syrup
1 cup white chocolate curls
¹/₄ cup fresh, whole raspberries
powdered Sugar

1.   Preheat the oven to 425°F. Line a baking sheet with parchment paper. Sift the flour and set aside. Crack each egg into an individual bowl and set aside.

2.   Combine the water, salt, butter, and almond extract in a heavy-bottomed saucepan, and bring to a boil. As soon as the butter is completely melted, remove from heat, add the flour, and beat quickly with a wooden spoon for 1 minute or until smooth. The mixture should pull away from the sides of the pan and form a ball.

3.   Beat in the eggs, one at a time. The mixture should be shiny, and slide off the spoon. Place the batter in a pastry bag fitted with a ¹/₂-inch plain tip. Pipe a 10-inch heart (approximately) onto the baking sheet. Pipe a smaller heart, just inside the first heart. And a third heart inside the second.

4.   Mix together the egg and salt. Using a pastry brush, paint the top with this egg glaze, and bake for 30 to 35 minutes, or until golden brown. Place on wire racks to cool.

5.   To make the filling: Whip the cream, using an electric mixer on a high speed, until soft peaks form. Sprinkle in the sugar, grated chocolate, and raspberries, and beat until stiff peaks form. Cover and refrigerate.

6.   To make the glaze: Melt the chocolate, butter, and syrup in the top of a double boiler over hot (not simmering) water, stirring continuously. Remove from heat and set aside to cool for about 30 minutes.

(continued)

Oven Temperatures

When baking with chocolate, oven temperatures need to be precise. Even the best ovens can loose calibration over time, so I recommend you buy and use a small oven thermometer. Then, be sure to keep an eye on it and adjust your oven's settings accordingly.

7.   Slice the heart. Spoon the raspberry chantilly cream on the bottom of the heart. Cover with the heart top, spoon the dark chocolate glaze on top, and sprinkle with white chocolate curls. Randomly place whole raspberries in and around the chocolate curls, and dust with powdered sugar.

Makes 8–10 servings

Chocolate Chip Baklava

Miniature chocolate chips enhance this classic Greek pastry of buttered phyllo dough, spiced walnuts and almonds, and flavored honey.

- *³/₄ cup miniature chocolate chips*
- *³/₄ cup walnuts, toasted and finely chopped*
- *³/₄ cup almonds, toasted and finely chopped*
- *¹/₂ cup superfine sugar*
- *¹/₄ teaspoon ground cinnamon*
- *¹/₈ teaspoon ground cloves*
- *1 pound phyllo pastry sheets, warmed to room temperature*
- *1¹/₂ cups butter, melted*

Syrup:
- *1¹/₂ cups water*
- *³/₄ cup light brown sugar, firmly packed*
- *³/₄ cup honey*
- *¹/₂ teaspoon cinnamon*
- *¹/₂ lemon, sliced*
- *¹/₂ orange, sliced*
- *1 tablespoon Grand Marnier*

1.   Preheat the oven to 325°F. Line a 15¹/₂-inch by 10¹/₂-inch by 1-inch jellyroll pan with parchment paper.

2.   Combine the chocolate chips, walnuts, almonds, sugar, cinnamon, and cloves. Set aside.

3.   Remove the phyllo pastry sheets from the package and cover with damp paper towels to keep them from drying out. Place 2 sheets in the prepared pan, and brush the top one with melted butter. Repeat 7 times, creating a pile of 16 sheets.

4.   Sprinkle a third of the chocolate chip mixture on top of the buttered phyllo pastry sheets. Cover with 6 more sheets, buttering every other sheet. Repeat two times. Cover with remaining phyllo pastry sheets, buttering every other sheet. Butter the top layer, and bake for 1 hour. Turn the oven off and leave the baklava in the oven for another hour.

5.   To make the syrup: Mix together the water, brown sugar, honey, cinnamon, lemon slices, and orange slices, in a heavy-bottomed saucepan. Bring to a simmer, stirring, over a low heat. Simmer uncovered for 20 minutes. Turn the stove off, remove the lemon and orange slices, and add the Grand Marnier.

6.   Remove the baklava from the oven and cut into 1¹/₂-inch squares. Spoon the syrup over the top. Place the pan on a wire rack to cool. When cool, cover with waxed paper, seal in foil, and set aside overnight.

Makes about 40 pieces

Peach Pecan Pastry

This simple, yet elegant, pastry swims in a white chocolate cream.

White Chocolate Cream:
4 ounces white chocolate
1 tablespoon butterscotch liqueur
1 cup heavy cream, chilled
2 tablespoons superfine sugar

Peach Pecan Pastry:
$^2/_3$ cup peeled, cored, and cubed fresh peaches
1 teaspoon lemon juice
$^2/_3$ cup dried cherries, chopped
$^1/_3$ cup light brown sugar
2 tablespoons peach liqueur
$^1/_3$ cup pecans, toasted and ground
$^1/_3$ cup pecans, toasted and chopped
8 sheets phyllo pastry dough
2 tablespoons butter, melted

1. To make the white chocolate cream: Melt the chocolate in the top of a double boiler over hot (not simmering), water, stirring continuously. Set aside to cool to room temperature. Stir in the liqueur.

2. Whip the cream, using an electric mixer on a high speed, until soft peaks form. Sprinkle in the sugar, beating until just combined. Fold in the melted chocolate. Set aside.

3. Preheat the oven to 400°F. Line a 15$^1/_2$-inch by 10$^1/_2$-inch by 1-inch jellyroll pan with parchment paper.

4. Coat the peaches in lemon juice as you cube them. Combine with cherries, brown sugar, and liqueur in a heavy-bottomed saucepan over a low heat. Bring to a simmer, remove from heat, and cool. Stir in the ground and chopped pecans. Set aside.

5. Remove the phyllo pastry sheets from the package and cover with damp paper towels to keep them from drying out. Place 2 sheets in the prepared pan, and brush the top one with melted butter. Repeat 3 times, creating a pile of 8 sheets.

(continued)

Take a Step Back in Time

The next time you're in France, visit Debauve & Gallais and taste a historical example of how confections were made in the early 1800s. Originally founded to produce and sell medicinal chocolates, this charming apothecary still has most of its original furnishings.

6.   Spoon the peach mixture down half of the length of the phyllo dough. Fold half the dough over the mixture, and seal under the bottom edge of the phyllo dough, creating a 15-inch log. Seal the ends and bake for 15 to 20 minutes, or until golden brown. Slice and serve with the white chocolate cream.

Makes 4–6 servings

Strawberry Blossoms

White chocolate cheese fills nests of phyllo pastry dough, which are topped with a bloom of fresh strawberries.

> *4 ounces white chocolate, finely chopped*
> *1 cup cream cheese, softened*
> *$1/2$ cup cottage cheese, warmed to room temperature*
> *1 egg, warmed to room temperature*
> *2 tablespoons sugar*
> *1 teaspoon lemon juice*
> *8 sheets phyllo pastry dough, warmed to room temperature*
> *2 tablespoons butter, melted*
> *2 cups fresh strawberries, sliced*
> *12 small whole strawberries*

1.   Preheat the oven to 350°F. Lightly coat 12 standard muffin-pan cups with butter and flour.

2.   Melt the chocolate in the top of a double boiler over hot (not simmering) water, stirring constantly. Set aside to cool to room temperature.

3.   Cream together the cream cheese and cottage cheese, using an electric mixer on a medium speed, until smooth. Add the egg, sugar, and lemon juice, and beat until thoroughly blended. Fold in the chocolate. Set aside.

4.   Remove the phyllo pastry sheets from the package and cover with damp paper towels to keep them from drying out. Cut 8 sheets of 12-inch by 15-inch phyllo pastry dough into 5-inch squares. Butter 1 square. Place another square on top, turning the square slightly. Butter the top. Repeat with 2 more squares, turning each slightly, to ultimately create a 16-point star. Gently fit into a muffin cup. Continue, creating 11 more phyllo pastry cups.

5.   Fill the phyllo cups three-quarters full with the cheese mixture, and bake for 10 to 15 minutes, or until the phyllo is golden brown and the cheese filling is firm. Cool on wire racks.

6.   Place the strawberry slices, tip side up, on top of the cheese filling, around the outside of each phyllo cup. Continue, arranging concentric circles of strawberry slices. Place a small whole strawberry, tip side up, in the center, and serve.

Makes 12 blossoms

Josephines

Let Napolean have his puff pastry— Josephine had a better idea . . . thin marbled chocolate bars separate layers of pastry cream and fresh berries.

Chocolate Truffles
page 48

Chocolate Turtles
page 90

Nestlé® Toll House® Cookies
page 96

Bittersweet Almond Biscotti
page 116

Chocolate Cream Pie
page 159

Classic Brownies
page 117

Heart-to-Heart Tart
page 170

Venetian Butter Cake
page 195

Chocolate Chip Cheesecake
page 202

Photo by Foodpix®

Mocha Dream
page 213

Peanut Butter Oreo Torte
page 218

Chocolate Pudding
page 249

Soufflé Chocolat
page 266

Teardrop Charlotte
page 268

White Knight Trifle
page 276

Chocolate Dipped Fruit and Cookies
page 337

Marbled Bars:

8 ounces bittersweet chocolate, tempered
2 ounces white chocolate, tempered

Filling:

2 tablespoons sugar
4 teaspoons flour
1 tablespoon cornstarch
2 egg yolks, slightly beaten
1 cup milk, warmed to room temperature
1/2 teaspoon pure vanilla extract
1/2 teaspoon almond extract
2 cups fresh blackberries

1. Cover a cookie sheet with waxed paper. Spread the bittersweet chocolate on the waxed paper, creating an 8-inch by 12-inch rectangle. Drizzle the white chocolate over the bittersweet chocolate and, using a sable painter's brush, lightly swirl the two chocolates together. Place in the refrigerator for 1 to 2 minutes. Score the chocolate, dividing the 8-inch side into 2-inch sections, and the 12-inch side into 4-inch sections. Refrigerate for a few more minutes, until set. Cut the chocolate along the score lines, and store in a cool place.

2. To make the filling: Sift together the sugar, flour, and cornstarch. Whisk in the egg yolk, beating until smooth and light. Set aside.

3. Bring the milk to a boil in a stainless steel saucepan. Slowly pour the hot milk into the egg yolk, whisking until all the milk is incorporated. Pour the mixture into the saucepan and, stirring continuously, bring to a simmer over medium heat. Continue stirring for 1 minute. Remove from heat and mix in the vanilla and almond extracts. Set aside to cool. Mash a few of the blackberries and fold into the filling. Cover and refrigerate.

4. When ready to serve, place the filling in a pastry bag, fitted with a 1/2-inch star tip. Pipe stars onto the top of 8 marbled chocolate bars. Top with fresh blackberries. Pipe more pastry cream on top of the fresh blackberries. Carefully place 4 of the pastry cream-covered bars on top of the other 4. Cover with the 4 remaining marbled chocolate bars and serve.

Makes 4 servings

What's Your Cacao I.Q.?

Can you match these plantation terms to their meanings?

1. Cacao mothers   A. Groves of cacao trees

2. Cacao walks   B. A blend of beans grown within one region

3. Cacao dance   C. One type of cocoa bean, from one specific area

4. Criollo   D. The rich inner meat of the cocoa bean

5. Cru   E. Tall trees that protect cocoa bean trees from the sun and wind

6. Cuvee   F. A tool used to split open the cocoa pods

7. Magra   G. A method of turning the cocoa beans while they dry

8. Nibs   H. the finest type of cocoa bean, also known
                     as caraque

9. Varietals

                 I. Blends of different types of beans, or beans
                    from different regions

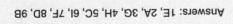

Answers: 1E, 2A, 3G, 4H, 5C, 6I, 7F, 8D, 9B

chapter seven

Cakes, Tortes, Fillings, and Frostings

When I was eight years old, my friend Renee had a birthday party. It was a pretty typical party with lots of friends, games, prizes, and presents. But when the birthday cake was served, my life was changed forever. It looked like an ordinary sheet cake, but underneath the thick buttercream was a chocolate chip cake! Now, this was in the 1960s when cakes were white, yellow, or chocolate. Period. But Renee's father was a professional baker, and I thought she was the luckiest girl in the world. My dad could make a pretty cool tree house, but *her* dad could make a chocolate chip cake. All these years later, even after I figured out all he did was add miniature chocolate chips to a basic cake batter, I still hold a special place in my heart for Renee, her father, and that chocolate chip cake.

So, the next time you make a light chocolate layer cake or dense chocolate torte, take the time and imagination to make it something special. You may create a memory that will last a lifetime.

Single Pan Cakes

Chocolate Flake Angel Cake

Heavenly light, this angel cake is divine on its own, and even better with a halo of June's Butter Fudge Frosting (page 231).

1¼ cups cake flour
1¾ cups superfine sugar, divided
½ teaspoon salt
12 egg whites, warmed to room temperature
1½ teaspoons cream of tartar
1 teaspoon pure vanilla extract
½ teaspoon pure almond extract
4 ounces grated semisweet chocolate

1. Preheat the oven to 375°F. Line the bottom of a 10-inch tube pan with parchment paper. Make sure the sides of the pan are dry and grease-free.

2. Sift together the flour, 1 cup of the sugar, and salt. Set aside.

3. Whip the egg whites with the cream of tartar and extracts, using an electric mixer on a high speed, until soft peaks form. Sprinkle in the remaining sugar, continuing to beat until stiff peaks form.

4. Sift a quarter of the flour mixture over the egg whites. Gently fold in. Repeat until all the flour mixture is incorporated. Gently fold in the grated chocolate. Be careful not to overmix or deflate the batter.

5. Pour into the prepared pan and bake for 35 to 40 minutes, or until a toothpick comes out clean when inserted in the

center of the cake. Cool the cake inverted. If your pan does not have built-in supports, place the pan over the neck of a bottle until completely cool.

Makes 10–12 servings

Cinnamon Mocha Chiffon Cake

Light and velvety, this chocolate chiffon cake has a rich espresso flavor with a hint of spice. For an added treat, top this cake with Grand Marnier Glaze (page 223).

$^1/_4$ cup nonalkalized cocoa powder
$^1/_4$ cup instant espresso powder
$^3/_4$ cup water, boiling
$1^3/_4$ cups cake flour
$1^3/_4$ cups superfine sugar, divided
2 teaspoons baking powder
1 teaspoon ground cinnamon
$^1/_2$ teaspoon salt
7 egg yolks, warmed to room temperature
$^1/_2$ cup light vegetable oil
2 teaspoons pure vanilla extract
7 egg whites, warmed to room temperature
$^1/_2$ teaspoon cream of tartar

1.   Preheat the oven to 325°F. Line the bottom of a 10-inch tube pan with parchment paper. Make sure the sides of the pan are dry and grease-free.

2.   Mix together the cocoa and espresso powders. Pour in the boiling water and stir

until evenly blended and completely dissolved. Set aside to cool.

3.   Sift together the flour, 1 cup of the sugar, baking powder, cinnamon, and salt. Add the cooled cocoa-espresso mixture, egg yolks, oil, and vanilla, using an electric mixer on a low speed, until thoroughly blended. Set aside.

4.   In a separate bowl, with clean, dry beaters, whip the egg whites with the cream of tartar, using an electric mixer on a high speed, until soft peaks form. Sprinkle in the remaining sugar, beating until stiff peaks form. Gently fold a quarter of the egg

(continued)

Creative Cuts

Who says a cake or torte needs to be round or square? A few cuts can create a hexagon or any number of interesting shapes. Let your imagination soar! You can make basic shapes even more intriguing by "gluing" additional pieces on with chocolate.

whites into the batter. Repeat until all the egg whites are incorporated.

5.   Pour into the prepared pan and bake for 1 hour, or until a toothpick comes out clean when inserted in the center of the cake. Cool the cake inverted. If your pan does not have built-in supports, place the pan over the neck of a bottle until completely cool.

Makes 10–12 servings

Leka's Gathering of Goddesses Cake

Here's a special, quick, easy, beyond deli-cious chocolate cake for all the goddesses who gather to snowboard (or participate in other activities) to raise money and aware-ness for the fight against breast cancer.

>   *³/₄ cup nonalkalized cocoa powder*
>   *2 cups sugar*
>   *2 cups flour*
>   *2 teaspoons baking soda*
>   *1 teaspoon baking powder*
>   *¹/₂ teaspoon salt*
>   *¹/₂ cup canola or safflower oil*
>   *1 cup hot coffee*
>   *1 cup milk*
>   *2 eggs, warmed to room temperature*

1.   Preheat the oven to 350°F. Lightly coat the bottom and sides of a 9-inch by 13-inch cake pan with butter and flour.

2.   Combine everything except the eggs, and beat for 2 minutes. Add the eggs and beat for 2 more minutes.

3.   Pour into the prepared pan and bake for 48 minutes, or until a toothpick comes out clean when inserted into the center of the cake. Cool in the pan for about 10 minutes, then finish cooling on a wire rack. Sprinkle with powdered sugar or serve with whipped cream and fresh raspberries.

Makes 10–12 servings

Torte Provence

Like the countryside of France, simplicity looks elegant with this fluted chocolate-pecan cake, crowned with fresh oranges and berries.

>   *8 ounces semisweet chocolate, finely*
>   *chopped*
>   *¹/₂ cup butter, softened*
>   *²/₃ cup sugar*
>   *1 teaspoon pure vanilla extract*
>   *¹/₂ teaspoon ground nutmeg*
>   *6 eggs, warmed to room temperature*
>   *1 cup pecans, toasted and finely chopped*
>   *¹/₄ cup flour*
>   *¹/₄ cup apricot preserves*
>   *2 tablespoons Grand Marnier*
>   *1 tablespoon superfine sugar*
>   *1 cup fresh orange sections, peeled*
>   *1 cup fresh strawberries*
>   *1 cup fresh raspberries*

1.   Preheat the oven to 350°F. Line the bottom of a 9-inch fluted baking pan with parchment paper. Lightly coat the sides of the pan with butter and flour.

2.   Melt the chocolate in the top of a double boiler over hot, not simmering, water, stirring continuously. Set aside to cool to room temperature.

3.   Cream the butter, using an electric mixer on a medium-high speed, until light and fluffy. Add the sugar, vanilla, and nutmeg. Adjust your mixer to a medium speed, and add the eggs, one at a time, until thoroughly blended.

4.   Fold in the cooled chocolate, pecans, and flour. Pour into the prepared pan and bake for 35 to 40 minutes, or until a toothpick comes out clean when inserted in the center of the cake. Cool on a wire rack.

5.   Combine the apricot preserves, Grand Marnier, and sugar in a heavy-bottomed saucepan. Bring to a simmer over a medium heat, stirring continuously. Remove from heat and set aside to cool.

6.   Invert the cooled cake on a serving dish. Mix together the fresh fruit and arrange on top of the cake. Using a pastry brush, paint the fruit with the Grand Marnier glaze.

Makes 10–12 servings

Venetian Butter Cake

Think of this as an ultrarich chocolate pound cake with the mystery and sophistication of Venice. This cake is delicious on its own, and even better when served with fresh peaches and Crème Mystique (page 224).

(continued)

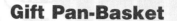

Gift Pan-Basket

For a friend who loves to bake, fill a baking pan with goodies as you would a gift basket. Here are a few tips:

1.   Deep round pans like bundt, tube, and springform pans work especially well.
2.   Place a decorative towel or napkins in the pan to make it more colorful and to protect the pan from scratches.
3.   Choose a theme for your gift. For example, include ingredients and tools needed for a special recipe, or all the basics, or exotic and hard-to-find surprises.
4.   Wrap in cellophane, and attach a small pastry tool to the bow!

*8 ounces bittersweet chocolate, finely
    chopped*
1¹/₂ cups butter, softened
*¹/₂ cup mascarpone cheese, warmed to
    room temperature*
1¹/₄ cups sugar, divided
6 egg yolks, warmed to room temperature
1 tablespoon dark rum
2 teaspoons pure almond extract
¹/₂ teaspoon ground ginger
2 cups cake flour
*6 egg whites, warmed to room tempera-
    ture*
¹/₈ teaspoon cream of tartar

1.   Preheat the oven to 350°F. Lightly coat the bottom and sides of a bundt pan with butter and flour.

2.   Melt the chocolate in the top of a double boiler over hot, not simmering, water, stirring continuously. Set aside to cool.

3.   Cream together the butter, mascarpone cheese, and 1 cup of the sugar, using an electric mixer on a medium-high speed, until light and fluffy. Adjust your mixer to a medium speed and add the egg yolks, one at a time, beating until thoroughly blended. Adjust your mixer to a low speed and blend in the rum, almond extract, ginger, and melted chocolate. Fold in the flour a little at a time.

4.   Beat the egg whites with the cream of tartar, using an electric mixer on a high speed, until soft peaks form. Sprinkle in the remaining sugar and continue beating until stiff peaks form. Fold a third of the egg whites into the batter. Repeat until all the egg whites are incorporated.

5.   Pour into the prepared pan and bake for 1 hour, or until a toothpick comes out clean when inserted in the center of the cake. Cool on a wire rack.

Makes 10–12 servings

Mocha Bean Fudge Cake

Intensely chocolate, this bundt cake is filled with mocha beans and chocolate chips, and is dusted with powdered sugar.

*4 ounces bittersweet chocolate, finely
    chopped*
1 cup sweetened condensed milk
2 cups flour
¹/₂ cup nonalkalized cocoa powder
¹/₄ cup instant espresso powder
1 teaspoon baking soda
¹/₂ teaspoon salt
¹/₂ cup butter, softened
³/₄ cup sugar
³/₄ cup light brown sugar, firmly packed
2 eggs, warmed to room temperature
1 teaspoon pure vanilla extract
1 cup milk, warmed to room temperature
1 cup semisweet chocolate chips
¹/₂ cup mocha beans
2 tablespoons powdered sugar

1.   Preheat the oven to 350°F. Lightly coat the bottom and sides of a bundt pan with butter and flour.

2. Melt the bittersweet chocolate in the top of a double boiler over hot, not simmering, water, stirring continuously. Set aside.

3. Bring the condensed milk to a boil in a heavy-bottomed saucepan over medium heat, stirring continuously until thickened. Remove from heat and fold in the melted chocolate. Set aside.

4. Sift together the flour, cocoa powder, espresso powder, baking soda, and salt. Set aside.

5. Cream together the butter and sugars, using an electric mixer on a medium-high speed, until light and fluffy. Adjust your mixer to a medium speed and add the eggs, one at a time, beating until thoroughly blended. Add the vanilla.

6. Adjust your mixer to a low speed and blend in the melted chocolate mixture. Alternate folding in the flour mixture and milk until lightly blended. Fold in the chocolate chips and mocha beans.

7. Pour the batter into the prepared pan and bake for 45 minutes, or until a toothpick comes out with moist crumbs when inserted in the center of the cake. Cool in the pan on a wire rack for 10 minutes. Remove from the pan and finish cooling on a wire rack.

8. Dust with powdered sugar before serving.

Makes 10–12 servings

Plating a Cake or Torte

"Plating" is a term used by caterers to describe decorating a plate before putting an individual dessert on it. Plating can magically turn a simple treat into an elegant creation.

1. To "dust" a plate, lightly sift cocoa powder, ground nuts, spice, or powdered sugar on it before adding the dessert.
2. Melted chocolate or sauces can be drizzled or piped on a plate in a defined or random pattern.
3. To "mirror" a plate, coat the entire plate with a fruit coulis or chocolate sauce.
4. Or mirror a plate, add drops of a contrasting sauce, and trace a toothpick through the drops to create hearts or a marbling effect.

Banana Nut Brownie Cake

Imagine a cake-size brownie, with chunks of fresh banana baked inside, topped with whipped cream and walnuts.

12 ounces semisweet chocolate, finely
   chopped
$^1/_4$ cup heavy cream, warmed to room
   temperature
1 cup butter, softened
$^3/_4$ cup sugar
$^3/_4$ cup light brown sugar, firmly packed
6 eggs, warmed to room temperature
2 teaspoons pure vanilla extract
2 cups flour
1 cup walnuts, toasted and chopped,
   divided
$^3/_4$ cup sliced and quartered fresh bananas
1 cup heavy cream, chilled
2 tablespoons superfine sugar

1. Preheat the oven to 300°F. Line the bottom of a 9-inch springform pan with butter and flour. Lightly coat the sides of the pan with butter and flour.

2. Melt the chocolate and cream in the top of a double boiler over hot, not simmering, water, stirring continuously. Set aside to cool.

3. Cream together the butter and sugars, using an electric mixer on a medium-high speed, until light and fluffy. Adjust your mixer to a medium speed and add the eggs, one at a time, beating until thoroughly blended. Add the vanilla.

4. Adjust your mixer to a low speed and blend in the melted chocolate. Fold in the flour, $^3/_4$ cup of the walnuts, and bananas, until lightly blended.

5. Pour the batter into the prepared pan and bake for 2 hours, or until a toothpick comes out with moist crumbs when inserted in the center of the cake. Cool in the pan on a wire rack for 10 minutes. Remove from the pan and finish cooling on a wire rack.

6. Whip the cream with the superfine sugar, using an electric mixer on a high speed, until stiff peaks just begin to form. Top the cake with the whipped cream and remaining walnuts.

Makes 10–12 servings

Pooh's Honey Crunch Cake

Rumor has it this chocolate honey streusel cake is Winnie-the-Pooh's favorite. So, the next time you're having a few friends over from the Hundred Acre Wood . . .

Streusel:
$^1/_2$ cup light brown sugar, firmly packed
2 tablespoons butter, chilled
2 tablespoons flour
1 teaspoon cinnamon
$^1/_4$ cup almonds, toasted and coarsely
   chopped
$^1/_4$ cup walnuts, toasted and coarsely
   chopped

$^{1}/_{4}$ *cup pecans, toasted and coarsely chopped*

$^{1}/_{4}$ *cup toffee bits*

Honey Cake:

1$^{3}/_{4}$ *cups flour*

$^{1}/_{4}$ *cup nonalkalized cocoa powder*

1 teaspoon baking powder

$^{1}/_{4}$ *teaspoon salt*

$^{1}/_{2}$ *cup butter, softened*

1 cup honey

1 egg, warmed to room temperature

2 teaspoons pure vanilla extract

$^{1}/_{2}$ *cup heavy cream, warmed to room temperature*

1 tablespoon powdered sugar

1 teaspoon alkalized cocoa powder

1. Preheat the oven to 350°F. Lightly coat the bottom and sides of a bundt pan with butter and flour.

2. Combine all the streusel ingredients with a fork or pastry blender, until crumbly. Set aside.

3. Sift together the flour, cocoa powder, baking powder, and salt. Set aside.

4. Cream together the butter and honey, using an electric mixer on a medium-high speed, until light and fluffy. Adjust your mixer to a medium speed and add the egg and vanilla, beating until thoroughly blended.

5. Alternate folding in the flour and cream until lightly blended.

6. Sprinkle half of the streusel mixture into the bottom of the prepared pan. Spoon half of the batter into the pan. Sprinkle with the remaining streusel over the batter. Spoon the remaining batter into the pan and bake for 30 to 35 minutes, or until a toothpick comes out clean when inserted in the center of the cake. Cool in the pan on a wire rack for 10 minutes. Remove from the pan and finish cooling on a wire rack.

7. Before serving, dust with powdered sugar and cocoa powder.

Makes 10–12 servings

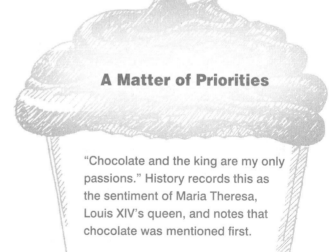

A Matter of Priorities

"Chocolate and the king are my only passions." History records this as the sentiment of Maria Theresa, Louis XIV's queen, and notes that chocolate was mentioned first.

Chocolate Ladyfingers

Ladyfingers are small pieces of cake, shaped like wide Popsicle sticks. They can be used for tiramisu, charlottes, trifles, and other specialties.

> *¹/₂ cup cake flour*
> *¹/₄ cup nonalkalized cocoa powder*
> *3 egg yolks, warmed to room temperature*
> *³/₄ cup superfine sugar, divided*
> *3 egg whites, warmed to room temperature*
> *¹/₈ teaspoon cream of tartar*

1. Preheat the oven to 400°F. Line a cookie sheet with parchment paper.
2. Sift together the flour and cocoa powder. Set aside.
3. Whisk together the egg yolks and ¹/₂ cup of the sugar until thick. Set aside.
4. Whip the egg whites with the cream of tartar, using an electric mixer on a high speed, until soft peaks form. Sprinkle in the remaining sugar and continue beating until stiff peaks form. Alternate folding the egg whites and flour mixture into the egg yolk mixture until lightly blended.
5. Place the batter in a pastry bag fitted with a plain ¹/₂-inch tip. Pipe 6-inch "fingers" (or whatever size or shape you desire), 1 inch apart, onto the parchment paper, and bake for 10 to 12 minutes. Cool on wire racks.

Makes enough to prepare 1 charlotte or tiramisu

Chocolate Pound Cake

Originally made with a pound of each main ingredient, we've reduced the amount of sugar and added chocolate for a dense buttery cake. This can be served as a loaf cake, or sliced (horizontally) and filled as a European-style layer cake.

> *¹/₂ pound (8 ounces) semisweet chocolate, finely chopped*
> *1 pound (2 cups) butter, softened*
> *¹/₂ pound (1 cup) sugar*
> *1 pound (6) eggs, warmed to room temperature*
> *1 teaspoon pure vanilla extract*
> *1 pound (2 cups) flour*

1. Preheat the oven to 350°F. Line the bottom of a 9-inch by 5-inch by 3-inch loaf pan with parchment paper. Lightly coat the sides of the pan with butter and flour.
2. Melt the chocolate in the top of a double boiler over hot, not simmering, water, stirring continuously. Set aside to cool.
3. Cream together the butter and sugar, using an electric mixer on a medium-high speed, until light and fluffy. Adjust your mixer to a medium speed and add the eggs, one at a time, beating until thoroughly blended. Adjust your mixer to a low speed and blend in the vanilla and melted chocolate. Fold in the flour a little at a time.
4. Pour into the prepared pan and bake for 1 hour, or until a toothpick comes out clean when inserted in the center of the cake. Cool on a wire rack.

Makes 10–12 servings

Wild Berry Shortcake

A slice of chocolate pound cake forms the base for a wild summer treat.

1 cup small fresh strawberries
1 cup fresh raspberries
1 cup fresh blackberries
1 cup fresh blueberries
6 tablespoons superfine sugar, divided
2 tablespoons wild berry liqueur
2 cups heavy cream, chilled
Chocolate Pound Cake (page 200)
$^1/_4$ cup powdered sugar, sifted

1.   Combine all the berries in a bowl; sprinkle with 2 tablespoons of the sugar and the liqueur. Gently mix, cover, and refrigerate for 1 hour.

2.   Whip the cream, using an electric mixer on a high speed, until soft peaks form. Sprinkle in 4 tablespoons of sugar and continue beating until stiff peaks begin to form.

3.   Divide the pound cake into 8 slices. Drizzle a little of the berry syrup over each slice and top with a pillow of whipped cream and a scoop of berries. Sprinkle with powdered sugar and serve.

Makes 8 generous servings

Chocolate Gifts for Antique Lovers

Original chocolatières, or chocolate pots, were made of copper, tin, pewter, or ceramic. The wide base allowed the pot to be placed on a stand over a heat source. A spout and wooden handle were provided to make pouring easier. And a hole was fashioned in the lid to hold the stirring stick or whisk.

As the popularity of chocolate grew, pots were fashioned in fine porcelain, silver, or gold, with matching cups and saucers. Artists competed for royal favor, designing the most elaborate set for Madame de Pompadour during the reign of Louis XV (and the most erotic for Madame DuBarry).

Cheesecakes

Chocolate Chip Cheesecake

We've added miniature chocolate chips to this New York-style cheesecake.

Crust:
1¹/₂ cups chocolate cookie crumbs
6 tablespoons butter, melted

Cheesecake:
3 pounds cream cheese, warmed to room temperature
1¹/₂ cups sugar
2 teaspoons pure vanilla extract
¹/₂ teaspoon pure almond extract
3 eggs, warmed to room temperature
2 egg yolks, warmed to room temperature
1 tablespoon lemon juice
1 cup miniature chocolate chips

1. Preheat the oven to 375°F. Line the bottom of a 10-inch springform pan with parchment paper.

2. To make the crust: Mix together the cookie crumbs and melted butter. Press into the bottom and up the sides of the pan. Bake for 15 minutes. Cool on a wire rack.

3. To make the cheesecake: Reduce the oven temperature to 300°F. Place a pan of water on the bottom rack of the oven, to help keep the cheesecake moist while baking.

4. Cream together the cream cheese, sugar, vanilla, and almond extract, using an electric mixer on a medium speed, until fluffy.

5. Adjust your mixer to a low speed and add the eggs, egg yolks, and lemon juice, beating until smooth. Adjust your mixer to a medium-high speed and beat for 1 more minute. Fold in the chocolate chips.

6. Pour into the prepared pan and bake on the center rack (over the pan of water) for 1 hour. Reduce the oven temperature to 250°F and bake for another hour. Turn the oven off and leave the cheesecake in the oven for 1 more hour. Remove from the oven and cool in the pan on a wire rack. When cool, cover and refrigerate overnight.

Makes 10–12 servings

Chocolate Cheesecake

Smooth and creamy, sweet and tart, and most importantly, chocolate—this is a marriage made in heaven for chocolate lovers and cheesecake lovers.

Crust:
1 cup graham cracker crumbs
¹/₂ cup pecans, toasted and finely chopped
6 tablespoons butter, melted

Cheesecake:
6 ounces bittersweet chocolate, finely chopped
2³/₄ pounds cream cheese, warmed to room temperature
¹/₂ cup heavy cream, warmed to room temperature
1¹/₂ cups sugar
2 teaspoons pure vanilla extract
5 eggs, warmed to room temperature
2 tablespoons alkalized cocoa powder

1. Preheat the oven to 375°F. Line the bottom of a 10-inch springform pan with parchment paper.

2. To make the crust: Mix together the graham cracker crumbs, pecans, and melted butter. Press into the bottom and up the sides of the pan. Bake for 15 minutes. Cool on a wire rack.

3. To make the cheesecake: Reduce the oven temperature to 300°F. Place a pan of water on the bottom rack of your oven to help keep the cheesecake moist while baking.

4. Melt the chocolate in the top of a double boiler over hot, not simmering, water, stirring continuously. Set aside to cool to room temperature.

5. Cream together the cream cheese, cream, sugar, and vanilla, using an electric mixer on a medium speed, until fluffy.

6. Adjust your mixer to a low speed and add the eggs, beating until smooth. Adjust your mixer to a medium-high speed and beat for 1 more minute. Fold in the melted chocolate.

7. Pour into the prepared pan and bake, on the center rack (over the pan of water) for 1 hour. Reduce the oven temperature to 250°F and bake for another hour. Turn the oven off and leave the cheesecake in the oven for 1 more hour. Remove from the oven and cool in the pan on a wire rack. Before serving, dust with cocoa powder.

Makes 10–12 servings

Good as Gold

European explorers were surprised to find that the Aztecs valued chocolate more than gold and used the small dark beans as currency. One or two beans would buy a simple meal, four beans a small animal, and one hundred beans a slave; for a mere ten beans, you could buy a night of pleasure.

Enterprising Aztec hucksters created one of the first forms of counterfeit currency by cracking the beans open and replacing the rich coveted nibs with dirt.

White Chocolate Cheesecake

Although this looks like a traditional cheesecake, it's sweeter and richer, thanks to lots of white chocolate.

Crust:
1¹/₂ cups vanilla cookie crumbs
6 tablespoons butter, melted

Cheesecake:
12 ounces white chocolate, finely chopped
2 pounds cream cheese, warmed to room temperature
¹/₄ cup heavy cream, warmed to room temperature
¹/₂ cup sour cream, warmed to room temperature
¹/₂ cup sugar
2 teaspoons pure vanilla extract
4 eggs, warmed to room temperature
2 cups white chocolate curls

1. Preheat the oven to 375°F. Line the bottom of a 10-inch springform pan with parchment paper.

2. To make the crust: Mix together the cookie crumbs and melted butter. Press into the bottom and up the sides of the pan. Bake for 15 minutes. Cool on a wire rack.

3. To make the cheesecake: Reduce the oven temperature to 300°F. Place a pan of water on the bottom rack of your oven to help keep the cheesecake moist while baking.

4. Melt the chocolate in the top of a double boiler over hot, not simmering, water, stirring continuously. Set aside to cool to room temperature.

5. Cream together the cream cheese, cream, sour cream, sugar, and vanilla, using an electric mixer on a medium speed, until fluffy.

6. Adjust your mixer to a low speed and add the eggs, beating until smooth. Adjust your mixer to a medium-high speed and beat for 1 more minute. Fold in the melted chocolate.

7. Pour into the prepared pan and bake on the center rack (over the pan of water) for 1 hour. Reduce the oven temperature to 250°F and bake for another hour. Turn the oven off and leave the cheesecake in the oven for 1 more hour. Remove from the oven and cool in the pan on a wire rack. Before serving, top with chocolate curls.

Makes 10–12 servings

Layer Cakes

Chocolate Sponge Cake

Use this versatile chocolate cake for ice cream rolls, custard or cream roulades, bombes, or layer cakes you want to soak with flavorings, liquors, or liqueurs.

³/₄ cup cake flour
¹/₄ cup nonalkalized cocoa powder
1 teaspoon baking powder
1 cup superfine sugar, divided
¹/₄ cup milk
2 tablespoons butter, cut into ¹/₄-inch cubes
3 eggs, warmed to room temperature
3 egg yolks, warmed to room temperature

1. Preheat the oven to 350°F. Line the bottom of an 8-inch or 9-inch layer cake pan with parchment paper. Or preheat the oven to 400°F, and line the bottom of an 11-inch by 17-inch or 12-inch by 16-inch sheet cake or jellyroll pan with parchment paper.

2. Sift together the flour, cocoa powder, baking powder, and 1/4 cup of the sugar. Set aside.

3. Warm the milk and butter in a heavy-bottomed saucepan, over low heat, stirring occasionally. Do not allow the mixture to simmer.

4. Whisk together the eggs, yolks, and remaining sugar in a bowl that can be used as the top of a double boiler. Place over simmering water and continue to whisk until warm. Remove from heat and whip, using an electric mixer on a high speed, until it cools and soft peaks form.

5. Gently fold in the flour mixture, a little at a time, until lightly blended. Add the hot milk mixture, folding until thoroughly blended.

6. Pour into the prepared pans and bake for 25 to 30 minutes if using a layer cake pan, or for 10 to 12 minutes if using a sheet cake or jellyroll pan. When done, the cake should spring back when lightly touched. Cool on wire racks.

Number of servings depends on how you use this cake.

Creating Even Layers for Your Cake

The first step in creating a beautiful layer cake is to cut even layers. Here's a trick that makes it easy and foolproof.

1. Remove the cake from the pan and refrigerate for 30 minutes. Then, place the cake on a flat work surface.
2. To make the top of the layer flat, shave off the top.
3. To create even layers, use a ruler to measure the height of the cake. Divide the height by the number of layers you want. For example, if the cake is 3 inches high, and you want a two-layer cake, your layers will each be 1 1/2 inches high.
4. Measuring from the bottom of the cake up, insert toothpicks around the side of the cake to mark each layer.
5. Using a serrated knife, gently slice halfway through the cake horizontally, just above the top layer of toothpicks.
6. Turn the cake a quarter turn and continue slicing. Repeat, turning and slicing, until each layer is evenly sliced.
7. Lay the layers on a flat surface, and use a dry, soft pastry brush to dust off any crumbs.

Filling and Frosting Your Cake

This is the fun part, especially when it comes time to lick the bowl.

1. Refrigerate your cake layers for 30 minutes.
2. Remove from the refrigerator and center your first layer on a cardboard cake round that is larger than the circumference of your cake.
3. Spread a layer of filling or frosting evenly over the top of the layer. Be sure to extend the filling or frosting to the edges of the layer.
4. If making a two-layer cake, place the second layer on top, and press down gently, leveling the cake. If making a three- or four-layer cake, repeat Step 3, adding the additional layers.
5. Using a spatula, remove any excess frosting from the sides of the cake. Refrigerate until the filling or frosting is set.
6. Remove from the refrigerator and dust any crumbs off the sides and top of the cake.
7. Using a metal spatula, spread a thin layer of filling or frosting on the top and sides of the cake. This will lock down any remaining crumbs and give you a smoother finish. Refrigerate until set.
8. Remove from the refrigerator and spread a generous layer of frosting on the top and sides of the cake. Refrigerate until set.
9. Remove the cake from the refrigerator and place the cake next to your serving plate. Slide a thin metal spatula or knife between the cake and the cardboard cake round. Slide a wide metal spatula (or two) under the cake. Lift and transfer the cake to the plate.

Devil's Food Layer Cake

This traditional chocolate layer cake got its name from the slight red hue cast by the cocoa powder, and its sinfully delicious flavor.

2¼ cups cake flour
1 cup nonalkalized cocoa powder
1 teaspoon baking powder
1 teaspoon baking soda
½ teaspoon salt
1 cup butter, softened
2 cups light brown sugar, firmly packed
2 teaspoons pure vanilla extract
3 eggs, warmed to room temperature
½ cup milk, warmed to room temperature
1 cup water, boiling

1. Preheat the oven to 350°F. Line the bottom of two 9-inch layer cake pans with parchment paper. Lightly coat the sides of the pans with butter and flour.
2. Sift together the flour, cocoa powder, baking powder, baking soda, and salt. Set aside.
3. Cream together the butter and brown sugar, using an electric mixer on a medium-high speed, until light and fluffy. Add the vanilla. Adjust your mixer to a medium speed and add the eggs, one at a time, beating until thoroughly blended.
4. Adjust your mixer to a low speed and alternate blending in the flour mixture and milk until lightly blended. Mix in the hot water just until smooth. The batter will be thin.

5. Pour into the prepared pans and bake for 30 to 40 minutes, or until a toothpick comes out clean when inserted in the center of the cake. Cool on wire racks.

Makes 10–12 servings

Buttermilk Layer Cake

This is a light chocolate layer cake that will allow your filling and frosting to be the star of the show. It's also a good choice to follow a rich meal.

4 ounces unsweetened chocolate, finely chopped
2 cups cake flour
1 teaspoon baking powder
1 teaspoon baking soda
¼ teaspoon salt
1 cup butter, softened
2 cups sugar
1 teaspoon pure vanilla extract
3 eggs, warmed to room temperature
1 cup buttermilk, warmed to room temperature

1. Preheat the oven to 350°F. Line the bottom of two 9-inch layer cake pans with parchment paper. Lightly coat the sides of the pans with butter and flour.
2. Melt the chocolate in the top of a double boiler over hot, not simmering, water, stirring continuously. Set aside to cool to room temperature.
3. Sift together the flour, baking powder, baking soda, and salt. Set aside.

(continued)

4.   Cream together the butter and sugar, using an electric mixer on a medium-high speed, until light and fluffy. Add the vanilla. Adjust your mixer to a medium speed and add the eggs, one at a time, beating until thoroughly blended.

5.   Adjust your mixer to a low speed and blend in the melted chocolate. Alternate blending in the flour mixture and buttermilk until lightly blended.

6.   Pour into the prepared pans and bake for 30 to 40 minutes, or until a toothpick comes out clean when inserted in the center of the cake. Cool on wire racks.

Makes 10–12 servings

Sour Cream Layer Cake

Slightly richer than a buttermilk cake, these chocolate layers will hold their own when partnered with strong-willed fillings and frostings.

> 4 ounces unsweetened chocolate, finely chopped
> 1/2 cup milk, warmed to room temperature
> 1 cup sour cream, warmed to room temperature
> 1 3/4 cups cake flour
> 1 teaspoon baking powder
> 1 teaspoon baking soda
> 1/4 teaspoon salt
> 3/4 cup butter, softened
> 1 3/4 cups sugar
> 1 teaspoon pure vanilla extract
> 3 eggs, warmed to room temperature

1.   Preheat the oven to 350°F. Line the bottom of two 9-inch layer cake pans with parchment paper. Lightly coat the sides of the pans with butter and flour.

2.   Melt the chocolate and milk in the top of a double boiler over hot, not simmering, water, stirring continuously. Cool to room temperature. Stir in the sour cream. Set aside.

3.   Sift together the flour, baking powder, baking soda, and salt. Set aside.

4.   Cream together the butter and sugar, using an electric mixer on a medium-high speed, until light and fluffy. Add the vanilla. Adjust your mixer to a medium speed and add the eggs, one at a time, beating until thoroughly blended.

5.   Adjust your mixer to a low speed and blend in the chocolate mixture. Slowly fold in the flour until lightly blended.

6.   Pour into the prepared pans and bake for 30 to 40 minutes, or until a toothpick comes out clean when inserted in the center of the cake. Cool on wire racks.

Makes 10–12 servings

Bittersweet Velvet Layer Cake

This is the ultimate layer cake for true connoisseurs—rich, elegant, and intensely chocolate.

> 6 ounces bittersweet chocolate, finely chopped
> 1/2 cup heavy cream, warmed to room temperature

1 cup mascarpone cheese, warmed to
    room temperature
1¹/₂ cups cake flour
¹/₄ cup nonalkalized cocoa powder
¹/₄ cup instant espresso powder
1 teaspoon baking powder
1 teaspoon baking soda
¹/₄ teaspoon salt
³/₄ cup butter, softened
1¹/₂ cups sugar
1 teaspoon pure vanilla extract
3 eggs, warmed to room temperature

1. Preheat the oven to 350°F. Line the bottom of two 9-inch layer cake pans with parchment paper. Lightly coat the sides of the pans with butter and flour.

2. Melt the chocolate and cream in the top of a double boiler over hot, not simmering, water, stirring continuously. Cool to room temperature. Stir in the mascarpone cheese. Set aside.

3. Sift together the flour, cocoa powder, espresso powder, baking powder, baking soda, and salt. Set aside.

4. Cream together the butter and sugar, using an electric mixer on a medium-high speed, until light and fluffy. Add the vanilla. Adjust your mixer to a medium speed and add the eggs, one at a time, beating until thoroughly blended.

5. Adjust your mixer to a low speed and blend in the chocolate mixture. Slowly fold in the flour until lightly blended.

(continued)

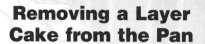

Removing a Layer Cake from the Pan

Here are a few tips for getting a cake out of a pan easily.

1. Before baking, line the bottom of the pan with parchment paper, and lightly coat the sides of the pan with butter and flour.
2. Cool the cake in the pan on a wire rack.
3. Slide a metal spatula or thin-bladed knife between the sides of the cake and pan.
4. Place a plate or cardboard round over the pan and invert the cake.
5. If you've used a springform pan, release the sides. If you've used a layer cake pan, gently tap the pan on the counter to release.

6. Pour into the prepared pans and bake for 30 to 40 minutes, or until a toothpick comes out clean when inserted in the center of the cake. Cool on wire racks.

Makes 10–12 servings

Chocolate-Chocolate Chip Layer Cake

Not only do you get a delicious chocolate layer cake, you get chocolate chips! This makes an extra special birthday cake for little ones.

> 4 ounces unsweetened chocolate, finely chopped
> $1/2$ cup cream, warmed to room temperature
> 2 cups cake flour
> 1 teaspoon baking soda
> $1/4$ teaspoon salt
> $1/2$ cup butter, softened
> $1^3/4$ cups sugar
> 1 teaspoon pure vanilla extract
> 3 eggs, warmed to room temperature
> $2/3$ cup milk, warmed to room temperature
> 1 cup miniature chocolate chips

1. Preheat the oven to 350°F. Line the bottom of two 9-inch layer cake pans with parchment paper. Lightly coat the sides of the pans with butter and flour.

2. Melt the chocolate and cream in the top of a double boiler over hot, not simmering, water, stirring continuously. Set aside to cool to room temperature.

3. Sift together the flour, baking soda, and salt. Set aside.

4. Cream together the butter and sugar, using an electric mixer on a medium-high speed, until light and fluffy. Add the vanilla. Adjust your mixer to a medium speed and add the eggs, one at a time, beating until thoroughly blended.

5. Adjust your mixer to a low speed and blend in the chocolate mixture. Alternate folding in the flour mixture and milk until lightly blended. Gently fold in the chocolate chips.

6. Pour into the prepared pans and bake for 25 to 30 minutes, or until a toothpick comes out clean when inserted in the center of the cake. Cool on wire racks.

Makes 10–12 servings

Marbled Layer Cake

Chocolate and vanilla cake batters swirl together in this elegant layer cake.

> 3 cups cake flour, divided
> 2 teaspoons baking powder, divided
> 1 teaspoon baking soda, divided
> $1/4$ teaspoon salt. divided
> $1/2$ cup nonalkalized cocoa powder
> 1 cup butter, softened
> 2 cups sugar
> 2 teaspoons pure vanilla extract
> 6 eggs, warmed to room temperature

1. Preheat the oven to 375°F. Line the bottom of three 9-inch layer cake pans with parchment paper. Lightly coat the sides of the pans with butter and flour.

2. Sift together 1½ cups flour, 1 teaspoon baking powder, ½ teaspoon baking soda, and ⅛ teaspoon salt. Set aside. In a separate bowl, sift together the remaining flour, baking powder, baking soda, salt, and cocoa powder. Set aside.

3. Cream together the butter and sugar, using an electric mixer on a medium-high speed, until light and fluffy. Add the vanilla. Adjust your mixer to a medium speed and add the eggs, one at a time, beating until thoroughly blended.

4. Divide the egg batter into 2 bowls. Fold the plain flour mixture into one. Fold the cocoa powder mixture into the other.

5. Pour slightly more than a third of the chocolate batter into 2 of the prepared pans. Pour slightly more than a third of the vanilla batter into the third pan. Randomly spoon the remaining chocolate batter onto the vanilla batter. Divide the remaining vanilla batter in half, and randomly spoon onto the chocolate batter. Gently swirl the batters together using the tip of a knife. Bake for 15 to 20 minutes, or until a toothpick comes out clean when inserted in the center of the cake. Cool on wire racks.

Makes 10–12 servings

White Chocolate Layer Cake

This is a light, white chocolate layer cake to complement your favorite fillings and frostings.

> 4 ounces white chocolate, finely chopped
> ½ cup heavy cream, warmed to room temperature
> ½ cup milk, warmed to room temperature
> 2 cups cake flour
> 1 teaspoon baking powder
> 1 teaspoon baking soda
> ¼ teaspoon salt
> ½ cup butter, softened
> ¾ cup sugar
> 1 teaspoon pure vanilla extract
> 3 eggs, warmed to room temperature

1. Preheat the oven to 350°F. Line the bottom of two 9-inch layer cake pans with parchment paper. Lightly coat the sides of the pans with butter and flour.

2. Melt the chocolate, cream, and milk in the top of a double boiler over hot, not simmering, water, stirring continuously. Set aside to cool to room temperature.

3. Sift together the flour, baking powder, baking soda, and salt. Set aside.

4. Cream together the butter and sugar, using an electric mixer on a medium-high speed, until light and fluffy. Add the vanilla. Adjust your mixer to a medium speed and add the eggs, one at a time, beating until thoroughly blended.

(continued)

5.   Adjust your mixer to a low speed and blend in the chocolate mixture. Slowly fold in the flour until lightly blended.

6.   Pour into the prepared pans and bake for 20 to 25 minutes, or until a toothpick comes out clean when inserted in the center of the cake. Cool on wire racks.

Makes 10–12 servings

Tiramisu

Traditionally, this immensely popular Italian dessert is made with layers of coffee and rum-flavored ladyfingers and mascarpone cream. For chocolate lovers, we use chocolate ladyfingers. And for an elegant graduation party at Stanford University, we prepared tiramisu in individual chocolate dessert cups.

>   *1 cup strong, hot brewed coffee*
>   *$1/4$ cup superfine sugar*
>   *2 tablespoons dark rum*
>   *2 tablespoons Kahlua*
>   *24 Chocolate Ladyfingers (page 200)*
>   *Easy Tiramisu Filling (page 226) or*
>   *Traditional Tiramisu Filling (page 227)*
>   *1 cup milk chocolate curls*

1.   Combine the coffee, sugar, rum, and Kahlua, stirring until the sugar is dissolved. Set aside to cool.

2.   Place 12 ladyfingers side by side, in the bottom of a 6-inch by 12-inch by 3-inch serving dish, and drizzle with half of the coffee mixture.

3.   Cover with half of the Tiramisu filling. Repeat, using the remaining ladyfingers and filling.

4.   Top with chocolate curls.

Makes 6–8 servings

Royal Ricotta Roulade

A chocolate sponge cake is painted with brandy syrup, stuffed with ricotta cheese and hazelnuts, and dusted with sugar and cocoa powder.

>   *Chocolate Sponge Cake (page 204)*
>   *2 tablespoons superfine sugar*
>   *$1/4$ cup water*
>   *2 tablespoons brandy*
>   *Royal Ricotta Filling (page 229)*
>   *2 tablespoons powdered sugar*
>   *1 tablespoon alkalized cocoa powder*

1.   Bake the Chocolate Sponge Cake in an 11-inch by 17-inch or 12-inch by 16-inch jellyroll pan.

2.   Simmer the sugar and water in a heavy-bottomed saucepan over low heat for 1 minute. Remove from heat and stir in the brandy. Set aside to cool.

3.   Using a pastry brush, paint the top of the sponge cake with the brandy syrup. Spread the Royal Ricotta Filling evenly over the top.

4.   Beginning at one of the narrow ends, gently roll the cake into a log shape. Slice off the ragged ends of the roulade and place, seam side down, on a serving dish.

5. Sift the powdered sugar, and then the cocoa powder over the top.

Makes 8–10 servings

Dante's Temptation

Who could resist this dark chocolate layer cake, slathered with dark chocolate frosting? Dante's hoping you can't! Once you taste its fiery frosting, you'll be back for more . . . and more . . .

>*Cream Cheese Frosting (page 232)*
>*Devil's Food Layer Cake (page 207)*
>*2 tablespoons cinnamon liqueur*
>*2 tablespoons tiny cinnamon candy hearts*

1. While making the frosting, add the cinnamon liqueur to the melted, cooled chocolate before adding the chocolate to the cream cheese mixture.
2. Fill and frost the layers of devil's food cake, creating lavish swirls, and randomly sprinkle the cinnamon hearts on top.

Makes 8–10 servings

Mocha Dream

In this European-style rectangular layer cake, coffee-flavored buttercream covers layers of light chocolate cake and rich chocolate cream.

>*Buttermilk Layer Cake (page 205)*
>*1/2 recipe Chocolate Ganache (page 225)*
>*Mocha Buttercream (page 230)*
>*18–20 mocha beans*

1. Bake the cake in an 11-inch by 17-inch half sheet pan, reducing the baking time by 5 to 10 minutes. When cool, slice into thirds, creating three 11-inch by 5 1/2-inch layers.
2. Fill with the Chocolate Ganache and frost with Mocha Buttercream. Place the remaining buttercream in a pastry bag fitted with a 1/2-inch star tip. Pipe lines, criss-crossing diagonally, across the top of the cake. Pipe a finishing line around the outside edge of the top of the cake. Place mocha beans in the crosshatch spaces.

Makes 10–12 servings

German Chocolate Cake

In addition to the traditional sweet coconut-walnut topping, we coat the sides of this cake with a milk chocolate frosting and milk chocolate chips, and top it with sparkling caramelized walnuts.

>*Sour Cream Layer Cake (page 208)*
>*German Chocolate Filling (page 229)*
>*1/2 recipe Sour Cream Frosting (page 232)*
>*1 1/2 cups milk chocolate chips*

Caramelized Walnuts:
1/4 cup sugar
2 tablespoons water
10–12 walnut halves

1. Bake the cake in two 8-inch layer cake pans, increasing the baking time by 5 to 10 minutes. When cool, slice each layer in half horizontally, creating four 8-inch layers.

(continued)

2. Spread a quarter of the German Chocolate Filling on top of one layer. Place another layer on top and spread with another quarter of the filling. Repeat until all layers are stacked and topped with filling.

3. Frost the sides of the cake with the Sour Cream Frosting, reserving some frosting, and gently press the chocolate chips into the frosting.

4. To make the caramelized walnuts: Combine the sugar and water in a small, heavy-bottomed saucepan. Cover and simmer for 2 to 3 minutes, over a medium heat. Remove the cover and continue simmering, without stirring, until the sugar turns an amber color. Remove from heat, dip the walnut halves, and place them on waxed paper to cool.

5. Place the remaining frosting in a pastry bag fitted with a ¹/₂-inch star tip, and pipe a decorative edging, wider than a walnut half, around the top rim of the cake. Place the walnut halves, evenly spaced, in the frosting.

Makes 10–12 servings

Crimson Velvet

For those very special occasions, this cake offers a hint of raspberry, and a touch of mocha, in a cloak of luxurious dark chocolate.

Bittersweet Velvet Layer Cake (page 208)
³/₄ cup raspberry preserves
2 tablespoons water
1 tablespoon raspberry liqueur

Mocha Ganache (page 226)
Dark Chocolate Coating (page 233)
1 cup bittersweet chocolate curls
12 fresh raspberries
2–3 tablespoons superfine sugar

1. Bake the cake in three 9-inch layer cake pans, reducing the baking time by 5 to 10 minutes. Set aside to cool.

2. Heat the raspberry preserves with the water in a heavy-bottomed saucepan over low heat, stirring continuously, until warm and smooth. Press the warm raspberry glaze through a strainer. Blend in the liqueur and, using a pastry brush, lightly paint the top of each cooled layer.

3. Fill and frost the cake with the Mocha Ganache. Refrigerate for 1 hour.

4. Cover the cake with the Dark Chocolate Coating.

5. Sprinkle the bittersweet chocolate curls on top of the cake.

6. Just before serving, coat the fresh raspberries with superfine sugar and scatter throughout the chocolate curls.

Makes 10–12 servings

Chocolate Chip Blizzard Cake

Miniature chocolate chips star in this cake- from top to bottom—which makes it a favorite for children of all ages.

Chocolate Chip Layer Cake (page 210)
Buttercream Frosting (page 229)
1 cup miniature chocolate chips

1. Bake the cake in three 8-inch layer cake pans, reducing the baking time by 5 to 10 minutes.

2. Fold the chocolate chips into the Buttercream Frosting. Fill and frost the cake.

Makes 10–12 servings

Strawberry Swirl Cake

Fresh strawberries snuggle into rich custard between, and on top of, layers of chocolate and vanilla cake. Strawberry shortcake was never this elegant or delicious!

Marbled Layer Cake (page 210)
4 cups fresh strawberries
Classic Custard Filling (page 228)
¹/₂ recipe Chocolate Buttercream (page 230)
1¹/₂ cups almonds, sliced and toasted

Glaze:
¹/₄ cup apricot preserves
2 tablespoons amaretto
1 tablespoon superfine sugar

1. Bake the cake in two 9-inch layer cake pans, increasing the baking time by 5 to 10 minutes.

2. Set aside 1 large whole strawberry. Wash, hull, and slice the remaining strawberries. Set aside.

3. Spread a quarter of the custard filling on one of the cake layers. Top with half of the strawberries. Cover with a quarter of the custard filling.

4. Place the other cake layer on top of the custard. Spread the remaining custard on top.

5. Frost the sides of the cake with the Chocolate Buttercream. Place the remaining buttercream in a pastry bag fitted with a star tip, and pipe swirls on top of the custard, around the outside rim of the cake.

6. To make the glaze: Combine the apricot preserves, amaretto, and sugar in a heavy-bottomed saucepan. Bring to a simmer over a medium heat, stirring continuously. Remove from the heat and set aside to cool.

(continued)

Decorating Party

For Valentine's Day, or any holiday, pour plain round, square, or heart-shaped chocolate boxes, and invite friends over to decorate them! Much like cakes, a contrasting color of chocolate can be piped on with decorating tips, or decorations can be "glued" on with a dab of warm chocolate.

7.   Arrange the remaining strawberries in a circle, side-by-side, inside the chocolate edging, with the tip sides toward the center of the cake. Arrange another circle, slightly overlapping the first. Continue to the center of the cake.

8.   Using a pastry brush, coat the strawberries with the preserves. Pipe a swirl of frosting in the center and top with a whole strawberry, tip side up. Press the sliced almonds into the side of the cake.

Makes 10–12 servings

Black Forest Cake

Cherries float in Chocolate Chantilly between layers of white chocolate cake, in this reverse variation of a classic.

> *White Chocolate Layer Cake (page 211)*
> *2 tablespoons superfine sugar*
> *1/4 cup water*
> *2 tablespoons kirsch*
> *1 1/2 cups dark, sweet cherries*
> *Chocolate Chantilly (page 224)*
> *1/2 cup white chocolate leaves*
> *6 ounces grated white chocolate*

1.   Bake the cake in two 8-inch layer cake pans, increasing the baking time by 5 to 10 minutes. Set aside to cool. Slice the layers horizontally, creating four layers.

2.   Simmer the sugar and water in a heavy-bottomed saucepan over low heat for 1 minute. Remove from heat and stir in the kirsch. Set aside to cool.

3.   Drain the cherries. Set 10 to 12 whole cherries aside. Slice the remaining cherries in half. Set aside.

4.   Using a pastry brush, lightly paint the top of each layer of cake with the kirsch syrup. Top one of the cake layers with a thin layer of Chocolate Chantilly and a third of the sliced cherries. Spread another thin layer of Chocolate Chantilly over the cherries. Repeat, adding two more layers.

5.   Add the fourth cake layer and frost the top and sides of the cake with Chocolate Chantilly. Place the remaining Chocolate Chantilly into a pastry bag fitted with a star tip, and pipe 10 to 12 large swirls around the outside edge of the cake. Top each swirl with a whole cherry. Arrange the chocolate leaves in the center of the cake, and gently press the grated chocolate into the side of the cake.

Makes 10–12 servings

Tortes

Cocoa Channel Torte

The beauty of this torte is in the simplicity of its design. We accessorize it just as simply, with Crème Mystique or a dollop of Chocolate Chantilly.

> *12 ounces semisweet chocolate, finely chopped*
> *1/2 cup butter, cut into 1/4-inch cubes*
> *4 eggs, warmed to room temperature*

1 tablespoon sugar

1 tablespoon flour

¼ cup alkalized Chocolate cocoa powder

1. Preheat the oven to 425°F. Line the bottom of an 8-inch springform pan with parchment paper.

2. Melt the chocolate and butter in the top of a double boiler over hot, not simmering, water, stirring continuously. Set aside to cool to room temperature.

3. Beat together the eggs and sugar, using an electric mixer on a high speed, until the eggs have tripled in volume. Adjust your mixer to a low speed and add the flour, mixing until lightly blended.

4. Fold a third of the egg mixture into the cooled chocolate mixture. Repeat until all the egg mixture is incorporated, being careful not to deflate the batter.

5. Pour into the prepared pan and bake for 15 minutes. Cool in the pan on a wire rack. The center will fall slightly as it cools.

6. Before serving, cut 6 strips of paper, 1 inch wide by 10 inches long. Place the strips on top of the torte in a random lattice pattern. Sift the cocoa powder over the torte, then carefully remove the strips of paper. Serve with Crème Mystique (page 224), or a dollop of Chocolate Chantilly (page 224).

Makes 10–12 servings

Leveling Your Torte

Most tortes bake or cool unevenly, with the sides higher than the center. Since, by design, they are denser than cakes, you can press a torte to make it level, rather than shaving what could be a significant amount off the top.

1. While still in the pan, gently press down the sides of the torte until they are level with the center.
2. Slide a thin-bladed knife between the sides of the torte and pan.
3. Place a plate or cardboard round over the pan and invert the torte.
4. If the torte is still not perfectly level, center the bottom of the pan on the top of the torte and press down gently.

THE EVERYTHING CHOCOLATE COOKBOOK

Angel Torte

This chocolate torte is slightly lighter than most, but just as delicious. As this torte cools, it will crack and collapse, creating a delicate, artful appearance.

> 4 ounces semisweet chocolate, finely chopped
>
> 2 tablespoons butter, cut into $^1/_4$-inch cubes
>
> $^1/_2$ cup brewed coffee
>
> $^1/_2$ cup alkalized cocoa powder
>
> 2 egg yolks, warmed to room temperature
>
> $^3/_4$ cup superfine sugar, divided
>
> 1 tablespoon butterscotch liqueur
>
> $^3/_4$ cup ground walnuts
>
> 3 tablespoons cake flour
>
> 4 egg whites, warmed to room temperature
>
> $^1/_8$ teaspoon cream of tartar
>
> 2 tablespoons powdered sugar

1. Preheat the oven to 350°F. Line the bottom of an 8-inch springform pan with parchment paper.

2. Melt the chocolate, butter, and coffee in the top of a double boiler over hot, not simmering, water, stirring continuously. Stir in the cocoa powder. Set aside to cool to room temperature.

3. Whisk together the egg yolks and $^1/_2$ cup of the sugar until thick. Add the butterscotch liqueur, chocolate mixture, ground walnuts, and flour. Set aside.

4. Whip together the egg whites and cream of tartar, using an electric mixer on a high speed, until soft peaks form. Sprinkle in the remaining sugar, beating until stiff peaks form.

5. Gently fold a third of the egg whites into the chocolate mixture. Repeat until all the egg whites are incorporated.

6. Pour into the prepared pan and bake for 35 minutes, or until a toothpick comes out with moist crumbs when inserted in the center of the cake. Cool in the pan on a wire rack. The center will fall slightly as it cools. Before serving, dust with powdered sugar.

Makes 10–12 servings

Peanut Butter Oreo Torte

This torte is both elegant and fun. A rich chocolate torte is covered in Peanut Buttercream and topped with Oreo cookies and crumbs.

> 4 ounces semisweet chocolate, finely chopped
>
> $^1/_2$ cup butter, cut into $^1/_4$-inch cubes
>
> 1 teaspoon pure vanilla extract
>
> 6 egg yolks, warmed to room temperature
>
> 1 cup superfine sugar, divided
>
> $^3/_4$ cup flour
>
> 6 egg whites, warmed to room temperature
>
> $^1/_4$ teaspoon cream of tartar
>
> Peanut Buttercream (page 230)
>
> 6 Oreo cookies, cut in half
>
> $^3/_4$ cup Oreo cookie crumbs

1.   Preheat the oven to 350°F. Line the bottom of a 9-inch springform pan with parchment paper.

2.   Melt the chocolate and butter in the top of a double boiler over hot, not simmering, water, stirring continuously. Set aside to cool to room temperature. Blend in the vanilla extract. Set aside.

3.   Whisk together the egg yolks and $1/3$ cup of the sugar until thick. Add the chocolate mixture and flour. Set aside.

4.   Whip together the egg whites and cream of tartar, using an electric mixer on a high speed, until soft peaks form. Sprinkle in the remaining sugar, beating until stiff peaks form.

5.   Gently fold a third of the egg whites into the chocolate mixture. Repeat until all the egg whites are incorporated.

6.   Pour into the prepared pan and bake for 45 minutes, or until a toothpick comes out with moist crumbs when inserted in the center of the cake. Cool in the pan on a wire rack. The center will fall slightly as it cools. When cool, cover and refrigerate overnight.

7.   Level the torte. Frost and decorate the torte with Peanut Buttercream. Arrange the Oreo cookie halves, cut side down, in a circle in the center of the torte. Gently press Oreo cookie crumbs into the side of the torte, and sprinkle any remaining crumbs on the top.

Makes 10–12 servings

Sienna Gold

If you like the world-renowned sacher torte, you'll love this variation. We've added ground hazelnuts to the chocolate torte, coated the sides with bits of honeycomb, and topped it with chocolate-coated apricots.

>   6 ounces semisweet chocolate, finely
>   chopped
> $3/4$ cup butter, cut into $1/4$-inch cubes
>   2 tablespoons praline liqueur
>   4 egg yolks, warmed to room temperature
> $3/4$ cup superfine sugar, divided
>   1 cup ground hazelnuts
>   2 tablespoons flour
>   4 egg whites, warmed to room tempera-
>   ture
> $1/8$ teaspoon cream of tartar
> $1/2$ cup apricot preserves
>   2 tablespoons water
>   1 cup dried apricots
>   4 ounces milk chocolate, tempered
>   Milk Chocolate Coating (page 233)
> $3/4$ cup crumbled honeycomb candy

1.   Preheat the oven to 350°F. Line the bottom of a 9-inch springform pan with parchment paper.

2.   Melt the chocolate and butter in the top of a double boiler over hot, not simmering, water, stirring continuously. Set aside to cool to room temperature. Blend in the liqueur. Set aside.

3.   Whisk together the egg yolks and $1/2$ cup of the sugar until thick. Add the

(continued)

chocolate mixture, ground hazelnuts, and flour. Set aside.

4.   Whip together the egg whites and cream of tartar, using an electric mixer on a high speed, until soft peaks form. Sprinkle in the remaining sugar, beating until stiff peaks form.

5.   Gently fold a third of the egg whites into the chocolate mixture. Repeat until all the egg whites are incorporated.

6.   Pour into the prepared pan and bake for 45 minutes, or until a toothpick comes out with moist crumbs when inserted in the center of the cake. Cool in the pan on a wire rack. The center will fall slightly as it

cools. When cool, cover and refrigerate overnight.

7.   Level the torte. Heat the apricot preserves with the water in a heavy-bottomed saucepan over low heat, stirring continuously, until warm and smooth. Press the warm apricot glaze through a strainer and, using a pastry brush, cover the top and sides of the torte. Set aside.

8.   Line a cookie sheet with waxed paper. Slice the dried apricots into $^1/_4$-inch strips. Dip the strips into the tempered chocolate and place on the waxed paper. (Don't try to straighten the strips; encourage them to crumple and curl.) Refrigerate for 5 minutes, or just until set. Set aside in a cool place.

9.   Cover the torte with Milk Chocolate Coating. Gently press the honeycomb into the side of the torte. Scatter the chocolate-coated apricot slices on the top of the torte.

Makes 10–12 servings

Café Noir Torte

If you love bittersweet chocolate, espresso, almonds, and Grand Marnier, this torte's for you.

> 6 ounces bittersweet chocolate, finely
>   chopped
> $^3/_4$ cup butter, cut into $^1/_4$-inch cubes
> 3 tablespoons Grand Marnier
> 3 tablespoons instant espresso powder
> 4 egg yolks, warmed to room temperature
> $^2/_3$ cup superfine sugar. divided

Level from the Start

Be sure to level your cake or torte batter after pouring it in the prepared baking pan. Spread the batter evenly with a spatula and gently tap the pan on a flat surface before putting it in the preheated oven. (Don't tap angel or chiffon cakes!)

¹/₂ cup ground almonds
¹/₄ cup flour
4 egg whites, warmed to room temperature
¹/₈ teaspoon cream of tartar
4 ounces almond paste
Dark Chocolate Coating (page 233)
³/₄ cup almonds, sliced and toasted
1 cup bittersweet chocolate curls

1.   Preheat the oven to 350°F. Line the bottom of a 9-inch springform pan with parchment paper.

2.   Melt the chocolate and butter in the top of a double boiler over hot, not simmering, water, stirring continuously. Set aside to cool to room temperature. Blend in the Grand Marnier and espresso powder. Set aside.

3.   Whisk together the egg yolks and ¹/₃ cup of the sugar until thick. Add the chocolate mixture, ground almonds, and flour. Set aside.

4.   Whip together the egg whites and cream of tartar, using an electric mixer on a high speed, until soft peaks form. Sprinkle in the remaining sugar, beating until stiff peaks form.

5.   Gently fold a third of the egg whites into the chocolate mixture. Repeat until all the egg whites are incorporated.

6.   Pour into the prepared pan and bake for 45 minutes, or until a toothpick comes out with moist crumbs when inserted in the center of the cake. Cool in the pan on a wire rack. The center will fall slightly as it cools. When cool, cover and refrigerate overnight.

7.   Level the torte. Place the almond paste between two sheets of waxed paper and, using a rolling pin, gently roll into a 9-inch circle. Place the almond paste on top of the torte and cover with Dark Chocolate Coating. Gently press the sliced almonds into the side of the torte and top with chocolate curls.

Makes 10–12 servings

Tuxedo Torte

This rich, dark chocolate pecan-based torte is topped with a white chocolate glaze and fresh strawberries dressed in chocolate tuxedos.

6 ounces semisweet chocolate, finely chopped
³/₄ cup butter, cut into ¹/₄-inch cubes
2 tablespoons Marc de Champagne
4 egg yolks, warmed to room temperature
³/₄ cup superfine sugar, divided
³/₄ cup ground pecans
3 tablespoons flour
4 egg whites, warmed to room temperature
¹/₈ teaspoon cream of tartar
White Chocolate Coating (page 233)
10–12 (same size) Tuxedo Strawberries (page 335)
¹/₂ cup white chocolate curls
³/₄ cup dark chocolate curls

1.   Preheat the oven to 350°F. Line the bottom of a 9-inch springform pan with parchment paper.

(continued)

2.   Melt the semisweet chocolate and butter in the top of a double boiler over hot, not simmering, water, stirring continuously. Set aside to cool to room temperature. Blend in the Marc de Champagne. Set aside.

3.   Whisk together the egg yolks and $^1/_2$ cup of the sugar until thick. Add the chocolate mixture, ground pecans, and flour. Set aside.

4.   Whip together the egg whites and cream of tartar, using an electric mixer on a high speed, until soft peaks form. Sprinkle in the remaining sugar, beating until stiff peaks form.

5.   Gently fold a third of the egg whites into the chocolate mixture. Repeat until all the egg whites are incorporated.

6.   Pour into the prepared pan and bake for 45 minutes, or until a toothpick comes out with moist crumbs when inserted in the center of the cake. Cool in the pan on a wire rack. The center will fall slightly as it cools. When cool, cover and refrigerate overnight.

7.   Level the torte and cover with White Chocolate Coating. Carefully slice the backs off the tuxedo strawberries and space them evenly around the outside edge of the top of the torte, with the cut side down and the tips pointed toward the center. Arrange the white chocolate curls in the center of the top of the torte. Gently press the dark chocolate curls into the side of the torte.

Makes 10–12 servings

Chocolate Truffle Torte

This world-class dessert is like no other. It is as rich and delicious as a chocolate truffle. Be sure to use your very favorite nibbling chocolate.

> *16 ounces bittersweet chocolate, finely chopped*
> *$^3/_4$ cup butter, cut into $^1/_4$-inch cubes*
> *6 egg yolks, warmed to room temperature*
> *1 tablespoon alkalized cocoa powder*
> *6 egg whites, warmed to room temperature*
> *$^1/_4$ teaspoon cream of tartar*
> *2 tablespoons superfine sugar*
> *Black and White Chantilly (page 225)*
> *Dark chocolate fans (optional) (page 333)*

1.   Preheat the oven to 425°F. Line the bottom of an 8-inch springform pan with parchment paper.

2.   Melt the chocolate and butter in the top of a double boiler over hot, not simmering, water, stirring continuously. Set aside to cool to room temperature. Whisk in the egg yolks and cocoa powder. Set aside.

3.   Whip together the egg whites and cream of tartar, using an electric mixer on a high speed, until soft peaks form. Sprinkle in the sugar, beating until stiff peaks form.

4.   Gently fold a third of the egg whites into the chocolate mixture. Repeat until all the egg whites are incorporated.

5.   Pour into the prepared pan and bake for 15 minutes. The torte should appear to be slightly undercooked. Cool in the pan on a wire rack. The center will fall slightly as it

cools. When cool, cover and refrigerate overnight.

6. Level the torte. Frost with Black and White Chantilly (page 225). Place the remaining chantilly in a pastry bag fitted with a star tip, and pipe large swirls or stars around the outside edge of the torte. Arrange the dark chocolate fans in the center.

Makes 10–12 servings

Fillings and Frostings

Grand Marnier Glaze

Curls of orange zest sparkle in this sweet glaze.

> ¹/₃ cup orange zest
> 1 cup water
> 6 tablespoons superfine sugar, divided
> ¹/₃ cup fresh-squeezed orange juice
> 3 tablespoons Grand Marnier
> 1 teaspoon pure vanilla extract

1. Bring the orange zest and water to a boil in a heavy-bottomed saucepan over medium heat. Boil for 3 minutes; remove from heat and drain.

2. Add 3 tablespoons of the sugar and the orange juice, and simmer over a low heat for 10 minutes.

3. Remove from heat and add the remaining sugar, Grand Marnier, and vanilla, stirring until smooth.

Makes enough to top a cake or torte

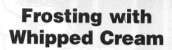

Frosting with Whipped Cream

Here are a few tips and tricks to help you when frosting with whipped or chantilly cream:

1. The heavy cream should be very cold before whipping. It also helps to chill the bowl and beaters.
2. Whip the cream just until stiff peaks *begin* to form; the whipped cream will continue to stiffen as you frost.
3. Use a cardboard round that is 1 inch larger than the circumference of your cake or torte.
4. Frost the sides at an angle, using the cardboard round as a guide, so the base is slightly wider than the top; this helps to support the weight of the cream.

Crème Mystique

The true mystique of this cream is that the flavor and consistency belies how easy it is to prepare. Use it in place of crème anglaise, or anytime you want to add an element of elegance to any chocolate dessert. This cream is also easy to customize by using a liqueur that will complement whatever it will be accompanying.

1 cup heavy cream, chilled
1–3 tablespoons superfine sugar
*1 teaspoon pure vanilla extract or 1 table-
   spoon liqueur*

1.   Whip the cream, sugar to taste, and vanilla or liqueur, using an electric mixer on a high speed, until the cream thickens but is still fluid (before soft peaks form).

Makes about 2 cups

Chocolate Chantilly

Chocolate whipped cream—quick and easy, and always popular.

¹/₂ cup alkalized cocoa powder
1 cup powdered sugar
2 cups heavy cream, chilled
1 teaspoon pure vanilla extract

1.   Sift together the cocoa powder and sugar. Set aside.
2.   Whip the cream (in a chilled bowl) using an electric mixer (with chilled beaters) on a high speed until soft peaks form. Sprinkle in the sugar mixture and vanilla, beating until stiff peaks just begin to form. Be careful not to overwhip.
3.   Fill and/or frost your cake or torte, or cover and refrigerate the chantilly.

Makes enough for a 9-inch layer cake or torte

Hot Slash

Here's the secret for slicing through delicate frostings and coatings without disturbing the smooth finish: Warm your knife under hot water, and dry it completely; then—slowly and gently—slice through the cake or torte. Let the warmth of the knife do the work.

Black and White Chantilly

Bits of dark chocolate are folded into sweetened whipped cream.

> 2 cups heavy cream, chilled
> $^1/_4$ cup superfine sugar
> 1 teaspoon pure vanilla extract
> $^1/_2$ cup bittersweet chocolate, grated

1. Whip the cream (in a chilled bowl) using an electric mixer (with chilled beaters) on a high speed until soft peaks form. Sprinkle in the sugar and vanilla, beating until stiff peaks just begin to form. Gently fold in the grated chocolate.

2. Fill and/or frost your cake or torte, or cover and refrigerate the chantilly.

> *Makes enough for a 9-inch layer cake or torte*

Chocolate Ganache

Not quite as sweet as Chocolate Chantilly, and slightly thicker and richer, this combination of chocolate and cream is also whipped before being used as a filling or frosting. You can also flavor this ganache with a liqueur that will complement your dessert.

> 12 ounces semisweet chocolate, finely chopped
> 3 cups heavy cream, warmed to room temperature
> 2 tablespoons liqueur (optional)

(continued)

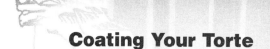

Coating Your Torte

The trick to creating a smooth coating on your tortes is to pour the ganache, rather than scooping and spreading, and to resist touching it up while setting.

1. After sealing your torte, warm your dark chocolate coating to 90 degrees, or your milk or white chocolate coating to 100 degrees. Your sealed torte should be set, but not cold.
2. Pour the coating evenly on top of the torte, encouraging it to spill over, coating the sides of the torte. Gently tip the torte or tap the cardboard round, if the coating appears uneven.
3. Working quickly, before the coating begins to set, cover any spots that didn't get coated using a warm metal spatula.

1. Melt the chocolate and cream in the top of a double boiler over hot, not simmering, water, stirring constantly. Set aside to cool to room temperature. Stir in liqueur (optional). Refrigerate until very cold.

2. Whip the ganache, using an electric mixer on a high speed, until it thickens and holds its shape. Be careful not to overwhip.

3. Fill and/or frost your cake or torte.

Makes enough for a 9-inch layer cake or torte

Mocha Ganache

Chocolate and espresso blend for this creamy whipped ganache.

> 12 ounces bittersweet chocolate, finely chopped
> 3 cups heavy cream, warmed to room temperature
> 3 tablespoons instant espresso powder

1. Melt the chocolate and cream in the top of a double boiler over hot, not simmering, water, stirring constantly. Set aside to cool to room temperature. Stir in the espresso powder. Refrigerate until very cold.

2. Whip the ganache, using an electric mixer on a high speed, until it thickens and holds its shape. Be careful not to overwhip.

3. Fill and/or frost your cake or torte.

Makes enough for a 9-inch layer cake or torte

Easy Tiramisu Filling

If you don't have time, or don't want to bother making a traditional tiramisu filling, try this quick and easy alternative.

> 2 cups mascarpone cheese, chilled
> 3 tablespoons superfine sugar, divided
> 1/4 cup dark rum
> 2 tablespoons Kahlua
> 1 tablespoon instant espresso powder
> 1 cup heavy cream, chilled

1. Beat together the mascarpone cheese and 2 tablespoons of the sugar, using an electric mixer on a medium speed, until smooth. Add the rum, Kahlua, and espresso powder, beating until thoroughly combined. Set aside.

2. Whip the cream, using an electric mixer on a high speed, until soft peaks form. Sprinkle in the remaining sugar, beating until stiff peaks just begin to form. Gently fold the whipped cream into the mascarpone mixture. Cover and refrigerate until cold.

3. Fill your layer cake, or create your tiramisu.

Makes enough to fill a 9-inch layer cake or tiramisu

Traditional Tiramisu Filling

This filling is so popular and delicious, we've used it to create trifles, choux pastries, and other fabulous desserts.

> 6 egg yolks, warmed to room temperature
> 3 tablespoons superfine sugar, divided
> 2 cups mascarpone cheese, warmed to room temperature
> $^1/_4$ cup dark rum
> 2 tablespoons Kahlua
> 1 tablespoon instant espresso powder
> $^1/_2$ cup heavy cream, chilled

1. Whisk together the egg yolks and 2 tablespoons of the sugar in a bowl that can be used as the top of a double boiler. Place over simmering water and whisk until hot. Remove from the heat and whisk in the mascarpone cheese. Fold in the rum, Kahlua, and espresso powder. Set aside to cool to room temperature.
2. Whip the cream, using an electric mixer on a high speed, until soft peaks form. Sprinkle in the remaining sugar, beating until stiff peaks just begin to form. Gently fold the whipped cream into the cooled mascarpone mixture. Cover and refrigerate until cold.
3. Fill your layer cake, or create your tiramisu.

Makes enough to fill a 9-inch layer cake, or tiramisu

Sealing Your Torte

Like cakes, tortes usually have lots of loose crumbs that can ruin a smooth finish. Most pastry chefs seal their tortes with some form of ganache before applying the final coating.

1. After leveling and removing the torte from the pan, refrigerate it for 30 minutes.
2. Remove the torte from the refrigerator and brush the crumbs off the sides and top using a dry, soft pastry brush.
3. Spread a thin layer of ganache (or coating) over the top and sides of the torte, filling cracks and locking down crumbs. Refrigerate just until set, before coating.

Zabaglione Filling

Some argue that tiramisu should be made with a zabaglione filling, in which sweet Marsala wine replaces rum and coffee flavorings. We've added grated chocolate, just for fun.

> 6 egg yolks, warmed to room temperature
> 3 tablespoons superfine sugar, divided
> 2 cups mascarpone cheese, warmed to room temperature
> 1/4 cup Marsala wine
> 1/2 cup heavy cream, chilled
> 1 cup grated milk chocolate

1. Whisk together the egg yolks and 2 tablespoons of the sugar in a bowl that can be used as the top of a double boiler. Place over simmering water and whisk until hot. Remove from the heat and whisk in the mascarpone cheese. Fold in the Marsala. Set aside to cool to room temperature.

2. Whip the cream, using an electric mixer on a high speed, until soft peaks form. Sprinkle in the remaining sugar, beating until stiff peaks just begin to form. Gently fold the whipped cream and grated chocolate into the cooled mascarpone mixture. Cover and refrigerate until cold.

3. Fill your layer cake, or create your tiramisu.

Makes enough to fill a 9-inch layer cake, or tiramisu

Classic Custard Filling

This makes a wonderful filling for chocolate layer cakes. You can also add fruit preserves for custom flavorings.

> 2 tablespoons cornstarch
> 1/2 cup milk, warmed to room temperature, divided
> 1 egg yolk, warmed to room temperature
> 3/4 cup heavy cream, warmed to room temperature
> 1/4 cup superfine sugar
> 1 teaspoon pure vanilla extract
> 1/4 teaspoon pure almond extract
> 2 tablespoons seedless fruit preserves (optional)

1. Dissolve the cornstarch in 1/4 cup of the milk. Whisk in the egg yolk. Set aside.

2. Combine the remaining milk, cream, and sugar in a heavy-bottomed saucepan. Bring to boil over a medium-low heat, stirring continuously. Whisk about 2 tablespoons of the hot cream mixture into the egg yolk mixture. Whisk the warm egg yolk mixture into the hot cream mixture. Continue whisking over a medium-low heat until the mixture thickens.

3. Remove from the heat and gently stir in the vanilla and almond extracts (and fruit preserves). Pour into a glass bowl and set aside to cool to room temperature. Cover and refrigerate until cold.

4. Fill your layer cake or spoon over fresh fruit.

Makes enough to fill a 9-inch layer cake

Royal Ricotta Filling

Decadent and earthy, this is a rich, sophisticated filling.

> 2 cups ricotta cheese, warmed to room
>   temperature
> ¹/₄ cup superfine sugar
> 1 tablespoon Frangelico liqueur
> ¹/₄ cup hazelnuts, toasted, skinned and
>   finely chopped
> 2 ounces grated dark chocolate

1.   Blend together the ricotta cheese, sugar, and Frangelico. Fold in the hazelnuts and grated chocolate.

2.   Fill and/or top your cake, torte, or roulade.

Makes enough for a 9-inch layer cake

German Chocolate Filling

Walnuts and coconut dominate this thick, rich, sweet topping. For a traditional German chocolate cake, partner this with your favorite chocolate layer cake.

> 1¹/₂ tablespoons cornstarch
> 1¹/₂ cups evaporated milk
> ³/₄ cup sugar
> ³/₄ cup dark brown sugar, firmly packed
> 9 egg yolks, warmed to room temperature
> 6 tablespoons butter, cut into ¹/₄-inch cubes
> 1 teaspoon salt
> 2 teaspoons pure vanilla extract
> 1 cup walnuts, toasted and chopped
> 1 cup sweetened shredded coconut

1.   Dissolve the cornstarch in the evaporated milk in a heavy-bottomed saucepan. Mix in the sugar, brown sugar, egg yolks, butter, and salt. Cook over a low heat, stirring constantly, until it thickens and begins to simmer.

2.   Remove from the heat and beat, using an electric mixer on a medium-high speed. Set aside to cool.

3.   Stir in the vanilla, walnuts, and coconut.

4.   Fill and/or top your cake or torte.

Makes enough for a 9-inch layer cake

Buttercream Frosting

This is a quick and easy way to make this classic filling and frosting. If you're used to store-bought buttercream, you'll be surprised by how much more delicious this version is. You can substitute the vanilla flavoring with your favorite liqueur to create a custom cake or torte.

> ³/₄ cup butter, cut in ¹/₄-inch cubes
> 1³/₄ cups powdered sugar
> ³/₄ cup heavy cream, chilled
> 2 teaspoons pure vanilla extract or
>   2 tablespoons liqueur

1.   Cream together the butter and sugar, using an electric mixer on a medium-high speed, until light and fluffy. Add the cream and vanilla (or liqueur), and continue to beat for 15 minutes.

2.   Fill and/or frost your cake or torte.

Makes enough for a 9-inch layer cake or torte

Chocolate Buttercream

Creamy and even more delicious than classic buttercream, you can also add your favorite flavoring to this recipe.

> *6 ounces semisweet chocolate, finely chopped*
> $1/2$ *cup butter, cut in* $1/4$*-inch cubes*
> $1^3/_4$ *cups powdered sugar*
> $3/_4$ *cup heavy cream, chilled*

1. Melt the chocolate in the top of a double boiler over hot, not simmering, water, stirring continuously. Set aside to cool to room temperature.

2. Cream together the butter and sugar, using an electric mixer on a medium-high speed, until light and fluffy. Add the cooled melted chocolate. Add the cream, continuing to beat for 15 minutes.

3. Fill and/or frost your cake or torte.

Makes enough for a 9-inch layer cake or torte

Mocha Buttercream

Chocolate and espresso combine to make a creamy, rich filling and frosting.

> *4 ounces dark chocolate, finely chopped*
> $1/2$ *cup butter, cut in* $1/4$*-inch cubes*
> $1^3/_4$ *cups powdered sugar*
> *2 tablespoons instant espresso powder*
> $3/_4$ *cup heavy cream, chilled*

1. Melt the chocolate in the top of a double boiler over hot, not simmering, water, stirring continuously. Set aside to cool to room temperature.

2. Cream together the butter, sugar, and espresso powder, using an electric mixer on a medium-high speed, until light and fluffy. Add the cooled melted chocolate. Add the cream, continuing to beat for 15 minutes.

3. Fill and/or frost your cake or torte.

Makes enough for a 9-inch layer cake or torte

Peanut Buttercream

Peanut butter remains one of the most popular flavors with both children and adults. Here's a way to use this usually whimsical flavor in an elegant way.

> $1/2$ *cup butter, cut in* $1/4$*-inch cubes*
> $1/4$ *cup creamy peanut butter*
> $1^1/_2$ *cups powdered sugar*
> $2/_3$ *cup heavy cream, chilled*

1. Cream together the butter, peanut butter, and sugar, using an electric mixer on a medium-high speed, until light and fluffy. Add the cream, continuing to beat for 15 minutes.

2. Fill and/or frost your cake or torte.

Makes enough for a 9-inch layer cake or torte

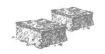

June's Butter Fudge Frosting

When I was growing up, we lived to lick the bowl when Mom made her signature frosting. And, when eating whatever it covered, we saved the frosting for last, swooning as each bite melted in our mouths.

> *8 ounces unsweetened chocolate, finely chopped*
> *$1/4$ cup butter, cut into $1/4$-inch cubes*
> *1 tablespoon light corn syrup*
> *1 cup evaporated milk*
> *2 cups powdered sugar, sifted*

1.   Melt the chocolate, butter, and corn syrup in the top of a double boiler over hot, not simmering, water, stirring constantly. Set aside to cool for a few minutes.

2.   Stir in the evaporated milk and powdered sugar.

3.   Fill and/or frost your cake or torte. If the frosting becomes too thick or dull, pour in a few drops of boiling water and stir.

Makes enough for a 9-inch layer cake or torte

Texturizing Frosting

Here are a few tips and tricks to add either texture or a smooth finish to your frosting:

1.   For a smooth finish, spread an even coating of frosting on the sides and top of your cake or torte. Warm a metal spatula by dipping it in hot water and drying it off. Lightly smooth the frosting with the spatula, rewarming as necessary.

2.   For a fun, lavish look, use a small, warm, metal spatula to create swirls all over your cake or torte.

3.   A plastic or metal pastry comb will help you create horizontal, vertical, diagonal, or curved lines in your frosting.

Smart Decorators Are Lazy Decorators

Investing in a decorating turntable (a professional-grade lazy Susan) will make frosting, coating, and decorating your cakes and tortes much more fun, and far easier.

I also find it helps to bring your project to eye level. This can be accomplished by building a simple platform out of a heavy, stable box if you prefer to stand, or by sitting down while you work.

Working with chocolate should always be fun, so use your imagination to invent practical ways to make your working area efficient and comfortable.

Cream Cheese Frosting

Sweet and tart, this fluffy dark chocolate frosting is rich and delicious.

> 8 ounces semisweet chocolate, finely chopped
> 1/4 cup heavy cream, warmed to room temperature
> 8 ounces cream cheese, warmed to room temperature
> 3/4 cup powdered sugar

1. Melt the chocolate and cream in the top of a double boiler over hot, not simmering, water, stirring constantly. Set aside to cool to room temperature.
2. Cream together the cream cheese and sugar, using an electric mixer on a high speed, until light and fluffy.
3. Adjust your mixer to a low speed and add the chocolate mixture. Adjust your mixer to a medium-high speed and beat until light and fluffy.
4. Fill and/or frost your cake or torte.

Makes enough for a 9-inch layer cake or torte

Sour Cream Frosting

Milk chocolate and sour cream create another sweet and tart contradiction in this rich frosting.

> 10 ounces milk chocolate, finely chopped
> 3/4 cup sour cream, warmed to room temperature

1.   Melt the chocolate in the top of a double boiler over hot, not simmering, water, stirring constantly. Set aside to cool to room temperature.

2.   Beat the sour cream, using an electric mixer on a medium speed, until smooth. Slowly add the melted chocolate, beating until creamy.

3.   Fill and/or frost your cake or torte.

Makes enough for a 9-inch layer cake or torte

Dark Chocolate Coating

This makes an exquisite, smooth coating for cakes and tortes.

> 10 ounces semisweet chocolate, finely
>   chopped
> $1/4$ cup heavy cream, warmed to room
>   temperature
> $3/4$ cup butter, cut into $1/4$-inch cubes
> 1 tablespoon light corn syrup

1.   Melt the chocolate, cream, butter, and corn syrup in the top of a double boiler over hot, not simmering, water, stirring constantly. Set aside to cool to room temperature.

2.   Cover your cake or torte.

Makes enough for a 9-inch layer cake or torte

Milk Chocolate Coating

Sweeter than a dark chocolate coating, but just as rich, this is a sophisticated finishing touch for milk chocolate lovers.

> 10 ounces milk chocolate, finely chopped
> $1/4$ cup heavy cream, warmed to room
>   temperature
> $1/2$ cup butter, warmed to room tempera-
>   ture
> 1 tablespoon light corn syrup

1.   Melt the chocolate, cream, butter, and corn syrup in the top of a double boiler over hot, not simmering, water, stirring constantly. Set aside to cool to room temperature.

2.   Cover your cake or torte.

Makes enough for a 9-inch layer cake or torte

White Chocolate Coating

If you use a high-quality white chocolate, this coating will actually be an elegant ivory color.

> 10 ounces white chocolate, finely chopped
> $1/4$ cup heavy cream, warmed to room
>   temperature
> $1/4$ cup butter, warmed to room tempera-
>   ture
> 1 tablespoon light corn syrup

1.   Melt the white chocolate, cream, butter, and corn syrup in the top of a double boiler over hot, not simmering, water, stirring constantly. Set aside to cool to room temperature.

2.   Cover your cake or torte.

Makes enough for a 9-inch layer cake or torte

The Magick of Chocolate

Witches and wizards use chocolate to infuse their potions with energy and joy. Fortunately, today's magick-makers have figured out that delicious ingredients work just as well as, if not better than, things like eye of newt, so many modern magic potions come in the form of tasty drinks, treats, and desserts!

Remember to cast a spell while brewing your potions—which simply means to verbally express how you want the potion to help you. And keep in mind that whatever you brew comes back to you threefold, so fill your potions with loving intent and your life will be filled with the same.

Here are some companion ingredients and their magick meanings, to help you design some brews of your own!

Almonds = Wisdom and Health
Allspice = Playfulness and Creativity
Apple = Health and Knowledge
Banana = Strength and Courage
Cherries = Learning and Friendship
Cinnamon = Friendship and Protection
Milk (or cream) = Strength and Health
Nutmeg = Memory and Dreams
Oats = Beauty and Abundance
Oranges = Happiness and Faithfulness
Peaches = Truth and Beauty
Raspberries = Love and Forgiveness
Strawberries = Romance and Playfulness
Vanilla = Love and Enchantment
Walnuts = Learning and Growth

chapter eight

Creamy
Creations

Creamy creations, to me, represent the greatest range of chocolate desserts: From hot steamed puddings to frozen soufflés, from light-as-air mousses to thick custards, and from elegant coupe glacée parfaits to simple scoops of ice cream.

Creamy creations also represent a great arena for experimentation. Fondue can be designed to duplicate a favorite cocktail. Marquises can be layered with other creamy creations. And ice cream . . .

Fondue, Pâté, and Marquises

Fondue di Saronno

A hint of almond flavors this thick, rich party treat.

> *³/₄ cup heavy cream, warmed to room temperature*
> *¹/₄ cup dark corn syrup*
> *12 ounces semisweet chocolate, finely chopped*
> *3 tablespoons amaretto liqueur*
> *angel cake, cubed*
> *fresh fruit, sliced or cubed*

1. Combine the cream and corn syrup in a heavy-bottomed saucepan, and bring to a gentle boil over medium heat.
2. Remove from the heat and add the chocolate, stirring until melted. Blend in the liqueur.
3. Place in a warmer or fondue pot and serve with angel cake and fresh fruit for dipping.

Makes 4–6 servings

Chocolate Pâté

Another party favorite, this chocolate treat has the consistency of pâté, and is wonderful when spread on plain wafer or shortbread cookies.

> *12 ounces semisweet chocolate, finely chopped*
> *¹/₄ cup butter, cut into ¹/₄-inch cubes*
> *¹/₂ cup heavy cream, chilled*
> *2 tablespoons superfine sugar, divided*
> *2 eggs, warmed to room temperature*
> *2 egg yolks, warmed to room temperature*
> *1 cup walnuts, toasted and chopped*
> *1 cup glazed cherry bits*

1. Lightly butter a loaf pan and line with plastic wrap, leaving an overhang on all sides.
2. Melt the chocolate and butter in the top of a double boiler over hot, not simmering, water, stirring continuously.
3. Whip the cream and 1 tablespoon of the sugar, using an electric mixer on a high speed, until soft peaks form. Cover and refrigerate.
4. Whisk together the eggs, egg yolks, and remaining sugar in a bowl that can be

used as the top of a double boiler. Place over simmering water and whisk until hot. Remove from the heat and beat, using an electric mixer on a medium speed, until the mixture cools and thickens. Fold the egg mixture into the chocolate mixture.

5. Fold the whipped cream into the chocolate mixture. Pour into the prepared pan, cover, and refrigerate overnight.

6. Remove from pan and place on a serving dish. Coat the sides with the chopped walnuts and top with glazed cherries. Serve as you would liver pâté with cookies instead of bread.

Makes 10–12 servings

Easy Mini Marquise

Individual milk chocolate marquises are crowned with hazelnuts, molded in fluted tart pans, and served with a bittersweet espresso sauce.

> *1/2 cup hazelnuts, toasted and chopped*
> *8 ounces milk chocolate, finely chopped*
> *2 tablespoons butter, cut into 1/4-inch cubes*
> *2 tablespoons light corn syrup*
> *1 tablespoon chocolate liqueur*
> *1 1/2 cups heavy cream, chilled*
> *2 tablespoons alkalized cocoa powder*

Bittersweet Espresso Sauce:
> *8 ounces bittersweet chocolate*
> *3/4 cup heavy cream, warmed to room*
>   *temperature*
> *2 tablespoons butter, cut into 1/4-inch cubes*
> *2 tablespoons instant espresso powder*

1. Lightly butter 4 to 6 individual fluted tart pans (approximately 1/2 to 3/4 cup capacity), and line with plastic wrap, leaving an overhang on all sides. Sprinkle the hazelnuts on the bottom of the tart pans and set aside.

2. Melt the chocolate, butter, and corn syrup in the top of a double boiler over hot, not simmering, water, stirring continuously. Set aside to cool to room temperature. Stir in the liqueur.

3. Whip the cream, using an electric mixer on a high speed, until soft peaks form. Cover and refrigerate.

4. When the chocolate mixture is cool, fold a third of the whipped cream into the chocolate. Repeat until all the whipped cream is incorporated.

5. Spoon the marquise mixture on top of the hazelnuts, cover, and refrigerate overnight.

6. To make the Bittersweet Espresso Sauce: Melt the bittersweet chocolate, cream, and butter in the top of a double boiler over hot, not simmering, water, stirring continuously. Stir in the espresso powder, and set aside to cool to room temperature.

7. Invert the molds onto serving dishes, remove the pans, and carefully peel off the plastic wrap. Dust the sides of the marquises with cocoa powder, and serve with Bittersweet Espresso Sauce.

Makes 4–6 servings

Aroma Therapy

When friends visit our "chocolate vault," a room specially designed to hold, and temperature controlled to protect, our couvertures and compounds, they never want to leave. The intoxicating aroma instantly puts them in a great mood.

It would be difficult to fill your home with fragrant couvertures or to live in the coolness they require, but you can come close to duplicating this euphoric atmosphere by lighting chocolate-scented candles. Here are a few nationwide sources:

Bare Escentuals—Chocolate hazelnut candles and "Kisses" perfume oil

(800) 227-3990 or
www.BareEscentuals.com

Illuminations—Mint chocolate chip and hot cocoa candles

1-800-CANDLES or
www.illuminations.com

Wicks 'n' Sticks—Chocolate fudge candles and potpourri wax

(888) 55-WICKS or
www.wicksnsticks.com

Mousses

Angel Mousse

Light and creamy, this dark chocolate mousse is a perfect finale for a rich meal.

> 12 ounces semisweet chocolate, finely
>   chopped
> ³/₄ cup heavy cream, warmed to room
>   temperature
> 3 egg whites, warmed to room temperature
> ¹/₃ cup superfine sugar
> White chocolate curls

1.   Melt the chocolate and cream in the top of a double boiler over hot, not simmering, water, stirring continuously. Set aside to cool to room temperature.

2.   When the chocolate mixture is cool, whisk together the egg whites and sugar in a bowl that can be used as the top of a double boiler. Place over simmering water and continue whisking until the egg whites are hot and the sugar is dissolved. Remove from the double boiler and whip, using an electric mixer on a high speed, until the meringue has cooled and increased in volume.

3.   Whisk the cooled chocolate to add air and lighten the mixture. Gently fold a third of the meringue into the chocolate mixture. Repeat until all of the meringue is incorporated. Spoon into serving glasses and top with white chocolate curls.

Makes 4–6 servings

Classic Chocolate Mousse

*Elegance in a glass, this traditional choco-
late mousse is ultrarich. The procedure for
preparing this dessert has evolved, to
prevent the danger of salmonella
poisoning.*

> *8 ounces semisweet chocolate, finely
>   chopped*
> *2 cups heavy cream, warmed to room
>   temperature, divided*
> *6 tablespoons superfine sugar, divided*
> *3 egg yolks, warmed to room temperature*
> *dark chocolate curls*

1.   Melt the chocolate and ½ cup of the
cream in the top of a double boiler over
hot, not simmering, water, stirring continuously. Set aside to cool to room temperature.

2.   Whip the remaining cream with
2 tablespoons of sugar until soft peaks form.
Cover and refrigerate.

3.   When the chocolate mixture is cool,
whisk together the egg yolks and the
remaining sugar in a bowl that can be used
as the top of a double boiler. Place over
simmering water and continue whisking until
the egg yolks are hot and have thickened
slightly. Remove from the double boiler and
whip, using an electric mixer on a high
speed, until the yolks have cooled and
increased in volume.

4.   Place the bowl in an ice water bath
and continue whisking until the mixture has
cooled and thickened a bit more. Be careful
that the mixture does not become ice cold.

5.   Whisk the cooled chocolate to add
air and lighten the mixture. Fold the egg
yolk mixture into the chocolate mixture.
Gently fold a third of the whipped cream
into the chocolate-egg yolk mixture. Repeat
until all the whipped cream is incorporated.
Spoon into serving glasses and top with
dark chocolate curls.

Makes 4–6 servings

The Sweetest Place on Earth

Hershey Town, USA, is a must-see
for everyone. There are rides and
attractions, and you'll learn how
chocolate is made, and about Milton
Hershey, the man behind the first
affordable chocolate bar.
    Hershey Town is located at
19 East Chocolate Avenue in
Hershey, PA, and is open during
the summer from 10:00 A.M. to
10:00 P.M. (800) HERSHEY.

Bitter Almond Mousse

Easier to make, but just as rich and delicious, this mousse is made with Italian cream cheese.

> 8 ounces bittersweet chocolate, finely chopped
> 1¼ cups chilled heavy cream, divided
> 2 tablespoons amaretto
> 6 tablespoons sifted powdered sugar, divided
> 1½ cups mascarpone cheese, warmed to
>   room temperature
> chocolate-coated slivered almonds

1. Melt the chocolate and ¼ cup of the cream in the top of a double boiler over hot, not simmering, water, stirring continuously. Set aside to cool to room temperature. Stir in the amaretto.

2. Whip the remaining cream with 2 tablespoons of the sugar until soft peaks form. Cover and refrigerate.

3. Beat the mascarpone cheese, using an electric mixer on a medium speed, until creamy. Sprinkle in the remaining sugar and continue to beat until thoroughly blended.

4. Whisk the cooled chocolate to add air and lighten the mixture. Gently fold a third of the sweetened mascarpone into the chocolate mixture. Repeat until all the mascarpone is incorporated.

5. Gently fold a third of the whipped cream into the chocolate-mascarpone mixture. Repeat until all the whipped cream is incorporated. Spoon into serving glasses and top with slivered almonds.

Makes 4–6 servings

Easy Viennese Mousse

Technically, this light, spiced mocha mousse is closer to a chantilly—but it's so delicious, your guests will never guess how quick and easy it was to make.

> 8 ounces milk chocolate, finely chopped
> 2½ cups chilled heavy cream, divided
> 1 tablespoon coffee liqueur
> 1 teaspoon pure vanilla extract
> 1 tablespoon instant espresso powder
> 1 teaspoon ground allspice
> ¼ cup superfine sugar
> milk chocolate curls

1. Melt the chocolate and ¼ cup of the cream in the top of a double boiler over hot, not simmering, water, stirring continuously. Stir in the coffee liqueur, vanilla, espresso powder, and allspice. Set aside.

2. Whip the remaining cream, using an electric mixer on a high speed, until soft peaks form. Sprinkle in the sugar, beating only long enough to incorporate.

3. Slowly pour a thin stream of the warm melted chocolate into the cold whipped cream while continuing to beat. This procedure causes part of the milk chocolate to blend into the whipped cream, as well as flecks of milk chocolate to form. Spoon into serving glasses and top with chocolate curls.

Makes 4–6 servings

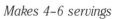

Rose Petal Mousse

Sweet and creamy, this light white chocolate mousse is a perfect delicacy for garden parties.

> *12 ounces white chocolate, finely chopped*
> *³/₄ cup heavy cream, warmed to room temperature*
> *¹/₄ teaspoon triple-strength rose water*
> *3 egg whites, warmed to room temperature*
> *¹/₄ cup superfine sugar*
> *fresh or sugared rose petals*

1. Melt the chocolate and cream in the top of a double boiler over hot, not simmering, water, stirring continuously. Set aside to cool to room temperature. Stir in the rose water.

2. When the chocolate mixture is cool, whisk together the egg whites and sugar in a bowl that can be used as the top of a double boiler. Place over simmering water and continue whisking until the egg whites are hot and the sugar is dissolved. Remove from the double boiler and whip, using an electric mixer on a high speed, until the meringue has cooled and increased in volume.

3. Whisk the cooled chocolate to add air and lighten the mixture. Gently fold a third of the meringue into the chocolate mixture. Repeat until all of the meringue is incorporated. Spoon into serving glasses and top with rose petals.

Makes 4–6 servings

Feeling Competitive

If you love designing desserts, you may want to start entering competitions. The rewards can be anything from recognition to cash prizes and international trips for two!

I recommend you begin with local events. If your community doesn't have one, see if one of your local service organizations would be interested in helping you plan one as a fundraising event.

Once you get your feet wet, watch for contest announcements in *Chocolatier* magazine, *Pastry Art and Design* magazine, gourmet food, women's, and family magazines.

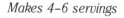

Eggnog Mousse

Ultrarich white chocolate mousse, flavored with brandy and Cointreau—a perfect treat for romantic snowed-in weekends.

> *1/4 cup orange zest curls*
> *2 tablespoons brandy*
> *1 tablespoon Cointreau*
> *1 teaspoon light brown sugar, firmly packed*
> *8 ounces white chocolate, finely chopped*
> *2 cups heavy cream, warmed to room temperature, divided*
> *1/2 teaspoon ground nutmeg, divided*
> *4 tablespoons superfine sugar, divided*
> *3 egg yolks, warmed to room temperature*

1. Combine the orange zest, brandy, Cointreau, and brown sugar in a small bowl. Set aside for 1 hour.

2. Melt the chocolate and 1/2 cup of the cream in the top of a double boiler over hot, not simmering, water, stirring continuously. Set aside to cool to room temperature. Drain the sweetened brandy and Cointreau into the chocolate mixture. (Save the orange zest curls for topping.) Add 1/4 teaspoon of the nutmeg, and blend.

3. Whip the remaining cream with 2 tablespoons of sugar until soft peaks form. Cover and refrigerate.

4. When the chocolate mixture is cool, whisk together the egg yolks and the remaining sugar in a bowl that can be used as the top of a double boiler. Place over simmering water and continue whisking until the egg yolks are hot and have thickened slightly. Remove from the double boiler and whip, using an electric mixer on a high speed, until the yolks have cooled and increased in volume.

5. Place the bowl in an ice water bath and continue whisking until the mixture has cooled and thickened a bit more. Be careful that the mixture does not become ice cold.

6. Whisk the cooled chocolate to add air and lighten the mixture. Fold the egg yolk mixture into the chocolate mixture. Gently fold a third of the whipped cream into the chocolate-egg yolk mixture. Repeat until all the whipped cream is incorporated. Spoon into serving glasses and top with the orange zest curls and remaining nutmeg.

Makes 4–6 servings

Florentine Mousse Towers

Creamy, easy white chocolate mousse is layered between Florentine cookies and served with fresh raspberries and blackberries.

> *10 ounces white chocolate, finely chopped*
> *1 1/2 cups chilled heavy cream, divided*
> *2 tablespoons wild berry liqueur*
> *16–24 Florentine cookies (page 108)*
> *1 cup fresh blackberries*
> *1 cup fresh raspberries*

1. Melt the chocolate and 1/2 cup of the cream in the top of a double boiler over hot, not simmering, water, stirring

continuously. Set aside to cool to room temperature. Stir in the liqueur.

2. Whip the remaining cream, using an electric mixer on a high speed, until soft peaks form.

3. Fold in the cooled chocolate. Place a cookie on a serving dish. Spoon a generous portion of mousse on top. Repeat two times, spooning slightly less mousse on each ascending layer. Top with a cookie and fresh berries, scattering more fresh berries around the tower.

Makes 4–6 servings

Parfait Crème Trois

Two varieties of chocolate mousse are layered with tiramisu filling in this three cream parfait.

¹/₂ recipe Bitter Almond Mousse (page 240)
¹/₂ recipe Easy Tiramisu Filling (page 226)
¹/₂ recipe Easy Viennese Mousse (page 240)
2 tablespoons each of dark, milk, and
*   white chocolate curls*

1. Fill 6 to 8 parfait glasses or champagne flutes a third full with Bitter Almond Mousse. Add a layer of Tiramisu Filling and a third layer of Viennese Mousse.

2. Top with mixed chocolate curls.

Makes 6–8 servings

The Wind and the Sun

All varieties of Theobroma cacao are relatively fragile, especially during the first five years of life. Although they thrive in extreme heat and humidity, direct sunlight can cause fatal damage. What's worse, a day of wind can destroy a cocoa plantation's production for years.

Today, coconut palms and banana trees are planted with the cocoa trees to provide shade and windbreaks. But planters in the Caribbean continue to hold their collective breath during hurricane season.

Grand Sabayon

We've added chocolate and a bit of whipped cream to this French Zabaglione to make it more like a fluid mousse.

> 8 ounces bittersweet chocolate, finely chopped
> 6 egg yolks, warmed to room temperature
> $^1/_2$ cup superfine sugar
> $^1/_3$ cup water
> 1 teaspoon pure vanilla extract
> 3 tablespoons Grand Marnier
> 1 cup heavy cream, chilled
> dark chocolate curls

1. Melt the chocolate in the top of a double boiler over hot, not simmering, water stirring continuously. Set aside.

2. Whip the egg yolks, using an electric mixer on a medium-high speed, until pale and thick.

3. Combine the sugar and water in a heavy-bottomed saucepan. Boil, uncovered, for 5 minutes over a medium heat.

4. Adjust your mixer to a medium speed and slowly pour a thin stream of the hot sugar syrup into the egg yolks, beating until blended. Increase the mixer speed to medium-high, and continue to beat until the yolks become lighter in color and thicker.

5. Adjust your mixer to a low speed and slowly add the vanilla, Grand Marnier, and melted chocolate.

6. Whip the cream, using an electric mixer on a high speed, until soft peaks form. Fold a third of the whipped cream into the chocolate mixture. Repeat, until all the whipped cream is incorporated. Spoon into serving glasses, and top with chocolate curls.

Makes 4–6 servings

White Chocolate Zabaglione

We've added white chocolate to this traditional Italian dessert of rich egg yolks and sweet Marsala wine.

> 4 ounces white chocolate, finely chopped
> 6 egg yolks, warmed to room temperature
> $^1/_4$ cup superfine sugar
> 6 tablespoons ($^1/_4$ cup + 2 tablespoons) Marsala wine
> white chocolate curls

1. Melt the chocolate in the top of a double boiler over hot, not simmering, water stirring continuously. Set aside.

2. Remove the top pot from a double boiler. In the bottom of the double boiler, heat water to a simmer.

3. While the water is heating, place the egg yolks and sugar into the top of the double boiler (away from the heat). Using an electric mixer set on a medium-high speed, beat until thickened.

4. Adjust your mixer to a medium-low speed and slowly add the Marsala wine. Place the mixture over the simmering water and continue beating until thickened.

5. Fold in the melted chocolate, spoon into serving glasses, and top with chocolate curls.

Makes 4–6 servings

Custards

Mad King Ludwig's Paskha

One of King Ludwig's residences was the inspiration for the castle in Disneyland, and for this dessert. We take dramatic creative license with this traditional Russian treat and mold it in tall, narrow, terra cotta pots to create individual white chocolate castles.

4 ounces white chocolate, finely chopped
1 cup small curd cottage cheese, warmed to room temperature
1 cup cream cheese, warmed to room temperature
2 tablespoons vodka
1 tablespoon blackberry liqueur
$1/4$ cup superfine sugar
$1/4$ cup, plus 12–18 fresh blackberries

Chocolate Sauce:
8 ounces semisweet chocolate
$3/4$ cup heavy cream, warmed to room temperature
2 tablespoons butter, cut into $1/4$-inch cubes
4–6 sprigs fresh mint
4–6 tablespoons dark chocolate curls
2–3 tablespoons powdered sugar, sifted

1.   Line 4 to 6 small, terra cotta flower-pots (approximately $1/2$ to $3/4$ cup capacity) with 2 sheets of cheesecloth. Leave the sides of the cheesecloth long enough to

fold back and cover the top of the pots when filled.

2.   Melt the white chocolate in the top of a double boiler over hot, not simmering, water, stirring continuously. Set aside to cool to room temperature.

3.   Combine the cottage cheese, cream cheese, vodka, liqueur, and sugar in a blender or food processor, and blend until smooth. (Or use an electric mixer on a medium speed.) Add $1/4$ cup blackberries and blend lightly.

4.   Fold in the white chocolate and spoon into the molds, being careful not to leave any air pockets. Smooth the top and

(continued)

A Smooth Guarantee

To prevent lumps from ruining your creamy creation, strain the delicacy through a fine mesh sieve before cooling and serving. Also, when refrigerating, be sure to place a piece of plastic wrap against the surface of creamy treats to prevent a skin from forming.

cover with the excess cheesecloth. Cover with plastic wrap and refrigerate overnight.

5.　The next day, make the chocolate sauce: Melt the semisweet chocolate, cream, and butter in the top of a double boiler over hot, not simmering, water, stirring continuously. Set aside to cool to room temperature.

6.　When ready to serve, remove the plastic wrap and fold back the cheesecloth. Invert on individual serving dishes, gently remove the mold, and carefully peel off the cheesecloth. Spoon a moat of chocolate sauce around each castle. Group three blackberries and a sprig of fresh mint in the

chocolate sauce. Top each castle with chocolate curls, and dust the chocolate curls and blackberries with powdered sugar.

Makes 6–8 servings

Coeur à la Crème

We've added bits of chocolate to this charming heart-shaped dessert; serve it with a fresh Raspberry Coulis.

Coeur à la Crème:
1 cup small curd cottage cheese, warmed to room temperature
1 cup mascarpone cheese, warmed to room temperature
¹/₂ cup sour cream, warmed to room temperature
¹/₂ cup heavy cream, warmed to room temperature
¹/₂ cup superfine sugar
4 ounces semisweet chocolate, grated

Raspberry Coulis:
2 cups fresh raspberries
¹/₄ cup powdered sugar
2 tablespoons raspberry liqueur

1.　To make the Coeur à la Crème: Line a Coeur à la Crème mold with 2 sheets of cheesecloth. Leave the sides of the cheesecloth long enough to fold back and cover the top of the mold when filled.

2.　Combine the first five ingredients in a blender or food processor, and blend until smooth. (Or use an electric mixer on a medium speed.) Fold in the chocolate.

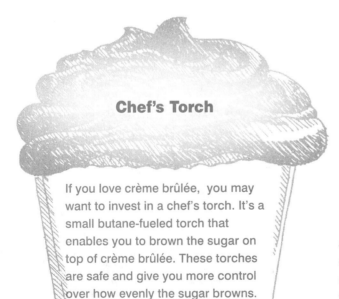

Chef's Torch

If you love crème brûlée, you may want to invest in a chef's torch. It's a small butane-fueled torch that enables you to brown the sugar on top of crème brûlée. These torches are safe and give you more control over how evenly the sugar browns.

Spoon the mixture into the mold, being careful not to leave any air pockets. Smooth the top and cover with the excess cheesecloth. Cover with plastic wrap and refrigerate overnight.

3.   To make the Raspberry Coulis: Combine the raspberries, sugar, and liqueur in a blender and process until smooth. Pour through a strainer to remove the seeds; cover and refrigerate.

4.   When ready to serve, remove the plastic wrap and fold back the cheesecloth. Invert on a serving dish, gently remove the mold, and carefully peel off the cheesecloth. Serve with chilled Raspberry Coulis.

Makes 6–8 servings

Café Crème Brûlée

Bittersweet chocolate and espresso make a delicious contradiction to the sweet caramelized sugar topping in this crème brûlée.

8 ounces bittersweet chocolate, finely
    chopped
2 cups heavy cream
2 tablespoons instant espresso powder
4 egg yolks, warmed to room temperature
1/4 cup superfine sugar
1/4 cup light brown sugar, firmly packed

1.   Preheat the oven to 300°F.
2.   Melt the chocolate and cream in the top of a double boiler over hot, not simmering, water, stirring continuously. Stir in the espresso powder and set aside.

3.   Whisk together the egg yolks and superfine sugar until thoroughly blended. Whisk a third of the chocolate mixture into the egg mixture. Repeat until all the egg yolks are incorporated.

4.   Spoon the crème into individual ramekins, and place in a baking pan. Pour warm water into the baking pan so that it comes halfway up the sides of the ramekins. Bake for 1 hour, or until a toothpick inserted in the center comes out clean. Chill.

5.   Before serving, preheat the broiler. Sprinkle the brown sugar evenly over each of the desserts. Place the ramekins back in the baking pan. This time, place ice water in the pan. Slide under the broiler only until the sugar caramelizes. Remove the ramekins from the pan and serve.

Makes 4–6 servings

Praline Brûlée

This spiced white chocolate custard is topped with pecans and caramelized sugar.

8 ounces white chocolate, finely chopped
2 cups heavy cream
2 tablespoons praline liqueur
1/2 teaspoon cinnamon
4 egg yolks, warmed to room temperature
3 tablespoons superfine sugar
4–6 tablespoons chopped pecans
1/4 cup light brown sugar, firmly packed

1.   Preheat the oven to 300°F.
2.   Melt the chocolate and cream in the top of a double boiler over hot, not

(continued)

simmering, water, stirring continuously. Stir in the liqueur and cinnamon, and set aside.

3.   Whisk together the egg yolks and superfine sugar until thoroughly blended. Whisk a third of the chocolate mixture into the egg mixture. Repeat until all the egg yolks are incorporated.

4.   Spoon the crème into individual ramekins, and place in a baking pan. Pour warm water into the baking pan so that it comes halfway up the sides of the ramekins. Bake for 1 hour, or until a toothpick inserted in the center comes out clean. Chill.

5.   Before serving, preheat the broiler. Sprinkle the pecans and brown sugar evenly over each of the desserts. Place the ramekins back in the baking pan. This time, place ice water in the pan. Slide under the broiler only until the sugar caramelizes. Remove the ramekins from the pan and serve.

Makes 4–6 servings

Crème Cocoa Caramel

This traditional crème caramel floats in a creamy chocolate-caramel sauce.

¹/₂ cup sugar
¹/₄ cup water
1 cup cream, warmed to room temperature
1¹/₂ cups milk, warmed to room temperature
6 eggs, warmed to room temperature
6 tablespoons (¹/₄ cup + 2 tablespoons)
*   light brown sugar, firmly packed*
1 teaspoon pure vanilla extract

Cocoa Caramel Cream Sauce:
¹/₂ cup heavy cream
1 cup sugar
¹/₂ cup water
1 tablespoon Irish Cream liqueur
3 tablespoons chocolate liqueur

1.   Preheat the oven to 300°F.

2.   Combine the sugar and water in a heavy-bottomed saucepan; cover and simmer for 2 to 3 minutes over medium heat. Remove the cover and continue to cook, without stirring, until the caramel turns a rich amber color. Divide between 4 to 6 individual ramekins. Set aside.

3.   Bring the cream and milk to a simmer in a heavy-bottomed saucepan over low heat.

4.   While the cream and milk are heating, whisk together the eggs, brown sugar, and vanilla until thoroughly blended. Whisk the hot cream mixture into the egg mixture.

5.   Spoon the custard through a sieve into each ramekin, without disturbing the caramel. Place the ramekins in a baking pan. Pour warm water into the baking pan so that it comes halfway up the sides of the ramekins. Bake for 1 hour, or until a toothpick inserted in the center comes out clean. Chill.

6.   To make the Cocoa Caramel Cream Sauce: Heat the cream in a heavy-bottomed saucepan over low heat.

7.   Combine the sugar and water in a heavy-bottomed saucepan; cover and

simmer for 2 to 3 minutes over medium heat. Remove the cover and continue to cook, without stirring, until the caramel turns a rich amber color. Whisk in the hot cream and set aside to cool to room temperature. Blend in the liqueurs.

8.   Slide a small, thin-bladed knife around the sides of each ramekin and invert each onto a serving plate. Spoon the sauce around each crème.

Makes 4–6 servings

Puddings

Pots de Crème

This sophisticated chocolate pudding is a perfect showcase for your favorite nibbling chocolate.

> 4 ounces semisweet chocolate, finely
>   chopped
> 4 egg yolks, warmed to room temperature
> 1 tablespoon superfine sugar
> 1¹/₂ cups heavy cream
> ¹/₂ cup milk
> 2–3 tablespoons chocolate curls

1.   Preheat the oven to 325°F.
2.   Melt the chocolate in the top of a double boiler over hot, not simmering, water stirring continuously. Set aside.
3.   Whisk together the egg yolks and sugar until the sugar is completely dissolved. Set aside.
4.   Combine the cream and milk in a heavy-bottomed saucepan and bring to a

simmer, stirring continuously. Slowly whisk the hot cream mixture into the egg yolk mixture. Slowly whisk the egg-cream mixture into the melted chocolate.

5.   Spoon the mixture into individual ramekins or pots, and place in a baking pan. Pour warm water into the baking pan so that it comes halfway up the sides of the ramekins. Cover the entire pan with heavy-duty foil and bake for 35 to 40 minutes. Remove the ramekins from the baking pan and cool on wire racks. Cover and refrigerate for 4 hours or overnight.

6.   Top with chocolate curls before serving.

Makes 4–6 servings

Chocolate Pudding

This old-fashioned dessert is delightful by itself, and wonderful in parfaits.

> 1 cup heavy cream
> 1 cup whole milk, divided
> ¹/₃ cup superfine sugar
> 6 ounces semisweet chocolate, finely
>   chopped
> 3 tablespoons cornstarch
> 3 eggs, warmed to room temperature
> 1 teaspoon pure vanilla extract

1.   Whisk together the cream, ¹/₂ cup of the milk, and sugar in a heavy-bottomed saucepan over medium heat. Bring to a simmer; remove from heat, and add the chocolate. Let stand for 5 minutes and then whisk until smooth.

(continued)

Chocolate Cookbooks

In addition to the books in other gift lists throughout this book, these are some of my favorites:

All-Butter Fresh Cream Sugar-Packed Baking Book by Judy Rosenberg

Chocolate from the Le Cordon Bleu Home Collection

Chocolate from the Kitchen Library of Williams Sonoma

Chocolate by Nick Malgieri

The Chocolate Bible by Christian Teubner, et al.

Death by Chocolate by Marcel Desaulniers

The Everything Dessert Cookbook by Lisa Shaw

Great Chefs Great Chocolate by Julia M. Pitkin

The International Chocolate Cookbook by Nancy Baggett

Spago Desserts by Mary Bergin and Judy Gethers

The Ultimate Encyclopedia of Chocolate by Christine McFadden

2. In a separate bowl, whisk together the remaining milk and cornstarch until smooth. Whisk in the eggs, one at a time, until thoroughly blended. Set aside.

3. Bring the chocolate mixture to a simmer over a low heat, whisking continuously to prevent scorching. Whisk a third of the hot chocolate mixture into the egg mixture.

4. Return the remaining chocolate mixture to the heat and slowly whisk the egg mixture into it. Bring the pudding to a boil, whisking continuously as it thickens.

5. Remove from the heat, whisk in the vanilla, and pour into serving dishes. To prevent a skin from forming on the top of the pudding, place a piece of plastic wrap directly on top.

Makes 4–6 servings

Spiced Steamed Pudding

This warm chocolate English treat is especially good on rainy winter afternoons. For an elegant presentation, serve surrounded by Crème Mystique (page 224).

> 4 ounces semisweet chocolate, finely chopped
> $^1/_2$ cup butter, cut into $^1/_4$-inch cubes
> 1 cup cake flour
> 1 teaspoon baking powder
> $^1/_4$ teaspoon ground cinnamon
> $^1/_4$ teaspoon ground cloves
> $^1/_4$ teaspoon ground allspice
> $^1/_4$ teaspoon ground ginger
> 1 egg, warmed to room temperature

¹/₂ cup sugar
¹/₂ cup cream, warmed to room temperature
2 tablespoons scotch whiskey
Crème Mystique (page 224)
1 ounce bittersweet chocolate, melted

1. Butter 6 individual steamed pudding molds. Put a rack in the bottom of a pot large enough to accommodate the molds.

2. Melt the semisweet chocolate and butter in the top of a double boiler over hot, not simmering, water, stirring continuously. Set aside.

3. Sift together the flour, baking powder, and spices. Set aside.

4. Whisk together the egg and sugar. Blend into the chocolate mixture. Fold in the flour mixture, cream, and scotch whiskey until lightly blended.

5. Spoon the pudding into the molds. Cover and seal the molds with heavy-duty foil. Place the molds on the rack in the prepared pot and carefully pour hot water into the pot so that it comes halfway up the sides of the molds. Simmer over a low heat for 1¹/₂ hours, or until set, adding water as needed.

6. Invert the individual puddings onto serving dishes. Spoon Crème Mystique around the puddings. In the Crème Mystique, place small evenly spaced dots of the melted bittersweet chocolate in a circle around the pudding. Using a toothpick, trace a circle through the center of each dot of chocolate, connecting the dots, to create a circle of hearts.

Makes 6 servings

Are You an Idea Person?

You can start a chocolate specialty company by "partnering" with a small local production house. A production house can be a manufacturer, retail candy store, or candy-making specialty shop. You would find and meet with caterers and party/wedding planners to come up with ideas for chocolate specialties based on the themes they've chosen and their budgets. You would find the molds and find or design the packaging. You would subcontract the molding of the chocolate to the production house and handle the pickup, packaging, delivery, and billing.

Steamed Peach Pudding

White chocolate and fresh peaches star in this steamed pudding, which is served with warm Cognac Cocoa Blanc.

4 ounces white chocolate, finely chopped
$1/2$ cup butter, cut into $1/4$-inch cubes
1 cup cake flour
1 teaspoon baking powder
$1/2$ teaspoon ground nutmeg
1 tablespoon fresh lemon juice
1 fresh peach
1 egg, warmed to room temperature
$1/4$ cup light brown sugar, firmly packed
$1/2$ cup cream, warmed to room temperature

Cognac Cocoa Blanc:
3 ounces white chocolate, finely chopped
$1/2$ cup evaporated milk
$1/4$ cup superfine sugar
$1/4$ cup light corn syrup
$1/4$ cup cognac

1. Butter a 1-quart pudding mold. Put a rack in the bottom of a pot large enough to accommodate the mold.

2. Melt the chocolate and butter in the top of a double boiler over hot, not simmering, water, stirring continuously. Set aside.

3. Sift together the flour, baking powder, and nutmeg. Set aside.

4. Place the lemon juice in a mixing bowl. Peel, pit, and lightly chop the fresh peach, tossing it in lemon juice as you work.

5. Whisk together the egg and brown sugar. Blend into the chocolate mixture.

Fold in the flour mixture, cream, and peaches until lightly blended.

6. Spoon the pudding into the mold. Cover and seal the mold with heavy-duty foil. Place the mold on the rack in the prepared pot and carefully pour hot water into the pot so that it comes halfway up the sides of the mold. Simmer over a low heat for $1^{1}/_{2}$ hours, or until set, adding water as needed.

7. To make the Cognac Cocoa Blanc: Place the white chocolate in a mixing bowl.

8. Whisk together the evaporated milk and sugar in a heavy-bottomed saucepan until smooth. Add the corn syrup and bring to a boil over medium heat, stirring continuously. Reduce the heat to low and cook for 5 minutes, stirring continuously.

9. Pour the hot milk mixture over the chocolate, and set aside for 1 minute. Whisk until smooth. Blend in the cognac. Serve warm over a slice of Steamed Peach Pudding.

Makes 6 servings

Sour Cherry Pudding Cake

While baking, a chocolate pudding magically forms on the bottom of this comforting snack cake.

4 ounces semisweet chocolate, finely chopped
1 cup flour
1 teaspoon baking powder
$1/2$ teaspoon salt
$1/2$ cup butter

1 cup sugar, divided
2 teaspoons pure vanilla extract, divided
¹/₂ cup buttermilk
1 cup dark cherries, drained
¹/₂ cup dark brown sugar, firmly packed
¹/₄ cup nonalkalized cocoa powder
1¹/₂ cups water, boiling

1. Preheat the oven to 350°F. Lightly coat the bottom and sides of a 9-inch square baking pan with butter and flour.

2. Melt the chocolate in the top of a double boiler over hot, not simmering, water, stirring continuously. Set aside.

3. Sift together the flour, baking powder, and salt. Set aside.

4. Cream together the butter, ¹/₂ cup of the sugar, and 1 teaspoon of the vanilla, using an electric mixer on a medium-high speed, until light and fluffy. Adjust your mixer to a low speed and add the buttermilk and flour mixture, beating until lightly blended. Fold in the melted chocolate and cherries.

5. Spread the batter evenly in the prepared pan. Mix the remaining sugar, brown sugar, cocoa powder, and the remaining vanilla with the boiling water, stirring until all dry ingredients are dissolved. Spoon gently and evenly over the batter, being careful not to create potholes in the batter.

6. Bake for 1 hour. Cool on a wire rack for 10 to 15 minutes. When serving, spoon some of the pudding over and to the side of the cake.

Makes about 9 servings

Thank the Irish

Irishman John Hannon was the first to successfully market cocoa beans in America. Arriving as a penniless immigrant in the early 1700s, Hannon had only a small sack of cocoa beans to his name. Believing in the promises of the new world, he sought and gained financial backing from a physician, Dr. James Baker, and then worked day and night establishing a market for this exotic delicacy (which was no small feat).

Dr. Baker remained a silent backer for fifteen years until Hannon lost his life while on a buying trip in the West Indies. However, under the doctor's care, the business continued to grow and, in 1895, incorporated under the name "Baker's Chocolate."

Frozen Creams

Frozen Chantilly Mousse

This iced chocolate mousse is wonderful alone, and even better when served with fresh fruit.

> 8 ounces semisweet chocolate, finely chopped
> 2 cups chilled heavy cream, divided
> 1/4 cup superfine sugar
> 1 teaspoon pure vanilla extract

1.   Melt the chocolate and 1/4 cup of the cream in the top of a double boiler over hot, not simmering, water, stirring continuously. Set aside to cool to room temperature.

2.   Whip the remaining cream, using an electric mixer on a high speed, until soft peaks form. Sprinkle in the sugar and vanilla, beating until stiff peaks begin to form.

3.   Fold a third of the whipped cream into the cooled chocolate mixture. Repeat until all the whipped cream is incorporated. Pour into a serving dish, cover, and freeze.

Makes 6–8 servings

Paradise Ice

This frozen white chocolate marquise is flavored with a rainbow of fruit.

> 12 ounces white chocolate, finely chopped
> 1/4 cup butter, cut into 1/4-inch cubes
> 2 tablespoons light corn syrup
> 2 tablespoons Key Largo liqueur
> 1 tablespoon orange liqueur
> 1 tablespoon grenadine
> 1 teaspoon lime zest
> 1 cup heavy cream, warmed to room temperature

1.   Melt the chocolate, butter, and corn syrup in the top of a double boiler over hot, not simmering, water, stirring continuously. Set aside to cool to room temperature. Stir in the liqueurs, grenadine, and zest.

2.   Whip the cream, using an electric mixer on a high speed, until soft peaks form. Cover and refrigerate.

3.   When the chocolate mixture is cool, fold a third of the whipped cream into the chocolate. Repeat until all the whipped cream is incorporated.

4.   Spoon into a 1 1/2-quart serving dish; cover, and freeze overnight.

Makes 6–8 servings

Ginger Walnut Frozen Soufflé

Candied ginger and toasted walnuts join milk chocolate for these frozen faux-soufflés.

> 8 ounces milk chocolate, finely chopped
> 1 1/2 cups heavy cream, warmed to room temperature, divided

2 tablespoons rum

$^1/_4$ cup superfine sugar, divided

1 egg, warmed to room temperature

3 egg yolks, warmed to room temperature

$^1/_4$ cup candied ginger, cut into small pieces

$^1/_2$ cup walnuts, toasted and coarsely chopped

1.   Measure a length of heavy-duty foil that will fit around each of six individual soufflé dishes or ramekins. Fold the foil in half lengthwise, and wrap around the top edge of each dish, creating a 3-inch height extension. Secure the foil to the dish, and place the empty dishes in the freezer.

2.   Melt the chocolate and $^1/_2$ cup of the cream in the top of a double boiler over hot, not simmering, water, stirring continuously. Set aside to cool to room temperature. Stir in the rum.

3.   Whip the remaining cream with 2 tablespoons of the sugar until soft peaks form. Cover and refrigerate.

4.   When the chocolate mixture is cool, whisk together the egg, egg yolks, and the remaining sugar in a bowl that can be used as the top of a double boiler. Place over simmering water and continue whisking until the egg mixture is hot and has thickened slightly. Remove from the double boiler and whip, using an electric mixer on a high speed, until the mixture has cooled and increased in volume.

5.   Whisk the cooled chocolate to add air and lighten the mixture. Fold the egg mixture into the chocolate mixture. Gently fold a third of the whipped cream, ginger, and walnuts into the chocolate-egg mixture. Repeat until all the remaining ingredients are incorporated. Spoon into the prepared dishes; cover and freeze overnight.

Makes 6 servings

Another Reason to Visit Hawaii

If you're planning a trip to Hawaii, be sure to include a visit to the "Big Island" where, in 1986, Jim Walsh established Hawaiian Vintage Chocolate, the first cocoa plantation in the United States.

Bitter Lemon Sorbet

Bits of bittersweet chocolate float in a tangy lemon sorbet for a very sophisticated flavor combination.

> $2^3/_4$ *cups water*
> $1^3/_4$ *cups light brown sugar, firmly packed*
> $^1/_4$ *cup fresh lemon juice*
> *1 tablespoon lemon zest, chopped*
> *1 teaspoon pure vanilla extract*
> *6 ounces bittersweet chocolate, finely chopped*

1.   Combine the water and brown sugar in a heavy-bottomed saucepan over a low heat, and stir until the sugar is dissolved. Set aside to cool to room temperature. Add the lemon juice, lemon zest, and vanilla; cover and chill.

2.   When the mixture is cold, add the bittersweet chocolate. Process in an ice cream freezer and serve.

Makes about 1 quart

Keoke Sorbet

Chocolate, coffee, and a splash of brandy come together in this frozen dairy-free treat.

> *3 cups fresh brewed coffee*
> $^3/_4$ *cup superfine sugar*
> *2 tablespoons brandy*
> *12 ounces semisweet chocolate*

1.   Combine the coffee and sugar in a heavy-bottomed saucepan over a low heat,

and stir until the sugar is dissolved. Set aside to cool to room temperature. Add the brandy.

2.   Melt the chocolate in the top of a double boiler over hot, not simmering, water, stirring continuously. Set aside to cool to room temperature.

3.   Blend together the coffee and chocolate mixtures; cover and chill.

4.   When the mixture is cold, process in an ice cream freezer and serve.

Makes about 1 quart

Cookies and Frozen Cream

Chocolate chips and chunks of Oreos star in this easy, faux vanilla ice cream.

> *2 cups heavy cream, chilled*
> $^2/_3$ *cup sweetened condensed milk, chilled*
> *2 teaspoons pure vanilla extract*
> $^3/_4$ *cup semisweet chocolate chips*
> $^3/_4$ *cup Oreo cookie chunks*

1.   Whip together the heavy cream, sweetened condensed milk, and vanilla, using an electric mixer on a high speed, until soft peaks form.

2.   Gently fold in the chocolate chips and cookie chunks.

3.   Pour into a 1-quart container, cover, and freeze overnight.

Makes about 1 quart

Easy Chocolate Ice Cream

For chocolate purists, this is a perfect showcase for your favorite nibbling chocolate.

> 12 ounces semisweet chocolate, finely chopped
> 3 cups light cream, divided
> 3 tablespoons superfine sugar

1. Melt the chocolate, 1 cup of the cream, and the sugar in the top of a double boiler over hot, not simmering, water, stirring continuously. Set aside to cool to room temperature.
2. When cool, whisk the remaining cream into the mixture; cover and refrigerate.
3. When cold, process in an ice cream freezer and serve.

Makes about 1 quart

Mint Krispy Ice Cream

Chocolate-coated Mint Krispys are added to this rich chocolate ice cream.

> 8 ounces semisweet chocolate, finely chopped
> 4 egg yolks, warmed to room temperature
> 1/2 cup superfine sugar, divided
> 1 cup heavy cream
> 1 cup milk
> 1/2 cup Mint Krispys, coarsely chopped*

1. Melt the chocolate in the top of a double boiler over hot, not simmering, water, stirring continuously. Set aside.
2. Whisk together the egg yolks and 1/4 cup of the sugar. Set aside.
3. Combine the remaining sugar, cream, and milk in a heavy-bottomed saucepan, and bring to a simmer over a medium heat.
4. Whisk about a quarter of the hot cream mixture into the egg yolks. Whisk the egg yolks into the remaining cream mixture.

(continued)

The First "Instant" Chocolate

As early as the seventeenth century, chocolate was blended with sugar and formed into small crude tablets called "Spanish rolls." These could easily be carried anywhere and dissolved in water to create a chocolate drink.

5. Cook over medium heat, stirring continuously, for about 5 minutes, or until thickened.

6. Remove from heat and fold in the melted chocolate. Cool to room temperature; cover and chill.

7. When the custard is cold, add the Mint Krispys, process in an ice cream freezer, and serve.

*Mint Krispys (available at See's Candies) are square, flat, dark-chocolate coated candies with a crisp mint-flavored center.

Makes about 1 quart

Gelato di Cioccolata

Cherries and pistachios are swirled through this chocolate Italian ice cream.

8 ounces bittersweet chocolate, finely chopped
$3/4$ cup light brown sugar, firmly packed
$1/2$ teaspoon unflavored gelatin
$1/4$ cup nonfat dry milk
$2^1/2$ cups milk
$3/4$ cup mascarpone cheese
$1^1/2$ tablespoons light corn syrup
2 tablespoons kirsch
2 cups cherry pie filling, drained
1 cup pistachios, coarsely chopped

1. Melt the chocolate in the top of a double boiler over hot, not simmering, water, stirring continuously. Set aside.

2. Mix together the brown sugar, gelatin, and dry milk. Set aside.

3. Whisk together the milk, mascarpone, and corn syrup in a heavy-bottomed saucepan over a low heat. Whisk in the dry ingredients, and bring to a simmer.

4. Remove from the heat and fold in the melted chocolate, kirsch, cherries, and pistachios. Cool; cover and chill.

5. When the custard is cold, process in an ice cream freezer and serve.

Makes about 1 quart

Buttered Rum Gelato

This buttery, white chocolate Italian ice cream is sprinkled with pecans and a pinch of nutmeg.

8 ounces white chocolate, finely chopped
$1/2$ cup light brown sugar, firmly packed
$1/2$ teaspoon unflavored gelatin
$1/4$ cup nonfat dry milk
1 teaspoon ground nutmeg
$2^1/4$ cups milk
$3/4$ cup heavy cream
$1^1/2$ tablespoons light corn syrup
2 tablespoons Butter Shots liqueur
$1/4$ cup white rum
1 cup pecans, toasted and coarsely chopped

1. Melt the chocolate in the top of a double boiler over hot, not simmering, water, stirring continuously. Set aside.

2. Mix together the brown sugar, gelatin, dry milk, and nutmeg. Set aside.

3. Whisk together the milk, cream, and corn syrup in a heavy-bottomed saucepan over a low heat. Whisk in the dry ingredients, and bring to a simmer.

4. Remove from heat and fold in the melted chocolate, liqueur, rum, and pecans. Cool; cover and chill.

5. When the custard is cold, process in an ice cream freezer and serve.

Makes about 1 quart

Glace Grand Chocolat

They say Italian gelato is the best ice cream in the world. I find French glace to be richer and more luxurious.

2¹/₂ cups light cream
¹/₂ cup superfine sugar
5 egg yolks
¹/₂ cup alkalized cocoa powder
1 tablespoon instant espresso powder
4 ounces semisweet chocolate, finely chopped
¹/₄ cup Grand Marnier liqueur

1. Whisk together the cream and sugar in a heavy-bottomed saucepan over a low heat, and bring to a boil.

2. Whisk the egg yolks until smooth. Whisk a third of the boiling cream mixture into the egg yolks. Return the cream to the heat and whisk in the egg yolk mixture.

Whisk until the custard thickens (about 15 seconds).

3. Whisk in the cocoa and espresso powders and the chocolate. Cool to room temperature; blend in the Grand Marnier. Cover and chill.

4. When the custard is cold, process in an ice cream freezer and serve.

Makes about 1 quart

Chocolate Monet Paintings

Reproductions of Monet's and other fine artists' paintings are created in edible chocolate by Hearts and Flowers. You can also send your favorite photo to them and have it turned into a chocolate masterpiece! Visit their Web site at *www.chocolateperfection.com,* or call the Advertising Specialty Institute at (800) 326-7378.

Melon Brandy Cups

Delicate sorbet and sweet cantaloupe fill delicate tuile cups.

1 cantaloupe

Tuile Cups:
$1/2$ cup butter, cut into $1/4$-inch cubes
$1/2$ cup sugar
$1/3$ cup dark molasses
$1/2$ teaspoon ground cinnamon
$1/4$ cup flour
2 tablespoons almonds, toasted and finely chopped
2 tablespoons brandy
$1/4$ teaspoon pure almond extract
2 ounces semisweet chocolate, melted
1–2 pints Keoke Sorbet (page 256)
4–6 tablespoons white chocolate curls
4–6 small, fresh, edible flowers

1. Scoop balls of cantaloupe using a melon baller. Cover and refrigerate.

2. Preheat the oven to 350°F. Line cookie sheets with parchment paper. Place 4 to 6 custard cups upside down on the counter.

3. Combine the butter, sugar, molasses, and cinnamon in a heavy-bottomed saucepan over a low heat. Bring to a boil. Remove from heat and whisk in the flour, almonds, brandy, and almond extract.

4. Spoon pools of batter onto the cookie sheets (about 2 heaping tablespoons each), and bake for 10 minutes. Place on wire racks to cool for 1 minute. Carefully peel each cookie off the cookie sheet while still warm and pliable, and place over the upside-down custard cups to form the bowls. Finish cooling on the custard cups.

5. Place the melted chocolate in a pastry bag fitted with a writing tip, and pipe swirls or zigzags on your serving dishes. Place a tuile cup on each plate. Place a scoop of sorbet in each cup. Add $1/2$ cup of cantaloupe balls, letting some topple out onto the dish. Top with white chocolate curls, and place a fresh flower(s) on the side.

Makes 4–6 servings

Derby Day Parfait

In the spirit of a mint julep, chocolate ice cream, flavored with mint candies, is layered with fresh strawberries and Kentucky fudge sauce.

Kentucky Fudge Sauce:
4 ounces semisweet chocolate, finely chopped
$1/2$ cup alkalized cocoa powder
$1/2$ cup sugar
$1/2$ cup evaporated milk
$1/2$ cup light corn syrup
1 tablespoon honey
3 tablespoons Kentucky bourbon

1–2 pints Mint Krispy ice cream (page 257)
2 cups fresh strawberries, sliced
sweetened whipped cream
4–6 Mint Krispys*
4–6 sprigs fresh mint

1.   To prepare the Kentucky Fudge Sauce: Melt the chocolate in the top of a double broiler, over hot (not simmering) water, stirring continuously. Remove from heat and set aside to cool to room temperature.

2.   Combine the cocoa powder and sugar in a heavy-bottomed saucepan. Stir in the evaporated milk, creating a thick, smooth paste. Add the corn syrup. Bring the mixture to a boil over a medium heat, stirring constantly. Remove from heat and fold in the melted chocolate, honey, and bourbon. Cool to room temperature.

3.   Place a small pool of sauce in the bottom of a parfait glass or champagne flute. Add a scoop of ice cream and a layer of strawberries. Repeat, topping with whipped cream, a Mint Krispy, and a sprig of fresh mint.

*Mint Krispy candies (available at See's Candies) are square, flat, dark-chocolate-coated mint candies that have a crisp center.

Makes 4–6 servings

Gelato Cassata Terrine

Italian ice cream is layered with whipped ricotta and zabaglione creams.

$^1/_2$ recipe Zabaglione Filling (page 228)
2 cups Gelato di Cioccolata, softened
    (page 258)

(continued)

Beware the Chocolate of Chiapa . . .

and of taking chocolate away from women! In the early 1600s, Spanish colonialists had become so addicted to chocolate that their servants would bring fresh cups to them throughout the long Catholic masses. The bishop enjoyed chocolate on a regular basis, but not during mass, and was angered by the distractions. He ordered those in attendance (who, at that time, were primarily women) to abstain. The bishop's command was ignored, obliging him to threaten excommunication and, ultimately, to use military force. Shortly thereafter the bishop died . . . after drinking a cup of chocolate.

Cassata:

4 ounces white chocolate, finely chopped

1/2 cup heavy cream, chilled

1 cup ricotta cheese

2 tablespoons amaretto

2 egg whites, warmed to room temperature

1/2 cup sugar

2 tablespoons alkalized cocoa powder

1/4 cup almonds, sliced and toasted

1. Lightly butter a 10-cup bundt cake mold and line with plastic wrap.

2. To make the Cassata: Melt the chocolate in the top of a double boiler over hot, not simmering, water, stirring continuously. Set aside to cool to room temperature.

3. Whip the cream, using an electric mixer on a high speed, until soft peaks form. Cover and refrigerate.

4. Blend together the ricotta cheese and amaretto, in a blender or food processor, or use an electric mixer on a medium speed. Set aside.

5. Whisk together the egg whites and sugar in a bowl that can be used as the top of a double boiler, over simmering water, until the mixture is hot and the sugar is dissolved. Remove from heat and whip, using an electric mixer on a high speed, until the mixture cools and increases in volume.

6. Fold the ricotta mixture and the cooled chocolate into the egg white mixture. Fold the whipped cream into the mixture; cover and refrigerate.

7. To make the Terrine: Spread the Zabaglione Filling in the bottom of the prepared pan. Add a layer of Cassata, and top with the softened gelato. Cover and freeze overnight.

8. To serve, invert onto a serving plate. Remove the pan and carefully peel off the plastic wrap. Dust with cocoa powder. Slice with a warm knife, and serve sprinkled with almonds.

Makes 8–10 servings

Coupe Glace

This is an elegant French version of an American ice cream sundae. When preparing a coupe glace, the hot fudge (or other sauce) and whipped cream are placed under, rather than over, the ice cream or gelato.

Bittersweet Fudge Sauce:

4 ounces bittersweet chocolate, finely chopped

1/2 cup alkalized cocoa powder

1/2 cup sugar

1/2 cup evaporated milk

1/2 cup light corn syrup

1 tablespoon instant espresso powder

Caramel Sauce:

3/4 cup heavy cream, warmed to room temperature

1 1/4 cups sugar

1/3 cup light corn syrup

1 1/2 cups sweetened whipped cream

1–2 pints Buttered Rum Gelato (page 258)

1.   To prepare the Bittersweet Fudge Sauce: Melt the chocolate in the top of a double boiler over hot (not simmering) water, stirring continuously. Remove from heat and set aside to cool to room temperature

2.   Combine the cocoa powder and sugar in a heavy-bottomed saucepan. Stir in the evaporated milk, creating a thick smooth paste. Add the corn syrup. Bring the mixture to a boil over a medium heat, stirring constantly. Remove from heat and fold in the melted chocolate and espresso powder. Cool to room temperature.

3.   To make the Caramel Sauce: Combine the cream, sugar, and corn syrup in a heavy-bottomed saucepan. Bring the mixture to a boil over a low heat, stirring with a wooden spoon only until the sugar dissolves. When the temperature reaches 244°F, pour the mixture into a stainless steel bowl or pot. Stir every few minutes while the mixture cools.

4.   Place a generous dollop of bittersweet fudge in a serving glass. Add a light layer of caramel. Pipe or spoon a pillow of sweetened whipped cream in the center, and top with a generous scoop of gelato.

Makes 4–6 servings

Glacée Moulin Rouge

This fairly simple dessert will dazzle your guests. A scoop of ice cream is drenched in dark chocolate liqueur and skirted with ruffles of rich chocolate mousse.

(continued)

Cacao Barry

Charles Barry was English, but when he decided to establish a chocolaterie in 1842, he chose Meulan, France, as his location. Cacao Barry grew to be the second largest chocolaterie in Europe, and was the first to introduce French chocolate to America's pastry chefs and chocolatiers. Their fine blend of beans is rich and consistent with traditional flavor identities.

In 1997, Cacao Barry merged with Callebaut to become Barry Callebaut. The new company continues to offer high-quality couvertures under both labels.

Cortés Conquers Chocolate

Although Columbus was the first to bring chocolate to Spain in the 1500s, the bitter, exotic delicacy did not capture the favor of King Ferdinand or Queen Isabella and was therefore ignored.

Twenty years later, after witnessing the fervor Montezuma felt toward chocolate, even in its bitter form, Cortés returned to Spain determined to reintroduce this treasure. Aware of King Charles V's passion for sweets, Cortés ordered that sugar and vanilla be added to the chocolate. In addition, when presenting the new drink, Cortés recounted stories of Montezuma's amazing sexual stamina after consuming the magic elixir.

1–2 pints Glace Grand Chocolat (page 259)
4–6 shots chocolate liqueur
Bitter Almond Mousse (page 240)
4–6 tablespoons white chocolate curls
4–6 maraschino cherries with stems

1. Place a large scoop of ice cream in a wide, shallow dessert glass. Press a 1-inch well in the top of the scoop using a ¹/₂-inch dowel or wooden spoon handle.

2. Fill the well with a shot of liqueur. The liqueur will spill out over the ice cream and form a moat.

3. Place the chocolate mousse in a pastry bag fitted with a ¹/₂-inch star tip, and pipe ruffles around the bottom edge of the ice cream (on top of the moat), and on top of the well (concealing the well). Top with chocolate curls and a cherry.

Makes 4–6 servings

chapter nine

Elegant Desserts

Don't be intimidated by elegant desserts; most are not as complicated as they look. The trick is to practice, practice, practice and to reward yourself with your efforts! Just remember: Never try to make an elegant dessert for the first time when your boss or mother-in-law is coming to dinner, use exceptional chocolate, and always relax and have fun.

Soufflés

Soufflé Chocolat

A delicate crust protects a creamy center in this heavenly chocolate soufflé.

> 8 ounces semisweet chocolate, finely chopped
> $1/4$ cup butter, cut into $1/4$-inch cubes
> 2 tablespoons chocolate liqueur
> 2 tablespoons water
> 4 egg yolks, warmed to room temperature
> $1/8$ teaspoon salt
> 2 tablespoons cognac
> 8 egg whites, warmed to room temperature
> $1/4$ cup superfine sugar

1. Preheat the oven to 375°F. Measure a length of heavy-duty foil that will fit around a $1^1/_2$-quart soufflé dish. Fold the foil in half lengthwise, and wrap it around the top edge of the dish, creating a 4-inch height extension. Secure the foil to the dish, and lightly coat the dish and collar with butter and superfine sugar.

2. Melt the chocolate and butter in the top of a double boiler over hot, not simmering, water, stirring continuously. Set aside to cool to room temperature. Mix together the chocolate liqueur and water, and blend into the cooled chocolate mixture.

3. When cool, whisk in the egg yolks one at a time, the salt, and the cognac. Set aside.

4. Whip the egg whites, using an electric mixer on a high speed, until soft peaks form. Sprinkle in the sugar, beating until stiff peaks begin to form. Fold a quarter of the egg whites into the chocolate mixture. Lightly fold in the remaining egg whites.

5. Pour into the prepared dish. Place the dish on a baking pan and bake for 30 to 35 minutes, or until puffed and golden. The soufflé should be baked around the outside edges and creamy in the center. Carefully remove the collar, and serve warm.

Makes 6–8 servings

Mocha Noir Soufflé

Dark chocolate pastry becomes lighter than air in these irresistible individual soufflés.

> 3 tablespoons butter
> 1½ tablespoons flour
> 1 tablespoon nonalkalized cocoa powder
> 1 tablespoon instant espresso powder
> ⅛ teaspoon salt
> ¾ cup milk, warmed to room temperature
> 4 ounces bittersweet chocolate, finely chopped
> 4 egg yolks, warmed to room temperature
> 1 teaspoon pure vanilla extract
> 6 egg whites, warmed to room temperature
> ⅓ cup superfine sugar
> powdered sugar

1. Preheat the oven to 400°F. Measure lengths of heavy-duty foil that will fit around each of six individual soufflé dishes. Fold the foil in half lengthwise, and wrap around the top edge of each dish, creating a 3-inch height extension. Secure the foil to the dishes, and lightly coat the dishes and collars with butter and superfine sugar.

2. Melt the butter in a heavy-bottomed saucepan over medium heat. Whisk in the flour, cocoa powder, and espresso powder until thickened (about 2 minutes).

3. Slowly add the milk and bring to a boil, whisking continuously. Remove from the heat and whisk in the chocolate until smooth. Whisk in the egg yolks, one at a time, and the vanilla. Set aside.

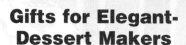

Gifts for Elegant-Dessert Makers

Gourmet kitchen shops are the best places to find high-quality specialty items for friends who make more sophisticated desserts.

- A dessert date at the restaurant of an award-winning pastry chef
- *Chocolate Passion* by Tish Boyle and Timothy Moriarty
- Soufflé dishes
- Charlotte molds
- Trifle dishes
- Bombe molds
- Springform pans
- Elegant serving dishes
- Decorator stand
- Domestic and imported couvertures
- Gourmet cocoa powders
- Flavoring liqueurs
- Exotic extracts
- Gourmet ingredients
- Candied violets
- Sugared rose petals

(continued)

4.   Whip the egg whites, using an electric mixer on a high speed, until soft peaks form. Sprinkle in the sugar and beat until stiff peaks begin to form. Fold a quarter of the egg whites into the chocolate mixture. Lightly fold in the remaining egg whites.

5.   Pour into the prepared dishes. Place the dishes on a baking pan and bake for 12 to 15 minutes, or until puffed. The soufflés should be baked around the outside edges and creamy in the center. Carefully remove the collars, dust with powdered sugar, and serve warm.

Makes 6 servings

Soufflé Ivoire

Creamy white chocolate is featured in this rich flourless soufflé.

6 ounces white chocolate, finely chopped
$1/4$ cup butter, cut into $1/4$-inch cubes
$1/4$ cup milk
4 egg yolks, warmed to room temperature
$1/8$ teaspoon salt
2 tablespoons cognac
6 egg whites, warmed to room
    temperature
$1/4$ cup superfine sugar
Crème Mystique (page 224)

1.   Preheat the oven to 375°F. Measure a length of heavy-duty foil that will fit around a $1^1/2$-quart soufflé dish. Fold the foil in half lengthwise, and wrap around the top edge of the dish, creating a 4-inch height extension. Secure the foil to the dish,

and lightly coat the dish and collar with butter and superfine sugar.

2.   Melt the chocolate, butter, and milk in the top of a double boiler over hot, not simmering, water, stirring continuously. Set aside to cool to room temperature.

3.   When cool, whisk in the egg yolks one at a time, the salt, and the cognac. Set aside.

4.   Whip the egg whites, using an electric mixer on a high speed, until soft peaks form. Sprinkle in the sugar and beat until stiff peaks begin to form. Fold a quarter of the egg whites into the chocolate mixture. Lightly fold in the remaining egg whites.

5.   Pour into the prepared dish. Place the dish on a baking pan and bake for 30 to 35 minutes, or until puffed and golden. The soufflé should be baked around the outside edges and creamy in the center. Carefully remove the collar, and serve warm with Crème Mystique.

Makes 6–8 servings

Charlottes

Teardrop Charlotte

Chantilly cream teardrops, speckled with dark chocolate, top rich chocolate mousse wrapped in chocolate ladyfingers.

24 Chocolate Ladyfingers (page 200)
Classic Chocolate Mousse (page 239)
$1/2$ recipe Black and White Chantilly
    (page 225)

1. Line the sides and then the bottom of an 8-inch springform pan with ladyfingers.

2. Prepare the mousse and pour into the pan, filling up to ¹/₂-inch below the tops of the ladyfingers. Cover and refrigerate until firm.

3. Place the Black and White Chantilly in a pastry bag fitted with a ¹/₂-inch plain round tip. Pipe teardrop shapes around the outside rim of the charlotte, with the points of the teardrops facing toward the center of the charlotte. Continue piping concentric circles of teardrops into the center of the charlotte.

Makes 8–10 servings

Butter Fudge Charlotte

Dark chocolate frosting simulates ladyfingers in this ultrarich charlotte.

> 8 ounces semisweet chocolate, finely
>   chopped
> ³/₄ cup heavy cream, warmed to room
>   temperature
> 1 cup butter, cut into ¹/₄-inch cubes
> 4 eggs, warmed to room temperature
> 1 cup superfine sugar
> June's Butter Fudge Frosting (page 231)
> 3 cups dark chocolate curls
> 1 teaspoon powdered sugar

1. Preheat the oven to 350°F. Lightly coat the bottom and sides of a charlotte pan with butter. Line the bottom of the pan with parchment paper.

Lindt

Swiss chocolatier Rudolphe Lindt was the first to blend additional cocoa butter into chocolate, creating a richer flavor and texture. Lindt also invented "conching," a method of continuously stirring and blending chocolate, at the end of the production cycle, to achieve the ultrasmooth texture we enjoy today.

The chocolaterie Lindt founded in the 1800s continues to make rich, exquisite couvertures, which can be purchased in small bars for nibbling, as well as in large slabs for making pastries and confections.

(continued)

Learn to Be a Chocolatier. . . in France!

For a very special gift for yourself or someone you love, plan a trip to France that includes a class at a world-renowned chocolate school. These schools offer short courses for aspiring professionals and for those who just want to have fun:

Ecole Gastronomique Bellouet-Conseil
48, rue de Sevres
75007 Paris, France
Phone: (011 33 1) 40.56.91.20
Fax: (011 33 1) 45.66.48.61

Le Cordon Bleu Ecole de Cuisine et de
    Patisserie
8, rue Leon
Delhomme, 75015 Paris, France
Phone: (011 33 1) 53.68.22.50
Fax: (011 33 1) 48.56.03.96

La Varenne Ecole de Cuisine
Chateau du Fey
89300 Villecien, (Burgundy) France
Phone: (011 33) 86.63.18.34
Fax: (011 33) 86.63.10.33

2.   Melt the chocolate, cream, and butter in the top of a double boiler over hot, not simmering, water, stirring continuously. Set aside.

3.   Whisk together the eggs and sugar until the sugar is completely dissolved. Whisk a third of the warm chocolate mixture into the egg mixture. Whisk the egg mixture into the remaining chocolate mixture.

4.   Pour into the prepared pan and bake for 50 to 60 minutes. The charlotte should still be soft under a thick crust. Cool on a wire rack, cover, and refrigerate overnight.

5.   To remove the charlotte from the pan, slide a warmed thin-bladed knife between the charlotte and the pan. Invert on a serving dish.

6.   Place the frosting in a pastry bag, fitted with a 1-inch star tip. Pipe simulated ladyfingers vertically around the outside of the charlotte. Top with chocolate curls, and dust with powdered sugar.

Makes 8–10 servings

Charlotte in Paradise

Paradise Ice fills a ring of delicate ladyfingers and is crowned with luxurious white chocolate curls.

24 Ladyfingers (page 200)
Paradise Ice (page 254)
3 cups white chocolate curls

1.   Line the sides and then the bottom of an 8-inch springform pan with ladyfingers.

2.   Prepare the Paradise Ice and pour into the pan, filling up to ½-inch below the tops of the ladyfingers. Cover and refrigerate until firm.

3.   Top with white chocolate curls and serve.

Makes 8–10 servings

Bombes

Grande Bombe

Chocolate sponge cake is painted with Grand Marnier syrup, topped with a dome of French chocolate ice cream, and decorated with chocolate ganache.

> ¼ cup superfine sugar
> 2 tablespoons water
> 2 tablespoons Grand Marnier
> Chocolate Sponge Cake (page 204)
> 2 recipes Glace Grand Chocolat, softened
>   (page 259)
> Chocolate Ganache (page 225)

1.   Combine the sugar and water in a small, heavy-bottomed saucepan. Cover, and simmer over a low heat until the sugar is dissolved. Remove from heat, cool to room temperature, and stir in the Grand Marnier. Set aside.

2.   Bake the sponge cake in an 8-inch layer cake pan. When the cake is cool, slice in half horizontally. Wrap and freeze

Explorer-Entrepreneur

After seeing the commercial impact chocolate had on the Aztec civilization and the social impact chocolate had on the nobility of Spain, explorer Hernando Cortés set about establishing cocoa plantations from Mexico to Trinidad and Madagascar, in the name of the Spanish crown.

Native American slaves were transported along with the trees to harvest and process the beans. Unfortunately, having little immunity to Western diseases, these workers soon perished, leaving a serious labor shortage. With much the same problem facing the sugar industry, plantation owners throughout the Caribbean began importing African slaves.

(continued)

one half for a future creation. Trim the remaining layer to fit inside a 2-quart domed bowl.

3. Lightly coat the inside of the bowl with butter, and line with plastic wrap.

5. Place the ice cream in the bottom of the bowl, being careful not to leave air pockets. Leave enough room at the top for the sponge cake layer.

6. Paint the sponge cake with the Grand Marnier syrup, and place the cake, syrup side down, on top of the ice cream. Cover and freeze.

7. Invert the bombe onto a serving dish, remove the mold, and carefully peel off the plastic wrap. Working quickly, place the Chocolate Ganache in a pastry bag fitted with a star tip, and cover the bombe in ganache. Serve immediately.

Makes 8–10 servings

Mini PB Bombes

Here's an elegant dessert that young ones will love. Chocolate ice cream covers peanut butter chocolate chip cookies, and is frosted with Peanut Buttercream Frosting.

> *¹/₂ recipe Peanut Butter Pleasers (page 99)*
> *Peanut Buttercream Frosting (page 230)*
> *Easy Chocolate Ice Cream (page 257)*
> *1 cup Reese's Pieces*

1. Bake the Peanut Butter Pleasers into 4-inch cookies. Set aside.

2. Place the frosting in a pastry bag, fitted with a ¹/₂-inch star tip. Set aside.

3. Place a cookie on each serving dish.

4. Place a large scoop of ice cream in the center of each cookie.

5. Working quickly, pipe stars all over the ice cream, from the base to the top. Surround the base of each bombe with Reese's Pieces, and serve immediately.

Makes about 6 servings

Rum Swirl Bombe

Marbled cake covers rich Italian gelato in this black and white variation.

> *Marbled Layer Cake (page 210)*
> *2 recipes Buttered Rum Gelato, softened (page 258)*
> *¹/₂ cup apricot preserves*
> *2 tablespoons white rum*
> *2 tablespoons superfine sugar*
> *¹/₂ cup white chocolate curls*

1. Lightly coat the inside of a 2-quart domed bowl with butter, and line with plastic wrap. Lightly butter the plastic wrap.

2. Bake the cake in two 9-inch layer cake pans. When cool, slice one layer in half horizontally. Wrap and freeze the top half for a future creation. Trim the remaining layer to fit inside the prepared bowl. This will be your base layer. Set aside.

3. Shave the top, bottom, and sides off the other layer and slice horizontally into ¹/₄-inch layers. Gently line the inside of the prepared bowl with these layers, being careful not to leave any gaps. Leave room at the top for the base layer.

4. Gently spoon the gelato into the bowl, being careful not to leave any air pockets. Place the base layer on top, cover, and freeze.

5. Combine the apricot preserves, rum, and sugar in a heavy-bottomed saucepan. Bring to a simmer over a medium heat, stirring continuously. Remove from the heat and set aside to cool.

6. Invert the bombe onto a serving dish, remove the mold, and carefully peel off the plastic wrap. Paint the entire bombe with the cooled glaze. Surround the base of the bombe with white chocolate curls, and serve immediately.

Makes 8–10 servings

Trifles

HRM Trifle

This classic British dessert layers cubes of cake with rich custard and fresh fruit in an elegant, straight-sided, clear glass serving bowl.

> Sour Cream Layer Cake (page 208)
> 2 recipes Classic Custard Filling (page 228)
> 1 cup heavy cream, chilled
> 2 tablespoons powdered sugar
> $^1/_2$ teaspoon pure vanilla extract
> $^1/_4$ cup brandy
> 2 cups fresh blackberries
> 2 cups fresh raspberries
> 2 cups fresh blueberries
> $^1/_4$ cup almonds, sliced and toasted

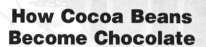

How Cocoa Beans Become Chocolate

After being harvested, the cocoa bean pods are split open, covered, and left in the sun, allowing the beans to ferment in their sugar-rich natural housing.

Next the beans are removed from the pods, dried, and packed in 110-pound sacks for shipment. Upon arrival at the chocolate factory, beans are carefully checked, sorted, and roasted according to blend specifications.

After roasting, the outer skins are removed and the nibs are broken down by a series of rollers. The nibs are then further ground into a paste, and blended with additional cocoa butter, sugar, vanilla, and an emulsifier. Finally, the mixture is conched (a grinding and blending process that produces a smooth, luxurious texture) and tempered.

(continued)

1. Bake the cake in two 8-inch square baking pans. When cool, cut the layers into bite-size cubes. Set aside.

2. Prepare the Classic Custard Filling without the optional fruit preserves. Cover and refrigerate.

3. Whip the cream, using an electric mixer on a high speed, until soft peaks form. Sprinkle in the sugar and vanilla and beat just until incorporated. Cover and refrigerate.

4. Place a layer of cake cubes in a straight-sided trifle bowl or any elegant clear serving bowl. Lightly sprinkle with brandy.

5. Add a layer of custard and a layer of blackberries.

6. Add a layer of cake cubes (sprinkled with brandy), a layer of custard, and a layer of raspberries.

7. Add a layer of cake (sprinkled with brandy), a layer of custard, and a layer of blueberries.

8. Top with the chantilly cream and toasted almonds.

Makes 10–12 servings

Harry Potter's™ Trifle

This trifle was inspired by the elegant feasts served at the Hogwarts School of Witchcraft and Wizardry . . . and by Harry's sweet tooth.

Chocolate Pound Cake (page 200)

Chocolate Spiders:
16 ounces semisweet molding chocolate
2–4 plastic chocolate molds for tiny spiders

Spiced Apples and Cherries:
2 tablespoons lemon juice
3 cups fresh, tart apples
2 tablespoons butter
3 tablespoons light brown sugar, firmly packed
1 teaspoon ground cloves
2 cups dark sweet cherries, drained
1 cup walnuts, toasted and coarsely chopped

Spiced Italian Meringue:
³/₄ cup sugar
¹/₃ cup water
6 egg whites, warmed to room temperature
¹/₄ teaspoon cream of tartar
1 teaspoon ground cinnamon
¹/₂ teaspoon ground cloves
3 tablespoons cinnamon liqueur
1 ounce semisweet chocolate, melted

1. Bake the cake in a loaf pan. When cool, cut into bite-size cubes. Set aside.

2. To make the chocolate spiders: Melt the chocolate according to the manufacturer's instructions. Stir the chocolate quickly and thoroughly. Place the chocolate in a pastry bag fitted with a small plain tip or a plastic squirt bottle. Fill the molds. Tap the molds on your working surface to release air bubbles. Refrigerate for 5 to 10 minutes, or until set. (The faster the molds are put in the refrigerator, the shinier your spiders will be.) Release from the molds and set aside in a cool place.

3. To make the spiced apples and cherries: Place the lemon juice in a mixing bowl. Peel, core, and cut the apples into bite-size pieces, tossing them in lemon juice as you work. Set aside.

4. Melt the butter and brown sugar in a heavy-bottomed frying pan, stirring continuously. Add the apples and cinnamon, and sauté, turning continuously, until golden. The apples should have a firm, but no longer crisp, texture.

5. Remove from the heat and gently mix in the cherries and walnuts. Set aside to cool to room temperature.

6. To make the spiced Italian meringue: Mix together the sugar and water in a heavy-bottomed saucepan. Bring to a boil over medium-high heat without stirring. If crystals begin to form on the sides of the pan, wash them away with a dampened pastry brush. Remove from the heat before the sugar begins to darken. If the syrup crystallizes, you must begin again.

7. While the syrup is heating, whip the egg whites, using an electric mixer on a medium speed, until frothy. Adjust the speed to high and sprinkle in the cream of tartar, beating until soft peaks form.

8. Adjust your mixer to a low speed and, very slowly, pour the boiling syrup directly into the egg whites. (Try not to pour the syrup against the sides of the bowl or through the beaters.)

9. Increase to a medium speed and continue beating until the meringue cools and stiff peaks begin to form. Add the cinnamon and cloves.

(continued)

Explorer-Entrepreneur

After seeing the commercial impact chocolate had on the Aztec civilization and the social impact chocolate had on the nobility of Spain, explorer Hernando Cortés set about establishing cocoa plantations from Mexico to Trinidad and to Madagascar, in the name of the Spanish crown.

Native American slaves were transported along with the trees to harvest and process the beans. Unfortunately, having little immunity to Western diseases, these workers soon perished, leaving a serious labor shortage. With much the same problem facing the sugar industry, plantation owners throughout the Caribbean began importing African slaves.

10. Place a layer of cake cubes in a straight-sided trifle bowl or any elegant clear serving bowl.

11. Add a layer of the apple mixture and a layer of the meringue. Sprinkle with chocolate spiders. Repeat 2 or 3 times more, filling the bowl.

12. Before sprinkling the final layer of chocolate spiders, place the melted chocolate in a pastry bag fitted with a writing tip, and pipe a spider web on top of the meringue.

Makes 10–12 servings

Trifle Parfaits

Dark chocolate biscotti and sweet mandarin oranges join a tiramisu filling in these individual trifles.

> 8–12 Bittersweet Almond Biscotti, crumbled (page 116)
> Easy Tiramisu Filling (page 226) or Traditional Tiramisu Filling (page 227)
> 2 cups mandarin orange slices, drained
> 4–6 mocha beans

1. Place a layer of crumbled biscotti in 4 to 6 parfait glasses or fluted champagne glasses. Add a layer of filling and a layer of oranges.

2. Add another layer of filling, a layer of biscotti, and a layer of oranges.

3. Top with a layer of filling, a sprinkling of biscotti, and a mocha bean.

Makes 4–6 servings

White Knight Trifle

For white chocolate lovers, this trifle contrasts tart raspberries with sweet cake and chantilly cream.

> White Chocolate Layer Cake (page 211)
> 2 cups heavy cream, chilled
> 1/4 cup powdered sugar
> 1 teaspoon pure vanilla extract
> 3 tablespoons raspberry liqueur
> 3 cups fresh raspberries
> 1 cup milk chocolate curls

1. Bake the cake in two 9-inch square baking pans. When cool, wrap and freeze one layer for another use. Cut the other layer into bite-size cubes.

2. To make the chantilly cream: Whip the cream, using an electric mixer on a high speed, until soft peaks form. Sprinkle in the sugar and vanilla, beating until stiff peaks form.

3. Place a layer of cake cubes in a straight-sided trifle bowl or any elegant clear serving bowl. Lightly sprinkle with raspberry liqueur.

4. Add a layer of cream and a layer of raspberries. Sprinkle with chocolate curls. Repeat 2 to 3 times more, filling the bowl, and serve.

Makes 8–10 servings

California Trifle

White chocolate brownies are featured with caramel custard, fresh apricots and strawberries, in this sweet trifle.

> 2 recipes White Chocolate Brownies
>   (page 122)
> 2¹/₄ cups heavy cream, warmed to room
>   temperature
> 1¹/₄ cups light brown sugar, firmly packed
> ¹/₃ cup light corn syrup
> ¹/₄ cup cornstarch
> 1 cup milk, warmed to room temperature,
>   divided
> 2 egg yolks, warmed to room temperature
> ¹/₂ cup superfine sugar
> 2 teaspoons pure vanilla extract
> ¹/₂ teaspoon pure almond extract
> 4 cups fresh strawberries
> 2 tablespoons fresh lemon juice
> 2 cups fresh apricots
> ¹/₄ cup white chocolate curls

1. Bake the brownies as directed. When cool, cut into bite-size cubes, and set aside.

2. To make the caramel custard: Combine ³/₄ cup of the cream, the brown sugar, and corn syrup in a heavy-bottomed saucepan. Bring the mixture to a boil over a low heat, stirring with a wooden spoon only until the sugar dissolves. When the temperature reaches 244°F, pour the mixture into a stainless steel bowl or pot. Set aside and stir every few minutes while the mixture cools.

3. Dissolve the cornstarch in ¹/₂ cup of the milk. Whisk in the egg yolks. Set aside.

4. Combine the remaining milk and cream and the sugar in a heavy-bottomed saucepan. Bring to a boil over a medium-low heat, stirring continuously. Whisk a few tablespoons of the hot cream mixture into the egg yolk mixture. Whisk the warm egg yolk mixture into the hot cream mixture. Continue whisking over a medium-low heat until the mixture thickens.

5. Remove from the heat and gently stir in the vanilla and almond extracts and the caramel mixture.

6. Pour into a glass bowl and set aside to cool to room temperature. Cover and refrigerate until cold.

7. Wash, hull, and slice the strawberries. Set aside.

8. Place the lemon juice in a mixing bowl. Peel, pit, and slice the apricots, coating in lemon juice as you work. Set aside.

9. Place a layer of brownies in a straight-sided trifle bowl or any elegant clear serving bowl. Add a layer of custard.

10. Place a ring of strawberry slices side by side, tip side up, against the side of the bowl. Fill with additional strawberry slices.

11. Add a layer of brownies, a layer of custard, and the sliced apricots.

12. Add a final layer of brownies, custard, and strawberries. Top with white chocolate curls and serve.

Makes 10–12 servings

Valrhona

Some say this exclusive, French boutique chocolaterie produces the finest chocolate in the world. I've found Valrhona to offer not only consistently exquisite couvertures, but also the most interesting and varied bittersweet and semisweet flavor selections.

Valrhona is very meticulous when selecting and processing beans. For example, they insist that the beans be dried in the sun, rather than in ovens (the fuel from the ovens can alter the flavor). Their blending choices are just as intense, producing grand cru and varietals that are revered for their aroma, body, and elegance.

Chocolate Pavlova

A circle of baked meringue is topped with a layer of rich cream and a layer of fresh fruit. This delicate dessert, created for the prima ballerina, Anna Pavlova, is even more elegant with a touch of chocolate and a hint of spice.

> 2 cups powdered sugar
> $1/4$ cup nonalkalized cocoa powder
> 1 teaspoon cornstarch
> 4 egg whites, warmed to room temperature
> $1/8$ teaspoon salt
> 1 teaspoon lemon juice
> $1/2$ recipe Easy Viennese Mousse (page 240)
> 2 cups mixed fresh fruit, peeled and sliced

1. Preheat the oven to 350°F. Using a dark pen or pencil, trace an 8-inch circle to use as a guide on the back side of a piece of parchment paper, and center the circle on a cookie sheet.

2. Sift together the sugar (reserve 1 tablespoon for topping), cocoa powder, and cornstarch. Set aside.

3. Whip the egg whites, using an electric mixer on a high speed, until frothy. Add the salt, beating until soft peaks form. Sprinkle in the sugar mixture, beating until stiff peaks begin to form. Add the lemon juice.

4.   Spoon the meringue onto the prepared pan, inside the 8-inch circle. Build the outside of the circle higher than the center, creating a 6-inch well.

5.   Bake for 5 minutes, then reduce the oven temperature to 250°F and continue baking for 1 hour. Turn off the oven and leave the meringue in the oven for 1 more hour. Finish cooling on a wire rack. The meringue may crack or collapse.

6.   When cool, pile the mousse in the center well and top with fresh fruit. (If you're using pears, bananas, or any other fruit that may darken, be sure to coat them in lemon juice.) Dust with the reserved powdered sugar and serve.

Makes 8–10 servings

Pavlova D'Amour

Formed in cupid's favorite shape, and topped with delicate white mousse, white peaches, and rose petals—this dessert will steal your heart.

> 5 egg whites, warmed to room
>   temperature
> 1/8 teaspoon salt
> 2 cups powdered sugar
> 1 teaspoon cornstarch
> 1 teaspoon white vinegar
> 2 tablespoons lemon juice
> 2 cups fresh Babcock peaches, peeled and
>   sliced
> 1/2 recipe Rose Petal Mousse (page 241)
> 1/4 cup fresh or sugared rose petals

(continued)

The Merry Monarch

When chocolate was introduced in England in the mid-seventeenth century, the "merry monarch" Charles II was an instant fan. The king's physician also touted the benefits of chocolate as a nourishing drink and as a cure for a hangover.

With these royal endorsements, exclusive chocolate houses, where the very rich could gather to socialize and savor this luxury, began to appear. Competition among these houses led to new ways to serve this drink, including varying the amounts of sugar and spices and replacing the water with milk and/or eggs.

1.   Preheat the oven to 350°F. Using a dark pen or pencil, trace an 8-inch heart to use as a guide on the back side of parchment paper, and center the heart on a cookie sheet.

2.   Whip the egg whites, using an electric mixer on a high speed, until frothy. Add the salt, beating until soft peaks form. Sprinkle in the sugar and cornstarch, beating until stiff peaks begin to form. Add the vinegar.

3.   Spoon the meringue onto the prepared pan inside the 8-inch heart. Build the outside of the heart higher than the center, creating a 6-inch well.

4.   Bake for 5 minutes, then reduce the oven temperature to 250°F and continue baking for 1 hour. Turn off the oven and leave the meringue in the oven for 1 more hour. Finish cooling on a wire rack. The meringue may crack or collapse.

5.   When cool, place the lemon juice in a mixing bowl. Peel, pit, and slice the peaches, tossing them in lemon juice as you work. Set aside.

6.   Pile the mousse in the center well and top with peaches and rose petals.

Makes 8–10 servings

Petites Jolies

These little beauties begin with a layer of chocolate speckled meringue baked atop a rich chocolate truffle torte. They're crowned with a chocolate-mint sabayon and tiny sparkling raspberries.

Chocolate Truffle Torte (page 222)

Meringue Pillows:
*4 egg whites, warmed to room
    temperature*
$^1/_8$ teaspoon cream of tartar
$^1/_2$ cup sugar
$^1/_4$ cup grated semisweet chocolate
$^1/_2$ recipe Grand Sabayon (page 244)*
2 cups fresh raspberries
$^1/_4$ cup superfine sugar

1.   Preheat the oven to 350°F. Line the bottoms of six 3-inch baking pans with parchment paper. Lightly coat the sides of the pans with butter and flour.

2.   Prepare the Chocolate Truffle Torte, divide between the six prepared pans, and set aside.

3.   To make the Meringue Pillows: Whip the egg whites and cream of tarter, using an electric mixer on a high speed, until soft peaks form. Sprinkle in the sugar, beating until stiff peaks begin to form. Gently fold the grated chocolate into the meringue.

4.   Spread the meringue over the tortes so that it completely covers the batter, sealing against the sides. Carefully create a small well in the center of each meringue, without breaking through to the torte.

5.   Bake for 25 to 30 minutes, or until set. Cool on wire racks.

6.   When cool, remove the cakes from the pans, remove the parchment paper, and place the cakes on serving dishes. Spoon the sabayon into the center well of each dessert. Coat the raspberries in superfine sugar, arrange on top of the sabayon, and serve.

*Replace the Grand Marnier with mint liqueur or $^1/_2$ teaspoon pure mint extract

Makes 6 servings

Marjolaine

Contrasting textures blend together in this modernized French classic, as chewy meringue wafers snuggle between creamy hazelnut mousse.

> 1 cup hazelnuts, toasted, skinned, and ground
> 1 cup almonds, blanched, toasted, and ground
> 2 tablespoons flour
> 1 cup superfine sugar, divided
> 7 egg whites, warmed to room temperature
> $^1/_2$ teaspoon cream of tartar
> $^1/_2$ recipe Classic Chocolate Mousse* (page 239)
> $^1/_2$ recipe Chocolate Buttercream** (page 230)
> Dark Chocolate Coating (page 233)
> $^3/_4$ cup almonds, toasted and coarsely chopped
> $^3/_4$ cup hazelnuts, toasted and coarsely chopped

1. Preheat the oven to 325°F. Line a 12-inch by 16-inch half sheet cake pan with parchment paper.

2. Mix together the ground nuts, flour, and $^3/_4$ cup of the sugar. Set aside.

(continued)

San Francisco Chocolates

San Francisco is renowned for two exceptional chocolates: Ghirardelli and Guittard. Italian chocolatier Domingo Ghirardelli brought his fine chocolate to the Gold Country (just north of San Francisco) in 1849, and supplied those seeking all that glittered with another form of gold. A few years later, in 1868, Etienne Guittard, skilled as a French chocolatier, opened a factory to provide San Francisco's bakeries and confectioneries with couvertures.

If you visit San Francisco, be sure to stop by Ghirardelli Square (near Fisherman's Wharf) where you can watch chocolate being made while you enjoy an ice cream sundae made with . . . Ghirardelli chocolate!

Designer Desserts

Can you match the names of these signature desserts to their design?

1. Chocolate Decadence

2. Dacquoise au Chocolat

3. Death by Chocolate

4. Dobosch Torte

5. Duchess of Parma Torte

6. Gateau l'Opera

7. Imperial Torte

8. Marjolaine

9. Reine de Saba

10. Sarah Bernhardt

A. Layers of hazelnut meringue, zabaglione buttercream, and dark chocolate buttercream are coated in a chocolate glaze.

B. A dense, intense torte served with raspberry coulis and sweetened whipped cream.

C. Layers of marzipan, chocolate cake, and chocolate buttercream, coated with chocolate glaze.

D. A rich single-layer chocolate and almond cake, coated with whipped ganache, a poured chocolate glaze, and sliced almonds.

E. Rectangular layers of almond and hazelnut genoise or meringue wafers, chocolate, buttercream, and praline are coated in buttercream and toasted nuts.

F. Seven very thin layers of genoise, separated by chocolate buttercream, are topped with a layer of crisp caramel.

G. An almond macaroon is topped with a teardrop of chocolate ganache and coated in dark chocolate.

H. Layers of sugar syrup-soaked almond genoise, coffee buttercream, and ganache are topped with a thin, solid chocolate plaque.

I. Layers of chocolate brownie, mocha mousse, and chocolate meringue are coated in a poured dark chocolate ganache.

J. Layers of almond or hazelnut meringue wafers and buttercream are coated with shaved chocolate or chopped nuts and topped with powdered sugar.

Answers: 1B, 2J, 3I, 4F, 5A, 6H, 7C, 8E, 9D, 10G

3. Whip the egg whites and cream of tartar, using an electric mixer on a high speed, until soft peaks form. Sprinkle in the remaining sugar, beating until stiff peaks begin to form.

4. Fold the nut mixture into the meringue. Spread in the prepared pan and bake for 30 to 35 minutes, or until golden brown. Cool on a wire rack.

5. When cool, remove from the pan and cut into 4 sections, creating 4-inch by 12-inch strips.

6. Place one strip on a serving plate, and top with mousse. Refrigerate until firm.

7. Repeat, layering two more meringue strips with mousse. Top with the remaining meringue strip and refrigerate until firm.

8. Frost the top and sides with a thin layer of buttercream, creating a smooth finish.

9. Cloak the top and sides with Dark Chocolate Coating. Place the remaining coating in a pastry bag fitted with a star tip, and pipe an edging around the top. Mix together the chopped almonds and hazelnuts, and press into the sides of the marjolaine.

*When making the mousse, add 1 tablespoon of Frangelico liqueur to the cooled melted chocolate and cream.

**Add $1/2$ teaspoon of pure almond extract to the Chocolate Buttercream recipe.

Makes 10–12 servings

The Legend of Montezuma

Cocoa beans weren't the only chocolate treasure brought back to Europe by early explorers. Exaggerated stories of how the Aztec king satisfied his entire harem after consuming golden goblets of chocolate inspired tabloid-like rumors of this new libation's power as an aphrodisiac. These stories captured the imagination of the royal courts, where kings and courtesans clamored for this exotic treat and, in turn, fueled more rumors of its erotic prowess.

Whether real or imagined, chocolate has continued to be revered for its seductive powers and still sparks the imagination of romantics everywhere.

Send Yourself a Gift Basket

When you deserve a special treat, why not send yourself a gift basket filled with chocolate surprises? Some of these sources even offer a plan that will automatically send you a surprise once a month!

Desserts Monthly
1400 West and 400 North
Orem, UT 84057
(800) 477-6575

Essentially Chocolate
15737 Crabbs Branch Way
Rockville, MD 20855
(800) FYI-GIFT

The Heavenly Chocolate Club
480-C Scotland Road
Lakemoor, IL 60050
(800) 800-9122

Praline Marjolaine

Layers of pecan meringue pastry separate rich chocolate buttercream in this variation of a tailored French classic.

2 cups pecans, toasted and ground
2 tablespoons flour
1 cup superfine sugar, divided
7 egg whites, warmed to room temperature
$^1/_2$ teaspoon cream of tartar
2 cups crumbled pralines or toffee bits
Chocolate Buttercream (page 230)
Dark Chocolate Coating (page 233)

1.   Preheat the oven to 325°F. Line a 12-inch by 16-inch half sheet cake pan with parchment paper.

2.   Mix together the ground pecans, flour, and $^3/_4$ cup of the sugar. Set aside.

3.   Whip the egg whites and cream of tartar, using an electric mixer on a high speed, until soft peaks form. Sprinkle in the sugar, beating until stiff peaks begin to form.

4.   Fold the nut mixture into the meringue. Spread in the prepared pan and bake for 30 to 35 minutes, or until golden brown. Cool on a wire rack.

5.   When cool, remove from pan and cut into 4 sections, creating 4-inch by 12-inch strips.

6.   Finely chop 1 cup of pralines or toffee bits. Set the remaining cup aside.

7.   Spread a third of the buttercream on top of one of the meringue strips, and sprinkle with a third of the chopped pralines or toffee. Repeat, ending with a strip of meringue.

8.   Frost the top and sides of the marjolaine with the remaining buttercream, creating a smooth finish.

9.   Cover the top and sides with Dark Chocolate Coating. Place the remaining coating in a pastry bag fitted with a star tip, and pipe an edging around the top. Press the remaining crumbled pralines or toffee bits into the sides of the marjolaine.

Makes 10–12 servings

Petites Marjolaines

With this recipe, we've turned a classic marjolaine into individual desserts for white chocolate lovers.

$\frac{1}{2}$ *cup pecans, toasted and ground*
$\frac{1}{2}$ *cup cashews, toasted and ground*
1 tablespoon flour
$\frac{1}{2}$ *cup superfine sugar, divided*
3 egg whites, warmed to room temperature
$\frac{1}{4}$ *teaspoon cream of tartar*
$\frac{1}{2}$ *recipe Eggnog Mousse (page 242)*
$1\frac{1}{2}$ *recipes White Chocolate Coating (page 233)*
1 cup white chocolate curls

1.   Preheat the oven to 325°F. Line 2 cookie sheets with parchment paper.

2.   Mix together the ground nuts, flour, and 3 tablespoons of the sugar. Set aside.

3.   Whip the egg whites and cream of tartar, using an electric mixer on a high speed, until soft peaks form. Sprinkle in the remaining sugar, beating until stiff peaks begin to form.

4.   Fold the nut mixture into the meringue. Place the meringue in a pastry bag fitted with a plain $\frac{1}{2}$-inch tip, and pipe 12 4-inch round disks. Bake for 15 to 20 minutes, or until golden brown. Cool on a wire rack.

5.   Stack 3 meringues, with a layer of mousse between each. Repeat, creating 4 desserts.

6.   Cover the tops and sides of each with White Chocolate Coating and top with white chocolate curls.

Makes 4 servings

Trademark Trivia

What chocolate company uses "La Belle Chocolatière," a painting by Jean-Etienne Liotard, as their company trademark? The painting depicts Prince Dietrichstein being served chocolate by his future wife.

Answer: Baker's Chocolate, since the mid-1800s, which also makes it one of the oldest trademarks in America.

From Madrid to Vienna

Chocolate was immensely popular in the court of the Holy Roman Emperor Charles VI. When this dynasty moved from Madrid to Vienna in 1711, chocolate was introduced to Northern Europe.

The Viennese were so impressed with this Spanish drink, they made it their own, and eventually became known for ultrarich cups of chocolate served with glasses of chilled water. When chocolate began to be used in pastries, the Hotel Sacher created what is still one of the most popular, and duplicated, tortes in the world.

Lunier

Think of this as an elegant ice cream cake. A meringue wafer and chocolate cake are layered with gelato. The cake is then coated in gelato and crumbled meringue.

Bittersweet Velvet Layer Cake (page 208)

Pistachio Meringue Pastry:

1 cup pistachios, ground
2 tablespoons cornstarch
1 cup superfine sugar, divided
6 egg whites, warmed to room temperature
$1/4$ teaspoon cream of tartar
1 quart Gelato di Cioccolata, softened (page 258)

1. Bake the cake in two 8-inch layer cake pans. When cool, wrap and freeze one layer for a future creation. Level and slice the other layer in half horizontally. Set aside.

2. Preheat the oven to 200°F. Using a dark pen or pencil, trace four $7^3/4$-inch circles to use as a guide on the back side of parchment paper. Center the circles on cookie sheets.

3. Mix together the ground pistachios, cornstarch, and $1/2$ cup of the sugar. Set aside.

4. Whip the egg whites and cream of tartar, using an electric mixer on a high speed, until soft peaks form. Sprinkle in the remaining sugar, beating until stiff peaks begin to form.

5. Fold the nut mixture into the meringue. Place the meringue in a pastry bag fitted with a ¹/₂-inch star tip. Pipe the meringue within the circles on the prepared cookie sheets, creating solid disks, and bake for 1 hour. Turn the heat off and leave the meringues in the oven for another hour. Finish cooling on a wire rack.

6. Line the bottom of a 9-inch springform pan with parchment paper. Place one of the 8-inch cake layers in the center. Spread a layer of gelato over the top of the cake, so that it also fills the sides.

7. Place one layer of pistachio meringue on top of the gelato. Spread a layer of gelato over the top of the meringue.

8. Place another layer of cake over the gelato. Frost the top and sides with gelato. Cover and freeze.

9. Crumble the remaining meringue layers. Carefully remove the ice cream cake from the pan. Cover the top and sides with crumbled meringue, and serve.

Makes 10–12 servings

Juin

This one's for you, Mom; a delicate almond meringue pastry, layered with a flourless chocolate cake and creamy chocolate-raspberry mousse, is wrapped in luxurious dark chocolate and topped with elegant dark and white chocolate ruffles.

Chocolate Cake:
8 ounces semisweet chocolate, finely chopped
¹/₂ cup butter, cut into ¹/₄-inch cubes
¹/₄ cup almond paste
¹/₂ cup superfine sugar, divided
6 egg yolks, warmed to room temperature
6 egg whites, warmed to room temperature

Almond Meringue Pastry:
2 cups almonds, toasted and ground
2 tablespoons flour
1 cup superfine sugar, divided

(continued)

A Dessert Date

One of the best birthday presents I ever received was a dessert date. A friend picked me up (in a limo!), and we went from gourmet restaurant to gourmet restaurant ordering only award-winning chocolate desserts!

You can also plan a dessert date around one special restaurant.

*7 egg whites, warmed to room
    temperature*
¹/₂ teaspoon cream of tartar
4 ounces semisweet chocolate, tempered
Angel Mousse* (page 238)
¹/₂ recipe Chocolate Ganache (page 225)
Dark chocolate and white chocolate ruffles

1. To make the Chocolate Cake: Preheat the oven to 350°F. Line the bottom of an 8-inch springform pan with parchment paper. Lightly coat the sides of the pan with butter and flour.

2. Melt the chocolate and butter in the top of a double boiler over hot, not simmering, water, stirring continuously. Set aside to cool to room temperature.

3. Cream together the almond paste and ¹/₄ cup of the sugar, using an electric mixer on a medium speed, until smooth. Add the egg yolks, one at a time, until thoroughly blended. Fold in the cooled chocolate mixture. Set aside.

4. Whip the egg whites, using an electric mixer on a high speed, until soft peaks form. Sprinkle in the remaining ¹/₄ cup sugar and continue beating until stiff peaks begin to form.

5. Fold a third of the egg whites into the chocolate batter. Repeat until all the egg whites are incorporated.

6. Bake for 30 to 35 minutes, or until a tester comes out with moist crumbs when inserted into the center of the cake. Cool on wire racks. Level the cake and slice in half horizontally. Set aside.

7. To make the Almond Meringue Pastry: Preheat the oven to 325°F. Line the bottom of two 8-inch layer cake pans with parchment paper.

8. Mix together the ground almonds, flour, and ³/₄ cup of the sugar. Set aside.

9. Whip the egg whites and cream of tartar, using an electric mixer on a high speed, until soft peaks form. Sprinkle in the remaining ¹/₄ cup sugar, beating until stiff peaks begin to form.

10. Fold the nut mixture into the meringue. Spread in the prepared pans and bake for 30 to 35 minutes, or until golden brown. Cool on a wire rack.

Cocolat

In 1976 French-trained Alice Medrich opened a small shop in Berkeley, CA, and forever changed America's appetite for chocolate. Cocolat offered real chocolate truffles. Frilly layer cakes were replaced with intensely chocolate tortes. Thanks to Alice, we transformed from sugar fanatics to chocolate connoisseurs.

11.   Cut a 4-inch by 28-inch strip of parchment paper and cardboard. Spread all but 1 teaspoon of the tempered chocolate evenly on the parchment paper, leaving a 1-inch margin on both narrow ends. Refrigerate, using the cardboard as a support, until firm enough to mold (about 5 to 10 minutes). If the chocolate gets too stiff, leave it at room temperature to soften.

12.   Place a layer of cake in an 8-inch springform pan. Cover with a layer of mousse.

13.   Add a layer of almond meringue and another layer of mousse.

14.   Repeat, stacking the remaining cake and meringue layers. Refrigerate until firm.

15.   Carefully remove the cake from the pan. Coat the sides with Chocolate Ganache, creating a smooth finish. (Reserve the remaining ganache for the top.)

16.   Leaving the chocolate on the paper (and holding the chocolate strip by the margins at the ends), gently place the chocolate strip at the base of the cake, wrapping it around the sides, on top of the ganache, (paper side out). Peel back both ends of the paper so you can overlap the ends of the chocolate strip. Warm the remaining teaspoon of chocolate and use it to "glue" the ends together. The strip should be taller than the cake.

17.   Spoon the remaining ganache onto the top of the cake, so that it comes within 1/2 inch of the top of the chocolate strip. Refrigerate until firm.

18.   Before serving, carefully peel the paper from the sides of the cake.

19.   Arrange dark chocolate ruffles, in the ganache, in a circle on top of and overlapping the outside rim of the cake. Add a circle of white chocolate ruffles, slightly overlapping the dark chocolate ruffles. Finish with another circle of dark chocolate ruffles in the center.

*Add 2 tablespoons of Chambord liqueur to the cooled chocolate and cream mixture while making the mousse.

Makes 10–12 servings

Theobroma Cacao

The cocoa bean tree received its scientific name in 1753 when a Swiss naturalist named Carl von Linne created a coding system for plants. He embraced the Aztecs' feelings toward chocolate, and chose a translation that means "food of the gods."

Razza

And for you, Dad, an artful chocolate torte is topped with a layer of mocha truffle ganache, which is covered with a layer of rich bittersweet mousse.

> Angel Torte (page 218)
> 10 ounces Guittard semisweet chocolate, finely chopped
> ³/₄ cup heavy cream
> 2 tablespoons Kahlua liqueur
> Bitter Almond Mousse (page 240)
> 3 cups dark chocolate curls

1.　Bake the torte in an 8-inch springform pan. Set aside to cool to room temperature.

2.　Melt the chocolate and cream in the top of a double boiler over hot, not simmering, water, stirring continuously. Set aside to cool to room temperature. Stir in the liqueur.

3.　Pour the cooled chocolate mixture into the fallen center of the cooled torte in the springform pan. Cover and refrigerate until firm.

4.　Line the bottom of a 9-inch springform pan with parchment paper. Lightly coat the sides of the pan with butter.

5.　Carefully remove the ganache-covered torte from the pan and peel the parchment paper off the bottom. Place the torte in the center of the 9-inch springform pan. Cover the top and sides with the mousse. Cover and freeze.

6.　Remove from the pan, place on a serving dish, and cover the top and sides with dark chocolate curls.

Makes 10–12 servings

Chocolate Boxes

Poured chocolate boxes are among my favorite specialty items. They are surprisingly easy to make and molds are available in a variety of sizes and charming shapes. In addition to round and square molds, you'll find molds for baby grand pianos, violins, crescent moons, houses, leaves, wreaths, top hats, hearts, and more.

chapter ten

Drinks and Libations

Chocolate began as a drink. By all accounts, it was a bitter, heavily spiced, sometimes greasy drink. But even in this form, it was coveted. Over the centuries, as chocolate grew in popularity, it transformed into candy, puddings, cakes, and pastries, and the focus strayed away from chocolate as a drink.

Today, the popularity of chocolate in its original liquid form is increasing. Gourmet coffees and cocktails include chocolate. And old-fashioned chocolate milk shakes and sodas are taking advantage of new quality couvertures and flavor combinations. For your next party, consider serving chocolate in the form of a liquid dessert!

Chocolate Syrups

Chocolate syrups can be used in a variety of hot and cold drinks. You can purchase premade chocolate-flavored syrup at any grocery store, but syrup made with your favorite nibbling (real) chocolate is far more flavorful.

Dark Chocolate Syrup

16 ounces semisweet chocolate, finely chopped
³/₄ cup water
6 tablespoons (¹/₄ cup + 2 tablespoons) sugar
¹/₂ cup light corn syrup
2 teaspoons pure vanilla extract

Milk Chocolate Syrup

16 ounces milk chocolate, finely chopped
³/₄ cup water
¹/₄ cup sugar
¹/₂ cup light corn syrup
2 teaspoons pure vanilla extract

White Chocolate Syrup

16 ounces white chocolate, finely chopped
³/₄ cup water
2 tablespoons sugar
¹/₄ cup light corn syrup
2 teaspoons pure vanilla extract

You can add additional flavorings to these basic chocolate syrups if desired: instant espresso powder (1 tablespoon), extracts (1 to 2 teaspoons), liqueurs (1 to 2 tablespoons), ground spices (¹/₄ to ¹/₂ teaspoon), or flavoring oils (2 to 3 drops).

1. Melt the chocolate in the top of a double boiler over hot, not simmering, water, stirring until smooth. Set aside.

2. Combine the water, sugar, and corn syrup in a heavy-bottomed saucepan over low heat. Bring to a boil, stirring continuously. Remove from heat, cool for 5 minutes, and blend in the melted chocolate and vanilla.

3. Store in an airtight container in the refrigerator.

Makes about 2 cups

Cold Drinks

Chocolate Milk Shake

There are two basic ways to make a chocolate milk shake. Using vanilla ice cream with chocolate syrup makes a sweet milk shake. For a truer chocolate flavor, substitute chocolate ice cream for vanilla and omit the chocolate syrup.

> *¹/₄ cup chilled chocolate syrup*
> *2 scoops vanilla ice cream*
> *1 cup ice cold whole milk*

1. Blend the ingredients together, using an electric blender or drink mixer, and pour into a chilled glass.

Makes 1 chocolate milk shake

Mocha Bean Shake

This mocha-flavored milk shake features bits of mocha bean candies.

> *1 scoop chocolate ice cream*
> *1 scoop coffee ice cream*
> *1 cup ice cold whole milk*
> *2 tablespoons mocha beans**

1. Mix together the ice creams and milk using an electric blender or drink mixer, blending until smooth.
2. Add the mocha beans to the milk shake. Blend for a few seconds more.
3. Pour into a chilled glass.

*Mocha beans are coffee-flavored chocolate candies, in the shape of coffee beans.

Makes 1 milk shake

Gifts for Chocolate Drink and Libation Makers

Kitchen departments of major department stores and larger kitchen specialty shops usually have a nice selection of drink and libation glasses and "tools."

- Old-fashioned milk shake glasses
- Hot chocolate mugs
- Café au lait cups
- Irish coffee glasses
- Cocktail glasses
- Daiquiri glasses
- Parfait glasses
- Hurricane glasses
- Pousse-café glasses
- Shot glasses
- Cocktail shaker
- Long-handled spoon
- Trays that make ice cubes in unique shapes
- Juicer
- Blender
- Ice crusher
- Gourmet chocolate syrups
- Chocolate liqueurs
- Sweetened ground chocolate
- "Sprinkles" (drink toppings)

Mystic Mint Milk Shake

Cookies and cream never tasted this good, especially on a hot afternoon.

2 scoops white chocolate ice cream
1 cup ice cold whole milk
1/2 teaspoon mint extract
3 Mystic Mint cookies (chocolate covered chocolate/mint cookies)

1.   Blend the ice cream, milk, and mint extract in a blender until smooth.
2.   Break up the cookies and add them to the milk shake. Blend for a few seconds more.
3.   Pour into a chilled glass.

Makes 1 milk shake

Chocolate Soda

There are two ways to make a chocolate soda. A traditional chocolate soda is made with vanilla ice cream and chocolate syrup. For an all chocolate soda, substitute chocolate ice cream for vanilla. And for a mocha soda, use coffee ice cream.
To duplicate an old-fashioned soda-fountain soda, use seltzer water, shot out of a charger.

1/4 cup chilled dark chocolate syrup
2 tablespoons ice cold whole milk
1/2 cup ice cold seltzer water or club soda
2 scoops vanilla ice cream
2 tablespoons sweetened whipped cream
1 teaspoon chocolate sprinkles
1 maraschino cherry

1.   Mix together the chocolate syrup and milk in a chilled soda glass.
2.   Add the seltzer water or club soda, and mix.
3.   Add the vanilla ice cream. Top with whipped cream, chocolate sprinkles, and a cherry.

Makes 1 ice cream soda

Mocha Float

This doesn't fizz like traditional floats, but on hot afternoons when you need a treat and a boost of energy, this super easy drink is guaranteed to perk you up.

2 scoops chocolate ice cream
ice cold coffee
2 tablespoons sweetened whipped cream
1/2 teaspoon sweetened ground chocolate

1.   Place the ice cream in a chilled glass.
2.   Add enough coffee to fill the glass.
3.   Top with whipped cream and sweetened ground chocolate.

Makes 1 float

Mocha Borgia Smoothie

Chocolate sorbet is blended with espresso and orange zest for this too-delicious-to-be-low-fat smoothie.

2 scoops chocolate sorbet
1 tablespoon dark chocolate syrup
1/2 cup coffee ice cubes
1 cold espresso

1 teaspoon orange zest
1 teaspoon shaved chocolate

1. Combine all ingredients except the shaved chocolate in a blender and mix until smooth.
2. Pour into a chilled glass and top with shaved chocolate.

Makes 1 smoothie

Hot Drinks

Hot Chocolate

Real hot chocolate should be made with your favorite nibbling chocolate, blended into a syrup, whole milk, and cream. If you're a white chocolate lover, use white chocolate syrup. And don't forget the marshmallows!

¹/₄ cup chocolate syrup
¹/₂ cup whole milk
¹/₄ cup heavy cream
5 miniature marshmallows
1 cinnamon stick

1. Place the chocolate syrup in a warmed mug. Set aside.
2. Heat the milk and cream together in a heavy-bottomed saucepan over medium heat, stirring constantly.
3. Just before the mixture boils, pour into the mug, and stir thoroughly. Top with marshmallows and serve with a cinnamon stir-stick.

Makes 1 serving

Pousse-Café Libations

Despite the name, pousse-café drinks do not necessarily contain a coffee-flavored liqueur. They are elegant layered libations. To design a pousse-café, you must consider the weight, textures, and colors of the liquors or liqueurs you plan to use, so that each layer floats on the one beneath and complements the layer above and below.

To pour a pousse-café, begin with a narrow, straight-sided cordial glass. Pour the base liquor or liqueur into the glass. Place the tip of a spoon against the side of the glass, just above the previous layer, back side up. Drizzle the next liquor or liqueur on top over the spoon. Continue until all layers have been added.

The Choice of Infamy

Marie Antoinette lost her head over chocolate long before she was sent to the guillotine. She kept a personal chocolatier, and preferred her chocolate flavored with orange flower water and orchid powder.

Madame du Barry insisted that her lovers drink chocolate before coming to call, to increase their chances of keeping up with her.

Napoleon insisted that chocolate accompany him on his military campaigns.

The Marquis de Sade wrote of chocolate's erotic powers.

And Casanova was convinced that when it came to seducing women, chocolate was even better than champagne. (Although he shamelessly used both.)

Cherry Cream Dream

This is an extra-special treat for extra-special little ones.

$^1/_4$ *cup warm white chocolate syrup*
3 *tablespoons grenadine*
$^1/_3$ *cup whole milk*
$^1/_4$ *cup heavy cream*
5 *miniature marshmallows*

1. Mix together the chocolate syrup and grenadine in a warmed mug. Set aside.
2. Heat the milk and cream together in a heavy-bottomed saucepan over medium heat, stirring constantly.
3. Just before the mixture boils, pour into the mug, and stir thoroughly. Top with marshmallows and serve.

Makes 1 serving

Café Mocha

If you prefer coffee to espresso, here's a way to start your day with a chocolate café au lait.

$^1/_4$ *cup warm chocolate syrup*
$^3/_4$ *cup hot, brewed coffee*
$^1/_2$ *cup whole milk*
$^1/_2$ *teaspoon sweetened ground chocolate*

1. Place the chocolate syrup in a warmed café au lait cup or large mug.
2. Add the hot coffee and stir until thoroughly blended.

3. Steam the milk until foamy. Pour the milk into the chocolate-coffee mixture, using a spoon to hold back the foam. Spoon a layer of milk foam on top and sprinkle with sweetened ground chocolate.

Makes 1 serving

LTS Mocha

Here's how I start my day when I don't have access to an espresso machine. It's a quick way to make an imitation espresso mocha. And I personally guarantee it will put you in a great mood.

1 generous teaspoon Suisse Mocha powder*
1 scant teaspoon instant espresso powder
1 cup hot brewed coffee
1 heaping teaspoon Haagen-Dazs vanilla ice cream

1. Mix together the Suisse Mocha and instant espresso powders in an Irish coffee mug.
2. Add the hot coffee and stir until thoroughly blended.
3. Microwave the mixture for 30 seconds on high. Add the ice cream.

*Suisse Mocha is one of the General Foods International Coffees.

Makes 1 serving

Chocolate "Beach Reads"

If you'd like a little chocolate in a light, fun, or heartwarming fictional read, "taste" one of these:

Chocolate Chip Cookie Murder by Joanne Fluke
Chocolate Jesus by Stephan Jaramillo
Chocolate Kisses by Margaret Brownley
Chocolate for a Woman's Soul by Kay Allenbaugh
Chocolate Sauce and Malice by Arline Potter
Dying for Chocolate by Diane Mott Davidson
Hot Chocolate by Suzanne Forster
Just Hand Over the Chocolate and No One Will Get Hurt by Karen Scalf Linamen
Like Water for Chocolate by Laura Esquivel
Love You to Death by Grant Michaels
Love Adds a Little Chocolate by Medard Laz

Espresso Mocha

For chocolate and espresso lovers, here's the only way to start the day.

>   2 tablespoons warm chocolate syrup
>   1 hot, single espresso
>   ³/₄ cup whole milk
>   2 tablespoons sweetened whipped cream
>   ¹/₂ teaspoon sweetened ground chocolate

1.   Mix together the chocolate syrup and espresso in a mug.

2.   Steam the milk until foamy. Pour the milk into the chocolate-espresso mixture, using a spoon to hold back the foam.

3.   Spoon a layer of milk foam on top and sprinkle with sweetened ground chocolate.

Makes 1 serving

Nirvana

When you're feeling overwhelmed, here's a sweet, spicy escape.

>   ¹/₄ cup chocolate syrup
>   1 hot, single espresso
>   ¹/₂ cup brewed coffee
>   1 cinnamon stick
>   ¹/₄ teaspoon whole allspice
>   ¹/₈ teaspoon whole cloves
>   ¹/₄ cup sweetened whipped cream
>   ¹/₂ teaspoon sweetened ground chocolate

1.   Combine the chocolate syrup, espresso, coffee, and spices in a heavy-bottomed saucepan over low heat. Cover and

heat for 10 minutes without letting the mixture boil.

2.   Remove the spices, pour into a mug, and top with whipped cream and ground chocolate.

Makes 1 serving

Liquor Libations

Chocolate and Whiskey

Whether it's bourbon, scotch, or whiskey, these strong-flavored grain alcohols are sparring partners for chocolate. Just a splash goes a long way.

Foolish Pleasure

For a Derby Day party, we added chocolate to a classic Mint Julep and named it after the first horse I ever bet on. (He won!)

>   2 ounces Mozart dark chocolate liqueur
>   ¹/₄ ounce fresh lemon juice
>   1 teaspoon superfine sugar
>   1 teaspoon water
>   3 fresh sprigs of mint
>   crushed ice
>   1 ounce Kentucky bourbon

1.   Mix together the chocolate liqueur, lemon juice, sugar, and water in a highball glass.

2.   Muddle in 2 sprigs of mint. (To muddle, gently mash the mint with the back of a bar spoon.)

3. Fill the glass with crushed ice, pour the bourbon over the ice, and garnish with the remaining mint.

Makes 1 libation

Ghost Buster

Cinnamon helps fend off evil spirits, while attracting friendship and passion. This fire and ice libation will help turn your poltergeists into friendly ghosts.

> 1 ounce Mozart white chocolate liqueur
> ¹/₂ ounce Jack Daniels
> ¹/₂ ounce Goldschlager
> ¹/₂ ounce peppermint schnapps
> ice

1. Pour ingredients into an old-fashioned glass filled with ice.

Makes one libation

Fat Tuesday

This mocha-orange-cherry treat is a tribute to the sweet excesses of the final day of Mardi Gras.

> 2 ounces Godiva dark chocolate liqueur
> 1 ounce bourbon
> 1 ounce Jamaican rum
> ¹/₂ ounce Cointreau
> ¹/₄ ounce grenadine
> 1 scoop coffee ice cream
> ¹/₄ cup sweetened whipped cream
> 1 tablespoon chocolate sprinkles
> 1 maraschino cherry

(continued)

Chocolate Liqueurs

Chocolate liqueurs make elegant gifts for chocolatiers, pastry chefs, and just plain chocolate lovers, everywhere. Some of the finer chocolate liqueurs are hard to find, but are well worth the search or special order. The easiest time to find them is around the fall and winter holidays.

Mozart—Chocolate and white chocolate liqueurs

Godiva—Chocolate and white chocolate liqueurs

Vandermint—Chocolate liqueur

Sheridan's—Vanilla cream and coffee chocolate double liqueur

Sabra—Chocolate-orange liqueur

Taam Pree—Chocolate truffle liqueur

Coquila—Chocolate liqueur

De Kuyper, Gaetano, Hiram Walker, and Leroux—each make a dark chocolate crème de cacao, and a "white" crème de cacao. White crème de cacao is technically clear.

1. Mix chocolate liqueur, bourbon, rum, Cointreau, grenadine, and ice cream in a blender until smooth.

2. Pour into a chilled parfait glass.

3. Top with whipped cream, chocolate sprinkles, and a cherry.

Makes 1 libation

Pralines and Cream

Chocolate, pecans, and a smooth peach-flavored bourbon; this libation is perfect for elegant summer garden parties.

1 ounce Godiva white chocolate liqueur
1 ounce Southern Comfort
1 ounce praline (pecan) liqueur
ice cubes
crushed ice

1. Place the ingredients in a cocktail shaker filled with ice.

2. Shake and strain into a cocktail glass filled with crushed ice.

Makes 1 libation

Candy Apple

If you love caramel apples dipped in chocolate, you'll love this rich after-dinner treat.

1 ounce crème de cacao
1 ounce apple schnapps
$^1/_4$ ounce butterscotch liqueur
$^1/_2$ ounce scotch
ice cubes

1. Place the ingredients in a cocktail shaker filled with ice.

2. Shake and strain into a cordial glass.

Makes 1 libation

Leprechaun's Folly

Chocolate, currants, and cherries disguise this whiskey-gin-rum concoction. After one of these, you'll be seeing rainbows everywhere!

1 ounce Mozart dark chocolate liqueur
1 ounce Irish whiskey
$^1/_2$ ounce sloe gin
$^1/_2$ ounce rum
$^1/_2$ ounce crème de cassis
$^1/_4$ cup fresh strawberries
$^1/_4$ ounce grenadine
1 teaspoon fresh lemon juice
1 teaspoon honey
$^1/_2$ cup ice
1 maraschino cherry for garnish

1. Mix all the ingredients except the cherry in a blender until smooth.

2. Serve in a chilled parfait glass garnished with a cherry.

Makes 1 libation

McCaffrey's Coffee

Always up for mischief, sneaking a little whiskey and a spoonful of whipped cream in her after-dinner coffee never failed to bring a twinkle to my little Irish grandmother's eye. I think she'd like this version of an Irish coffee even more.

1 ounce Mozart dark chocolate liqueur
¹/₂ ounce Irish whiskey
¹/₂ ounce butterscotch liqueur
1 cup fresh brewed coffee
¹/₄ cup chantilly cream
chocolate curls for garnish

1. Combine the chocolate liqueur, Irish whiskey, butterscotch liqueur, and coffee in an Irish coffee glass.

2. Top with chantilly cream and chocolate curls.

Makes 1 libation

Chocolate and Rum

Cocoa beans and sugarcane have grown together since the beginning of time, so it's not surprising that chocolate and rum blend so well together in pastries and in libations.

BK's Chocolate Pudding

Like its designer (a successful, high-powered friend who holds executive board meetings on jet skis), this serious chocolate libation is all about fun.

3 huge scoops chocolate ice cream
1¹/₂ ounces Kahlua
2 ounces Bacardi dark rum
¹/₄ cup sweetened whipped cream
1 tablespoon Hershey's chocolate syrup
1 tablespoon salted Planter's cocktail
peanuts, chopped

1. Mix the ice cream, Kahlua, and rum in a blender until smooth.

2. Pour into a chilled milk shake glass.

3. Top with whipped cream, drizzle with chocolate syrup, and sprinkle with peanuts.

Makes 1 libation

Tavarua

Easily the most enchanting of the South Pacific islands, Tavarua is the inspiration for this elegant tropical libation of chocolate, almonds, and coconut.

(continued)

Death by Chocolate

Long before 20th century pastry chefs were designing decadent chocolate desserts "to die for," European nobility was slipping poison into goblets of rich chocolate cocktails to do away with husbands, lovers, and enemies. The luxurious flavor and texture of chocolate, with the help of added spices, masked the drink's lethal intent.

2 ounces Mozart white chocolate liqueur
1 ounce light rum
¹/₂ ounce amaretto
¹/₂ ounce coconut cream
¹/₂ cup ice
shaved, semisweet chocolate for garnish

1. Mix the chocolate liqueur, rum, amaretto, coconut cream, and ice in a blender until smooth.
2. Pour into a chilled parfait glass.
3. Garnish with shaved chocolate.

Makes 1 libation

Chocolate Daiquiri

If you love strawberries dipped in chocolate, you'll love this icy treat.

1 ounce Godiva white chocolate liqueur
1 ounce light rum
¹/₄ cup sliced fresh strawberries
¹/₄ ounce fresh lime juice
¹/₂ cup ice
¹/₄ cup grated semisweet chocolate

1. Mix all ingredients except the grated chocolate in a blender until smooth.
2. Blend in the grated chocolate.
3. Serve in a chilled hurricane glass.

Makes 1 libation

Enchanted April

This is a perfect libation for afternoons when you want to dream about moving to a villa in Tuscany.

1 ounce Mozart white chocolate liqueur
¹/₂ ounce amaretto
¹/₄ ounce apricot liqueur
1 ounce rum
2 ounces light cream
ice

1. Place ingredients in a cocktail shaker filled with ice.
2. Shake and strain into a cocktail glass.

Makes 1 libation

Tiramisu

This Italian dessert is so popular, we had to turn it into an after-dinner drink.

¹/₂ ounce Kahlua
¹/₂ ounce Godiva white chocolate liqueur
¹/₂ ounce dark rum
¹/₂ ounce whipped mascarpone (Italian cream cheese)
grated milk chocolate for garnish

1. Layer Kahlua, chocolate liqueur, and rum in a pousse-café or cordial glass.
2. Top with a dollop of whipped mascarpone.
3. Sprinkle with grated chocolate.

Makes 1 libation

Hot Buttered Rum

This libation should be served in front of a crackling fire on a stormy afternoon.

> 1 recipe Hot Chocolate, made with white
>   chocolate syrup (page 295)
> 1 ounce butterscotch liqueur
> 1 ounce light rum
> ¹/₄ cup sweetened whipped cream
> 1 dash nutmeg

1.   Make the hot chocolate in an Irish coffee glass, omitting the marshmallows.
2.   Blend in the butterscotch liqueur and rum.
3.   Top with whipped cream and nutmeg.

Makes 1 libation

The REV

This hot libation was designed by our wild best friend and contractor to get everyone charged for the Samuels/Smith and Voudy Way Custom Mountain Bike Invitational.

> 1 double espresso Mocha (2 shots of
>   espresso) (page 298)
> ¹/₂ ounce Goldschlager
> 1 ounce Kahlua
> 1 ounce rum

1.   Prepare the espresso mocha in an Irish coffee glass, without the whipped cream and ground chocolate.
2.   Add the Goldschlager, Kahlua, and rum.

3.   Top with whipped cream and ground chocolate.

Makes 1 libation

Chocolate and Tequila

I couldn't imagine blending chocolate with tequila until one of our clients requested margarita truffles, which turned out to be delicious. Like whiskey, this product of the blue agave plant can overwhelm chocolate; a little goes a long way.

Smugglers' Blues

The more popular chocolate became throughout the world, the more it was taxed, which spawned a lively trade in smuggled chocolate. Unfortunately, word of this coveted delicacy did not spread as quickly to pirates, who regularly dumped precious cocoa beans, thinking them to be sheep dung.

White Chocolate Margarita

This started as a truffle for a Cinco de Mayo party, and grew into a frozen libation.

> 2 ounces Godiva white chocolate liqueur
> 1 ounce tequila
> $^1/_2$ ounce triple sec
> juice of $^1/_2$ lime
> 1 cup ice
> white chocolate curls for garnish

1. Mix all ingredients except chocolate curls in a blender until smooth.
2. Pour into a chilled margarita glass.
3. Top with chocolate curls.

Makes 1 libation

Cabo Cooler

Sweet chocolate and coffee liqueurs disguise the tequila kick in this frozen libation.

> l ounce Coquila chocolate liqueur
> 1 ounce Kahlua
> $^1/_2$ ounce Cuervo Gold tequila
> 1 cup ice

1. Mix all ingredients in a blender until smooth.
2. Pour into a chilled margarita glass.

Makes 1 libation

Scout's Tequila Mockingbird

Don't you think Scout would prefer her Tequila Mockingbird with chocolate?

> 1 ounce Godiva white chocolate liqueur
> $^1/_2$ ounce tequila
> $^1/_2$ ounce crème de menthe
> 1 cup ice
> sprig of fresh mint for garnish

1. Mix the first 4 ingredients in a blender until smooth.
2. Pour into a chilled margarita glass.
3. Garnish with the sprig of mint.

Makes 1 libation

Temptress

Beware! The chocolate, wild black currants, and cinnamon in this frozen libation will tempt you into drinking more.

> 2 ounces Mozart white chocolate liqueur
> $^1/_2$ ounce tequila
> $^1/_2$ ounce crème de cassis
> $^1/_4$ ounce cinnamon liqueur
> 2 ounces light cream
> $^3/_4$ cup ice

1. Mix all ingredients in a blender until smooth.
2. Serve in a chilled margarita glass.

Makes 1 libation

Caribbean Sunrise

This libation adds chocolate and a float of Galliano to a classic tequila sunrise.

> 1 ounce Coquila chocolate liqueur
> $1/2$ ounce tequila
> $1/4$ ounce grenadine
> 4 ounces fresh squeezed orange juice
> $1/2$ ounce Galliano
> ice

1. Pour all ingredients except the Galliano into a highball glass filled with ice.
2. Top with a float of Galliano.

Makes 1 libation

Wild Bill's Orange Coma

This sweet, chocolate-orange slush is perfect for reunion weekends with life-long friends.

> 1 ounce white crème de cacao
> $1/2$ ounce white tequila
> $1/2$ ounce white rum
> $1/2$ ounce vodka
> $1/2$ ounce triple sec
> 4 fresh squeezed orange juice ice cubes
> 1 ounce light cream

1. Mix all ingredients in a blender until smooth.
2. Serve in a chilled margarita glass.

Makes 1 libation

Montezuma's Nitecap

This is a more civilized version of the spicy xocolatl (bitter water) Montezuma drank before visiting his harem.

> 2 ounces Coquila chocolate liqueur
> $1/2$ ounce tequila
> $1/4$ ounce cinnamon liqueur
> 1 single espresso
> 1 cup fresh brewed coffee
> 1 cinnamon stick

1. Combine the chocolate liqueur, tequila, and cinnamon liqueur in a goblet.

(continued)

J. S. Fry & Sons

In the late 1700s, after being denied entry to universities and most professions due to his allegiance to the Quaker faith, Englishman J. S. Fry turned to trading in cocoa beans. He was the first to grind the beans using steam power and use Van Houten's press to create cocoa powder. Fry hoped that he could persuade others to drink cocoa rather than "demon" gin.

2.   Add the espresso and coffee.

3.   Garnish with the cinnamon stick.

Makes 1 libation

Chocolate and Vodka

This colorless, almost flavorless alcohol, originally distilled from potatoes, works well in chocolate libations when you want to add an invisible kick.

Avalanche

We designed this sweet mocha slush in the middle of a heat wave, dreaming of snowboarding seasons to come.

> shaved ice (or snow!)
> $^1/_2$ ounce Butter Shots
> 1 ounce vodka
> 1 ounce Kahlua
> $^1/_2$ ounce Irish Cream liqueur
> 4–6 ounces ice cold chocolate milk
> shaved chocolate for garnish

1.   Fill a frozen pint glass with shaved ice.

2.   Pour the remaining ingredients over the ice in the order given. (Don't stir!)

3.   Garnish with shaved chocolate.

Makes 1 libation

Mudslide

Warning! One sip of this mocha milk shake, and your problems, inhibitions, and resolve will start to slide away.

> $^1/_2$ ounce Godiva dark chocolate liqueur
> $^1/_2$ ounce Irish Cream liqueur
> $^1/_2$ ounce Kahlua
> 1 ounce vodka
> 4 ounces milk
> 1 scoop chocolate ice cream
> 1 scoop coffee ice cream
> grated chocolate for garnish

1.   Mix all ingredients except the grated chocolate in a blender until smooth.

2.   Pour into a chilled parfait glass.

3.   Top with grated chocolate.

Makes 1 libation

Chocolate Goddess

If chocolate is the food of the gods, chocolate and fruit (and vodka and rum!) must be the drink of the goddesses.

> 1 ounce Godiva white chocolate liqueur
> 1 ounce vodka
> $^1/_2$ ounce light rum
> $^1/_2$ cup fresh strawberries
> $^1/_2$ ounce fresh lime juice
> $^1/_4$ ounce grenadine
> $^1/_2$ cup ice
> 1 orange slice for garnish

1.   Mix all ingredients except the orange slice in a blender until smooth.

2.   Pour into a chilled parfait glass.

3.   Garnish with the orange slice.

Makes 1 libation

Frozen Banana

If you love frozen bananas coated in chocolate, you'll love this milk shake.

> 1 ounce Godiva white chocolate liqueur
> 1 ounce vodka
> 1 ounce banana liqueur
> 1 teaspoon almond syrup
> 1 scoop vanilla ice cream
> ¼ cup fresh sliced bananas
> ¼ cup sweetened whipped cream
> 1 tablespoon semisweet chocolate curls
> 1 tablespoon almonds, roasted and coarsely chopped

1. Mix the first 6 ingredients in a blender until smooth.
2. Pour into a chilled hurricane glass.
3. Top with whipped cream, chocolate curls, and almonds.

Makes 1 libation

White Chocolate Russian

This classic drink has always needed chocolate.

> 1 ounce Kahlua
> 1 ounce vodka
> ice
> 1 ounce Mozart white chocolate liqueur

1. Place the Kahlua and vodka in a cocktail shaker filled with ice.
2. Shake and strain into an old-fashioned glass filled with ice.
3. Float the chocolate liqueur on top.

Makes 1 libation

The Catholic Controversy

You would think the Catholic Church would have objected to chocolate based on its reputation for inspiring passion or because of the many incidences of church officials being poisoned with the help of chocolate. But when controversy erupted it was a matter of commerce, the debate taking the form of whether chocolate was a food or a drink.

The Jesuits, traders of chocolate at the time, claimed it was a mere beverage, therefore clearing the way for clergy and parishioners to continue buying and drinking it during the ecclesiastical fast. The Dominicans, however, argued that chocolate was far more substantial, and should be excluded during this holy period. This debate raged for two centuries before the Jesuits prevailed.

Chocolate Martini

Shaken or stirred, this is the only way for chocolate connoisseurs to drink a martini.

*1 ounce white (clear) crème de cacao
2 ounces vodka
1 splash vermouth*

1. Place ingredients in a cocktail shaker filled with ice.
2. Shake and strain into a chilled cocktail glass.

Makes 1 libation

The First Ad for Chocolate

"In Bishopsgate Street, in Queen's Head Alley, at a Frenchman's house, is an excellent West India drink, called Chocolat, to be sold, where you may have it ready at any time; and also unmade, at reasonable prices." *The Public Advertiser, 1657*

Insatiable Passion

If you have a passion for chocolate and raspberries, try this sophisticated cocktail.

*1 ounce Mozart white chocolate liqueur
1/2 ounce Chambord liqueur
1 ounce vodka
2 ounces half-and-half
ice*

1. Place ingredients in a cocktail shaker filled with ice.
2. Shake and strain into a chilled cocktail glass.

Makes 1 libation

Chocolate and Gin

Distilled with juniper berries, this deceptively potent alcohol has the potential of stealing the spotlight from chocolate, so use it with care.

The Great Gatsby

You know he threw extravagant parties. Did you know this is the drink he served?

*2 ounces white (clear) crème de cacao
1 ounce gin
ice cubes
crushed ice
1 lemon twist for garnish*

1. Place the crème de cacao and gin in a cocktail shaker filled with ice cubes.

2. Shake and strain into a cocktail glass filled with crushed ice.

3. Garnish with the lemon twist.

Makes 1 libation

Noble House Sling

This libation adds chocolate to a traditional Singapore sling.

> 1 ounce white (clear) crème de cacao
> 2 ounces gin
> 1 ounce fresh lime juice
> $^{1}/_{2}$ ounce grenadine
> ice
> club soda

1. Mix the crème de cacao, gin, lime juice, and grenadine in a highball glass.

2. Fill with ice and club soda.

Makes 1 libation

Endless Summer

This blend of chocolate and watermelon, with a hint of orange and almonds, is a perfect dessert drink for summer barbecues.

> 2 ounces Godiva white chocolate liqueur
> 1 ounce gin
> $^{1}/_{2}$ ounce melon liqueur
> $^{1}/_{4}$ ounce triple sec
> $^{1}/_{4}$ ounce amaretto
> $^{1}/_{4}$ cup fresh watermelon
> 2 scoops white chocolate ice cream

1. Mix all ingredients in a blender until smooth.

2. Serve in a chilled hurricane glass.

Makes 1 libation

Mandarin Ice

This exotic slush combines chocolate with orange and ginger.

> 1 ounce Mozart white chocolate liqueur
> 1 ounce sloe gin
> $^{1}/_{2}$ ounce triple sec
> $^{1}/_{4}$ ounce ginger liqueur
> $^{1}/_{4}$ cup mandarin orange slices
> 1 cup ice

1. Combine all ingredients in a blender and mix until smooth.

2. Serve in a chilled daiquiri glass.

Makes 1 libation

Key West

Chocolate, tropical liqueurs, and gin blend to mirror the casual elegance of this intoxicating town.

> 1 ounce Mozart white chocolate liqueur
> 1 ounce gin
> $^{1}/_{2}$ ounce Key Largo liqueur
> $^{1}/_{2}$ ounce blue curaçao
> ice

1. Place ingredients in a cocktail shaker filled with ice.

(continued)

2. Shake and strain into a cocktail glass filled with ice.

Makes 1 libation

Bella Donna

This libation of chocolate, hazelnuts, and peaches is best when sipped by candlelight in a bubble bath.

> 1 ounce Godiva white chocolate liqueur
> ¹/₂ ounce gin
> ¹/₄ ounce Frangelico
> 3 ounces peach nectar
> ice

1. Place ingredients in a cocktail shaker filled with ice.
2. Shake and strain into a cocktail glass.

Makes 1 libation

Black Irish Martini

An Irishman joining Her Majesty's Secret Service inspired this jet-set libation.

> 1 ounce Mozart dark chocolate liqueur
> ¹/₂ ounce Irish Cream liqueur
> 2 ounces gin
> ice

1. Place ingredients in a cocktail shaker filled with ice.
2. Shake and strain into a chilled cocktail glass.

Makes 1 libation

A Ration of Chocolate

For the soldiers of World War II, Hershey formulated a chocolate bar with a longer shelf life and a higher melting point by replacing the cocoa butter with vegetable fats. Hershey then produced over 3 million of these bars, which the military called "Ration D."

Brandies and Champagne

Wine country's finest is a wonderful companion to chocolate.

Midnight Caller

Intense and mysterious, this libation will intoxicate your senses and ignite your imagination.

> 1 ounce Mozart dark chocolate liqueur
> 2 ounces Grand Marnier

1. Warm the chocolate liqueur and Grand Marnier in a brandy snifter.

2. Serve at midnight with an intimate confession.

Makes 1 libation

Scarlett's Secret

If only Rhett had figured out how Scarlett really liked her brandy . . .

>   2 ounces Mozart white chocolate liqueur
>   1 ounce cognac
> $^1/_2$ ounce Chambord liqueur

1. Warm a brandy snifter.
2. Swirl all the ingredients together in the brandy snifter.

Makes 1 libation

Writer's Muse

When writer's block sets in and your deadline draws near, relax and treat yourself to this creative jump-start.

>   1 Espresso Mocha (page 298)
> $^1/_2$ ounce Mozart dark chocolate liqueur
> $^1/_2$ ounce Kahlua
> $^1/_2$ ounce Grand Marnier

1. Prepare the Espresso Mocha in an Irish coffee glass, without the whipped cream and ground chocolate.
2. Add the chocolate liqueur, Kahlua, and Grand Marnier.

3. Top with whipped cream and ground chocolate.

Makes 1 libation

Chevalier

If brandy and soda is your favorite cocktail, try this sparkling dessert drink.

>   1 ounce white (clear) crème de cacao
>   1 ounce Korbel brandy
>   crushed ice
>   club soda
>   1 lemon twist for garnish

1. Swirl the crème de cacao and brandy in a brandy snifter.
2. Add the ice and soda.
3. Garnish with the lemon twist.

Makes 1 libation

Brandy Alexander

This has been a favorite of chocolate lovers for many years.

>   1 ounce dark crème de cacao
>   2 ounces brandy
>   1 ounce heavy cream

1. Place ingredients in a cocktail shaker filled with ice.
2. Shake and strain into a brandy snifter.

Makes 1 libation

Chocolate Eggnog

This rich libation came to life when we were asked to design an eggnog that would be easy to make, safe from salmonella poisoning, and very chocolate.

    2 ounces Godiva white chocolate liqueur
    1 ounce brandy
    1/2 ounce Cointreau
    1/4 ounce butterscotch liqueur
    4 ounces light cream
    ice
    2 tablespoons sweetened whipped cream
    1 dash nutmeg

Dogs and Chocolate

No matter how much you like to spoil your dog, don't give him or her chocolate; even a small piece could be lethal. Chocolate contains theobromine, a natural chemical that, in dogs, can cause effects similar to an overdose of amphetamines.

1. Place ingredients except whipped cream and nutmeg in a cocktail shaker filled with ice.
2. Shake and strain into an Irish coffee glass.
3. Top with whipped cream and nutmeg.

Makes 1 libation

Moonlight and Lightning

This libation is best when sipped during a summer lightning storm, in the moonlight.

    1 large fresh strawberry
    1 ounce white (clear) crème de cacao
    ice-cold Mumms Cordon Rouge

1. Wash and hull the strawberry. Place it in a fluted champagne glass.
2. Add the crème de cacao and champagne, filling the glass.
3. Wait until you've finished the champagne to eat the strawberry.

Makes 1 libation

Chocolate and Liqueurs

Liqueurs have always been a favorite flavoring ingredient for chocolate confections and pastries. If you don't have time to bake or temper, serve one of these chocolate libations for dessert.

Angel's Kiss

Dark chocolate and white chocolate, layered with cherry liqueur—what could be more heavenly for a chocolate lover?

> $^1/_2$ *ounce Godiva dark chocolate liqueur*
> $^1/_2$ *ounce maraschino liqueur or grenadine*
> $^1/_2$ *ounce Godiva white chocolate liqueur*

1. Layer each liqueur, in the order given, into a pousse-café glass.

Makes 1 libation

Dolce Rosa

This sweet little libation is for my Italian grandmother, whose greatest pride and pleasure was the love of her family.

> *2 ounces Mozart white chocolate liqueur*
> $^1/_2$ *ounce amaretto*
> *a few drops of triple-strength rose water*
> *3 ounces light cream*
> *ice*
> *fresh or sugared rose petals for garnish*

1. Place ingredients except rose petals together in a cocktail shaker filled with ice.
2. Shake and strain into a cocktail glass.
3. Garnish with rose petals.

Makes 1 libation

Golden Corniche

This is the chocolate style to which we should all become accustomed.

> *1 ounce Mozart white chocolate liqueur*
> $^3/_4$ *ounce Galliano*
> *1 ounce light cream*
> *crushed ice*

1. Mix all of the ingredients except ice in a blender until smooth.
2. Pour into a chilled cocktail glass filled with crushed ice.

Makes 1 cocktail

Grasshopper

This classic libation makes a wonderful dessert, especially on hot summer nights.

> *1 ounce Godiva white chocolate liqueur*
> *1 ounce crème de menthe*
> *1 ounce light cream*
> *ice*

1. Place ingredients in a cocktail shaker filled with ice.
2. Shake and strain into a cocktail glass.

Makes 1 libation

Banana Split

For the kid in all of us, here's a grown-up banana split!

> 2 ounces Godiva white chocolate liqueur
> 1 ounce banana liqueur
> $^1/_4$ ounce butterscotch liqueur
> $^1/_4$ cup fresh strawberries
> 2 scoops vanilla ice cream
> 4 tablespoons dark chocolate syrup
> $^1/_4$ cup sweetened whipped cream
> 1 tablespoon toasted almonds, coarsely
>   chopped
> 1 teaspoon chocolate sprinkles
> 1 maraschino cherry

1. Mix the chocolate liqueur, banana liqueur, butterscotch liqueur, strawberries, and ice cream in a blender until smooth.

2. Fill a third of a chilled milk shake glass with the ice cream mixture. Add 2 tablespoons chocolate syrup. Add a second layer of ice cream mixture and chocolate syrup. Add a third layer of ice cream mixture.

3. Top with whipped cream, almonds, chocolate sprinkles, and a cherry.

Makes 1 libation

Robert's Peak

A favorite of our favorite rock climber, this will warm you on the coldest night, and it's even better when prepared over the campfire.

> 1 recipe Hot Chocolate (page 295)
> $^1/_2$ ounce peppermint schnapps
> 1 splash Jack Daniels
> sweetened whipped cream or marshmallows

1. Make the hot chocolate in an Irish coffee glass.

2. Add the peppermint schnapps and Jack Daniels.

3. Top with whipped cream or marshmallows.

Makes 1 libation

Heart Hug

Whenever your heart needs a hug . . .

> 1 recipe Hot Chocolate, made with white
>   chocolate syrup (page 295)
> $^1/_2$ ounce Godiva white chocolate liqueur
> $^1/_4$ ounce cinnamon liqueur
> $^1/_4$ cup chantilly cream
> tiny cinnamon hearts for garnish

1. Make the hot chocolate in an Irish coffee glass, omitting the marshmallows.

2. Add the chocolate and cinnamon liqueurs.

3. Top with chantilly cream and cinnamon hearts.

Makes 1 libation

chapter eleven

Decorations and Specialties

Chocolate can create a thousand mistakes, and cover even more. I always keep lots of chocolate decorations on hand for those days when, even though I've done everything right, the chocolate dessert I've created decides to throw a temper tantrum. (Smother anything in chocolate curls and no one will guess it didn't turn out quite right.)

I also keep lots of specialties and decorations on hand to quickly turn an ordinary dessert (I confess, even a store-bought emergency backup) into something special. A simple scoop of ice cream served in a chocolate cup or molded specialty is a dazzler. Put a chocolate bow on top of a slice of pound cake and Sara Lee's name will never come up. And strawberries dressed in chocolate tuxedos will make you a legend.

Dessert Toppings

Dusting and Stenciling

One of the easiest ways to decorate with chocolate is to sift a fine coating of cocoa powder onto your dessert. This technique is sometimes called dusting with chocolate. To take this technique one step further, you can create a design on the top of your dessert by sifting cocoa powder through a stencil.

1. You can use a paper doily as a stencil, or you can create a custom stencil by cutting a design out of sift paper or light cardboard.
2. If the top of your dessert is dry, you can lay the stencil directly on top. Place the cocoa powder in a fine mesh sieve and gently tap, rather than shake, a thin even layer of cocoa powder over the stencil. Take care to use a minimal amount of cocoa powder. You want an even coverage, but if you use too much, the design will blur when you remove the stencil. Then slowly lift the stencil up, being careful not to disturb the design.
3. If the top of your dessert is moist or sticky, rig a frame that will hold the stencil above your dessert. You can do this by placing the dessert in a pan that is slightly larger and taller, or by arranging glasses or boxes around the dessert, upon which the stencil can rest.

If you've never used a stencil, it's a good idea to practice first by stenciling onto waxed paper. Once you've stenciled a few desserts, you'll have a feel for how much cocoa powder to use and what stenciled designs look best.

Pamela Asquith   Truffles & other Chocolate Confections

Peaches
&
DREAMS

Serves 2
100 calories

Serves 2
70 calories

10 oz apple cider
3-5 peach slices
4 large strawberries
1 banana
1/8 tsp of cinnamon

VANILLA
1 Frozen banana
1 cup milk
1 tsp vanilla extract

PINA COLADA

Serves 2
185 calories

1 6oz container nonfat coconut yogurt (frozen)
½ banana (frozen)
½ of a 20oz can crushed pineapple
1 cup nonfat milk

STRAWBERRY

5 large strawberries
6oz. light (reduced sugar) fat free strawberry yogurt (frozen)
aka one container of Yoplait

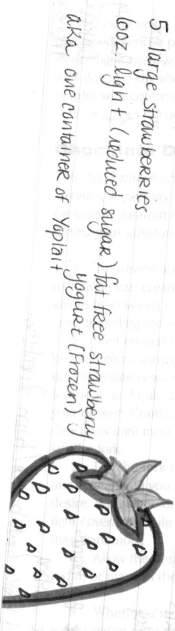

Mystery Solved

When I _____ _____ choco-
_____ _____ became
_____ was a mystery to me how
something so rich in cocoa butter
could be so drying. I talked to several
chocolatiers who wondered the same.
Common sense finally kicked in when
I realized the same emulsifiers that are
added to chocolate to absorb the
greasiness of cocoa butter or other
_____ naturally absorb our skin's oils.

To protect your hands, wear thin
synthetic surgeon's gloves when
working with chocolate. Wearing
gloves will also help insulate your body
heat from the chocolate, and you'll be
less likely to leave fingerprints.

When you're finished, use hand
lotion enriched with cocoa butter!

6. Peel the bits of chocolate off the waxed paper and store to melt and use again, or save to break up and sprinkle on other desserts (instead of the chocolate flavored sprinkles grocery stores sell.

Piping with Chocolate

Perhaps one of the most widely used decorating techniques is piping with chocolate. This can be used to create a wide variety of designs, including initials.

This technique requires a pastry bag, fitted with a writing tip, or a squeeze bottle with a very small opening. Once again, use high-quality couverture for the best results.

1. Place the melted chocolate, while still warm, in the pastry bag or bottle, and draw the design you desire. The easiest, and most popular, designs for piping are straight or diagonal lines, crosshatches, and swirls.

2. If you want very fine lines, choose a tip with a very small opening, make sure your chocolate is very warm and fluid, and work quickly.

3. If you prefer heavier lines, let the chocolate cool a bit and work more slowly, or select a tip with a slightly larger opening.

4. If the base glaze or coating on your dessert has not yet set, the chocolate you pipe on top will melt into the base. If you want the decoration to sit on top of the base, wait until the base has set to decorate.

As with stenciling, if you've never piped chocolate, practice on waxed paper; you can recycle the chocolate, or use it for nibbling! I still practice sometimes before decorating my desserts, particularly if it's a precise design, just to get warmed up.

Chocolate Filigree

This is a lovely decoration, and surprisingly simple if you have a template. Chocolate filigree is chocolate piped in a delicate, usually loopy, design, and placed vertically or horizontally on a dessert. Filigree pieces can be small (an inch or two in diameter) for individual desserts, or large enough to cover a cake or torte. You can even create multidimensional decorations by piping flat pieces and gluing them together with melted chocolate.

1. The easiest way to create chocolate filigree is to place a picture of the design you'd like to duplicate on a flat surface under a sheet of waxed paper or cooking-grade acetate.

2. Place melted chocolate in a pastry bag fitted with a writing tip, and trace the design. Allow the filigree to set in a cool room, or refrigerate for 3 to 5 minutes.

3. Carefully remove the filigree from the waxed paper or acetate with a metal spatula. Try not to touch the piece too much, to prevent fingerprints and melting.

4. Place on a dessert, or store in an airtight container in a cool place. If you need to stack the pieces, place a piece of waxed paper between each layer.

Chocolate Appliqués

Similar to filigree or stained glass, with this decoration you pipe an outline of an object (for example, a butterfly) and then color in the center with a contrasting color of chocolate.

1. Place a picture of the object you want to copy on a cookie sheet or jelly-roll pan under a sheet of waxed paper or acetate.

2. Place melted chocolate in a pastry bag fitted with a writing tip. Outline the object.

3. Allow the outline to set in a cool room, or refrigerate for 3 to 5 minutes.

4. Place melted chocolate of another color (for example, if you've piped an outline in dark chocolate, use white or milk chocolate) in a pastry bag fitted with a writing tip. Lightly fill in the area within the outlines with chocolate.

5. Quickly lift and tap the cookie sheet after you fill each small object or each area of a larger object; the newly piped chocolate should spread and flatten, filling in any small gaps.

6. Refrigerate for 3 to 5 minutes, or until set.

7. Carefully remove the appliqués from the waxed paper or acetate, with a metal spatula.

8. Handle and store these decorations as you would Chocolate Filigree (page 318).

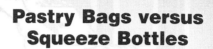

Pastry Bags versus Squeeze Bottles

I prefer squeeze bottles to pastry bags for most decorating and specialty projects. Squeeze bottles give you more control, they can be placed in the microwave oven for gentle rewarmings, and they are much easier to clean.

When you're finished with your project, empty as much chocolate as possible from the bottle. Place the bottle in your refrigerator. When the chocolate is set, squeeze or roll the bottle to break up the chocolate, and tap it out of the bottle. With this technique, very little chocolate washes down the drain.

Grated Chocolate

Grated chocolate can be folded into a batter, much like chocolate chips, or used to decorate desserts or drinks.

1. Chill a bar or block of couverture. Line a jellyroll pan with waxed paper.
2. Draw the chocolate over the holes of a stainless-steel hand-held grater onto the waxed paper.
3. Store the grated chocolate in an airtight container, in a cool place.

Shaved Chocolate

Shaving chocolate with a vegetable peeler or a knife is one way of creating chocolate curls.

1. To create the smallest chocolate curls: Chill a bar or block of couverture. Line a jellyroll pan with waxed paper.
2. Prop the chocolate on the edge of the jellyroll pan so that the curls will fall onto the waxed paper. Draw a vegetable peeler over the chocolate lightly and quickly.
3. For slightly larger curls: Allow the chocolate to warm slightly at room temperature. Draw the vegetable peeler over the chocolate a little more slowly, applying a little more pressure.
4. For wider chocolate curls: Prop a block of chocolate on the edge of a jellyroll pan lined with waxed paper.
5. Place a large chef's knife at the base of the chocolate block. Hold the handle of the knife with one hand and the tip of the blade with the other, so the blade of the knife is parallel to the surface of the chocolate. (If you've never used this technique, place a cardboard sleeve over the tip of the knife so you don't cut yourself.)
6. Draw the knife up from the base of the chocolate block. Once again, the temperature of the chocolate and the amount of pressure you apply will determine the size and weight of the shaved curls.
7. Store shaved chocolate in an airtight container, in a cool place.

Chocolate Curls

The other method for creating chocolate curls is to spread and scrape melted chocolate. With this technique, you can use one type of chocolate, creating solid color curls, or you can blend chocolate of different colors, creating marbled, feathered, or striped curls. For a scraping tool you can use a spatula, chef's knife, plastic putty knife, or almost anything with a clean, dry straight edge.

1. For this technique you will need stainless-steel cookie sheets or jellyroll pans with perfectly flat, clean backs. Warm the pans on a low heat in your oven. This prevents the melted chocolate from cooling too quickly while spreading a thin layer. Be careful not to let the pans get too hot; you should be able to handle them without oven mitts.

2.   To create solid color curls: Spread the melted chocolate in a thin (approximately ¹/₈-inch-thick), even layer on the back of the warmed pans. Tap the pans gently to release air bubbles and to smooth the finish.

3.   Refrigerate for about 15 to 20 minutes, or until set. Remove from the refrigerator and warm at room temperature until you can scrape the chocolate without it cracking or splintering. If it gets too warm, refrigerate it for a few more minutes.

4.   The size and shape of the curls depends on the scraping tool you use, the temperature of the chocolate, and the angle at which you scrape. The wider the blade or straightedge, the wider the chocolate curls. The softer the chocolate, the tighter the curl. The sharper the angle of your blade, the tighter the curl. For example, to create chocolate cigarettes, scrape at a 45-degree angle.

5.   Secure the pan so it will not slide or shift as you scrape. Place your scraping tool at the top of the pan and gently slide your scraping tool over the chocolate. Place the curls on your dessert or in an airtight container layered with sheets of waxed paper.

Striped Chocolate Curls

1.   To create curls with thin stripes: Warm the pans, as instructed on page 320.

2.   Spread a thin layer of chocolate on the back of a pan. Chill until set.

Jobs in Chocolate

Here are some ideas for job opportunities within the chocolate industry:

1.   *Confectionery Shops* are a delicious place to begin, where you'll be serving, packing, and selling chocolate confections.
2.   *Specialty Shops* will acquaint you with the tools, equipment, and ingredients needed for candy-making or cake-decorating. In many instances, these shops also offer classes, or have a small production facility attached.
3.   *Production Houses* will give you hands-on opportunities in working with chocolate. In most, you'll learn how to temper, mold, fill, and enrobe.
4.   *Distributors* are always looking for energetic and knowledgeable sales reps.
5.   *Manufacturers* have opportunities in buying, marketing, production, and sales.

(continued)

3. Scrape a series a fine lines into the chocolate using a pastry comb. If you're having trouble keeping the lines straight, place a metal ruler or straightedge alongside the chocolate to guide your pastry comb.

4. Lift and gently tap the excess chocolate onto waxed paper to recycle.

5. Spread a contrasting color of melted chocolate over the remaining chocolate lines. Refrigerate until set and scrape as instructed in steps 4 and 5 on page 321.

6. For wider stripes: Melt contrasting colors of chocolate separately. Using pastry bags fitted with plain 1/4-inch tips, pipe parallel stripes of chocolate about 1/4 inch apart on the back of warmed pans. Using a spatula, carefully spread the lines so they blend together. Proceed as you would for solid color curls.

7. For random stripes: Melt contrasting colors of chocolate separately. Spread a thin layer of chocolate on the back of a warmed pan. Randomly drizzle a contrasting color of chocolate on top. Proceed as you would for solid color curls.

Feathered Chocolate Curls

1. To create a feathered effect: Warm the pans as instructed on page 320.

2. Spread a thin layer of chocolate on the back of a pan.

3. Working quickly with a contrasting color of chocolate, pipe evenly-spaced parallel lines of chocolate, using a pastry bag fitted with a writing tip.

4. Using a toothpick or small sable paintbrush, gently run a line, perpendicularly, from left to right, through one of the piped lines. Change direction, running a line from right to left, through the next piped line. Repeat, alternating directions, until all the lines are feathered.

5. Tap, chill, and scrape, as you would for solid color curls (see page 321).

6. To create feathered hearts: Pipe or spoon small circles of chocolate in a parallel line. Run a toothpick or brush through the center of the circles to create a line of hearts. Tap, chill, and scrape, as you would for solid color curls.

Marbled Chocolate Curls

1. To create a marbled effect: Warm the pans as instructed on page 320.

2. Spread a thin layer of chocolate on the back of a pan.

3. Working quickly with a contrasting color of chocolate, lightly pipe random lines or swirls of chocolate using a pastry bag fitted with a writing tip. (Or drizzle the contrasting color on top.)

4. Using a toothpick or small sable paintbrush, gently swirl the chocolates together.

5. Tap, chill, and scrape, as you would for solid color curls (see page 321).

Chocolate Fans

Chocolate fans can be made with pure chocolate for a crisp look, or with chocolate dough (see page 331) for a

softer look. In either case, they can be made in a variety of sizes and designs.

1. Warm a pan, melt and spread the chocolate, and chill as you would for solid, striped, feathered, or marbled chocolate curls.

2. After chilling, brace the pan to prevent it from shifting as you work. Hold the bottom of a spatula or straightedge blade in one hand and the top edge in the other, at a slight angle (about 10 degrees) to the pan.

3. Scrape sections of the chocolate in a slight arc, or fan shape, with one end of the scraper moving faster than the other. One side of the fan should have soft ruffles, while the other should come together in a tight gather. Gently pinch the gathered end before chilling again to set.

Chocolate Leaves

Chocolate leaves are fairly simple and fun to make. They can also be made in a variety of shapes and sizes to reflect the season or theme of your dessert. They can be scattered, placed symmetrically, or even clustered in a large, open, rose bloom shape.

Be careful to use leaves of edible plants that are clean, dry, and free of pesticides.

1. Line several cookie sheets or jelly-roll pans with waxed paper.

A Royal Advantage

Chocolate was enjoyed from the early 1500s to the mid-1600s almost exclusively by the nobility of Spain. Small amounts had found their way to Italy and the South of France, but not to any of the royal French palaces.

When a marriage was arranged between Maria Theresa of Spain and Louis the XIV, the French expected the usual payment of political advantages, gold, art, and precious gems. They never imagined the treasure they were about to receive. Maria Theresa, having a passion for chocolate, ordered that a vast amount accompany her. When she introduced her rich Spanish drink at the court of Versailles, she quickly became the most popular member of royal society.

(continued)

2. Paint the top (shiny side) of the leaves with melted chocolate, using a paintbrush, small pastry brush, or your finger. Be careful not to get any chocolate on the edges of the leaves, which will make it more difficult to peel the leaf off after the chocolate has set.

3. Place the leaves chocolate side up on the waxed paper. Refrigerate until set.

4. Gently peel the fresh leaves off the chocolate leaves, and place on your dessert, or store in an airtight container layered with waxed paper.

Chocolate Cutouts

Chocolate cutouts can turn a simple dessert into something special. They can also help you incorporate a theme into your dessert.

1. Proceed as you would for solid, striped, feathered, or marbled chocolate curls.

2. Refrigerate for a few minutes, until firm but not yet set.

3. If you are using metal cookie cutters to create shapes, gently press the cookie cutters into the chocolate. If you need squares, rectangles, or triangles, score the chocolate with a knife. Chill until set.

4. Remove from refrigerator, fit the cookie cutters (or knife) into the preformed shapes, and gently cut through the chocolate. Place on your dessert, or store in an airtight container, layered with waxed paper.

Molded Specialties

Chocolate Molds

Another method for creating shaped chocolate uses chocolate molds. Today, most chocolate molds are made out of a heavy, pliable clear plastic. Molds are available in a myriad of shapes and sizes, including sports, entertainment, special interest, and professional themes. Even some of your favorite characters are licensed.

Molding chocolate can be fun and easy, so easy that it's a great project for little ones. You can use either tempered couverture or chocolate that is specially formulated for molding. Molding chocolate is available at most craft and specialty shops, in a variety of flavors and colors.

1. Be sure your chocolate molds are clean and dry. If new, wash the molds with warm, soapy water. Dry with a soft towel, being careful not to scratch the mold. To be sure the molds are absolutely dry, blow them with a hair dryer on a warm or cool (not hot) setting.

2. Temper or melt the molding chocolate according to the manufacturer's instructions. Stir the melted chocolate thoroughly.

3. Place the chocolate in a pastry bag fitted with a plain tip or in a plastic squeeze bottle. (I prefer using squeeze bottles—they're easier to fill, use, and clean.)

4. Fill each cavity *almost* full with chocolate. (If the cavity overflows, your chocolate

pieces will not have a clean, sharp edge.) Gently tap the mold to release air bubbles and flatten the surface of the chocolate.

5. Immediately place the mold in the refrigerator. The faster you cool the molds, the shinier your chocolate pieces will be.

6. When set, hold the mold upside down over waxed paper. Gently twist the mold as you would an ice cube tray. The chocolates will release. Decorate your dessert, or store in an airtight container layered with waxed paper, or wrap each piece in confectioners' foil.

Multicolored Molded Chocolate

The design of many chocolate molds is simple, requiring only one color of chocolate to create the piece. However, sometimes, to create a more interesting effect, you may want to marble the chocolate in the mold. Chocolate hearts, for example, are far more beautiful when marbled.

In addition, some molds have a more intricate design that invites you to layer colors of chocolate. For example, if the mold is of a cartoon character, you may be able to pour its eyes, nose, and mouth in colors different from the one you use for its face.

Molding chocolate is available in several colors. You can also add powdered colors to white chocolate. Do not use liquid food coloring or gel coloring that contains any form of liquid; these will cause your chocolate to seize.

Cadbury

In 1824, Englishman John Cadbury opened a coffee, tea, and chocolate shop in Birmingham, England, and was among the first to pioneer affordable chocolate for the commoner, by offering bars of Cadbury's French Eating Chocolate for 2 shillings. He also found a way, using one of Van Houten's presses, to remove every trace of cocoa butter from chocolate, creating the first pure cocoa powder. Together with his sons, Cadbury built a "company village," where employees lived as well as worked, and were provided with health care, education, and housing. (Milton Hershey followed this model when designing what would become Hershey, Pennsylvania.)

(continued)

1. To create a marbled effect: Melt contrasting colors of chocolate separately, and place the melted chocolate in separate pastry bags or squeeze bottles.

2. Alternate the colors of chocolate you use when filling each cavity. When you tap the mold the chocolates will blend together in a marbled effect. You can also swirl the chocolates together with a paintbrush. (Be careful not to use a toothpick or any other object that could scratch the mold.) Proceed as you would with solid color molds.

3. To layer colors: Carefully fill the deepest section within each cavity. Tap the mold, and refrigerate until set.

4. Fill the next layer of sections, or the remaining cavity, with a contrasting color of chocolate. Proceed as you would with solid color molds.

Chocolate Cups

Chocolate cups can also turn a simple dessert into something special. There are a variety of plastic molds available to help you create cups, you can use paper cupcake liners to create chocolate cups, or you can use a free-form method.

Molded Cups

Plastic molds are available in many shapes and sizes, from small shot glasses to large dessert cups. As with other molded shapes, you can use either tempered couverture or molding chocolate. Couverture will give you a thinner, more flavorful cup. Molding chocolate is easier to work with, especially if you're just getting started.

1. Wash and thoroughly dry your molds.

2. Temper your couverture, or melt molding chocolate according to the manufacturer's instructions.

3. Pour only enough chocolate in each cavity to coat the sides and bottom of the mold. Tip and turn the mold to coat the sides of each cavity. If there is too much chocolate in any of the cavities, turn the mold upside down over waxed paper, and allow the excess to drip out. Wipe away any chocolate that has spilled over the sides of the cavities onto the top of the mold. (This will give your cups a clean edge.)

4. Refrigerate until set. Gently twist the mold to release the cups. Use or store in an airtight container, between layers of waxed paper, in a cool place.

Watson and Martin Cups

These elegant little cups were designed by and for my favorite event and gift specialists. Tiny chocolate liqueur cups are filled with truffle ganache, capped with couverture, and topped with chocolate initials.

1. Plastic molds in the size and shape of shot glasses are available at (or can be ordered through) most specialty shops.

Make the cups as instructed on page 326. Or, you can buy chocolate liqueur cups through specialty shops or distributors.

2. Prepare the truffle ganache as directed in Chapter 3. You can use any flavor. You can also use a white chocolate liqueur cup with a dark chocolate ganache, or vice versa. Place the ganache in a large squeeze bottle with a $^1/_4$-inch opening at the tip, or a pastry bag fitted with a plain tip. Fill each cup $^7/_8$ full of truffle ganache. The ganache should be cool, but fluid enough to fill the cup without leaving air pockets. The top should also flatten easily when the cup is gently tapped. Refrigerate until firm.

3. Melt couverture or molding chocolate that is the same color as the chocolate cup. Place in a squeeze bottle or pastry bag fitted with a small plain tip. Add a layer of couverture on top of the truffle ganache that extends over the edges of the chocolate cups. Be careful not to use too much chocolate; you don't want this layer to spill over the sides of the cup, but it's very important to seal the truffle ganache inside the cup (so refrigeration is not necessary), and to create a smooth top on your cup. Tap gently to smooth, and refrigerate until set.

4. To make initials that are consistent in size and design, you can buy plastic initial frosting "stamps" at most craft and specialty shops. These are designed for you to press letters into frosting to use as

Peter and Nestle

In 1875 Swiss chocolate pioneer Daniel Peter created a new sensation using Henri Nestle's condensed milk. Just after the turn of the century, they brought Nestle Chocolate and Confections to the United States, where milk chocolate became America's favorite. Today, Nestle's Chocolate provides consumers with popular candy bars, while Peter's Chocolate offers Swiss-quality, American-made couvertures. (Both are divisions of the Nestle Food Company.)

Nestle's also makes a delicious sugar-free blend of chocolate liquor, cocoa butter, and Maltitol, similar in quality to a couverture, which can be used for pastries and confections.

(continued)

a guide for writing messages like Happy Birthday. Use these to gently press an initial into the top of each cup. (You can also draw initials freehand.)

5.   Melt couverture or molding chocolate in the same or a contrasting color. Place in a pastry bag fitted with a writing tip or a squeeze bottle. Trace the pressed initial with the chocolate, or draw an initial freehand. Refrigerate just until set. Serve in foil confectionery cups.

Cupcake Cups

You can also use paper standard or mini cupcake liners to create chocolate dessert

Thinning Compound

If your molding chocolate gets too thick, add a few "paramount crystals." These waxy bits are made out of the same fat substance found in most molding chocolates, and will thin your compound safely and effectively. (You should not have need for these if using couvertures.)

cups. Be sure to have the matching metal pans to support the cups while the chocolate is setting.

1.   Make sure your paper liners are clean and dry.

2.   Temper your couverture, or melt molding chocolate according to the manufacturer's instructions.

3.   Paint a thin even coating of chocolate inside of each paper liner using a paintbrush or small pastry brush. Be careful not to press too hard; you don't want to flatten any of the tiny pleats in the liners. Place each painted cup in the metal cavity of a cupcake pan.

4.   Refrigerate until set. Repeat, painting one or two more layers. Refrigerate for an hour, then cover and refrigerate overnight. Gently peel the paper off the chocolate cups and use or store.

Ruffled Cups

You can also create chocolate cups in a free-form manner. One method is to wrap paper cups with waxed paper, and then to dip the cups in melted chocolate. This creates a ruffled or loosely pleated chocolate cup.

1.   Line cookie sheets or jellyroll pans with waxed paper. Cut squares of waxed paper that are twice the size of the paper cups you plan to use. For example, if you are using 6-ounce cups, the waxed paper squares should be 12 inches by 12 inches.

2.   Center a paper cup on top of a square of waxed paper. Loosely tuck each corner of the paper into the cup, creating pleats. (Be careful to leave the paper loose; if it's too tight, the chocolate may crack when removing the paper. Hold the paper in place with a rubber band around the top edge of the cup.

3.   Place the melted chocolate in a bowl that will accommodate the depth of the finished chocolate cup you desire. Dip the bottom of the cup into the melted chocolate and place on the prepared pan. Refrigerate immediately, for 1 hour. Cover (without removing the paper) or place in an airtight container, and refrigerate overnight.

4.   Remove from refrigerator, and gently remove the paper cup and waxed paper. Use immediately, or store in an airtight container in a cool place.

Tulip Cups

Another free-form method is to dip balloons in chocolate, creating a smooth tulip-shaped cup. Be sure to choose small, sturdy balloons, and to wash and thoroughly dry them before using.

1.   Line cookie sheets or jellyroll pans with waxed paper. Fill the balloons about two-thirds full with air.

2.   Temper your couverture, or melt molding chocolate according to the manufacturer's instructions.

3.   To create solid color chocolate cups: Place the melted chocolate in a

(*continued*)

Pouring Cups

The trickiest part of making cups is pouring just the right thickness of chocolate for the sides and bottom. If the chocolate is too thin, the cup may crack when filled. If the sides are too thick, the cup will look clumsy, the chocolate may overpower its contents, and your guests will have a difficult time breaking the cup to eat it.

I recommend using a dark chocolate molding chocolate when you're just getting started; it's the easiest to work with. As your expertise grows, you can move on to tempered couvertures.

wide, shallow bowl. Coat the bottom and part of the sides of each balloon in the chocolate, turning and dipping the balloon to create the tulip shape.

4.   Place each balloon on the prepared pan, with the knotted end of the balloon up. Be sure to place the balloon so that the shape of the cup you've created is level. Some of the chocolate will gravitate down to form the cup's base.

5.   Refrigerate for 1 hour. Cover and refrigerate overnight. Gently pierce the balloon with a pin near the knot to deflate the balloon. Remove the balloon, and use the cup immediately, or store in an airtight container in a cool place.

6.   To create marbled or streaked chocolate cups: Place a puddle of chocolate (about $1/2$ cup) on a marble slab. Drizzle or marble a contrasting color of chocolate on top. Dip and roll the balloon as instructed above.

Chocolate "Punch" Bowls

A chocolate bowl filled with fruit salad or small scoops of ice cream makes a very elegant centerpiece for a dessert buffet. I recommend you practice molding smaller chocolate bowls before attempting this advanced project, and that, for your first punch bowl, you use semisweet molding chocolate.

Choose a high-quality, smooth-sided plastic bowl in the size and shape you prefer. Be sure your bowl is clean, dry, and free of scratches.

1.   Melt couverture or molding chocolate. Make sure both the bowl and the chocolate are at room temperature. If the bowl is cooler than the chocolate, the chocolate will not spread smoothly or evenly. Pour only enough chocolate in the bowl to create a *thin* coating on the sides and bottom. Tilt and turn the bowl, covering the sides. If any chocolate spills onto the rim of the bowl, wipe it clean, creating an even edge. Refrigerate for 5 minutes only.

2.   Repeat twice more, refrigerating after each coating. Set aside in a cool place overnight.

3.   Place a towel covered with waxed paper over a flat surface. Turn the bowl upside down just above the waxed paper. Gently pull the sides of the bowl away from the chocolate; the chocolate lining should pop out easily. If it does not, you may have tempered the chocolate improperly and you will have to begin again. Fill the bowl with fruit salad, truffles, ice cream, trifle filling—any dessert you desire, or store in a cool, dry place until needed.

Chocolate Dough Specialties

Chocolate Ribbons

Chocolate ribbons can be created in two ways: either by rolling chocolate dough with a rolling pin, or pressing the dough through a pastry maker. Once made, ribbons can be used to wrap a cake or torte, or to make and accompany chocolate bows.

1. To create ribbons using a rolling pin: Knead the chocolate dough.

2. Place the kneaded dough between two pieces of waxed paper, and roll with a rolling pin, as you would pastry dough. When the dough reaches the thickness you desire, cut into ribbons. Use right away, or store in an airtight container between layers of waxed paper.

3. To create ribbons using a pastry press: Knead 1-inch to 2-inch balls of chocolate dough. Flatten the balls into disks. Using the largest setting on your pastry maker, press each disk. Adjust your pastry maker to the next largest setting and press the disks again. Continue, reducing the size gauge on your pastry maker each time, until the dough becomes the depth you desire. Cut the flattened dough into the lengths and widths you need.

Fettuccine di Cioccolata

Here's a fun twist on spaghetti and meat-balls. Chocolate dough is formed into the size and shape of fettuccine, and topped with cocoa powder-coated truffles!

1. Process the chocolate dough according to the directions for chocolate ribbons. Cut or process the dough in the shape of fettuccine. Place the chocolate fettuccine on a serving platter, as you would the pasta version.

2. As an option, you may want to spoon some Crème Mystique (page 224) on top.

3. Form chocolate truffles into meatball shapes and coat with alkalized cocoa powder. Scatter on top of the fettuccine.

Chocolate Bows

Chocolate bows can be used to decorate desserts . . . and presents!

1. Create chocolate ribbons as directed on page 331. To create a 4-inch bow, cut 4 lengths of ribbon $3/4$ inch wide by 9 inches long.

2. Overlap and gently press the ends of each ribbon together, creating circles or loops.

3. Place one loop on a piece of waxed paper, positioning the ends, which were pressed together, in the center and on the bottom of the loop. Gently press the center of the top part of the loop down into the ends of the ribbon. This will create the first two loops of the bow.

4. Place another loop perpendicularly on top of the first loop, again pressing the top center down.

5. Continue, placing the remaining two ribbons between the first two, pressing down the centers. You should have eight bow loops when finished.

6. Gently form the loops of the bow, up and out. Chill until set.

Chocolate Roses

Chocolate roses are charming and deli-cious. They are easily created, one petal at a time.

1. Prepare and knead the chocolate dough.
2. Roll the dough into ¼-inch balls. Press the balls into flat rose petal shapes (basically round). Also roll small cone-shaped pieces to use as the center of the rose.
3. Wrap one petal around a cone. Curve the top of the petal out slightly, like a rose blooming naturally. Add another petal, overlapping the first. Continue, with each petal opening slightly

wider. For a small bud, use just a few petals. For larger roses, keep adding petals. Chill to set.

Chocolate Pom-Pons

As an alternative to chocolate roses, you may want to decorate with chocolate pom-pons.

1. Prepare chocolate ribbons as directed on page 331. Cut the ribbons into 1-inch by 8- to 16-inch lengths.
2. Fringe one long side of each ribbon by making ½-inch cuts, ¼ inch apart.
3. Gently roll the fringed ribbon, starting at one of the short ends. When rolled, squeeze the base with your thumbs and fore-fingers to make the pom-pon open. Chill until set.

Chocolate Fans

As mentioned before, chocolate fans can be made with pure melted chocolate or with chocolate dough. Making fans with chocolate dough creates a softer, more luxurious fan.

1. Prepare chocolate ribbons as directed on page 331. Cut the ribbons into the desired width and length.
2. Gently pleat the ribbons.
3. Pinch one end of the pleated choco-late dough, and gently spread the opposite end slightly to create the fan. For an even softer look, trim the corners of the fanned end into a curve. Chill until set.

Starter Kit for Kids

"Yummy Chocolate Bugs," by Curiosity Kits is a great starter kit for kids. It comes with a reusable mold and all the molding chocolate and tools your kids will need to create and decorate yummy chocolate bugs! Look for these kits at learning stores, or on the Web at *www.curiositykits.com.*

Chocolate Dough

By adding corn syrup to chocolate, you create a substance similar in texture to pastry dough (or play dough). Chocolate dough can be used to create chocolate flowers, ribbons, bows, pom-poms, and more. It can also be used to wrap cakes and tortes.

1. To make the chocolate dough: Line a jellyroll pan with heavy-duty plastic wrap, leaving enough at either end to fold over and cover the chocolate dough after it is poured in.

2. Stir $1/3$ cup of light corn syrup into 12 ounces of melted bittersweet or semisweet chocolate, or stir $1/4$ cup of light corn syrup into 12 ounces of milk or white chocolate.

3. Spread a thin layer of the chocolate mixture into the prepared pan, and cover with plastic wrap. Cool at room temperature for several hours or overnight.

4. Divide the chocolate dough into four pieces, and knead each piece as you would pastry or bread dough, until it is pliable. The dough may seem too hard at first, but your hands will warm it as you knead, making it more manageable. If the dough seems too soft, place it in the refrigerator for a few minutes.

Playing with Chocolate Dough

For special play days or gift-making parties, mix up a batch of chocolate dough for your little ones.

You can use a base of white chocolate and add powdered coloring to create a variety of colors. The kids can use plastic cutting and shaping tools from nonedible dough makers, or they can just use their fingers and imaginations. These creations make wonderful gifts and adorable treats.

Dipped Specialties Coating with Chocolate

Fresh strawberries dipped in chocolate are always a crowd-pleaser. So are tart dried fruit slices coated in sweet, creamy chocolate. And plain shortbread cookies dipped in chocolate become elegant companions for coffee or ice cream.

Dipping fruit or cookies is very simple, especially if you use chocolate formulated for molding, which doesn't need to be tempered. There are a few tricks that make dipping fruit foolproof. . . .

Dipping Fresh Strawberries

When choosing strawberries to dip, select berries that are a red, ripe color all the way up to the base of the leaves. If there is a white or pale green rim around the top, they will not be as flavorful. Long-stemmed berries are the easiest to dip, but you can use any size or variety. Long or short, be careful not to pull any of the leaves off while dipping.

1. Line cookie sheets or jellyroll pans with waxed paper.
2. Wash and *thoroughly* dry each strawberry. It is essential that the berries are dry, even under the leaves. Even one drop of moisture will cause the chocolate to seize.

3. Pour tempered couverture or melted molding chocolate into a small bowl that is deep enough to accommodate the size of the strawberries you're dipping, and stir thoroughly.

4. Gently gather the leaves of the strawberry, holding the leaves up out of the way. Dip each strawberry, coating three-quarters of the berry, and place it on the prepared pan. Refrigerate immediately for a shiny result. Refrigerate only until set, then store in a cool place. Do not store the dipped strawberries in the refrigerator, as condensation will form on the chocolate.

Dipping and Decorating Fresh Strawberries

To create an even more enticing treat, chocolate-dipped strawberries can also be decorated with chocolate sprinkles, tiny chocolate curls, nuts, spices, or colored sugar crystals.

1. Line cookie sheets or jellyroll pans with waxed paper.

2. Prepare what you plan to use for decorations (make chocolate curls, chop or grind nuts, etc.).

3. Wash, *thoroughly* dry, and dip each strawberry.

4. Sprinkle the decoration on each strawberry immediately after dipping it, while the chocolate is still warm and receptive, then chill.

Double-Dipping Fresh Strawberries

Double-dipping or even triple-dipping fresh strawberries is fairly simple. You can dip the berries vertically to create horizontal striping, at a diagonal, or using a combination of vertical and diagonal dips. Use your imagination and have fun.

1. Line cookie sheets or jellyroll pans with waxed paper.

2. Wash and *thoroughly* dry, each strawberry.

3. Temper couverture, or melt molding chocolate, and dip each berry in one color of chocolate, holding the leaves out of the way. Chill until set.

4. When the first chocolate is firmly set, dip each berry in a contrasting color of chocolate. Chill and store, as directed on page 335.

Tuxedo Strawberries

These are showstoppers. Fresh long-stemmed strawberries are dressed in chocolate tuxedos. Of all the specialties we prepare, these are my favorite. I think of them as members of a symphony orchestra; some big, some small, some fat, some thin. (If long-stemmed strawberries are not available, you can use large strawberries; it's just a little more difficult to hold onto them while dipping.)

(continued)

1.   Line cookie sheets or jellyroll pans with waxed paper.

2.   Wash and *thoroughly* dry, each strawberry, as instructed on page 334.

3.   Place the strawberries on a paper towel. Decide which side is the most attractive, and on which side each strawberry rests with the best balance.

4.   Temper white couverture, or melt white molding chocolate. White chocolate will create each strawberry's "shirt." Holding the leaves up out of the way, dip the front side of each strawberry. Place the strawberry chocolate side up on the prepared pan, and chill until firmly set.

5.   Temper semisweet couverture, or melt dark molding chocolate. Dark chocolate will form each berry's "jacket." Once again, holding the leaves up out of the way, dip one side of a strawberry at a diagonal, partially covering the white chocolate. Dip the other side at a diagonal, partially covering the white chocolate. The white chocolate should now be in the form of a solid "V," flanked on each side by dark chocolate. Chill until set.

6.   Place tempered dark chocolate or melted dark molding chocolate in a pastry bag fitted with a writing tip.

7.   To create the bow ties: In the center of the top of the white chocolate "V," draw a horizontally elongated "*x*." Draw lines connecting the far ends of the "*x*," creating two tiny triangles. Fill in both triangles with chocolate.

8.   Add 2 to 3 tiny dark chocolate buttons below the bow tie, by lightly dabbing the white chocolate with the end of the writing tip. (Cute, huh?)

9.   Serve on an elegant, doily-covered serving platter.

Raspberry Crowns

Fresh raspberries are set in chocolate atop a light chocolate wafer. These delicate little bites are lovely alone, or can be used to top other desserts.

1.   Line cookie sheets or jellyroll pans with waxed paper. Place flat round chocolate wafers on the waxed paper.

2.   Temper couverture, or melt molding chocolate. Spoon a small pool of chocolate on top of a wafer. Place fresh raspberries tip side up in the chocolate, covering the top of the wafer. Repeat, topping all the wafers with chocolate and raspberries. Refrigerate until set.

3.   Working with one crown at a time, spoon more chocolate on top of the raspberries. (You don't want to completely cover the raspberries, you just want to spoon enough to hold another layer of berries.) Add a smaller circle of raspberries on top. Refrigerate until set.

4.   Spoon a little more chocolate in the center of each crown and top with one more raspberry. Refrigerate until set. Dust with a tiny bit of powdered sugar.

Frozen Banana Bites

These are even more fun than frozen bananas on a stick. Thick slices of fresh banana are dipped in dark chocolate and topped with chopped almonds.

1. Line cookie sheets or jellyroll pans with waxed paper.
2. Toast and coarsely chop almonds. Temper couverture, or melt molding chocolate.
3. Peel and slice fresh bananas into bite-size disks. Dip each slice of banana into the chocolate, using a dipping fork, and place on the prepared pan. Top with chopped almonds, and freeze until set. Serve in paper or foil confection cups, or place in an airtight container and store, layered with waxed paper, in the freezer.

Dipping and Decorating Dried Fruit

Although dried apricots seem to be the most popular dried fruit to dip in choco-late, any dried fruit can be coated in chocolate or dipped and decorated.

One of my favorite decorations is to place sliced toasted almonds in a fan shape over the chocolate coating. Another is to dip dried apricots in white chocolate and sprinkle with nutmeg.

1. Line cookie sheets or jellyroll pans with waxed paper.

2. Prepare what you plan to use for decorations (grated chocolate, chocolate sprinkles, spice, nuts, cocoa powder, etc.).
3. Temper couverture, or melt molding chocolate. Dip each slice of dried fruit in the chocolate, and place on the prepared pan, flat side up. (The side of the fruit that was once next to the pit should be against the waxed paper.)
4. Sprinkle the decoration on each slice of dried fruit immediately after dipping, while the chocolate is still warm and receptive. Chill and store as directed on page 335.

A Tuxedo Strawberry Party

When strawberries are in season, throw a party to teach your friends how to make tuxedo strawberries! This is a treat that crosses all age and gender lines. Everyone I've ever met loves them and is even more delighted when shown how to make them.

Dipping and Decorating Cookies

Any variety of cookies can be dipped, or dipped and decorated. Before dipping, dust any crumbs off the cookie to prevent them from contaminating your dipping chocolate.

1. Line cookie sheets or jellyroll pans with waxed paper.
2. Prepare what you plan to use for decorations (grated chocolate, chocolate sprinkles, spice, nuts, cocoa powder, etc.).
3. Temper couverture, or melt molding chocolate, and dip each cookie in the chocolate.

Money Hungry Monarchs

In 1660 the first English tax was imposed on chocolate to raise money for the many pleasures of Charles II. Thirty years later, to boost the income of William and Mary, another law was passed requiring all sellers of chocolate to buy a special license.

4. Sprinkle the decoration on each cookie immediately after dipping, while the chocolate is still warm and receptive.
5. Place on the prepared pan, decorated side up, and chill.

Chocolate-Coated Spoons and Cinnamon Sticks

These make wonderful package toppers when slipped into a cellophane bag and tied with a ribbon. They also make perfect hostess gifts when arranged in a tin or mug. And they are always delightful companions to a cup of coffee or hot chocolate.

If you want to flavor your chocolate-coated spoons or cinnamon sticks, be sure to use specially formulated flavoring oils, available at most specialty shops. Do not use liqueurs or extracts—they will cause your chocolate to seize. Flavoring oils are available in tropical and citrus fruit flavors, mint, and spice flavors, and even fun flavors like toasted marshmallow.

If you're dipping plastic spoons, choose heavy, high-quality spoons. We prefer gold metallic plastic spoons to white. If you're dipping cinnamon sticks, be sure they're fresh and clean. And make sure both spoons and cinnamon sticks are dry before dipping.

1. Line cookie sheets or jellyroll pans with waxed paper.

2.   Temper couverture, or melt molding chocolate. Dip the bowl of each spoon, or a third of each cinnamon stick in chocolate.

3.   Place on the prepared pan, and refrigerate until set.

Chocolate Finger Paints for Kids

When you want to give your little ones a special treat, let them finger-paint with chocolate! They can paint cookies, a pan of brownies, the top of a cake (single layers or sheet cakes work best), or even just a sheet of waxed or parchment paper. The best part is, they can eat their creations!

Chocolate is very drying to the skin, so when your little ones are done, rub lotion into their hands after washing.

> *16 ounces white chocolate, finely chopped*
> *2 tablespoons light corn syrup*
> *1/4 cup butter, cut into 1/4-inch cubes*
> *1 cup heavy cream, warmed to room temperature*
> *powdered coloring for chocolate*

1.   Melt the chocolate, corn syrup, butter, and cream in the top of a double boiler over hot, not simmering, water, and stir until smooth.

2.   Divide the chocolate into different bowls and blend in the powdered colors. Powdered coloring is highly concentrated, so sprinkle in just a tiny bit at a time until you achieve the color you desire. If the color gets too dark, add more white chocolate. Set aside to cool to room temperature, stirring occasionally.

3.   Dip and draw! If the chocolate gets too thick, blend in a little warm cream and stir until smooth.

Chocolate Finger Paints for Adults

And when you want to give yourself a special treat . . .

> *16 ounces semi-sweet chocolate, finely chopped*
> *2 tablespoons light corn syrup*
> *1/4 cup butter, cut into 1/4-inch cubes*
> *1 1/2 cups heavy cream, warmed to room temperature*
> *1/4 cup liqueur*

1.   Melt the chocolate, corn syrup, butter, and cream in the top of a double boiler over hot, not simmering, water, and stir until smooth. Set aside to cool to body temperature. Stir in the liqueur, or divide the chocolate into two or more bowls and blend a different flavor of liqueur into each.

2.   Dip and draw!

Index

Everything® **Get Published Book**
$12.95, 1-58062-315-8

Everything® **Get Ready For Baby Book**
$12.95, 1-55850-844-9

Everything® **Golf Book**
$12.95, 1-55850-814-7

Everything® **Guide to New York City**
$12.95, 1-58062-314-X

Everything® **Guide to Walt Disney World®,**
Universal Studios®, and
Greater Orlando
$12.95, 1-58062-404-9

Everything® **Guide to Washington D.C.**
$12.95, 1-58062-313-1

Everything® **Herbal Remedies Book**
$12.95, 1-58062-331-X

Everything® **Homeselling Book**
$12.95, 1-58062-304-2

Everything® **Homebuying Book**
$12.95, 1-58062-074-4

Everything® **Home Improvement Book**
$12.95, 1-55850-718-3

Everything® **Internet Book**
$12.95, 1-58062-073-6

Everything® **Investing Book**
$12.95, 1-58062-149-X

Everything® **Jewish Wedding Book**
$12.95, 1-55850-801-5

Everything® **Kids' Money Book**
$9.95, 1-58062-322-0

Everything® **Kids' Nature Book**
$9.95, 1-58062-321-2

Everything® **Kids' Puzzle Book**
$9.95, 1-58062-323-9

Everything® **Low-Fat High-Flavor**
Cookbook
$12.95, 1-55850-802-3

Everything® **Microsoft® Word 2000 Book**
$12.95, 1-58062-306-9

Everything® **Money Book**
$12.95, 1-58062-145-7

Everything® **One-Pot Cookbook**
$12.95, 1-58062-186-4

Everything® **Online Business Book**
$12.95, 1-58062-320-4

Everything® **Online Investing Book**
$12.95, 1-58062-338-7

Everything® **Pasta Book**
$12.95, 1-55850-719-1

Everything® **Pregnancy Book**
$12.95, 1-58062-146-5

Everything® **Pregnancy Organizer**
$15.00, 1-55850-336-0

Everything® **Resume Book**
$12.95, 1-58062-311-5

Everything® **Sailing Book**
$12.95, 1-58062-187-2

Everything® **Selling Book**
$12.95, 1-58062-319-0

Everything® **Study Book**
$12.95, 1-55850-615-2

Everything® **Tarot Book**
$12.95, 1-58062-191-0

Everything® **Toasts Book**
$12.95, 1-58062-189-9

Everything® **Total Fitness Book**
$12.95, 1-58062-318-2

Everything® **Trivia Book**
$12.95, 1-58062-143-0

Everything® **Tropical Fish Book**
$12.95, 1-58062-343-3

Everything® **Wedding Book, 2nd Edition**
$12.95, 1-58062-190-2

Everything® **Wedding Checklist**
$7.95, 1-55850-278-5

Everything® **Wedding Etiquette Book**
$7.95, 1-55850-550-4

Everything® **Wedding Organizer**
$15.00, 1-55850-828-7

Everything® **Wedding Shower Book**
$7.95, 1-58062-188-0

Everything® **Wedding Vows Book**
$7.95, 1-55850-364-1

Everything® **Wine Book**
$12.95, 1-55850-808-2

Everything® is a registered trademark
of Adams Media Corporation

$12.95, 304 pages, 8" x 9 ¼"

Your friends and
family will be amazed
with what you can do!

- Tutorials on the most
  popular programs
- Simple instructions to get
  your home page started
- Maintenance routines to
  keep your site fresh
- And much, much more!

$12.95, 320 pages, 8" x 9 ¼"

A pregnancy book
that really does
have everything!

- Extensive medical
  evaluation of what's
  happening to your body
- Exercise and diet tips
- 40-week pregnancy
  calendar
- And much, much more!

Now Available!
Only $9.95 each

For more information, or to order, call 800-872-5627
or visit www.adamsmedia.com/everything
Adams Media Corporation, 260 Center Street, Holbrook, MA 02343